How
the
Light
Gets in ...

Ring the bells that still can ring.
Forget your perfect offering.
There is a crack in everything.
That's how the light gets in.
(from "Anthem", Leonard Cohen)

Anthology of Poetry from Canada

Túr Cohen*

Is uaigneach mé, sa túr amhrán seo
ach tá focail fhiána fhiara i ndiaidh sleamhnú tríd an *dure*
is ní thuigim iad, cé go bhfuil siad fíor;
ah, cultúr ársa aisteach do mo tharraingt siar.

Is báite mé, sa chúr focal seo
ach tá snámh in aghaidh an easa ar mo thoil go fóill
is tuigfidh mé iad, fiú má théann daor
orm cultúr ársa aisteach a thabhairt i dtír.

Tá an oíche ag teacht, tá an bás ag teannadh,
"tá mé tá tú tá sé" ar an iPod agam
fiú má cheannaím ciall, nach mbeidh sé mall, rómhall?
Scairt sa dorchadas, teilifís don dall?

Chaith mé blianta anseo, ag cumadh liom
gan ceol an tuisil ghinidigh ina chabhair dom
ach tá fonn ag teacht ó oileán thiar,
guthanna geala Gaeilge do mo tharraingt ó *The Echoing Years*.

* Foilsíodh dánta Gaeilge sa díolaim ó Cheanada agus ó Éirinn dar teideal
The Echoing Years. Bhí dánta le Leonard Cohen sa rannóg Ceanadach. I
gcomhrá le Louis de Paor faoin iontas agus faoin bhród a bhí orainn beirt as
a bheith in aon leabhar le Cohen, luaigh de Paor go b'fhéidir gur cuireadh
cóip den leabhar chuig Cohen agus go raibh ár gcuid focal Gaeilge i ndiaidh
sleamhnú isteach sa teach s'aige i nganfhios d'éinne. Chuir an tsamhail sin
ag cumadh mé...Más féidir, is fearr na focail thuas a chanadh le fonn an
amhráin *Tower of Song* de chuid Cohen.

* Poems in the Irish language were published in the anthology from Canada
and Ireland *The Echoing Years*. Some poems from Leonard Cohen appeared
in the Canadian section. In a conversation with Louis de Paor about how surprised and delighted we were to be published in the same book as Cohen, de
Paor mentioned the possibility that Cohen had probably been sent a compli-
mentary copy, and that our Irish words had slithered in his door unbeknownst
to anyone. That image set me off composing...if possible, the above words
should be chanted to the tune of Cohen's *Tower of Song*.

Philip Cummings

How the Light Gets in ...

Anthology of Poetry from Canada

EDITED BY

John Ennis

Centre for Newfoundland and Labrador Studies

School of Humanities, Waterford Institute of Technology, Ireland

Note on the editor:

John Ennis is the author of thirteen books of poetry. He is Head of School of Humanities at Waterford Institute of Technology, where he is also chair of the Centre for Newfoundland and Labrador Studies. His last long poem was *Oisin's Journey Home*, a piece in praise of the workers who built and served Newfoundland's railway. He has acted as editor for *Poetry Ireland Review*. He served on the Executive of Poetry Ireland for eleven years and taught Creative Writing for ten years. Awards have included The Patrick Kavanagh Award in 1975, numerous firsts in the Listowel Open and The Irish American Cultural Institute Award in 1996. In 2008, Memorial University at Sir Wilfred Grenfell College awarded him an Honorary Doctorate in Law.

"O felix culpa . . ."
from the Easter Liturgy

How the Light Gets in
First published in 2009 by

The Centre for Newfoundland & Labrador Studies,
School of Humanities Publications, Waterford Institute of Technology.

Printed and bound in Ireland by eprint Limited, Dublin.

Cover illustration by Aidan Dunne, Waterford, Ireland.
Like his brother, deceased writer Séan, Aidan Dunne hails from St. John's Park in
Waterford City. Aidan holds a Licentiate from the Royal Photographic Society and
works mostly as a freelance photographer. His work was exhibited at The Temple Bar
Millennium Exhibition. He has completed a number of commissions for Waterford
Healing Arts Trust, which culminated in a major solo exhibition entitled *After the
Storm*. His work forms part of Waterford City Council's Art Collection. He is working
on a photographic series for landscapes, old roads and pathways being subsumed into
urban planning. His art as photographer: "Just a matter of opening my eyes to what is
already around me."

Graphic design and layout by Jackie Raftery, Ireland.
Jackie Raftery is a graphic designer with some twenty years experience in the field. She
lectures in Graphic Reproduction and Origination at Waterford Institute of Technology.
She is presently engaged in postgraduate fine art research on the Jokob Locher's 1497
Latin translation, *Stultifera Navis* (*The Ship of Fools*), by Sebastian Brant, an
incunabulum which is housed in the Chester Beatty Library in Dublin. Artwork based on
her research practice will form part of the Chester Beatty collection.

ISBN 0-9540281-8-X

to Dr. Stephanie McKenzie,
whose daring spirit and entrepreneurial drive
made these anthologies possible

Stephanie McKenzie

Aidan Dunne

Jackie Raftery

Gerald Squires, The Last Church in the Bay, St. Kieran's

Almost reverently
we walked among the rocks
of the holy church
and worshipped roses
in the dead yard
and came again to the cove
as they did after rosary
in the green and salty days

from "St. Leonard's Revisited", Al Pittman

Appreciation

First of all, a big thank you to Leonard Cohen for allowing us to use a line from one of his songs as the title for this anthology.

Thanks to the many colleagues in the School of Humanities and its departments at Waterford Institute of Technology, who assisted in any way with this project, in particular Christine O'Dowd Smyth for her liaison with the French-language poets included; Janice Simmons of the Poets' House at the Institute for making contact with Rhode Island School; Ray Cullen, acting Head of Languages, Tourism and Hospitality and staff in Culinary Arts for hosting the Waterford launch; Liam Rellis at the Centre for Newfoundland and Labrador Studies; Samantha Thomas in Waterford and Oxford; staff in Art & Design at the Institute including Jackie Raftery, Christine Simpson, Joy Rooney, Martin Quigley, Sheila Naughton and Lorenzo Tonti; Emmanuel Jakpa; Dermot Aylward and staff in Educational Services; last, but by no means least, the administrative staff in the School of Humanities at Waterford, including Norah Fogarty, School Administrator, along with Hannah, Caroline, Dorothy, Laura, Margaret, Martin and Maria.

Further thanks to Ambassador Patrick Binns, Maria O'Reilly and staff at the Canadian Embassy in Dublin; Agnes Aylward and Kristy Clarke, INP; Max Middle, Michael Pittman, Garrett Fitzgerald, Paul Casey, Maureen Kennelly, Leon Litvack; Armand Garnet Ruffo; Joanne Arnott; Michael Coyne and Kent Jones at Sir Wilfred Grenfell College, Corner Brook, and Susan Doyle at Rhode Island School, as well as all the student artists involved. An especial thanks to Tony and Kalle Ryan.

While every effort has been made to ensure that biographical and bibliographical details recorded in this book are accurate, the editor does not claim this work to be fully authoritative and wishes to apologise in advance for any errors or omissions in the acknowledgements and referential material provided. Any corrections notified will be acknowledged and incorporated into any future edition of the work. Every effort has been made to trace the holders of copyright, but if copyright has been inadvertently breached in any case, copyright holders should contact the publisher.

John Conway, Conquest, Rural Municipality of Fertile Valley

the lone and level prairies

Contents

Sheri Benning

E. D. Blodgett

Beverley Brenna

Heather Brett

Tom Dawe
from *Where Genesis Begins* (Breakwater Books, 2009)

Rosanna Deerchild
from *this is a small northern town* (The Muses Company, 2008)

Jeramy Dodds

Don Domanski

John Donlan

Mike Doyle

Matthew Hollett

George Johnston

Elis Juliana

Barbara Klar

Carl Leggo

Brenda Leifso

Tim Lilburn

Andrea MacPherson

Randall Maggs

Alice Major

David Manicom

Stephanie McKenzie

W. H. New

Jeff Park

Elizabeth Philips

Sharron Proulx-Turner

Matt Rader

Monty Reid

Peter Sanger

Crystal Sikma

Sue Sinclair

Carolyn Smart

Andrew Suknaski

Anne Szumigalski

John Terpstra

Mildred Tremblay

Yvonne América Truque

Michael Trussler

Diane Tucker

Jacqueline Turner

Alan R. Wilson

David Zieroth

**Artists (Illustrations, Paintings & Photography:
in order of appearance in text):**

Walking In Elysium

For some years now, I've been walking in Elysium. I'd got a sense of it years ago reading Michael Crummey's "Her Mark" where Ellen Rose surveys her earthly estate:

> Bounded above by the sky, by the blue
> song of angels and God's stars.   Below by the bones of those who
> made me.
> I leave nothing else. Every word I have spoken the wind has
> taken, as it will take me. As it will take my grandchildren's children,
> their heads full of fragments and my heart not among those. The day
> will come when we are not remembered. I have wasted no part of my
> life in trying to make it otherwise ...

Not that Canada is at the end of the earth, though I did have that sense of vertigo in Vancouver, on my own, looking out to sea. And the clarity of the air was sometimes disorientating for this mortal. Not, of course, that the country's Elysian plains, or prairies, are in any sense, *that*, Elysium, for the struggling people who live midland in the decimated farmlands. Gary Geddes rightly rounds on any simplistic notion of Canada as peace maker, "a nation of gentle saints", rather he points to its tradition of "noisy compromise". Perhaps, though, there is a parallel with Newfoundland, something special about the land, its own earned *dúchas*. As Adrian Fowler noted in a few words for the cover of *However Blow the Winds* (2004), it was to a large extent the Irish and English poor, who together prizing their freedom, peopled the province. Similarly, on the mainland, decent people fleeing the manifold tyrannies of Europe, or wherever, sought out Canada and made it their home. Something of their original goodness must permeate the national psyche and, of necessity, filter down into its verse.

Not that the First Nations could take such advent lightly. Theirs were the sacred grounds of a shared native Elysium of the Great Spirit. A white aggression bred from Genesis knew neither stopping nor sharing. Ongoing tensions still colour these pages. What happened in Newfoundland still cries out to heaven in the words of poet, Joan Crate:

> New-found-land the title,
> a joke, a riddle, and
>
> *What shall we do with -*
> me; a suspended sentence.

("Loose Feathers on Stone", for Shawnandithit, a long poem where Crate's persona joins hands with that of the last Beothuk).

On the poetry front, it has become apparent to me that no anthology, however ambitious, or series of anthologies, can ever deplete the Canadian fields. Each book offers a particular armful of poems gathered at a particular juncture of time and opportunity, governed by the eye that sees and hand that picks. Such contingencies. An initial request broadcast across the eastern province brought in hundreds of manuscripts. Only a fraction constituted *The Backyards of Heaven* (2003) governed as we were with inadequate budgets. I can still see submissions in piles languishing to window sills.

All the while, I became conscious of voices in verse outside the province of Newfoundland and Labrador. Some of the poets from the province included in the two volumes mentioned made a living in other parts, Toronto or Montréal, for instance. Pratt was an early example. At the March Hare Festival, I met poets from BC, twice the distance from Europe, major voices like Lorna Crozier and Susan Musgrave. Talk inevitably led to other names in the trade. I began to read wider then. I first got a sense of the immensity of Canadian space from Jan Zwicky, and it was somehow hugely consolatory. Odd names started to appear in the verse, like *Brandon, Limerick* . . . What were such doing in Canadian verse? Maybe there was a buried hinterland of Irish connections? Certain enclaves in Montréal and across Québec and in the west were mentioned. So, the prospect of a third anthology, one spanning coast to coast was discussed and shelved, and discussed and shelved for the umpteenth time as preposterous. An earlier attempt (by others) appeared to have vanished without trace. Not that any anthology would in any way be restricted to "Irish" voices; early on, Stephanie McKenzie laid down a marker on this and she was right; for instance, against what was intended on one grants front, First Nations from Newfoundland & Labrador were as comprehensively included as we could manage in *The Backyards of Heaven* (2003). Chief Misel Joe came on Irish tour. Stephanie McKenzie found the funding for a five-city trip for her compatriots to Ireland, the poets of Newfoundland and Labrador.

But *Canada*? An anthology comprising *Canada and Ireland*? In one rash moment, the decision was taken to proceed. A research grant from The International Council for Canadian Studies made research visits possible on both sides of the Atlantic. Colleagues were helpful with names and advice, often totally contradictory; lists were arrived at and torn up and replaced, until some consensus was reached for both sides allowing us to proceed. Duly launched in Ireland and Canada in 2007 and 2008, the 1280-page *The Echoing Years*, as it became known, the third part of the trilogy, might have concluded the effort. The penultimate launch was at Congress of the Humanities and Social Sciences in UBC.

It was then I came across the well-stocked poetry shelves of UBC Bookstore. *All these new names I'd never even heard of?* It was not that my colleague editors were unaware of such names: such a range simply could not have been accommodated in *The Echoing Years*. I spent a few hours browsing on the hoof and made enough selections of new work to blow credit cards and cash with just about enough to see me watered and back. The ridiculous sprang to my lips as I sat down mid-day outside O'Mahoneys for a bite with Stephanie. "Count me out!" said Dr. McKenzie bringing down her cigarette on the ash-tray with the force of excommunication. Got the books back and started serious reading. On reading Joanne Arnott's "Conception", I knew I had the *fiat* I needed. At a Leonard Cohen concert on a dark rain-washed magical evening in mid-summer Dublin, I heard his song "Anthem" as if for the first time and I knew I had my title if I could procure permission for it. And so on to David Zieroth. The in-between is history, other leads, and hundreds of emails. On getting wind of the venture, Randall Maggs emailed me on another insomniac bleary-eyed night declaring me "incorrible". I had not the heart to tell him to add the "-gi-" bit. Later, last October, when they awarded me an Hon. Doctorate of Laws at SWGC for my previous labours, and after Rex Browne had driven me to Glenburnie to see the house where that intrepid Campus Principal, John Ashton from Barnsley, spent his last days with Sheila, Rex took me to Stephanie's office. I presented her two volumes of possibles. Without a word, she took the lot, left them behind a press and resumed her reading. Only then did I realise fully I was on the right track, — reinforced by Fred's warm reception for *The Echoing Years* in *Poetry Ireland Review* (*PIR* 95). Soon Kent Jones and his art students at SWGC, Susan Doyle with hers at Rhode Island and colleagues and students at Waterford had become absorbed with another version of the Illustrated Manuscript. If not quite *The Leabhar Mòr* or *The Great Book of Ireland*, still on the same trail. The absence of my colleagues on the editorial scene on this occasion allowed me to include their work, which I admire anyway, this time without conflict of interest. So concludes for me the formal anthologies. Sixty-five soon, grandfather now, I tell my "kids" I'm near the age of liberation, — to resume "To-morrow to fresh woods, and pastures new."

Meanwhile, back to Elysium, where E. D. Blodgett's fine *Elegy* presumes a living community of spirits past and present (like Al Pittman's *West Moon*):

> only ghosts will cross
> the landscapes that compose
> the soul
>
> until my soul
> becomes
> a ghost

people lingering in the mind with all the resonance of Glück and his blessed spirits. Somewhere in this landscape, John Donlan might enthuse with Hopkins: "long live the

weeds and the wilderness yet". In this case, Donlan lives for half the year on a lake north
of Kingston, Ontario, surrounded by one hundred and seventy-seven acres of wilderness.
Elise Partridge describes him as having the reverence of Wordsworth combined with
the tenderness of John Clare for creation in his verse. His poem "Columbine" is
dedicated to Susan Musgrave's partner, Stephen Reid, the subject of *The Stopwatch
Gang*, an account of a gang of bank robbers. Perhaps these latter had read too much
Pound, whose discourse on banks is relevant to our times. Speaking of Pound, old
Ezra must surely enthuse over the pictographs of young poet Matthew Hollett, whose
superb line "helios brings morning to corner brook" took *The Backyards of Heaven*
into allegro maestoso, its final movement. Matthew Hollett's pictographs appeared in
Shift & Switch, an exciting new anthology of experimental verse, whose concerns are
as much mathematical as metrical, and whose *oeuvre* for specialists in Irish medieval
verse will recall the latter's similar obsession with the laws of pre-Einstein Physics, it
being the work of poets (no shrinking violets) to reflect and re-inforce the powers that
held the universe together. The pictograph links also with the genesis of First Nations
wonder in its first articulations.

An important criterion in any piece of writing is the apparent truth or emotional
veracity of its contents. Poetry is no exception. In the realm of characterisation,
symbolic cardboard types fold as quickly as their makers. Allegorical types survive
through the details of portrayal. The real soon create their own ambience.

Again and again, throughout the poets, whose work can only be sparingly represented
in the following pages, people walk off with the poems constructed to contain them. I
have been fortunate to meet salt-of-the-earth fathers, mothers, sons, daughters and
neighbours, heroes and villains and sometimes animals, broken down trucks and
lawnmowers in their midst. The pages of the following are alive with the real, as
opposed to the literary: Bachinsky, Benning, Connolly, Dawe, Deerchild, Dempster,
Donlan, Doyle, Gottfriedson, Johnston, Leggo, MacPherson, Maggs, McKenzie,
McLeod, McWhirter, Philips, Rader, Rhodes, Rogers, Sinclair, Smart, Suknaski,
Trussler, Tucker, Wilson, Zieroth and others in between, say, Szumigalski's partner
cowering in silence, Suknaski's own father warts & all, his Dunc and Babe
McPherson, Rhenisch's Evelyn in BC, the raw power and affection of Rader's old
mustang, the burial of the horse in Philips, Connolly's "Aunt Olive Amongst the
Heavy-Petters", Riggs as remembered by Tom Dawe, people and circumstance
touching the raw nerve. Decent fair folk, people the author of *Piers Plowman* could
rub shoulders with, or Chaucer, speaking of whom I'd refer readers to the 252-page
The Office Tower Tales (The University of Alberta Press, 2008), Alice Major's *tour de
force*, a kind of high-rise office *Canterbury Tales* up and down the escalators and in
places people must meet perforce "in an age not so much evil as incoherent".

What was surprising to this reader was the number of poems in contemporary volumes addressing issues of the individual soul, spirit or individual psyche, however one wishes to define that chemistry. Old biblical forbears are done and dusted to walk again in the poems of Carla Funk, a kind of observant Penelope or Nazarene Mary in her sewing room. Samson and Delilah breathe again, good old fashioned Gluttony, obese as you like, finishes last in the race of the seven deadly sins while the St. Thomas in everyone is addressed in "Love Poem for a Skeptic". In a memorable re-visioning of the Healer, Himself, Harold Rhenisch envisages Him as the saviour of small engines at the garage door in "Hymn for Small Engine Repair". Rhenisch also writes what must be a hymn for whales, getting to the task before Brendan the Navigator. Mike Doyle has a poem "Written on the Soul"; Elis Juliana remembers "A holy moment"; Barbara Klar's eloquent "Prayer" calls for the strength of the bear in adversity; Brenda Leifso has a sequence "Prayer for Rain"(unlikely to find many imitators on this side); Andrea MacPherson finds a space in her European travels "where [I] will learn to pray", Randall Maggs writes of Sawchuck (reviled by fans one week, idolised the next) slumped before the statue of the virgin in "Dinner at the Priest-House" where dropping the apostrophe s has a curious effect); Diane Tucker's poem "while praying" takes place outside a shower; Sheri Benning's "Descent from the Cross" makes extraordinary use of the blank page; it appears Tim Lilburn and Stephanie McKenzie have a soft spot for Jesuits in "Fr. Paul le Jeune, S.J., in the Forest" and "First Vision of Father Marquette" respectively; David Zieroth remembers a time he could pray and not thereafter (well, maybe, as we'll see):

> I planted, and prayed
> for the market to hold, and when
> it failed I stopped praying
> and never began again ...

In "Dogwood Tree in Winter", Mildred Tremblay considers the many falls of her father in his last years:

> The sound of crashing
> in this house terrorizes me. Jesus
> only fell three times.

Her humour in "Jehovah", when two ardent young men call to her door bent on conversion, has her heading to the hills for sanctuary, while "Thee" as a no-holds barred love poem has its familiars in the "Thys" and "Thous" still current on the tongues of Sunday. John Terpstra surveys "The Little Towns of Bethlehem"...

If a Christian *mythos*, therefore, informs both imaginative thought, structure and emotive thrust in poems for many, its ancient contemporary in the catacombs, Orphism, imbues the work of Graham Good in no small measure in his elegant translations of Rilke's late poetry in *The Sonnets to Orpheus*. Writing of a part of the world where God for years was much trumpeted, if not much in evidence among the savageries of the warring parties (in the words of Richard Murphy in *The Battle of Aughrim*, — a kind of native Irish Batoche, —

> ...They know little about God
> But something of the evil exploded by the word),

George McWhirter at the end of his remarkable poem for his sister on the Shankhill Road in Belfast, who survived the bombs but not her cancer, writes "God bless you, Lily", an ending that is authentic, apt and earned (*"Pensée Poème Assay* for my Sister"). Few poets would get away with such verbal sweep in Ireland: were it not for the ghost of Joyce frowning on any such after him in his toast to Tim Finnegan, in matters of the spirit, Blanaid Salkeld put paid to any such creeping revisionism in her poem "Leave us Religion" in its lands where archeological warehouses are packed to capacity with the toes of monks and cranial memorabilia as highways inch forward.

When I first considered setting out on the anthology trail for Canada, I collected as many recent anthologies of Canadian poetry as I could. As a teenager, way back, I had Ralph Gustafson's *Penguin Book of Canadian Verse* (1957), and primal echoes of F. R. Scott's "Old Song" and its spacious music, —

> a quiet calling
> of no mind
> out of long aeons
> when dust was blind
> and ice hid sound
>
> only a moving
> with no note
> granite lips
> a stone throat

have long striated my own mind. Gustafson's strictures on the verse he saw as Canadian were quite purist though: "There are no Aphrodites in Canadian poetry — the seafoam is too cold". He advised on poetic conditions linked to the seasonal and geographical contingent, — a spare lyricism and metaphysical wit were to be cultivated, with the Laurentian Shield preferably as backdrop. What he would have made of the tropical imagery of Jan Conn in *Jaguar Rain* and *Botero's Beautiful Horses* must remain conjecture. What is very obvious to this reader is that Canadian poets will come and go imaginatively as they please; the world today is very much every poet's oyster anyway and foreign treasures may well be appropriated back home in a manner parallel to or replacing the imperialist mindset. At one memorable Hare Concert in Gander, Anita Best announced that she was on a one-woman crusade against Irish cultural imperialism; she then proceeded to sing songs in Irish. Like Seamus Heaney (whose every line is enriched by his undergraduate studies in Linguistics), Jan Conn's scientific education informs the precise reportage of her poems; her *anam cara* is Margaret Meade, orchid hunter in Brazil from the 1950s to the 1980s. Jungle, jaguar and the human imagination in a ravenous hunger for the exotic comprise the imaginative trinity of Conn's memorable poetry. I found the Canadian poetic enriched by many other seams from abroad as well: Shane Rhodes with his Hispanic themes; Brenda Leifso's excursions into Greek mythology with chilling empathy, "The Maenads Prepare for the Hunter"; the entirety of Tim Lilburn's *Orphic Politics*; the poems of Bolivian poet Yvonne América Truque (who later settled in Montréal) translated into French by Jean-Pierre Pelletier; the Afro-Caribbean Papiamentu of Curaçao writer Elis Juliana translated by Hélène Garrett. Jeramy Dodds wishes "Happy Birthday to Carl Linneaus, 300 Years Old" while Heather Brett from Newfoundland and living a near lifetime in Ireland takes her poems from our midland landscapes. Mary Dalton's riddles have an Anglo-Saxon provenance: they at once tease and fret, like a good detective novel in haiku, opening up lots of cul-de-sacs. One has got to test Mary's road to be taken against a lifetime of experience. A marvellous sense of Wordsworthian pantheism pervades the *oeuvre* of Sue Sinclair. A pantheism here not of Constable oaks, but of inanimate things that appear about to speak to the reader. Tables and chairs have a halo of a Joycean *quidditas* about them. The breaker on the cover of *Breaker* appears to be coming at us with a mind's eye of its own. A certain new humour, as in "Dawn till Dusk", sometimes makes her world that bit less disquieting:

> We awaken to find the house
> waiting for us,
> patiently grazing
>
> in a field, chewing
> the same mouthful of grass
> as always …

Elizabeth Philips could not have written some of her best poems without Keats at her shoulder. One of her poems is entitled "To Keats". Never mind if it's forty below and

> an implacable
> prairie winter cracks the floor joists …

she continues to savour "the soft-dying day". She is a poet who thrills in opposites and the richly apposite. Her "River Edge" is pure Keats, too, loading every rift with ore and the detritus of the thaw. Canadian poets look to mainland Europe, also, for imaginative sustenance or umbiblical anchor: Andrea MacPherson visits the Celtic Isles seeking forbears; Stephanie McKenzie immerses herself in Van Gogh. Earlier, *The Echoing Years* took from "Forests of the Medieval World" (Don Coles in olden-year France and Germany) while Carmine Starnino etymologised his Italian tongue in

"On the Obsolescence of Caphone." Dominique Gaucher writes in French on the subject of journeys savouring the atmosphere of cities Vienna, Sofia, Bucharest and more besides. Francis Catalano's translations of the Italian poet, Valerio Magrelli, earned him the national John Glassco Award in 2006.

In its own way, *The Echoing Years* helped to bridge the gap between old and new worlds with its inclusion of twelve poets from Eastern Europe translated by Irish poets. And is Sawchuk, the archetypal hero of hockey (and father who keeps facing the day to put bread on the table for his kids), not from Ukrainian stock?

Such cultural cross-fertilisation has always made for greatness: Keats taken with the Grecian urn, Coleridge away with Kubla Khan until the knock on the door from Porlock. Ireland's greatest treasure, *The Book of Kells*, could not have come into being had not church artists from Byzantium travelled west in an iconoclastic time (the miniature had limited possibilities with a faithful who liked to adore their saints tall). In turn, the Irish monks, formerly slave traders, their faces quite well made up it seems with berries in fashion, marched back across Europe well-stocked now with hymns and quills, illuminating the Word in latinate manuscripts this time in dark ages in monasteries built by their own hands, forgetting sometimes to erase their Gaelic snarls from the margins if the bell for supper was late, again.

There is one trait or physical distinctiveness of Canada that is immediately apparent to visitor and reader alike; the sense of utter spaciousness in landscape and art. This dimension colours both book titles and contents as well as thematic fixations. At the centre of it is a sense of "the sacred essence of life", a phenomenon Kim Anderson identifies in the work of Joanne Arnott but which probably owes all to a continuing First Nations consciousness. Joanne Arnott writes eloquently of her struggle for space, establishment of that sacred space that is the self and the individual spaces between herself and her children. Yet, having established space, the poet is lost without its plenitude in "Gone Not Gone":

> With the kids gone
> I sleep in a messy house
>
> that I may wake up
> with the illusion
>
> *not gone*

Michael Trussler stakes out his own space, apart, in *Accidental Animals*, yet every line, and the spaces between them, are over-run with his absent children as he still in imagination seeks to amuse them. Issues of personal space inform Brenda Leifo's masterly "Letter to Kirk: Vancouver" as surely as they did the equally impressive

Catherine Hunter poem "Two Thousand and Two" we were fortunate to come across for *The Echoing Years*. At the heart of this spatial focus is often a quietist, tender, meditative tone on the losses and gains of the spirit, as in the poems of Michelle Desbarats, in for instance, her lines on the death of an animal, "The Miracle of Beside a Dog". There is a quality of unaffected openness about all this that is refreshing. Crystal Sikma can write a beautiful tender love poem, "Driving down into Qu'Appelle". The Qu'Appelle Valley has long been an important otherworld crossroads for First Nations and immigrant Canadians. See a title by an Irish poet, "Driving into . . .X", and one might expect a demolition job on the landscape whatever the location. One might wait a long time for a title like Anne Szumigalski's *When Earth Leaps Up* to emerge from the Irish midlands (though "exiled" by work I confess I've yet to read from any of the *thirty* anthologies pioneered by Heather Brett). Sometimes the issue of space can be haunting, as in the lack of space one might have accorded someone. Anne Szumigalski was by all accounts a most generous person and mentor to many young poets, yet she regrets hugely the lack of space accorded a partner in "Untitled ('When I think of him …')"

In reading anthologies of Canadian Poetry, I was particularly struck by a statement in the *15 Canadian Poets X 3* anthology by Gary Geddes referring to a constant aimed at in Canadian poetry one could easily overlook or take for granted: an essential decency of spirit. Without this quality embedded in the psyche on a grand scale, Canada as a nation could not have become the kind of gentle giant it has largely become in world affairs (many would pray that it retains this position, for everyone's survival if for no other reason). This quality comes to the fore in verse in different ways. It is the bedrock from which David Manicom speaks in *Desert Rose, Butterfly Storm*. Where, really, anymore is the "home of the free, home of the brave?" In a poignant re-take of Robert Duncan's "A Poem beginning with a Line by Pindar" and emulating the latter's ode formations, Manicom touches base with north-american thinking on unbridled militarism, armament rhetoric and contemporary savagery. Wilfred Owen is dead a long time and the dialectic between his two protagonists in "Strange Meeting" might never have been spoken. The humiliations at Guantánamo shocked a whole continent. The bloody mess that Iraq became. The U.S. standoff at United Nations that made the razing of Gaza another muscle flex in the exercise of strategy. Manicom is drawn back to Eliot's *Wasteland* to locate a co-relative for the times we live in, in an attempt to get to grips with contemporaneity. Eliot prefaced his long poem with "NAM Sibyllam quidem Cumis ego ipse oculis meis vidi in ampulla pendere, et cum illi pueri dicerent … / With my own eyes I saw the Sibyl suspended in a glass bottle, at Cumae, and when the boys said to her: 'Sibyl, what is the matter?' She would always respond: 'I yearn to die.'"

> Hoover, Roosevelt, Truman, Eisenhower –
> where among these did the power reside
> that moves the heart?

wrote Duncan in the section "The Thundermakers descend," and Manicom rejoins in "Gameboy" set against the background of new fundamentalisms:

> JehovahYahwehJesusOsamaAllahGeorge
> What is this particular fucking prayer-faced ruse
> All about?

He invokes Yeats who clearly saw in "The Second Coming" the nazi monster, while we continue blithely unaware at the brink of extinction, — like the callow boys, on their way to grow up for another war far away, or the immolative car bomb someone else decides, with all the calculation of prayer, — still questing the Sibyl on the human condition.

Which is not to say there are not lesser conflicts nearer home, or the playout of these continuing on prairie or in any small northern town in Canada or Ireland. Alice Major in her poem "What is buried under the walls" speaks of a woman's voice with "anger ripped from her throat" arraigning her residential street at 3am:

> You're on Indian land, man.
> You're all on fucking Indian land, man.
> This is fucking Indian land.

The treaties have long been made and broken and whatever re-verified into our time, but hurts still linger and fester, whether these be of historical recentness or part of the contemporary reality. Readers of Newfoundland literature cannot but be aware of the hold the fate of Shawnandithit and the last of her people still has on the popular imagination. Joan Crate's long poem "Loose Feathers on Stone" from *Foreign Homes* (Brick Books, 2001) is dedicated to Shawnandithit, the poem note referring to "The Beothucks, a First Nations tribe of Newfoundland ... the victims of European disease and genocide". If one is to judge from the poetry of Rosanna Deerchild, ("cousin comes in from the bush"), Garry Gottfriedson ("Strep-throat"), Neal Mcleod ("1895, Batoche"), Sharron Proulx-Turner ("anxiety of influence") or Janet Marie Rogers ("Check Point"):

> another day
> young ones wait outside
> without coats
>
> without kisses goodbye
> for late buses
> to take them
> to racist schools...

— the past, or remnants of the past still linger today. This time there can be no excuse for decent people not to take a stand on basics at every opportunity if any bedrock of decency be true. One of the most poignant and shattering moments in compiling

The Backyards of Heaven (2002 – 2003) was our wait for permissions faxed to us from
The Labrador as First Nation Innu trekked from Davis Inlet to Natuashish, beside whose
circumstance our own concerns were as nothing. In UBC Bookstore, I saw shelves and
shelves of stories and studies re-living and expunging a ruthless residential system,
which religion supported and bolstered, during which time some one hundred native
languages were systematically extinguished. In the face of such holocaust, the *bata stick*
looks benign. The mind baulks trying to come to terms with the enormity of the scale of
extinction. Yet, somehow from this dustbowl of tears, a re-flowering of First Nations
culture in life and in the arts emerged. This re-emergence is examined in depth by poet
Stephanie McKenzie in her study *Before the Country: Native Renaissance, Canadian
Mythology* (University of Toronto Press, 2007) in the context of the late nineteen sixties
and early nineteen seventies. The continuing re-surgence (and here I can only refer to
voices in poetry) can be gauged by the inclusion of eight First Nations poets in *The
Echoing Years* along with the additional six included here (excluding Suknaski, who
writes with eloquence on First Nations heroes and circumstance). Inadequate, but better
to light the candle than to curse the darkness. What is remarkable to this reader is the
depth of First Nations tolerance despite all. Joanne Arnott sees her poems, from one
angle, as opportunities for mothers (First Nations and other) to compare notes. In the
introduction to *MOTHER time*, she asks, "In later years, were your teen-aged sons
handcuffed and tasered by sadistic 'peace officers'? Or were their lives transformed by a
human, dressed as a police man, being touched by a human, dressed in criminal clothes?
Our stories, spoken truly, are essential: food and drink, fresh air, room to grow?" An old
wisdom asserts, "the truth will set you free". Neal McLeod acknowledges the evil
committed by both white and First Nations in the past and the need now for new modes
of reconcilement. He pays tribute to the "brave white kids" who came to his
neighbourhood to take on his team in hockey ("James Smith Hockey Arena"). First
Nations, it appears, pick their battles more carefully today. A little subversion can go far.
Neal McLeod has an uncle smoke his pipe through a sermon on hell and damnation. The
Jesus-obsession is neatly critiqued in another church context, by the words of McLeod's
great-great-great-grandfather, a Cree-Dene from the Cold Lake area of Alberta:

> he said, he couldn't understand why
> they would talk about Jesus
> when they killed him
> he used to think
> they were afraid
> they would be punished

Such recalls the Irish folktale tradition of the priest-on-horseback versus the raggy boy
on foot and their exchanges: "Where is God, boy?" / "Why, did ye lose Him?" where
an exercise in cathechism is boomeranged back on one in the saddle of faith.

In *Gabriel's Beach*, Neal McLeod finds his own redemptions. His uncle was one of many First Nations to win praise for bravery on the beaches of Normandy. To that extent, they became members of a collective withstanding tyranny on a global scale. They earned the respect, if not the full rights, of people back home. In the poet's case, mosôm Gabriel is a model for personal re-generation. Sometimes the context of the uncle's exploits will have a familiar ring with the *Táin*: in a contest that lasts over three pages, Gabriel and his opponent take breaks to see to the health and sustenance of the other, in scenes that echo with Ferdia and Cúchulainn. In a book that is as excoriatingly confessional of himself, as it is celebratory of the Cree nation, he recalls in "Words for my Sons" a time when "[T]he ancient river was so dry in my soul that [I]could no longer cry" and pays tribute: "Our women have been strong in their stories, but we have been weak in our silence. Remember, it is our grandmothers who helped us survive". Women like the grandmother of Sharron Proulx-Turner, who like a silent Penelope, continued reading the blanket in her hands knowing one day her house would be restored, the heroic return. Of the eight First Nation poets featured in *The Echoing Years*, five were women with four out of six in this volume. It's not, of course, as if First Nations are short of male heroes to dwell on. McLeod, himself, recalling Batoche ("1885, Batoche"), remembers how the old men sent the young people away, then

> old men fought
> told jokes, teased, chided
> each other
> as bullets cut
> bodies into the earth

Strange, then, that whatever common ground was initially established between white and First Nations was partly achieved by other outcasts once from nearer home. Recognising an archetypal forbear in the poem "Song About", Joanne Arnott muses:

> … maybe you remember her
>
> she married nice gaelic men
> she married herself
> into the white race …

When I first made contact with Sharron Proulx-Turner, the poet wondered if it was because another ancient forbear of hers was Irish (she honours also the French connection). Not at all. Sharron's titles are awesome, and fascinate, before one even gets into the text.

The Irish do have something else in common with First Nations today; a parental preoccupation with education; an education for their children at all costs. Colleagues from Canada have been amazed at the privations Irish parents will put up with to finance their "kids" through third level and beyond. John Conway in his marvellous book of photographs from Saskatchewan, his native province, *Saskatchewan Uncommon Views*, recalls how he heard a chief say that just as buffalo meant life to their ancestors in the past, it was education, "getting an education," that was buffalo today for his young people.

When I visited Ottawa last summer on the way back from Congress of the Humanities and Social Sciences at UBC in Vancouver, poet and professor at Carleton, Armand Garnet Ruffo kindly drove me round the city to see the sights. As we looked down on the massive locks connecting the Ottawa Canal with the Ottawa River, he pointed to a space beneath the cliffs on the other side. "If you and I had been here at the time, we'd have had our labouring shacks down there". Later, I saw close by hidden away under some trees, an old lichened celtic cross, with three symbols, - the pick, the wheelbarrow and the mosquito. But I could see no monument to First Nations. This only bears out the opening lines of Joan Crate's "Loose Feathers on Stone":

> There is no stone, or word, or prayer to mark
> Our fleet lives, our staggering deaths ...

Or maybe as ex-celts, we're just better at erecting crosses.

Speaking of Saskatchewan a minute ago, I'd refer readers to *FAST FORWARD NEW SASKATCHEWAN POETS* (Hagios, 2007), a memorable anthology and apparently the first in twenty-five years. I've chosen from the work of the following poets therein: Sheri Benning, Beverley Brenna, Neal McLeod, Jeff Park, Mansel Robinson, Crystal Sikma and Michael Trussler. Had space, time and opportunity allowed I could have picked the lot. Mansel Robinson considers the politics of poetry readings in his poem "A Poet Prepares". If he's not careful, he could end up like Paul Durcan addressing empty chairs. Poets Sheri Benning, Barbara Klar (editor), Neal McLeod and Michael Trussler have since published full volumes which are drawn on for this work. Speaking of their anthology, editors Barbara Klar and Paul Wilson point to this new swathe "looking up from the prairies toward possibility and a broad world view". Perhaps, too, it is salutary to remember Kavanagh's advice in "Epic" as he surveys the Homeric goings on in Monaghan:

> I made the Iliad from such a local row.
> Gods make their own importance.

And how in any real sense could there ever really be *post-prairie?* According to Yeats, it takes a lifetime to get to know even a field. What then of the prairies? The poet's eye "in fine frenzy rolling" is at home there as anywhere. There are ample poems to prove it. Of course, poets writing of the prairie have their own difficulties with editors "in important places" if the editor in Don Kerr's poem "Editing the Prairie" is anything to go by:

Well, it's too long for one thing
and very repetitive.
Remove half the fields.
Then there are far too many fences
interrupting the narrative flow.
Get some cattlemen to cut down those fences.
There's not enough incident either,
this story is very flat.
Can't you write in a mountain
or at least a decent-sized hill?
And why set it in winter
as if the prairie can grow nothing
but snow. I like the pubic bush
but there's too much even of that,
and the empty sky filling all the silences
between paragraphs is really boring.
I think on due consideration
we'll have to return your prairie.
Try us again in a year
with a mountain or a sea or a city.

The best poets stand in awe of their subject as if in perpetual wonderment. As with Pygmalion, poets get a sense of the poem watching them. John Steffler speaks of the verse of Sheri Benning (from Saskatoon, now studying in Scotland) "drinking the world in – in its darkness and loveliness and nameless potencies." The great archetypal nexi move like girders under *Thin Moon Psalm*: mother and child, sister and sister, lover and lover, father and daughter in waves of sorrow, loss and hope. As always, what's lost is ever more haunting than what's been accrued:

We undress, hold each other urgently; heat of our bodies
a false certainty. Tired and dumb, we whisper small words,
I love you, I love you, pebbles to dam the tide of coming morning.
Forgive us. We don't know how. Love is not inevitable — ...

...In the morning we take a cab to the airport.
Sky, a bloodless face we can't read, suspect it might be judging us.
We think we might've lacked courage the night before,
though we don't say...

Two other poets in whom *Eros* excels are Barry Dempster and Monty Reid. Dempster's *Love Outlandish* is just that: a traversing of the A to Z of relationships. Irish readers will probably find parallels in the searing honesty of his work with that of mid-life James Simmons in marital breakdown. On the outlandish theme, he is a kind of Erasmus into *Praise of Folly* number sixty-seven. "One moment they [lovers] are excited, the next depressed, they weep and laugh and sigh by turns; in fact they truly are quite beside themselves". Dempster's heart is essentially that of the big-hearted father in "Devotion" considering the inert body of his wife:

> He picked up her hand which lay in her lap
> like a heap of mousy bones
> and, lifting it to his lips, kissed the abyss.

Monty Reid also specialises in the alphabet of love. His partner (as an introductory note tells us) left Luskville, a phantom settlement on the Ottawa River in western Québec and returned to Alberta "nursing a suite of dissatisfactions." The poet can only murmur plaintively that he never forgot his partner's birthday, but must nurse an inventory of loss:

> ...we were together 32 years
> let's say we had sex on average two times a week
> allowing for absences or sick leave
> or the above average holidays
> and that hi-rate first year
>
> that would be 32 times 52 times 2
> equals 3328
>
> and the nipple
> still rises
> to the tongue
>
> times 2

Sofia Omelkovica from Latvia provides two illustrations for a moment of tenderness and lingerie falling from past times of "the heart /... that delicate necklace with its solitaire".

Heather Brett is a Canadian poet living in Ireland. She has done our own hinterland no small service; her guiding hand has edited or co-edited a staggering thirty books of young people's writing across the flat midlands in places like Laois, Offaly, Westmeath and Longford, centres off the beaten track of, say, a Yeatsian Sligo or a Joycean Dublin, to name but two well-heliconized watering holes.

Other poets with a local connection include Jacqueline Turner who finds it no bother to re-work *The Faerie Queene*. If Spenser in his day drew on the relative spaciousness of North Cork, so does this poet, with a cocktail of genres, embrace the greater curvature of Horseshoe Bay. The poems of Mike Doyle, a Canadian now for some thirty years, still draw on an Irish, or London-Irish perspective. A critic with publications on William Carlos Williams and James T. Baxter, Doyle is very much an own stylist in his poems purveying comedy in universal mortality as in "Raking Shaking". Stephanie McKenzie has spent some time in Ireland as lecturer, editor and researcher. Her poem "Reading a Two-Day Old George Elliott Clarke's *Execution Poems*" has for location Marquette in the U.S. In the poem, she feeds and burps the baby (called Alana, *Ir.* A leanbh / O My child! O My darling!) of a housemate so that the latter can take a shower (her partner from South America has been detained at some border or other). Feeding a baby, a task many a parent does, perhaps while watching CNN or SKY News to Herodian explanations as to why the murder of children in Gaza was necessary. Clarke's *Execution Poems* is an extraordinary *tour de force;* I regret not having it all included in *The Echoing Years.* Since then *Black* has appeared to no less acclaim and should be sought out too. Here, I've given space to a much younger writer, Keita Demming, and his poem,"Blackness" from *We Have a Voice: An Anthology of African and Caribbean Student Writing in BC.* This discursive poem is perhaps best read in the socio-political discourse of the new era on the continent heralded by Obama. Don Domanski, a native of Cape Breton Island, now lives in Nova Scotia, the location of George Elliott Clarke's *Execution Poems.* What Irish poet would dare a title like *All Our Wonder Unavenged*? There is no poem of Domanski that's not luminous at heart.

"Be transported", warns Gary Geddes, when reading the work of Elizabeth Bachinsky (it is as well to remember we're still in Elysium). Jeanette Lynes writes of the "strange dark music of what it means to be human" as a constant in Bachinsky. Her world is anywhere and everywhere, a place of marriage-hunting small-town girls and burst condoms with consequences, where the men are noticeably dependable. A virtuoso across the stock-in trade of poetic forms and metres, the poet even leaves these one-pagers in her dusty wake with her long two-sister trans-Canada road poem "Drive", a kind of pedal-down all female *Bonny & Clyde* at the limits of emotion, tears and fevered transit. Bachinsky is blessed, too, with a wicked sense of humour as in "St. Michael".

Douglas Barbour and Sheila A. Murphy, two poets cycling in tandem across the days to create a poem occupy a rare space: the everyday musings of each dovetailing with the other in seamless transit down the pages in luminous conjunction. A curious (in the Marvellian sense) experiment that succeeds, their duet in verse challenging the void, the inevitable fall, the nihilism in the heavens over the next rise:

> their notes flew over
> what is rumoured to be darkness

One of the big events in Canadian Poetry in 2009 must be the launch at The Hare of Tom Dawe's *Where Genesis Begins.* This book is lovingly introduced by Martina Seifert, DAAD-Lektorin, German Studies, at QUB, and shepherded by Stan Dragland's indepth study of the poet's work at the end, illuminated all the while by the work of Gerald Squires (the Jack B.Yeats of Newfoundland). Taking its cue from the Kavanagh poem "To a Man after the Harrow", the book keeps motley company with among others on stage, Lot's Wife, Thoreau, Asters, Riggs and The Last Keeper

---

surveying Ottawa. I once saw Tom Dawe (a modest, quiet and subversive man) hold the audience in his palm at a concert in Corner Brook, – rolling in the aisles is more apt, as he dissected the follies of politics and politicians: that is, before the Hare Police (in deference to Al and other seven-minute celebs in the line-up) inveigled him off stage. He was doyen of Waterford schoolchildren at his workshops here. The audience at his reading took him to themselves as he stumbled with emotion in his poem on John Clare.

Sometimes the verse of Jay MillAr is that of subversive bristling naturalist. Perhaps he cuts loose fewer times than he should. There is more than a trace of Wordsworthian pantheism in the genes of his poems. This urban business is too much with us. But, then, there is the Lake Shore.

George Johnston, a poets' poet, heeds Yeats's injunction: "Sing [only] whatever is well made", an attention to craft at all times. In the service of celebrating the ordinary across a spectrum of experience, he is a master of diction, tone and nuance, complex form and metre. Acquiring a status akin to Don Francisco Giner de los Ríos (as fondly remembered by Antonio Machado) as mentor, apparently, Johnston's own "Farewell to Teaching" evokes a resonance with O'Carolan's famous lament or the 1792 *Sgarúint na gCompánach.*

But home is where the heart is. Andrea MacPherson in *Away* may recognise in spirit the estrangement of forbears in reverse, like a pilgrim back to first principles, as she traverses countries of the old world. Her gaze is young and constant, sharp yet benign, at once quiet and incisive. In the end, in parched Karterados, she's homesick, longs for home, Canada ("the geography of bougainvillea"):

> I dream of the places I will go once home:
> thick rainforests, yards of lilac and rose bushes
> circular parks with lagoons ...

One doesn't have to read far into Carl Leggo (earning his bread in Vancouver) to discover where his heart is. His poem beginning, "After a semester in Memorial, I returned home with Lana..." could well step off the pages and the illustrious company of the *romance* genre poets in medieval Spain. His father, so well captured in "Lilacs", has just passed on.

The question of terminal sickness, or mortality, as it beckons to those in their prime is always a challenge. *Orphic Politics* by Tim Lilburn is an extraordinary work. In this reader's experience, never was there such a triumphant descent into Hades recorded for an Orpheus in full stride. An Orpheus facing the first-last shock of mortality through illness. The book's incantatory rhythms and primal imagery (in a cascade of personal and social contexts) take the reader, like Eurydice, through the shadowy catacombs of the soul. Will it all end in bleak tears like the original? The cover of the book in its life-sensuousness is a gospel in itself.

Francis Catalano works his own crepuscular world in the second book of a penthology titled *Le Crepuscule des Lieux / The Twilight of Places* due to appear in 2009 or 2010.

Night Work The Sawchuck Poems by Randall Maggs is also a descent into the heart of darkness of the vulnerable hero, in this case the famed hockey goalkeeper. Bardic in its scope and sweep, *Sawchuck* demanded a new language and Maggs forged it for him. In Waterford, and elsewhere in Ireland, and in Canada, people had the privilege of watching, hearing and perhaps adding to this long poem in the making (both countries share a passion for the historically related encounters of hockey and hurling). In this sense, its making had all the provenance of the original epic recited in community, added to and deleted in the communal mind on the rock of veracity. All the feedback probably helped to make the poem the best seller it became, running to new editions and outselling at one stage Cohen and Shakespeare. At a Seán Dunne Festival reading in Waterford, I turned to Kennelly and said,"Why aren't we doing this?" It's not as if every summer Sunday till September fails to witness yet another Gaelic triumph or put-down in packed stadia, glory or humiliation in a space and time as tight as any Grecian unity. Why write of Greek heroes when those of the Kingdom go largely unsung? Seán Ó Tuama's great two-pager on Christy Ring points to a wider dereliction. Why not take on the prose of Tom Humphries, if we're able to? For players more professional for many, as loyal, free, unpaid *amateurs* than some professionals themselves.

Kevin Connolly's "I Really Need Ted Lilly To Throw The Hook" also belongs to this world, coming as it does in the wake of "Double Suicide". Anyone, anywhere, who joins the Sunday or Saturday afternoon or evening faithful, the tens of thousands following the Barnsleys or Westmeaths of football, who have seen Dessie Dolan attempt frees into the Nazi salutes, or fists, of Hill 16, will appreciate this poem:

> We're up two and I'm sick to death of losing.
> It's Posada, never an easy out, but the hook
> is there for Lilly. It's the seventh and his old team,
> the 250-million-dollar Yankees, have beaten the
> shit out of us all week ...

Down from Kavanagh's Seat by the canal, at the embassy launch of her novel, *Outlander*, Gil Adamson, Connolly's partner, placed her man in the forefront of Canadian poets. Who among the packed seats dared to stand up to contradict the six-foot novelist? Except one voice to quip, "If you want to push your novel, go marry a poet" referring to Connolly's refusal to accept the defeat of a manuscript gathering dust, all the while exhorting his partner to move a story that despite publisher rejection after rejection went on to become the multiple award winner it has become. Connolly's *Revolver* has already won its own praise with his earlier *drift* (2004); a comparison with Whitman by one critic may not be farfetched. Another quote has Connolly treading the highwire between "elation and cynicism, joy and grief, terror and love".

Unfortunately, time and circumstance are all too short to allow me to expand more fully on the pleasures of reading the poets in the collections drawn on for this book. This volume can in no way be taken as a canon of contemporaneity in Canadian poetry. It merely represents one *anthos-logia* from the broad field of work out there for the picking and the pleasure. What could be selected within the timespan available. Waiting longer, or reaching further, to collect that extra *anthos* jeopardizes the enterprise as it is. Websites open out on vistas of more individual publications and other anthologies. It is a boundless perspective. Like the old man on Patmos, one could keep gathering and choosing, but there's enough here to be going on with. People *must get their hands on the books* and read them in their entirety, otherwise the anthology becomes the lazy man's read. There is also the skewed nature of this exercise; on more than one occasion I altered the sequence in the originals for the sake of this entity. I seek the forbearance of poet and publisher in this matter.

Elysium... Diane Tucker's *Bright Scarves of Hours* belongs to this shimmering landscape: poems that celebrate veiled grace and contrariness, that list a fascination with recipes, holiday snapshots and the reciprocities of car-pooling and invite the eyes of neighbours in to view the love making of husband and wife ("to husbands and wives"):

> Cast off the dim years of doing it in the dark.
> Let the watered light spread across your backs, your bellies.
> In the history of all the world there has never
> been a belly like that one. There never will be again.

Alan R. Wilson is no stranger to the Pleiades. His *Sky Atlas* for purveyors of the sonnet lists eighty eight in the genre celebrating eighty-eight constellations. Another *tour de force* under the stars that influence our minutiae no less than the tidal pull of the moon.

A particular pleasure was to come across the long poems of W. H. New and David Zieroth, *Along a Snake Fence Riding* and *The Village of Sliding Time* respectively. The first links eight voices along the perimeter of love and loss; the second fairly hurtles with pace, its speed in counterpoint to the staid village lives it depicts.

So, from Arnott to Zieroth, this book moves. In the latter's poem "Had I Stayed on the Farm" the *fiat* of Joanne Arnott's "Conception" leads to the child, the boy in this instance, an archetypal One moving among us again who must get lost, straying off on his own, not in any temple, but

moving along the ditches for days
trapping muskrat and living on
chokeberries and bulrushes
sleeping by a little fire of sticks

until he returns, charting already his own path to immolation,

as someone else, burnt and smoky
his sisters silenced by the strides he took
to reach the pump, the way he drank
from the barn well, his hands
a mesh of little nicks and cuts
where the cries of the animals
had entered him ...

John Ennis, Waterford, February 2009.

Joanne Arnott

from *Mother time* (Ronsdale Press, 2007)

Conception

He lifted her flowered pocketbook from the small pub table
that rose like an island between them. He grasped the small
metal tag on one side, and slowly unzippered the wallet, up,
across, down. Looking inside, he found the second, inner
pocket, and touching the small metal tag, delicately, he
opened the zipper.

He reached for the coin on the table, picked it up with
his pale hand, and placed it inside the inner compartment.

She watched him, transfixed.

Slowly, he closed the inner pocket, the coin held safe.
Then, still with a gentle hand, he closed the outer zipper.
Finally, he placed the flowered pocketbook once more on the
table between them.

She looked at her pocket book for a while, then looked
across the table at him. He met her gaze for a moment, then
glanced away.

"So," he asked, "shall we go?"

"Yes," she responded.

She picked up her pocketbook, all dusky rose, and held
it close to her breast.

"I am ready," she said.

Birth / Wide / Spread

thighs widespread
a compact head
coming down
out of my belly
into

World

this is the first descent

within the context of
my body
formlessness bestirred herself
into form

a whole true human
doubly embodied
then moving down out of

my wide open vulva
my cunt
my lips spread so wide
they might split

the crowning

Energy

I am pulling down from the sky
through the crown of my head

the gift of goddess is
the miracle of body

the miracle of birth and body
the miracle of energy channelled
in a straight line
from crown to crown

through me

the complexity
of becoming

we may never be
this close again, but here
pure
a primal moment

head sliding snug against
cunt/muscle/bone

small cheerful sounds
you are making
I am hearing
your mouth
still enclosed in me
words of parting
greeting

birth/wide/spread

with passage of the head
the hard work of belly and hips
is done

your slippery
body leaves

a wide wake
of pleasure

passing through me

White Solids, Pink Shadows

He gets me where I'm most vulnerable,
in bed, early in the morning,
sucking on my breasts and sprawling
all over my body.

You're too heavy for me,
I mumble.
*Get off. Move over. Lay
beside me.* No,
he wants to do it just
like
this.

The failing brush with intimacy turns into
early morning pushing and shoving,
I end up
telling him to fuck off and
leave me alone. *Just get the hell
out of my room*
I yell
and then he starts slapping me.

This pisses me off.

Because I am bigger,
because I am stronger,
because I am nine times his age
and sleepy
and madder than hell,
inevitably
I win.

A final stinging slap
raises a welt on his
tiny brown butt, white solids
exactly the shape
of three maternal fingers
that connected real well.

Pink shadows demarcate
the shape of each
distinctive finger.

All morning, all afternoon
endless streams of ancient
moments of terror
and childish despair
wash up through my body.

He recovers hours
before I do,
his laughter ringing

through rooms,
the marks on his body fade
into almost
nothing.

He asks me to nurse and we sit
in an armchair together.

I think about being a child
being grown up.

His tenderness reminds me
never to give up.

I search for some plan of action
that might actually begin

to change things.

Decade One

There was a time
when I worried
that the rest of my life
would be spent
drawing little dinosaurs
at your request

I worried
I would be changing
your diapers
forever

Those worries passed
half a lifetime ago
new worries trickled in
swelled
passed in their turn

What I learned from you
stays with me, your little voice
moaning, *all right*
I will
teaching me over
and over again
about domination

Your look of wonder
sitting up in bed
when I, exhausted
by your endless river
of words, asked, "Can't you
lay there quietly
and tell yourself stories
in your head?"
I didn't know
I could do that
you said
our world changed
ever after

The lessons
in precision, like the time
you asked to nurse and I replied
"we need to lay down
for that," and you said *okay*
and stretched out
on that grey suburban sidewalk
ready for me

And all those tender hours
spent with your brothers
the elder, the younger,
your father
your mother
calling us out
inviting us in
wandering off without us

circling back
again

Love when you choose
is a palpable, focussed flow
like the jetting stream
of a firefighter's hose

Articulated wit–
you can bring us to the edge–
a power you are learning
to discriminate with,
use with discretion: less and less
do you find yourself
calling forth
unexpected storms

You arrived
in our lives
in a great hurry
like a thunderbolt
descending
into a family dance
of humour
and of love

When I hurt
I want to bite
and this was true
in the deep of the night
when you were born

"I need something
to bite on," I said
and your auntie, dog-lover
that she is
disappeared from view
then returned
with a rolled-up newspaper

This I declined
so she took it away
and pulled from the closet
a blue plastic oar
for me to gnaw upon

Again, I eschewed her choice
and thus in the very moments
of your birth
I had to pause
and think very carefully
about what exactly it was
that I required

"Please bring me
a clean
cloth diaper," I said
and she did
and I bit down
and you peeked out
and your dad
made of his hands
a cradle
to catch you

Every bit as much
as you were wanted then
you are wanted now

Every bit as much
as you were integral to us
you are integral to us

Ten years old
may seem like
neither here nor there

But you are a boy
resplendent with joy
and I dare you

to show yourself
to the world
to shine your light
to celebrate
as I most definitely do
your life

Remember when I bought
all those dictionaries
last year?

Grab one, son,
because I want you to know
exactly

what is in this
birthday package:
Love, your mom

As a Good Jaguar Should

today I have been
a good mother
my son and I
spent time among
the trees   first
I taught him
how to climb a tree
then   I taught him
how to kill a goat
then   I taught him
always to drag his kill
off to a private place
to feed
and to snarl
at untimely visitors
as a good jaguar should

Thirteen

like a shaggy bear
on the bench in the booth
beside me
he turns restlessly
lays down his head to sleep
then surges up
and orders another plate
of food

I listen
to the poetry man
sing out his heart for his mom
and hear this boy-bear beside me
sucking the last drops of water
from his glass

Separation

My parents are like
crows in the trees who
throw down their voices

Some birds will bounce
right up to you
eat from your hands

But those crows call
and come just so close
turn heads to examine

if you throw food
they will bounce away
take flight

My sons are like flotsam adrift
now seen, now gone again

I do what I can to
gather them up

and fail,
and fail again

My sons are like sweet promise
on the horizon

beauteous colours that enchant
I do not know

do they rise?
do they set?

My husbands are like
the end of the night
in the bar room

after all of the pick-ups
have happened
the partiers gone

My husbands are like
a thousand echoing chapters

row upon row upon row of him
sitting

head in hands

Gone Not Gone

With the kids gone
I sleep in a messy house

that I may wake up
within the illusion

not gone

Grandmother

hawk
starling
robin
crow

through springtime dawns
where winter cold
sighs and fades
and summer warmth
draws near and
takes place

morning after morning
opens grey
buds swell into presence
birds shelter in the wind
songful
full of quarrel
commissioning with voices
the coming of the day

my grandmother
lay dying
someone's infant child, parents
long fled
someone's adolescent girl
long pants in the snow
jaunty tilt of head
someone's bride to be
in courtship by the pig stye
fence
someone's young mum
someone's middle aged
domestic
someone's
old woman

your father loved
to sing
your husband played
the piccolo
your children sang
in church choir
your granddaughters sing
across the final hours
of your use
of breath

my grandmother
lay dying
all of the ages of self
gathered onto one bed
an old, old woman
with handmaidens
who loved to touch
her face
and the crown of her head
who loved to kiss her forehead
her cheek
her neck
as she had done for us
countless times

no longer will I search
my grandma's pockets
for a treat
I search your sightless
eyes
your falling silent
breath

no longer will I see
the bright lines of laughter
dawn across your face
while life still moves

between us
I hold your hand
I love you

a final chance to be with you
in life
all I can do
is watch
and touch
and sing
the final evening

soft as a caress
grandmother
has flown

Song About

this is a song patterned
after a song sung
for centuries

maybe you recognize it

it is a rhyming song
but the rhymes are
in another language

maybe you can hear them

it is a song sung
by a native mum
to her babies

maybe you recognize her

she sang it to her baby who
sang it to her baby
who sang it

maybe you remember her

she married nice gaelic men
she married herself
into the white race

maybe you recognize me

she sang it to her baby who
sang it to her baby
in silence

maybe you can hear me

this is a song patterned
after a song sung
to a baby

maybe you recognize it

it is a song about
it is a song about
a sound caught
in a mother's throat

it is a song about
it is a song about

a song caught
in a mother's throat

it is a song about
it is a song about
it is a song about

Elizabeth Bachinsky

from *Home of Sudden Service* (Nightwood Editions, 2006)

PACK

We learned to sell ourselves early in life. Got badges
for good sales and how to sew. The deft among us praised
for the perfect square knot, we chanted, feverishly
fumbling, *Right over left, left over right and under...*

Polite, our socks yanked tight up under our knees,
we made vows to the Queen. We really meant them.
Our secret hand signals, our hierarchy,
we were like the Freemasons, only smaller.

We were made to circle a mushroom. Not sure why.
The moms, let's not forget the moms—
automatons, pre-programmed to pick up
and drop off and pick up again.

O, they'd crowd in the corner of the gym
unable to pick out their kid from a distance.
All that competition! *Here, here! Over here!*
you'd scream—as if screaming would set you apart.

Later, we would be waitresses, work in factories.
Sell beautiful things we ourselves could not afford.
Later, we'd bury our mothers—every one of us.
Plant mushrooms in the dirt. Circle them.

Brian Macbeth

OF A TIME

When the voices of children are heard on the green
And laughing is heard on the hill,
My heart is at rest within my breast
And everything else is still.

William Blake, "Nurse's Song," *Songs of Innocence*

Here is the place where I grew up:
a ridge of high cold mountain surrounds
a flat town set deep
into a valley. Thirty thousand
people live here, three of them
my own. I am lucky; we keep horses:
two big bays with quick eyes
and soft coats that gleam when I brush them.
I have friends. I bridle my animal
and ride out to meet them. Together, we ride
over pastures into the pale forest light.
Our galloping: our bodies' thrilled moment,
staunch cedars whipped into a green haze,
our paths chopped to bits by hooves.
Now, into the ravine, we lean back
in our saddles, feel our muscles
heat with strain as our horses' haunches dig in
to the bank. We go down, feet thrust
firm in our stirrups as we hit the muddy
water and then—we are light!
Is it possible that such a beast can swim?
He weighs a ton (at least!) but here
he is, his expectant ears pricked forward,
forward, as he glides through the murk.
The trees have made a room for us,
surround our sounds, the sounds of girls
swimming with horses.
How far we are from the town. How
we animate ourselves.

HOW TO BAG YOUR SMALL-TOWN GIRL

Those small-town girls they like to marry early
you know. Can't wait to settle down, have
a kid or two. What they wouldn't give
for a solid man, one who's ready
to rein it in—that rampant prick—and stick
close to home, a good father, provider
and lover, a tall drink of water
who's cool when the pickup's bust, stick
shift stuck in second gear or the condom's broke
again. But there's no such thing as too much man
to handle. Those girls, they like them rough
around the edges, tough boys who'll never balk
at next month's rent with heart enough to love
a woman right, again and again and again.

HOME OF SUDDEN SERVICE

The last year of high school, I got a job
as a pizza delivery person, drove burning hot
stacks of Hawaiian-with-extra-cheese around
all night in my Volkswagen Rabbit. The radio
always playing something like "Smoke
on the Water" or "Crazy on You," and I smoked
so many cigarettes my pointer finger started
turning really yellow. After a while, they let me work
in the kitchen too. Squirting bottles of sweet
tomato sauce onto discs of dough.
I quit that place for the coffee shop with
the medical/dental and got an apartment
with Angel right away, which was about time.
The first month, we made love
in every room. I worked my ass
off in the coffee shop and got myself promoted
to shift supervisor after only four months;
Angel got on full-time at the shop.

So I got my Dogwood and I got pregnant.
Didn't seem to be any reason not to, especially
with the mat leave, and we weren't wrong.
Cole's three-and-a-half now. I have to leave him
with Mom on the days I go to work.
I try to get a lot of early shifts so I can spend
nights with Angel and Cole, but it's hard.
There aren't that many supervisors at the shop,
so I have to work a lot of nights anyway.
It's a lot of responsibility. On my days off
I take Cole to visit his dad at work.
Cole loves a truck up on a jack.
Whenever we show up, we wait for Angel
in the office. There's a sign out front that reads
Home of Sudden Service, but sometimes
it takes him a while to notice us.
When he looks out from under the truck
and sees us, though, he gives
us this shy kind of smile, as if we're his secret
and heat passes through my body like a wave.
Sometimes I think he's still getting used
to the idea of us. When he comes home, he's filthy,
but I love the smell of him, he smells like my father
used to when he came home from work.
I don't know... is that fucked up? I don't think so.

OUTCASTS

> *Search out the early misfit who at school,*
> *sickly for love and giddy with his sex*
> *found friendship like a door banged in his face,*
> *his world a wasteland and himself a fool.*
>
> P.K. Page, "Outcasts"

Across your halls, your double-wide classrooms,
stood gangs of boys in hooded sweatshirts,
jeans and T-shirts artfully arranged
to maximize their apathetic charm
or, perhaps, the leanness of their arms
and backs, their heavy-lidded eyes too full
of your body to ignore: fervent boys
whose gazes promised lecherous intent
and afternoons of fumbled love. But to
search out the early misfit... who at school

among us had such courage? He stood
in his own shadow, his brow a constant line
across his face. You will remember him
as you knew him: not at all, though,
he watched you with the haunted eyes
of a scolded child from the rim of his math text-
book, read the lines your body made under
your clothes. How desperately he loved the
long pale hair that fell to your back like flax,
sickly for love and giddy with his sex;

and yet, his hangdog looks did nothing to
inspire your love. You didn't see, but he
still saw, saw how at night you lay beneath
those undeserving boys, despair rising
in his throat. How could he speak? Too shy
to even say your name aloud or place
his hand beside your hand, he had no words
for what he had to say, and you were gone
besides, too high to care if he, enraged,
found friendship like a door banged in his face.

I tell you, seek him out—or one as like
as you can find; and if he's grown enough
to take your hand, I tell you: give it up.
If you still feel, after all that you have felt,
let go your faux sophistication.
Embrace him. If he unravels like a spool
of thread, so much the better to remind
you of your own pent need. Tell him again
the story of the years you did at school
your world a wasteland, and yourself a fool.

FOR THE PUNK ROCK BOYS

The stars engraved your names indelibly
as ink under my skin, you valley boys:
Sean and Shaun and Michael, Paul and Steve.

How often fifty fingers tried to free
my half-formed breasts on nights you boys,
like stars, engraved your names indelibly

with knives into the bark of a pine tree
or a park bench. The parks filled with your noise.
Sean and Shaun and Michael, Paul and Steve,

how strange you were, above me—strange like thieves
one frightens in a heist. You were just boys
with stars engraved, like names, indelibly

along your boyish veins. You stood out green
under your flesh. You tasted like a choice.
Sean and Shaun and Michael, Paul and Steve,

you wore your anger as you wore your need,
as politic or fashion, such little joy—
and yet, the stars inscribed your names. *Indelibly,*
Sean and Shaun and Michael, Paul and Steve.

ST. MICHAEL

> *And in my heart there stirs a quiet pain*
> *For unremembered lads that not again*
> *Will turn to me at midnight with a cry.*
>   Edna St. Vincent Millay

Once, I slept with this guy
from work. His name was
Michael. He was seventeen,
and I wasn't much
older. I brought him
home with me after
a shift at the coffee shop
where we'd been
squirting whipped cream
on top of mochas
for eight hours or so.
He didn't want to spend
the night. Didn't want
to upset his mom who was
waiting for him to come
home—which was fine
with me. He came;
I leaned onto my elbow,
looked over at him, and he
sighed
just like in Millay's poem,
so we did it again. He tasted
sweet, like something you'd stir
into your coffee.
He told me his father was a man
of the cloth. I didn't know
what that meant to him
or what it was supposed
to mean to me. I put his cock
in my mouth; he went home
anyway. Soon after,

he quit the coffee shop
and got a job landscaping
and I didn't see him again.
Now, I hear, he teaches
English at a Catholic school
in the suburbs. He was
so lovely when he was a boy.

AT FIFTEEN

after Irving Layton

Their chests like planks, bellies
like planks,
I want to undress boys
as a carpenter undresses

a block of pine.
Their clothes, shed like shavings,
smell of aftershave, of pine.
I want them naked, contrapposto,

still as posts. They are so polished
beneath their shirts and jeans.
They are so lean, penises
rearing, eager, impatient as ponies.

Young men: all edges, jut of hip, whip of spine.
What temperamental instruments they are,
what clichéd agonies they moan,
my mouth on them now
and then gone.

Brian Macbeth

MARY HILL

Terrifying, to sit behind the wheel of the car I'd financed
with my father's blessing one Sunday afternoon, him having had

enough of shuttling me. Period. Terrifying, in that one is meant
to drive forward and always look where one is going

and me always uncertain and then certain of something larger
than myself, having imagined that sometime, almost certainly, I

wouldn't *see* anything at all: no line of cars ahead on the freeway,
no oversized inflatable hamburger buffeted in a wind atop

a fast-food franchise, no green-blue horizon or stand of cedar, just this
thank-you-and-collect-your-things *nothing*. Terrifying,

like how salvage is almost slavish, or voice is almost vice.
He'd told me "debt builds

character," meaning "get a job," so I did and drove that car
to get there. Twenty minutes to the warehouse and back, either way,

until I knew that road so well I could drive it with my eyes closed,
so I did,

some eighty kilometres an hour, ten seconds between off-ramp
and concrete divider. "Ten, nine, eight..."

Douglas Barbour & Sheila A. Murphy

from *Continuations* (The University of Alberta Press, 2006)

iv.

out toward the fading light
of day gone, star fallen's
feather drift's a fire inscribed imploded
but beyond bibliograph
spoken's dream said outward
flare offers freedom as gift

practice, fever, strongarm, fate,
the lavish choices drift from fire
the salsa has imploded
here goes speaking on a bet,
a flare, a roster or a feeble
rose to centre what we favour

fate fêted felt as always
already done beforehand's
not what we bargained for
forests fall unheard there
as the river fills
with land thrown out to sea

with sea itself tossing
the lighted trinkets smothered
by momentum tainted near
the frost of havens heard
as land below
the weeds of a priori

choice? a sleight of
hand or brand name
the weight of it
buckles iron and oil
as the slick sticks
life to rock and won't let go...

v.

... commandments spawn likely ingenuity
pronouncing antithetical disjunction
everywhere and from each spigot
of new grace indented
things to have obsessed on
as adults might do when hurt

when were they hurt
those obsessive ones coming
to the same conclusion again
and again disjunctive in fear
and trembling on the verge of
breaking from commands meant

comatose commands tweak live
young, old guilts very plural
in obsession, coming to the same
fear lined with vibrati chock
flavored with verge and nearly
broken in anticipation of the hurt

and can't take it this time
again yet do each time
twisted further into use
less repetition spoken
on the couch again   again
they wait for the shock of

only flowers, less shrill
than thought   previous things
furtively perhaps press in
on nerves and foster
longing for the couch again
st ore/d filaments   of what

mouth opens to silent snow
falling so gently   beyond

transparence   transference
discretion   each frozen flower
blossoming above a hand
held nervous out and opening...

vi.

... and who listens anyway
in the huge auditorium
darkness empty or full
do they   putative   hear
a complex music or the
shattered sense of syntax surprised

and even further into dis
connection, do they veer
back to intended selves,
or is the fall more sharply carved,
so a dividing line, once crossed,
becomes the defining moment

viii

a pulse is caught
pounding as prelude
to the old / making
a floor recalled
to status letters
transformed into thought

underfoot it shakes a shambles
as grooving into some new
beat beaten drum call
to dance beyond thought
thought beyond hierarchy
s call and response

a wafer thin drum tone
begins, then dance in flux
becomes scale model of desire,
the motive of percussion,
without event to stimulate
incessant seasons

modal of desire sharpened
against the rough beat
beat beaten floor bounce
bacchanal / backchannel
converse of shook foil
feel the shiver of skin beat

the slender drift of swan across
thin water passes gravity
toward rhythm shaken
from sleep's desire, glimmer
of crushed reflection
linking floor to tops of trees

x.

... how 'we' called
culled from swept into
what's there   thought
less of   under mind
but not lost in bold
strokes   the the there

one take taken / bold strokes
minded mindful culling from / toward
mantra cooling ferment
of idée fixe
better all the time / the same /
thought there

host not lost   not
gone from mind caught

catching now in tangled muchness
felt in every body motive
action there   mantraed
mandala   worlding

as the spring bird feeds
the autumn bird / a tangled winter
motive secular in action
equals the occasion
to relax upon / caught
host chancing benediction

let be the swash of
colour   let be
its moment   bird
in bush flash   tone
tangles   trompe
l'oeil   brushed   stroked

one is smitten by
the beauty of mistakes
their unintended grace,
their swift resilience,
their resemblance to intention
shifted by a truer mind

no one knows   none
will say   or should
they will get it wrong
take laughter love   take
hold 'error'   its resilience
the grace of   gone now again...

xi.

the everything available
occurs not for the asking
division's infinitely unnatural

but for growth upon the edge
of cliffs where scenes never are
so beautiful as to be taken

and setting sail subjects
the blue below to deeper ruts
running through a safety sought
elsewhere   a place there
blessed if token
taken away from minds made up

breath guides, the mind elides
a past too dark
to leverage rhetoric
too richly dressed and
dight as words step out
fitfully across the dark ...

xiii.

nothing perfectly
becomes / an accident until /
craft segregates the markings
that have whitened / loss
coursing / through foster
placement / randomly sustained

all those lost ones let go
whereof   wherever
accident allows / a gape
of love / a clutching of
the mother / the lines
owed to the paper placing there

the gap / a glove / would touch /
the *is* written on cellophane /
a random mother matched to
a lost child / lines drawn

placed to accidental
session after session / held in time

then moving out / and in
to systems transparent   and incised
with being (t)here
where mother and child (re)unions
sung below the mid / rash call
of leader / ship of the line

tines leave their tuning
a transparent shade etched
onto ritual, the clash
of wills eventually finds
parallel parades calling
for motion, being the motion...

... I want to gather something
white as silence is
presumed, I want to kneel
upon an afternoon's resiliency
night's own earned green
onscreen as wide as sentences resumed

and open to the clear
interpret via all roads lead
from / why is to the call?
I'd sit within that silence
reading all its changes
hearing those sweeter melodies

inclusive of harmonious clarity
the roads one reaches via
silence / within which changes
have interpreted the strand
of song / heard from the sweetness
leading to a reading of the call

xiv.

...her picture in a year when she
seemed beautiful, even sounded
from the page the voice of
a deserved stretched focus,
placed beside the current look of years
the eye eventually releases

time to flow / how beauty
only seems at every moment
in her life to sound the currents
of opinion continuing to change
focus   what an eye untrusting
opens to time after time

she felt, she melded with
surroundance, one infers continuing
as an act of trust, until
the eye needs no more, and
the beauty says itself,
when focus is at last entrusted

to the movements a figure
constructs outward
an aural surround
to dance that space as if
a trust in every next step
instructs beauty's terrible reach

or beauty's most desirable mistakes
that sprawl new purity into
the space aural as figured
speech, practice of trust,
instructive in movement
as the outward ceases to yield fear

but yields to it / beauty's realm re
named as trust   lost to

dusty 'justice' / stories of
death dealt out for someone
s sake as 'the beauty of
the weapons' mis-takes again

apart from winter pear, these
winter temperatures turn elemental
weaponry with muscles flexed
to the point of an unyielding indifference
disguised as dedication, justice,
pressing forward into stories

frozen solid / the 'as if' of
narrative refused   an absolute
zero of muscled movement
all that lovely body
ing forth gone into the
world of righteousness ...

xv.

...what is the point of aspiration,
is there a place to which dance finally
arrives, the step merely a metaphor
for something, perhaps a world within
the chosen calling that eventually confiscates
what inherently is there

taken away it goes further
than believed and the feet stumble
slowly to a stop beneath
the great blossoming chestnut tree
leaning toward seed reaching
out to the dancing stars

collaborating as the standstill snow
feeds earth its topmost layer
beneath which seeds won't stop

the breakthrough planned for
slow rising to stars from chestnuts,
their great shine ...

xxii.

... given as gone / into the world
clouded as salted (Carthage
in flames   again and again)
written on the wind
instruments playing up a
storm troping against angst

shelter comes as figment
and again the wind
plays tutti insistently
as an instrumental urge
to self against the storm
requiring all the instruments

in tandem   song
lines scribed against figments
of imagination's lack
backed into corners
homemade twisted beams
tornadoed darkly toward silence

just before what strikes
comes an unearthly negative
of the strike itself
when something very like imagination
will unmake home twist line after
line into hideous song

silenced in the mist
gathering slowly and with
what gravity flowing
to cover all bodies in

shrouded knowledge they'll
'study war no more'...

xxiv.

... folded the soft page
plies implies a field
of yellow leaves
read and fallen (stars
angst against concrete
listed but unheard

is a fleck of quiet
just about a field beneath
the stars or is there folding
that resists the listed
leaving of the sur
faces implied

any resistance plied surface
faded in ambiguous circumstance
not with standing fast but
stood up   left for dead
lined scrolls of names
gone down gone far beyond

surfaces stand until
surfaces are lost as scrolls
named circumstantial gone and
possibly beyond the fade
of dull resistance far
from lines with ambiguity

Sheri Benning

from *Thin Moon Psalm* (Brick Books, 2007)

What it tastes like
(Frost)

In near dark,
when she's almost
asleep. Smell of coming
rain, wet wool. A spore
of the farm rises in her.
Animals, shadow-pulse.
Her father in the barn.
Rubber boots. Manure.
Open door cedar-light.
Kitchen window weeping
the beet soup loam, sweat
of someone you love. Hands
thick with work and cold
around a hot bowl. Autumn
dusk in bled cloud – loose
straw, spilled oil, a concrete floor.
Steam's in-between-breath pause.
Stars, tin, a drink of well-water.

> *as when you pull a stone from the river,*
> *and hold it in you palm. The light is wrong.*

Sleeping Blue

The night before I leave there is a storm. Wind, a train
down Nevsky that runs past us before we can turn
to see what it is. Street dirt bites our eyes,
sunset culled by fists of cloud.

We undress, hold each other urgently; heat of our bodies
a false certainty. Tired and dumb, we whisper small words,
I love you, I love you, pebbles to dam the tide of coming morning.
Forgive us. We don't know how. Love is not inevitable –

when we meet what can't be named, that we choose to love
is a kind of grace that shades everything. Like the soft shadows
of night-snow turning winter into a sleeping-animal blue.

In the morning we take a cab to the airport.
Sky, a bloodless face we can't read, suspect it might be judging us.
We think we might've lacked courage the night before,
though we don't say.

Sometimes I will dream of return, but in the dreams, clouds entropy.
Wind shears your face. And instead of coming home with bread and wine
to find me reading at our kitchen table, a candle gutters
and you will walk away.

At the airport we sit on the steps, share a cigarette.
Without thinking you reach over to wipe something from my lip,
hold your finger there. Later you help me carry my bags through customs,
yell an insult back at the guards before you kiss each of my eyelids,

and promise we'll meet soon. Forgive us, we lack courage.
Don't know how to hold the pose of letting go. But the grace
of the moment on the step, your finger, pressed to my lip,
its small shadow – a sleeping-animal blue.

Mikiskaw

The fire which torments us becomes the rose;
our suffering shall be something beautiful.
                    – Larry Benning, study notes on *Four Quartets*, 1967

Fall. Running through cougar-shadow light and the clove smell of summer's
death-simmer. Blade of winter held at my throat so I can't see it, only feel its
thin sting on the mothskin of my neck. Soon poplars will be pleading hands
with nothing to hold,

fear-chocked throats. Remember my father in the hospital last year. Muscle
of his work decayed until I found my own body–breastbone wicker-ridge, colt
knee bulge. Holding his driftwood bones, hands, a hollow gray, the colour left

when wind peels back light, I had never hated someone more. His limbs
naked but for the whispery hospital cotton, that last bloodless leaf's cling-by-
the-nails desperation. Running now in viscous harvest-sun,

I remember that Cree trappers have a word for this season to come, for the
heldbreathness between gilded leaves and mother-curves of snow, the waiting
for ice to swell at lake's temples.

Bird-bones

Air screamed through your bird-bones as you flew
from your snowmobile, into a field of snow and stubble,

once an inland sea. Your spine unhinged.
I stand around the corner of your hospital room,

Andrew, listen to my father sing as he holds your quivering legs.
What emerges from our bodies cracked open? The stiff door

of an abandoned farmhouse: orbit of dust,
flurry of dark wings. Propelled

by the thrum of your heart you landed
in a prairie of frozen stars, my father's song –

the one he sang to me when I fell here, heart-first
and screaming, into the sudden rush of sky.

Descent from the Cross [1]

Rembrandt, 1634
Hermitage Museum
St. Petersburg, Russia

1

The face in Rembrandt of the man pulling Christ off the cross. It's my father
pacing from the machine shed to the barn. Night diffuse with the silence of *I
have nothing*. Empty-arm begging of autumn fields beneath sky. Dry snow —
flaked stars, moths of reflected light. Wheat two bucks a bushel. Harvest dust-
thin. His body a reed flexed with work and frost. In the middle of his life, a
grief that stops blood.

In the painting, a woman holds a candle. The worn-cotton glow of the
yardlight poorly cloaking the black of night. The man pulling Christ off the
cross is thinking nothing. Not *what should I do? what should I do?* because to
look it in the eye is to die. He's just standing, now in the barn, the heat of
sleeping breath, straw, manure. His bloodless face drifts in the cadence of
animal-pulse. Across his shoulders a burlap sack of feed. Against his cheek,
silence where a heart once beat.

Fidelity

"At last the fidelity of things opens our eyes"
                    – Zbigniew Herbert

Once my sister was sick. So much had happened to her body
over which she had no say; it lay dormant in her sinew for years.

But then, the aftershock –

I sat beside her when they slipped her body into the MRI.
I wanted to hold her, but couldn't, so I prayed

as though I was a bargain-hunting pauper willing to trade up
glass beads and feathers, something as useless as my life,

for her safety. As though a prayer could be anything
other than a plover's nest in marram grass, vulnerable

to what is always devastatingly unknown.
That night, driving in Saskatoon, she didn't believe

the moon could look like it did, so I drove her to the edge of the city's halo.
Hemmed in by wheat and barley, glow of a bare bulb in the root cellar

of August dusk, we hung our heads out the car windows
into cricket hum. Stars and there it was –

moon, a cupped palm, sallow,
and ready to receive.

What it tastes like
(Salt)

In the smeared light
of a hardware store,
urine smell of burning
coffee. Against some hip,
the dead-leaf crush of a diaper.
It rises in her. Shadows
threshed by noon sun

implying nothing. A fly
in a bowl of bloated cereal,
sweet milk. Jack-in-the-box
cartoon-caw of a TV left on
a room away. Her father
in a harrow-cloud of brittle
earth. Lilacs, like swollen
lips, in a jam jar. Yesterday's
boiled potatoes. Carrots
in the sink. The metal
taste of dirt. Her mother
in the kitchen, crying.

> *Her body won't forget. Ridge of skin*
> *after the sloughing of a scab.*

Dance

My brother wakes me to tell me about his night: breath,
whiskey, smoke, starred December sky. How he danced

with a woman the way I once showed him —
he too misses a body scarred by the same steep

path of birth. We now live a country apart.
Dancing together is rare. Slow hum of heat

echoes the shape of him, lifts me
from a dream of drowning in that creek

west of our farm, where our thirst for return
began, the fetal glow of my face in reeds —

I refuse to let go of the home
we were cast from so I can begin

to breathe. His clove breath,
starred sky, echo of heat,

tell me of night. We now live
a country apart, dancing is rare.

He wakes me to forgive me
for believing my despair

is like no other despair.

The colour of

The shameless meandering of leaves, the colour of
some slow jazz trumpet, of yeah-i-loved-you-so-
what-ness. A half-step off, semitone descent.

Somewhere someone is desperately in love with you.
He's trying to slough the shiver of loss with manual labour.
He's painting houses and with every brush stroke he is stabbed
by a memory of *the thinnest blue song*.

How he told you your eyes are the colour of the distance
within an embrace *the thinnest blue song*, in the spring
of a city where the sun doesn't set; between the sky
and the Neva at midnight, *the thinnest blue song*,
that time you took a boat along the Fontonka canal.

His words and the fumes are rotting his brain
as he paints someone's damned house all day, watches
CNN all night, wonders whose bed you're sleeping in, hums
the thinnest blue song the thinnest blue song

and you in this shameless meandering of leaves, the colour of
some cliché for pride, of hold-your-head-high as you fall
at a half-step-off chromatic pace.

November Light:

1
November light, without a home –
back-bent, on the corner of Whyte and 105th
in a torn jean-jacket, cigarette-smoke gray, muttering
at passersby about the darkness that is coming.
Few listen. Few even turn their heads.

2
Light of that aborted pig fetus in the dusty quart jar
at the back of the grade ten Biology cupboard.

3
Afraid to open your mail? Shadows
under your eyes? When you think,
do you just get sad?

4
Not October light, the whisky-jack drunk
on fermented crabapples dancing in the dying
flames of the apple tree.

5
Of bone-ash and clay,
which harden into something that can shatter.
If you must, speak in hushed tones.

6
The doe's coat turns dun so she can hide
in the spaces cut by bare aspen branches near
the Saskatchewan river. Only her wet-eyed stare
is visible. November light, something unseen
watching.

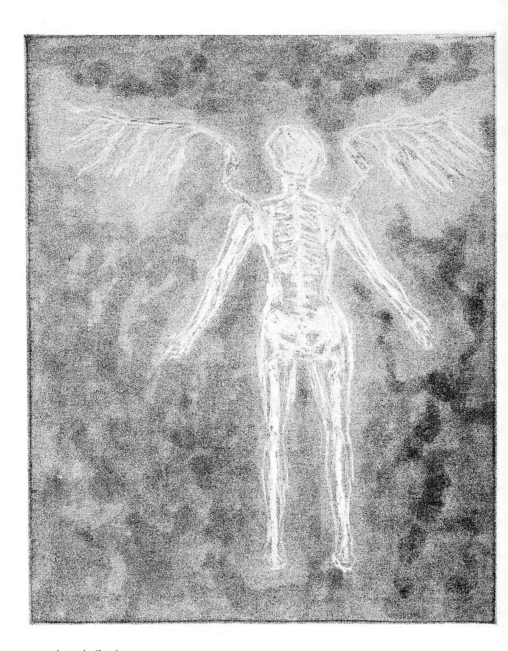

Amanda Goodyear

Bones in the wings

When he kissed me between my shoulder blades,
I thought how the bones in the wings of birds,
are as fragile as the skim of first frost
on pasture grass – early morning,
late August.

Wolverine Creek

Fall. When scraped fields
show us the empty-
cathedral air inside us.

Shrew sounds of leaves,
bleeding at a pace the eye can't hold.
As a child standing in willow kindle,

grasses the yellow of grandma's dying
arms, watching geese harrow a sky made
more blue by the radiance of decay,

asking for a sign –
*if you are there, spell this
in the furrow of geese*

and always unable to decode
their flight, to find the equation, a basket
to heap meaning, grandma's apron full of chokecherries,

small questions, *why in death the smell of estrus?*
But soon the geese over Wolverine,
the creek that doglegs our land.

Standing in their wake,
mind made small by another's height,
left with the imprecision of loss –

strewn chokecherries, their bee-sting
taste. Learning we reckon only through
loss: the place where we begin.

The Breath of Looking

i)

The great horned owl underfeather you found
suspended on brome teaches you about the near
imperceptibility of grief. About thinness.
How light, hardly snared by down,
filters through and changes just-so
and so grief wears you, makes
you its slight shadow.

ii)

The great horned owl underfeather teaches you
about the eyes of someone you long for. How if they could
stroke you, they would be as graceful as the almost
weightless. How if you could look at the sky
through them, you would feel smaller,
but not less.

iii)

The great horned owl teaches you that the knack for
flight has something to do with silence. Its wings polish
planes of air; distance shimmers in their wake. In the after-
weep hiccoughing hearts of poplar leaves, how
to feel the silk breath
of looking.

St. Benedict's Rule

You make tea for a man who was your lover.
Where once there was desire, now a palm-sized heartbeat,
pleasant to hold. Open wings of frost on the window.

He waits at a table the colour of old teeth.
Outside the abbey's kitchen (a killdeer's nest
in fescue) a blizzard has cried itself to sleep.

Snowdrifts, wide-eyed, torn, at the corners of doors.
Whisper-light of lamp, soft-furred shadow,
metronome-breath of sleep.

You feel the thread of his gaze weave
a tapestry of the ablution that you are
performing for him:

gnawed-on kettle's lost key rattle; damp
cheek of steam; small sounds of pouring water, words
that you murmur when you think no one is looking.

Bark and flower steeping in veined
Wheat Pool mugs. All scraps of shed clothes
from a grandmother's rag-bag, the smell of farm-

chapped hands, diesel, cured clover,
still in her worn poplin, in his worn flannel.
Once he was your lover,

he lived in a cabin on the border
of the abbey's halo. After vespers you'd go
to him. Stars, eyes of birch craning into night.

Wind in evergreens,
a lucid dream, Wolverine Creek
untethered from gravity by sleep.

He lit stubs of old altar candles, showed you how
to play the guitar. Spice of his hair as he knelt before
you: beeswax, wool, smoke. Moon, a blade

sharpened so many times its light grown
soft. The care he took: willow-
balm for feet and hair,

each button
undone, each finger
warmed beneath his tongue.

E. D. Blodgett

from *Elegy* (The University of Alberta Press, 2005)

… One of your letters lay
open beside me
on a table as if

forgotten and then found
again because the light
of afternoon had changed

or was it I who was
suddenly open then
who had not seen what you

had said of you and me
of what you too forgot
and then recalled surprised

I want to write to you
and ask you why you do
not die and ask you then

why there is nowhere I
can send what I might ask
before forgetting you…

… I take another note
of yours into my hands
to gaze upon the sketch

that holds up the words
its inability
to speak gazing at me

as if it were a child
that had just been born
its tongue unused to seize

the shape of words and so
it merely utters *o*
its mouth taken by

astonishment before
falling mute again
the only answer I

can muster is an *o*
that only I can hear
your sketch unable to

take in the least sound
as children who are deaf
or children but still born

How did I dare to say
that I would be the one
that would forget you

rather I should ask
what do rivers recall
when they go down to sea

so I stare at the sea
and know that I am not
recalled or known or seen

A small object of yours
was placed into my hands
I saw it was a stone

that you would carry in
the hope it would protect
you moving over the earth

I tried to make it warm
but it refused and lay
inertly in my hand

without you to keep
it warm it must be just
a stone and cold and dead

I want your hand in mine
without it I will be
a stone too and cold ...

... So when at night I say
my prayers who will be there
to hear what I might say

not you not God but just
myself and I have heard
all these murmurs before

that fill the air inside
my room and cling to all
the objects there unsure

of what their purpose is
prayers are only us
and in them we become

someone else who
fills a larger space
with more uncertainty ...

...A leaf is nothing else
without the barest sense
of where its life comes from

it hangs upon a branch
in sun and rain and dark
its capability

its being there alone
neither forsaken nor
waiting and being is

all that it can be
nor does it know where it
might be but in the air

its only movement from
the wind   its stillness from
the parting of the wind...

...Without my knowing how
I have become grass
and it takes root inside

my soul beneath the stars
which fill my soul's sky
but they remain so far

nearest then is grass
and its fragility
that is in me as I

must be in it   the smell
of its autumnal weight
gently rising in me

if I lie down here
it will be in the fall
of all mortality ...

...So my waking turns
to sleep deep as the sea
with all that it has borne

a solitary bird cries out
against the starry sky
its unaccompanied song

music does not fall
from its mouth but only light
falling through the dark

until it falls into
my heart as if it were
its only place to fall

music of light has no
melody known but when
its presence is announced

nothing remains untouched
turning to light within
the dark that silently

withdraws becoming just
the shadow of the dance
its finalities

the gift that gives the soul
its bright necessities
among the floating stars

Beverley Brenna

from *FAST FORWARD NEW SASKATCHEWAN POETS* (Hagios, 2007)

Sport Fishing at St. Brieux

The water boils with tiny pickerel,
bodies churning
in and out of St. Brieux's bowl.

Restless boats sulking in the reeds,
men stand braced with Pilsner
lifting fish that from a distance flash like dimes.

Ed Corveau is one of them,
cap a screwed on tribute
to the Montréal Canadians.

Ed's wife has left him,
run off to the other side of town
with Luc the Banker.

Thinking of his empty house,
Ed rips the pickerel from his hook,
its mouth a torn stem.

He throws it back,
bends to watch the blue white stomach twist,
the fins like mottled petals, sinking

and he thinks of her before the wedding
on her graduation night
how he pinned an orchid to her dress.

Betrayal

The house they built together
now defies her,
paper peeling
from cracked walls,
floorboards shifting with the tugging wind.

Nights she lies alone
and sifts through sounds
she cannot name
the rising fear
that someone's there.

Room by room, she piles furniture
in windows, doorways, thin arms stiff
as branches; hiding in the kitchen –
cans stacked just inside the door –
she counts preserves by candlelight.

But sleeping here beside the stove
cannot prevent the walls from entering her dreams,
calling moist obscenities
What is it you want? she whispers
even as her children come to pack her things.

Heather Brett

from manuscript in progress

Transvestite, seated

after Diane Arbus

There are points to be considered here:
Light and highlights,
horizontals, straights and narrows,
that levelled, complaisant gaze:
the cross on the tee
of transvestite,
the hangbeam of the y in boy.

The mantle leads,
right-angled neck against relaxed shoulder
or the other way about. Thigh to shy knee,
the sheen of nylon stocking.
A scribbled strip of edge along the seat:
Black patent shoe.
Ruled flooring, tongue and lip of groove.

I cannot sleep.
Beams across the ceiling underline it.

The Formation of Ice Crystals

for Paul

It's early, before nine
and minus five in Omagh.
Then a side road
over the flattened hills
towards Fermanagh.

Rime frost follows the fog,
frozen air weighted,
a halo around every tree
inhaling light,
a white lei along every branch
a caught breath over every bush.

This hush has stalked me
for weeks,
cold numbing of rehearsed words,
ice crystals on my tongue
chilling my speech.
A chance to acclimatise
adjust to all things cold.
The future bleak,
bereft and abundant
in one and the same breath.

When I said space,
I really meant distance.

Oh Ireland

for Katie and Margaret McAleese

The second leaving,
a Spring day in March
and a railway station in the north
and the very last time you see your sister.
She gets an hour off from the mill
to say goodbye forever.
Then Belfast, the docks, the pier awash with tears.
A boat to Southampton
for the liner out.
You're on your own now,
the first leaving back
when you fell for the protestant,
threw your hat in with the other crowd,
broke free from every sort of rope
that bound convention.

March sea, the cheaper fare.
A full week moored to your cabin
while the ocean swells,
falls back,
waves tilt and thicken with ice.
Ireland behind you,
the Atlantic below
and a new found coastline beckons.
Those were the years of telegraphs and distance
thin airmails and funerals,
snow drifts, and lamps for the darkness.
All the leaving and the waiting,
to go or get there or even return,
two sides of the same tossed coin
a silver bright half-crown,
or perhaps, that unfamiliar dollar.

Instinct

for my son, Greg

Morning, early, the last wet breath
then an instant of startling clarity
before the burnish
that slightest of blush on the backdrop;
a promise.

My son, the man:
always the blonde child
laughing from the water.
Always the young pietà
I cradled

The last breath.
Dusk swallows delicately
all the birdsong,
the flowers stretch,
the red-bronze day.

Cinnabar Moth and the Messenger

When the grass is this long
I rise early,
metallic rasp of pheasant,
insistent muffle
of a collared, cooing wood pigeon:
trillings and twitterings
placed so lightly in the
backdrop of the settling day;
the whole morning
slowly and surely balancing,
bracing and flexing to enfold
these many hours.

Grass cool and damp
springs, clover purples
between my toes like bruised
and cream chrysanthemums.
My friend the scientist says
that for every 10,000 stems
there is only one four-leafed clover,
some odds then, luck to be plucked at random.
And I think of the travelling blacksmith,
his gift of a horseshoe and one nail
that I toted back to the kingdom,
Gower and Franklin on my mind.

Light floods the sky, a tint of yellow promise,
something aqua rising.
Ragwort stalks the garden, laden
with inch-long, voracious caterpillars,
black and amber larvae
black and red in their formal wear,
evening cape and gothic collar.
A messenger lands,
cocks his head and his eyes hold.
Whatever comes, he says,
won't be pleasant:
can't be undone.

daughter...

above the sink, on the windowsill
I have placed your photograph.

At least once a day, I stand here
gazing in on you.

That one time I dreamt of you,
you were wearing sky blue,

your hair a blond sheaf
falling: you turned towards me

and your smile was knowing.
Everything and all that we are.

Each day, I tell you how sorry I am,
notice how your voice is fading.

I only moved here last September,
I still paint a little, still write.

Why is it that I can't hear you?
It's like you're behind

a wall of thick glass,
a snow globe, where you're always twenty,

always smiling.
Is it me? Have I stopped listening?

I put the knives away,
fold over the dishcloth.

Francis Catalano

de Le Crepuscule des Lieux

Désert désir

Le ciel   en petites coupures, à plates coutures
     que tranche la ligne-hache des montagnes acérées arides
       retailles de papier voltigeant bleu
par-delà les pics ocres, les socles esthétiques
     avions de guerre furtifs dissimulés
       dans les pétroglyphes
    ici-bas un noyau de pêche irréel
       roule irrégulier   irradié
sur la voie carrossable chauffée
     par les pneus, les noeuds
      par le peu d'âme   le trop plein de rien
    dans les réservoirs d'essence
et les réserves d'indiens

          (vers Monument Valley)

The west, ouais, oui, ouest
      où est l'est, à l'ouest   ouais
         aller où l'ouest est
d'ici à san, à alex   aller avec alex
    vers l'est aztèque ou avec lou vers l'ouest
   le toit ouvrant   le soleil dedans
     à l'apex, au texaco
taches d'huile à l'est de l'essence
      the west, the best, ouais
    eighty-eight, sixty-six, at least, the east
     est estival, est estimé, est stomacal
         et tests dans l'ouest
    des amants on the road
l'ouest, oui, et les aimants
    yes, yes, yes,...

(I don't North)

Le blanc vin   et l'herbe vert-bouteille
et le roc   les ocres   les profils ogres
                        aigle jaune safran
          buvant une courbe
          de soleil   survole
des coyotes hot   des poissons frétillent
     et les lacs apache   et roosevelt
le blanc vin blond
          dans le verre tournoie   verdoie
le même aigle   jaune safran
     fonce vers le *nihil*   le vide
          serres serrées, boucle bouclée
                        un lézard pétrifié dans l'idem
une pluie de proies   crochu
     le bec-cible et branchu et fourchu et fichu
Arizona, as is que fend un pionnier
          pioche à hauteur de joue du pion
     du grand chef   du cavalier   du roi
et mat   et regarde   et prend garde
                et cætera

          (Le blanc vin et l'herbe vert-bouteille)

La Terre est un litchi (il appert)   vu du bleu
                                   hublot sec ovale
vu de l'objectif-géode   la Terre est un canyon
          plateau de lumière   derrière
     les microbes changent de peau les planètes leur plan
          dieu-serpent, serpent-dieu
sur la route en lacet   écrasé par un pneu
par ce peu d'âme qui roule
          la Terre veut, la Terre peut
     la Terre sauve-qui-peut
par une mue de Kyoto,
zen le fruit sur la branche fléchissante
          apache hachis

                (Sur une branche fléchissante)

Passe un train-scie polychrome
        une file Malévitch de rectangles Kandinsky
le long d'un vers volumétrique de Sandburg
train-train, locomotive, nature morte vivante
        imperturbable hache
        inexorable hachis de cailloutis
moteurs à combustion, explosion du roc
        érosion du corps et de l'âme
siècles attachés un à un au mouvement sans frein
        sans entrain   vers le programme-progrès
        sous la fourchette-assiette
et surtout, surtout   bonnes bises aux bisons

                (« Freedom is cheap » C. Sandburg)

J'ai la nette sensation   d'être une auto louée
        vouée au lave-auto   auto-auto
      faite pour rouler   *que* pour rouler
            auto non à soi, auto à tous
        que tout le monde conduit
on pose sa signature, laisse le volant à un autre
c'est comme la langue, ça sent le neuf
              mais c'est usagé
          on monte, descend
on remet les clés au suivant
qui y va de sa conduite, avec son style, son technolecte
        langage illimité, air climatisé, GPS, lecteur CD
        pourvu qu'à la remise du véhicule
            les niveaux — du sens? des sens? de la langue? —
                      soient les mêmes qu'au début
            à moitié plein   à moitié vide
peu importe   à moitié
dans la moiteur de l'été

             (Devant la baie de San Diego)

Si le soleil est l'oeuf la Terre — je m'en veux —
                    est le rond du poêle
une spirale aspire les mots, les casse
                    il convient avant le silence
de casser la coquille des mots, leur substance
          s'étend   comme la mer
les mots   les jaunes   le soleil s'étendent aussi
grillant sur le vieux rond de poêle en spirale
                    altitude zéro Terre
                    degré absolu
faisant en sorte que le poème prenne, s'uniformalise
     pour qu'il redevienne blanc
comme le silence d'avant
          avant la bouche de l'univers

                    (Tous les Waffle House du monde)

Fumé le fumier miscellanées peyotl, whisky & tobacco
          font effet le sol, *soil, oil*
les fruits et légumes bio
          poussant dans les sillons   de l'encéphale
sont des protocerveaux   protubérances du
Colorado en action, déviation déniée   vol à vau l'eau
                                             vol à vau de mirage
          d'un hyperdivorce post-ironique d'oiseaux
trois cents caplets d'un anti-diarrhéique   chutant
                    d'un trou dans les nuages-iguanes
          qui éblouit le toit ouvrant
d'autant ouvrant qu'en chemin
                    la fiente s'annihile
          s'autofertilise, éclôt
                    ô raison merdique
tassée toute   dans le comprimé imagination

                    (Fumé le fumier)

Jan Conn

from *Botero's Beautiful Horses* (Brick Books, 2008)

In Bolivia Once

In Bolivia it took me five years to traverse a river.
Could be today I'm in a demolition derby or a boot camp,
my young lover about to turn 50, my serenity my anxiety.

Here's a toy dog, here's a little pool it laps—
with the moon and a forest scene including nearly nude
female, essence of beauty, incremental at best.

Same moon later on the darkened ridge, heaven needs editing.
In an old movie the moment's eclipsed and during the black-out
we're kissing like crazy, hiding from the director's assistant.

This month punishes my teeth. November, after the hawks
have migrated and the rock climbers descended
at sunrise, a bit stiff in the shoulders from holding up the stars.

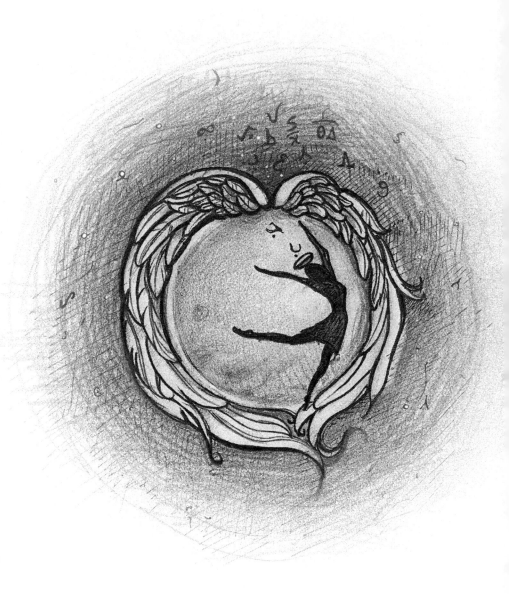

Michelle Lee

The Clipped Language of Mathematics

I

Tom in printed shirt and black jeans defines, in the clipped language
of mathematics, the inverse of a matrix,

a forced translation of the life of a star. How I love you *alpha* and
beta, yes and even the square root of a window

where outside is blossoming the delirious magnolia
and crepe myrtle, the shy queen,

or a red-tailed hawk is dismembering a squirrel.
$N=1$ hawk a random sample so insignificant we throw it away.

II

The boulder: russet, pitted—worn out by history.
A fragment of the moon, exhausted by lovers' laments,

witness to untold numbers of tired metaphors.
Beneath the boulder the woman with lavender hair

and violet eyes holds a pose for the sculptor.

Her calm demeanor, top of her class at Miss Elkington's charm school, but
boulder beats telephone book balanced on top of the head

for keeping the spine erect. In her mind she's hurtling through
outer space, no sign of gravity. Speaking to the stars in Arabic

and explaining the dreaded sum of squares,
the approximation of the approximation...

There are more than enough stars, like an audience, to satisfy sample size.

for Christine Kowal Post

Fragrance of the Moon

Ghost of Buddy Bolden strolling Shell Beach, moonstruck,
scattering high silver cornet notes. Outscatting the moon.

Notes blown so pure and loud they create new tides—the now-famous
Bolden Tide carries away sleeping babies and old men

melancholic in their nursing homes.

*

Fragrance of the moon:
white musk or cold, like new snow on granite. Leads

to drinking, dancing solitary at midnight. Oh, give me a kiss,
a honeydew, a spray can of *Moonlight on Demand.*

Those glow-in-the-dark stars I mailed to my nephew, belatedly,
for his birthday on the Ides of March, I saw them last night,

they made the Dog Star howl, they stole Cassiopeia's heart.

Brian Macbeth

Spanish Insane Asylum, 1941

By spoon or by force bright red food enters my mouth.
A black pig exits with an apple.
I feel prehistoric. Lindora, the nurse, insists it's a transitory phase.
What if my ears really do become arrestingly large leaves?

I think I will hire a pair of sculptors or brick masons
to carry me around in a closed litter today.
Tribal men in grey cloaks arrive and leave.
In the basement the double-headed serpent is training
to do figure eights.

In the middle of the arched bridge she halts
and lets her hair fall into the roiling water.
Each morning her three bluebottle flies attach to her wrists
and take her for a stroll.

Don't bother me. I'm painting tablecloths with meaningful symbols.
Erasing my father.
She gave me a set of pearls and then took them back.
She dresses me in tulle.

This ward is filled with quietly and noisily desperate souls.
In my left side there's an electric plug,
and my heart is lying by itself on a striped towel.
The resident squids spend their long days
reporting my every move.

Hanging over your head is a large pair of scissors.
When they should be sleeping, what do the townspeople of Santander do?
It's all the same, the storm principle.
The head on the back of the chair speaks to me.
Some days I prefer the darkness.

                              *

Today the bison of Altamira thunder through the clinic.
We're near the sea, we inhale its rogue aroma night and day.
We're frightened by its suck and gurgle, treacherous depths.
I yearn for the burned down 15th century town,

the stone buildings. Father Stone, I'll be yours tonight.

Can I return to Paris now,
to Mr. Birdman? Brilliant crimson feathers frame his face.
Is he mine or yours?
An elderly king in sapphire shoes is pulled along on a flat
horse-faced cart.
Is he going to the races or to hell?

She hides turkeys, smothered in gravy, beneath her bed.
I learn to speak owl.
There are many anorexics here but I'm not one of them.
He wants to be able to see through the wall
and inside my body to my uterus. It's ultramarine.

I'm a handsome man with too many secrets,
striding down a flight of stairs.
There's a family of cards in the room next to mine.
Queens of Hearts is the only one to speak. The others
moan and whistle, giggle and hum.

*

...it's just my skin is not my skin anymore.
One attractive inmate keeps stroking my index finger.
If I concentrate hard enough I can disguise myself as a horse.
Or I could live the remainder of my life as a pogo stick.

The tide comes in and now they want to ship me to South Africa.
No, says the doctor. He wants to cram my veins
with yellow Jell-O.
My mind is alive with ghosts.
She puts slivers of mirror on my toast.

In my insect net I catch songs and voices. Of course
I don't listen to them!
She built a labyrinth in my room
so I cannot find my way out of bed.
All the inmates drink tea in the afternoons
out on the patio, with their nurses on leashes.

The priest tried to visit me but I saw the tiny devils all over his jacket.
His visiting card tasted of dark chocolate.
To reach our pills left on a sand bar
with our name on it, we all have to swim
in the dreaded ocean. I have the farthest to go.

for Marlene Belfort

The Hydraulics of Rabbit

At fifteen I sketch RABBIT
not rabbit. Something
from nothing. Ink on thin paper, nearly translucent.
See lagomorph, see me.
Beneath rabbit's shadow, love is not
a many-splendoured thing but remote
and mathematical, dark blue in hue.
A hydraulics puzzle. The hind legs jacked up
on special levers, twitch of ears and nose the result
of many fine wires.

My father, water. My mother, on fire.
Scorching the doorframe of the kitchen.
Jump little lagomorph, jump!
Into the convent, behind grey walls.
All those ominous watchers.
At the arched windows
the nuns wave good-bye, white
handkerchiefs billowing in a hot wind,
when I'm accepted into Real Academia.
The same wind, years later, chases me across the Atlantic.

Erin Gerrity

Tower Song (A Poem in Celebration of Darwin's Birthday)

I

She dwells alone in a medieval town, in the 21st century, how
is this possible? A stern-looking woman with a feather

tucked into the brim of her flat black hat. In front of her
an anonymous goateed man with a bulging sack of live birds

that escape one by one as he cycles along.
Behind her, young golden-haired girls in choir gowns,

more tentative, ride among the birds, pedaling
sedately but with rebellion in their hearts,

a jewel illuminating their secret desires. Away they go!
To the tower!

II

Somewhere outside time and mind,
the golden-haired beauties embroider the mantle of the world.

Some madman or genius conducts their weave
in time with high clear notes, a composition for flute such as Rampal

plays in the afterlife. They leap
into one of the boats sailing away on the

crystalline seas at the horizon—too many orange triangles
in the tower, and outside the sky is mutinous and unruly.

We see an animal (species unknown), a lobster, a nautilus wherein abide
three golden birds. The animals are docile and mild, for which we have

Mr. Blessed-are-the-Meek to thank. Evolution, we say, and at the same time
someone insists on Lamarck's inherited musculature. It's akin to watching

a ping-pong match with an infinite number of balls in the air, or an
outmoded TV show we once sang along to, when we were much

younger, of course, but now we might be tempted again, if only to save
Darwin from such a ridiculous fate. *My* childhood, we shout,

stamping our feet.

III

One young woman flees to a new dimension, standing upright
with her arm linked to his in a boat made of thunderclouds,

lightning to steer by. She wasn't at ease in the tower,
wanting a different life, much improved, enchanted, constructed,

glorious, the weather not to be trifled with. The sky striated and hot,
despite the lateness of the hour, and he, cast from a heaven

in which we do not believe, conjures a sail from his linen cloak.
They are headed toward a mountain, whispering

because of what might be within hearing or firing range. After all,
they have run away and now they are shocked to see themselves

up ahead and from the back, but younger. Frightened,
determined, nothing can stop them. They enter the lit cave.

Brian Macbeth

Eros

Handsome marble statue, fig-leafed, upright
on a pedestal in a fountain in a courtyard paved
with slate flagging and last year's leaves. Eros,
we guess, his irises gleaming emerald,

his torso taut as a drum. Beyond the courtyard
it's early spring, lilacs with their heady scent,
everywhere the luxury of novel, riotous growth.
I wonder what you are doing in Paris tonight,

and with whom. I wonder how we conjured a love
that became so swollen and discordant. Your borrowed
views of women, sweetheart, were positively archaic.
Don't ask how I'm doing because I've had a bad day

on the lip of a volcano, exploring the ruins of Cuicuilco
in the searing Mexican sun, the mysteries of Paraclesian
alchemy turning my brain into a knot.
There remain streets of blasted statuary

and rubble between us, my darling,
despite our shared history of surrealist art,
decalcomania and Freudian psychoanalysis.
Long past midnight Eros steps cautiously out of his pool

and approaches a door, knocking discreetly, meets
a striking dark-haired woman, doffs his fig-leaf
and you can guess the rest, except he doesn't
return to the fountain or the century that created the courtyard.

Brian Macbeth

Cametá

I recall the little town of Cametá,
how in the mornings the butter yellow walls of our room
would be radiant, light pouring in, farther in,
unstoppable. Then the mango trees wired with speakers
would crackle, daylong, Chico Buarque and English songs
from the 60s and 70s filled with saudade.

How do we survive the past, its long stutter
running beyond us as clouds fleeing overhead
on a windy day seen from the top of a hill. Then erase
one by one the hill, the wind, the clouds. One's private Chagall,
blue figure of dream, or the nightmare dragon with its
large malevolent eye, glistening in the cold rain.

Once I rowed a wooden boat
to a cobalt island, where all the rocks were shades
of blue. I dreamed this again and again.
Perhaps I was trying to grow up but could not,
for the blue was the blue of raw feelings, confusion, somehow
mixed in with my mother's sudden death.

South along the Tocantins
our last stop was Cametá, where we all nearly drowned
when the boat hit a partly-submerged island, throwing us
overboard into the tall tangle of water plants, the black
turbulent water. Afterward, still in shock,
we ate a late dinner, telling the story over and over.

My mother's last Christmas, 1975, I was
the only child who didn't come, and I have always wished
I had been with her when they came to take her away,
and then carried her ashes to the graveyard in Toronto.

How calm the water looked, later,
as we walked by the untroubled shore, unable to sleep,
and the stars glittered hard and sharp, Orion
wheeling far away to the east—

Brian Macbeth

Rumour of Silk

Tonight I should take the roan from the stables
and go, leave the old capital of San Salvador,

and my green-eyed beauty. She is wild, and longs for silk.
In the whole of southern Brazil, not a single silkworm.

Nor even a seed of a mulberry tree.
In the rainforest, it is said, everything grows.

I know the cannonball tree—its provocative crimson flowers,
and the ceiba with its secrets. The capoeira master

said I should travel north to Manaus. Where the two rivers meet
in ink blue and terracotta, I may find a rumour of silk.

Kevin Connolly

from *Revolver* (House of Anansi Press, 2008)

Antonia is not the Plasterer

1

Agnes, Betsy, Cornelius and Dexter each voted for a class president.
Dana is the cousin of the girl who attends Lincoln.
Pat studied the spelling list with Mickey and the other girl, but both
did better in the contest than he did.
Lauren is a female, and the other two animals are male.

2.

Five students in each class (Bob, Cathy, Dan, Ed, Faye) are each the
best at a certain subject.
Jorgenson used to work at Giant Corp. but then got a better offer
from the company where she's working now.
The animal in the Tacoma Zoo, which is not the aardvark, can
climb trees.
Ingram is younger than Lathem.

3.

Antonia, Colleen, Emmanuel and Gustav, whose last names are Dewey,
Hamilton, Kennedy and Shaw, are a biologist, a flight attendant, a
magician and a plasterer.
The person who voted for Hough is taller than Betsy and the person
who voted for Grant.
The girl who attends Carver used to live next door to a boy
named Nelson.
Jackie did better in the contest than Mickey did.

4.

Amherst, Bartlett, Croft, Davies and Enders each listened to a
rebroadcast of an old radio program (*Fibber McGee and Molly, The Green
Hornet, Jack Benny, The Lone Ranger, The Shadow*).
Lauren is larger than the animal who lives in the house.

Cathy and the student who is the best at handwriting had lunch at
school with Bob and the student who is best at geography.
Litton, who has been with the same company for twenty years,
worked her way up from the bottom.

5.
Five animals (aardvark, bear, cheetah, elephant, zebra) live in zoos in
different cities (Detroit, Houston, Omaha, San Diego, Tacoma).
Debbie is younger than Harold but older than King and Art.
Shaw, who is not Antonia, is very good at her work, which is not part
of the building industry.
Agnes did not vote for Hough.

6.
Dana, Ephram, John and Martha attend four different schools (Adams,
Carver, King, Lincoln).
Pat studied the spelling list with Mickey and the other girl, but both
did better in the contest than he did.
Enders didn't listen to the Jack Benny program.
The animal who lives in the barn is angry at the mouse who tricked
him yesterday.

7.
Art, Bob, Cathy, Debbie and Harold have last names of Green, Ingram,
Jones, King and Lathem.
The president of Big Co. and his wife go golfing several times a year.
The fastest animal is in the San Diego zoo.
Neither Amherst nor Croft listened to a comedy program.

8.
Bobby, Jackie, Mickey and Pat finished in first, second, third and
fourth places in a spelling contest.
Bartlett listened to a program about the Old West.
Lauren is larger than the animal who lives in the house.
Dan and the student who is best at handwriting walked home from
the school with the student who is best at reading.

9.

Figure out who (Jorgenson, Kiley, Litton, Tyler) is the president of
which company (Big Co., Giant Corp., Mammoth Co., Super Co.).
The striped animal is not in a zoo in the southern part of the country.
Jones is older than either of the other men, but is younger than Green.
Kennedy, who is not the magician, is older than Hamilton and is
younger than Emmanuel.

10.

Lauren, Norman and Peter are a cat, a dog and a mouse. They live in
a barn, a garage and a house.
Dan, Cathy and the student who is best at spelling walked to school
with Ed and the student who is best at geography.
The president of Big Co. and his wife go golfing several times a year.
Antonia is not the plasterer.

11.

Match them up from the clues below.
Match up the student and the subject from the clues below.
Match up everything from the clues below.
Match them up from the clues below.
Match up each animal with the zoo where it lives.
Match each person with the school attached.
Match the first names with the last names.
Figure out how each person did in the contest
        and whether the person is boy or a girl.
Kiley doesn't know the president of Mammoth Co. but has heard of him.
Figure out who is what and who lives where.

Clean Head

for Daniel Jones

To you it's a pincer, to the crab
it's just the crutch that keeps him up
nights, upright in a sudden current,
or the force that backs him into

the metaphor of a very famous poet,
or the thing that gets him boiled
and quartered over drawn butter.
Like tattooing and piercing is cool,

but if I pulled a knife, ran it over my face
diagonally, maybe nicked an eye
or something — because I thought I'd
look dead windswept — everyone who

knows me would fear for my sanity.
An ominous sign, they'd say, like
a radical change in hairstyle, a
cry for help favoured by the suicidal.

And it's true — the one friend I know
who killed himself died with a clean
head and a fresh prescription.
But illness is not the sum of it. Not really.

Really it's about still caring — about
what duels you, scares you to death.
Seconds tumbled smooth like stones.
Nauseous flyboy stumbling to the tarmac,

as if the sudden quiet, this sense of being
grounded, was all new to him.

Aunt Olive Amongst the Heavy-Petters

When she's not talking, and that's rare enough even with the
goiter, she can't hear a thing — a plus for an old girl who,
unlike her kin, ends one bottle before opening another.
There's glass plastered into garden walls, a threat of poison
tossed in with the carp and lettuce and marine lilies.
Throw as many googlies as you like — there's no one to lob
your balls back, not like at Normandy, not like the B of B.

There's Herbert, rangy brother, rung twitchy by the Blitz and
fled for Spain; sister Doris trapped by jealousy and duty
and bingo; two sons and their brood of boys — too
young and squirmy to kiss you properly,

though you remember the pier as it was, before the moribund
casino and manmade "recreation" pond, crowds so big then
young lovers risked the low tide for a bit of privacy.
Salt on a lip's kiss, little hands shoved up under your jumper.
Who could resist their boldness, who'd want to? The rejected
and leftover, sunlit cads, and best — the hungry boys,
dead and buried in their minds already, improbably reprieved.

Thirty-One

Your skin is pierced with hunted hearts
I trifled with and left for lost.
Their full wings, airy arts?
Frail instruments I took for ghosts.

How many trawled and bleachy drips
have strangled on those fingertips?
Ditties for the dead, speaking parts,
which now seem less-than-pretty trips

downriver, where they peddle frowns.
Past grasses any current drowns,
you followed every line I tossed
with swallows only you could dodge.

All skin I took, I swallow freely now,
and you (all heart) scale every rib of me.

Double Suicide

However fondly devised, there's something feral
about it: that identical strangers would want out

in the exact increment it takes to push past reason,
that one wouldn't love it more than another, his fix
on her the narcotic that makes her miss her stop.

Of course, it's a matter of assumption — your lover
wouldn't let it go, but surely Christ or somesuch might
— it not really *your* idea, him that hopeless about the lost
job, lost hope, lost baby, lost chance to fix Dad
finally, for what he did or didn't do.

Photos being photos, they record the watcher's tones.
No soliloquy outthinks its author. Still, the camera
captures blinds, bodies, bed, and the swallowed logic:
destroy her as she'd destroyed him, or surely would
have, faced with the sight of her dead.

I Really Need Ted Lilly To Throw The Hook

We're up two and I'm sick to death of losing.
It's Posada, never an easy out, but the hook
is there for Lilly. It's the seventh and his old team,
the 250-million-dollar Yankees, have beaten the
shit out of us all week. Faced with a real
pitcher, they're driving up the count,
knowing it's Speier or Ligtenberg or Frasor
to follow, who never seem to get a call, or
forgot how to pitch the minute they put on the
stupid new uniform. High fastball . . . strike. Change,
down the shoot, whiff. Fastball, fishing, off the plate.

And now I really need Ted Lilly to throw the hook.
It changes nothing, but it's suddenly important now.

Mary Dalton

from *Between You and the Weather* (Running the Goat Press, 2008)

A second skin—
my oily demeanour
between you and the weather.

*

A miniature planet,
I glow with a watery light.
See my lines of longitude;
see my small beard
and my single green horn.

*

Oh you may judge it bluster,
but I'm the most stupendous of travellers.
They talk of me from the Pole to Cape Horn.
All a-quiver, they dub me prima donna,
say I relish melodrama,
savour a tornado, or a good typhoon.

*

I'm your open sesame,
your abracadabra.
Your own greedy Gollum.
Compact, rectangular,
your pal at the bazaar.
Depend on me
and I'll go for your jugular.

*

You dare call me drudge?
Think again, mister.
As shadows lengthen
I'm witch-horse,

the scarecrow's mother,
the lurker in the corner.

*

An old man, an infant:
my emblems.
I run through the fields like a hare.
I run my fingers through your hair.

*

Muscle of water.
Speckled lunge.
Anti-freeze in my blood,
iron, a gold ring and a
small pig in my belly,
I charge the depths.

*

A pale-faced patron,
I've paid your salary.
At your table a regular.
But I harbour grim secrets:
I've served the torturer;
I've put that flush in your cheek.

*

A jumbled alphabet,
I'm a means to your saying.
A skittering creature
at rest by my side.

*

I'm a cold-hearted dazzler,
an albino chameleon—
now light as a feather,
now hefty, a burden.
I warn you now:
it'll end in tears.

*

A breathing apparatus,
I gave the Irish their letters.
Some folks cleave to me,
thwarting my killers.

       *

Oh, it's all very well—
when you're tired or you're down
you creep to my altar,
slide into my trance.
You know how
to push my buttons.
Then for days you ignore me.
One day you'll find it
harder to leave me.
It's your comfort I think of—
I squat here and wait.

       *

I'm a small bass fiddle,
cow-swallower,
king of the slime,
the plague's first note.

       *

Coffin or cradle—
the waves decide.

       *

A rumble, a murmur.
A spring erection, rosy,
unfurling quick to
crinkly green fans.

       *

Small as a flicker,
huge as a mountain.
Wind's my fickle friend.
Tame me, I'll serve you.

Turn your back, I'll
devour you
and all that's about you.

      *

There was a bruising at my making.
After, I seethed.
I can make folks glad,
or I can steal their brains.

      *

I am an old beast,
an ancient howl
caught in my throat.
When I utter
from my flared mouth,
all the lost cry out.

      *

Michelle Lee

I'm a jaunty fellow,
a sparkling guest
in my thin white suit
and my jolly red hat.
Invite me in,
you'll wish you hadn't.
A convicted thief,
I'm hard to evict.

*

I know the secrets of trees,
but there's a terrible blank
at my heart.
Like a burnt-out comedian
I rely on other's lines.

*

I'm invisible,
yet changeable.
I'm light as eider
and fierce as a tiger.
I've four lieutenants
to do my bidding.

*

Wesley Bates, Woman on the Shore

You coaxed me up out of the sea—
you've always needed me—
probed bowels of the earth,
all just to cull me.
I've built up vast empires.
Lethal and vital,
I'm a matter of tears.

                    *

Once the woods were home;
I had a sure footing.
Now I've learned to love flux.
Where it's all ups and downs
I'm the wind's painted plaything.

                    *

A small tent—
a bar across.
A gateway:
avatar of beginnings.
                    *

Me, a thing of wisps and flutters,
a green hand?
Guess again.
I am the ancient one,
the survivor.
I launch my messengers
all over the earth.

                    *

Gerald Squires, Lot's Wife

Tom Dawe

from *Where Genesis Begins* (Breakwater Books, 2009)

Lot's Wife

Flat character. Cutout
illustration for a Sunday school lesson:
                    disobedient woman.
We never even knew
her name.

But flesh her out, remembering
all flesh harks back
                    to fire,
imagine reasons
for her looking back. Grant her
at least curiosity.

Some say two married daughters remained
in the holocaust.
But the story leaves room
                    for options:
What about other relatives
and friends? What about enemies?
Was she bored with God and religion?
Indifferent? Stuck in a rut? Sick of her lot?
Perverse? Tired of taking orders from patriarchs?
Did she have lovers
burning for her in Sodom?
Did somebody in the smoke
                    call out her name?

Irit, like the child in the fairy tale,
stooping furtively,
pocketing bright pebbles
                    for the way back.

Big bang over her shoulder. Irit
swerving, staring back into genesis.

Irit, woman as landscape.
                    Salt of the earth.

Alone on the barrens,
by a solitary leaning rock,
I sometimes hear her name
chirping
in my head.

Thoreau

(for Enos Watts)

I thought of you today
in that hush
after a woodpecker
somewhere across the swamp
had stopped drumming
leaving woods and fields
no longer what they were.

You who claimed
that all sound
even our speech
is the beginning
of pregnant silence.
You listening to the rhythm
of your own drummer
long after the flicker
had flown.

You in the ticking
of your mother's clock
carved wooden grandfather
behind her in the hall

when as a child
she used to get out of bed
after midnight
secretly
sitting on a summer doorstep
savouring the world's silences
and growing up
in the lilt of warm evenings
falling in love
with quietude
along Concord's Virginia Road
when lowing of distant cattle
carried brooks and meadows
and landscapes altered
in the strains of Joe Merriam
local farmer
not as familiar anymore
whistling to his horses
in the dark.

Years later in your cabin
on Walden Pond
you listening
to a faint steam whistle
becoming bumblebee
inside a flower
and an unknown flute player
far off in the dusk
expanding the remoteness
of the universe
another Krishna
piping the planet
into place again.

You always receptive
to the world's harp strings
right where you were.
Your pulse in time

with beetle tick
and cricket chant.

Your wakeful local night
more meaningful
than any long journey.

Asters

With summer gone
and you in the fall of something,
suddenly turn one day,
look over your shoulder,
and there they are,
stars in a ditch.

You whose ancestors,
before any chaos
of Michaelmas,
once knew a goddess
who cried
petals of patience
and afterthought
down to a parched world.

In stardust you were young once,
in love, on a shaman's path
to divination,
your quest for charms
and panacea
coming on.

Today, in another September,
alone on a back road,
you glimpse purple markers,
galaxies underfoot,
reminders

that no explosion,
this side of the first big blast,
could better the silent one,

when these petalled asteroids
        and all
                their relatives
collided with
receptive earth.

Bess

On goat-tramped hills
outside walled towns
in ancient times,
you might have been
the one cast out
to carry plague away.

Further north,
in remote hamlets,
you might have been
village whore, bog-maiden,
noose around neck,
riding rough tumbrel
into oblivion.

In the New World
of Puritans,
you might have been
a scarlet woman
tempting church elders,
labelled by scripture
for prison, stock or scaffold.

For me,
you are a recurring memory

of a trip
to old St. John's.
In a scent of grapes and gasoline
my uncle's loaded drunk,
staggering along.
I'm six years old,
stumbling to keep up,
your raucous voice
calling out to him
through snow squalls
in from the Narrows.

"Sam...Sam...
Ya knows
what I wants now...
me skin."

Suddenly, as you swing from an alley,
he's snarling, cursing,
punching you to the ground.
You crumble like a reefer.

He starts to run
and I run after him,
crying, afraid to look behind.
Pain pricks my ribs.
The wind scrapes
like a splitting-knife.
Drifting snow blurs everything.

So many years ago now,
I still hear him
laughing
on the way home
when I ask
who took your skin away,

poor outport exile,
beaten street-beater,
lady of the flies.

All those winters gone.
A child's question
still jigging in my mind.

The Last House

According to legend,
a bird fluttered
into the great hall
of feasting one night,
above all the music and chatter,
window to window –
then was gone.
And the harpist looked up, singing
our life is like that,
one brief, bright moment
between two darknesses.

This morning I am alone
on the abandoned island,
in the last house standing.
The fires are out,
the music gone.
The feasters have left the table.

I followed something
up from landwash,
small, ruffled, grey,
flitting in through a warped
doorframe,
out another.

In from buttercups
and rat-tails
strumming
on the wind.

Out into sea light
and strings of morning glories
tuned along cellar stones.

Fogscape

(for Stan Dragland)

Loren Eiseley once said
the fog made him feel free,
unobserved,
himself,
gave foretaste
of what it means
to become ghost.
How wonderful
he might have felt
in Newfoundland.

Once, on the Cape Shore,
I heard a woman say
she found "company" in the fog,
the way things shifted
each time she looked up
to that gap in the hills
where her son walked off
one morning years ago,
on his way to the mainland.

Alone today, on a headland,
I wonder if anyone or
anything sees me
ghosting near lighthouse
and solitary grave
of the keeper's daughter,
young woman of another century,
still
in this place

where the wind ties knots
in tuckamore.

Salt on my lips,
reminding me again
of origins,
luminous abstractions
of first chaos.
Fog eradicates horizon.
Surf pounds rock.
Sea birds haggle
somewhere.

I am brushed out
in the immense flow
of a Turner landscape
where solid forms
are sacrificed,
smashed
in a sun-wobbling vortex
of silver,
strangely liberated
in my insignificance.

Riggs

Riggs always waited for the Lord's Day
to bother people,
sauntering from house to house,
asking to use the telephone.
Eventually, after warnings
from the welfare officer,
nobody would let him
make a call back home
to the outport that always
hung up on him anyway.

But Riggs still waited for Sunday.
For this, he tolerated the pills of Monday,
slumbering it all into Tuesday
when a bus packed him and the others
off to a rec-center
for darts and shuffleboard.
He snaked and laddered
through Wednesday and Thursday,
bingo cards blurring
into months on a calendar.

On Friday, when the aroma
of fish-sticks floated up corridors,
he became more familiar.
Sometimes the old mariner in him
rose up to corner a guest,
recounting once more
years ago at the ice

when the captain called him aside
to say: "You're a good man, Riggs."

Saturday night, alone in his cubicle,
stripped for a bath,
he watched his torso in a mirror,
contours of the bumpy shoulder
shaped in childhood by a blow
from his father's pitch-fork.
And the old man
glaring back at him
from Man-O-War Gulch,
that place in the north
where men sometimes went ashore
for bare-fisted boxing matches
to settle disputes
over fishing berths.

Riggs longed for Sunday.
Against whatever waited

he had the Lord's Day
and a number
scrawled on cigarette paper
deep in his pocket.

Tea Room

A simple abode. Utensils few,
plain, unassuming.
Nothing extra in the room
but a bunch of flowers,
a picture on the wall.
Even a bit of poverty.
A singing kettle,
the distant sound of water falling,
wind blowing.

My mother's place
out on the headland
almost qualifies.
She still there at eighty-odd,
tranquil, reverent, solitary,
telling me over again,
still crafting
that story about the time
her uncle had tea
with a poor fisherman in Toslow,
the best he ever tasted –
from an old tin can.

The two of us,
over steaming cups,
philosophers
at a plain table.

In my mother's house
are many
mansions.

Cowboys

He was a few years older than the rest of us
but that never stopped Frank, the Catholic boy,
from joining us sometimes for a game of
cowboys.
How easy those days of white cloud
when granite beach became prairie,
and dry kelp rolled by
like tumbleweed.

On his last day with us,
he arrived with half a muzzleloader
and the eye sockets of a gas mask
from an abandoned cellar.
He lit us a small fire, outlaw style,
in the ribs of a caplin-skiff.

That was the day the priest came
and took him away,
without a word.
We knew little then
what it meant
to have a girl
in trouble
on the Cape Shore.

Just like that,
the Lone Ranger was unmasked,
dragged up through a cabbage patch
by a frail, sickly fellow
in a black frock.

And nobody,
not even Hopalong Cassidy,
Red Ryder or the Cisco Kid
could do a thing
about it.

No way at all
for any good cowboy
to go.

Solomon Kane

beloved principal of the old school,
was an outport legend.

Sometimes in a rage,
he'd leave the room,
race over to the merchant's shop,
dip his strap
into the pickle barrel.

Solomon Kane, master
of the bloody switch,
respected for pounding
Euclid, arithmetic
and the Laws of Moses
into students' heads.

Today his last homily
towers up through nettles
on a tombstone
in an abandoned churchyard.
"The dead in Christ
shall rise first."

He waits deep down
in glacial clay,
pinned by the prongs
of juniper roots,

still teaching.

Slips

"Slips" he always called them,
moving away from us
in woodsy October sunshine,
rabbit snares coiled
and bulging in his pockets.

This is years ago.
Mother is spreading a picnic blanket.
I cry after Father,
but Mother comforts me,
explaining he won't be long.
Waiting, I toss chuckley pears
into a swift brook,
watching them
swirl away.

He returns in a scent of turf,
squashberries and pipe tobacco,
sitting on the blanket
to tell me things:
I learn that rabbits
turn white for winter,
their feet are lucky,
and a brace is two.

Now, many years later,
just the two of us
in his hospital room
on a snowy afternoon,

he in his final dementia,
a Lear of sorts, babbling
in his own
great storm,

and I, crying inside,
wanting to follow him
again.

"A great place for slips," he says,
indicating the white walls
and the long, fluorescent corridor.
"Rabbit paths all over the place."

"Do the doctors catch any?"
I ask, playing along, and

just for a second or two,
the old hunter arrogance surfaces,
the planter's entrenched resentment
of all authority:

"They wouldn't catch shit,"
he snarls.

The Last Keeper

He has kept a light,
but not the proud, familial one.
The lanes are safe now.

Not like in the day of
those men looking down from frames
on the cold, grey wall.

They had their shipwrecks,
storied rescues and storms;
they were sometimes heroes.

He has kept a light,
the great silver arc rotating
through dutiful days;

careful records too:
caplin-scull counts, bird-calls
low in evening light,

and sketches of shells,

watercolours, sea-carved
landscapes abounding.

Now, in his last week,
as decreed by Ottawa,
he has seen a sign:

a trout ring appearing
at last in the small pool
he stocked three years ago.

Just for a moment, today
by his pruned rose-bush,
he feels the ancestors

looking down on him.
He straightens up suddenly,
peers off to sea.

He has kept a light. Ottawa
and the ancestors both
can go to hell.

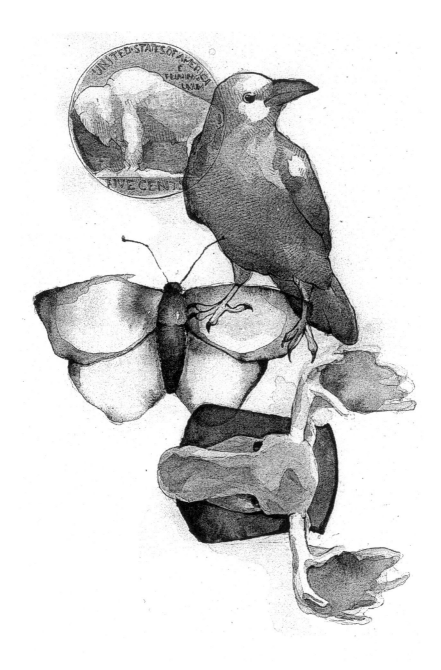

Ida Floreak

Rosanna Deerchild

from *this is a small northern town* (The Muses Company, 2008)

indian bay

my brothers and sister
forge a parental note
buy a pack of smokes
hustle a drunk
into buying them
a six-pack for a beer

they sit on the bleachers
behind indian bay
smoke   drink   talk shit
about other kids
each other and this shitty town
watch the sun melt away
radio full blast   creedance warns
there's a bad moon on the rise

later they laugh jostle for room
on the narrow sidewalk
then lean heavy on each other
sneak past the escalating war
between mama and daddy
in the kitchen

drag a dresser across
the bedroom door
turn up the record player
drown out the sound
of small bombs exploding
downstairs

my brothers and sister
are a ragged rebellion
cap a beer off the window ledge

pass a cigarette back and forth
take long drags   the smoke slips out   drifts
across the moon on the rise
over indian bay

rain

dark hair falls
down her back
straight and neat
full moon face
high cheek bones
small pert mouth
smooth olive skin

auntie claimed my sister
as her own   burnished her
with love   told her
hold your head up
my girl hold it high

walked with those words
until she was 9
and mama took
her back to help
around the house

daddy calls her too proud
brings home a green dress
from the neighbour's garbage
tries to make her wear it
but she won't

not even when he beats her
keeps her in her room
to hide the bruises
she misses church
then school
a week passes

i wait until everyone
is asleep   go down the hall
stand at her door   listen
for her breathing   scratch
at the wood until she lets me in
we lay together   listen to rain falling
i tell her bed time stories
promise to build her an ark

static

he takes apart radios
all kinds clock radios
stereos walkmans tape
recorders   all dissected
my brothers tiny pliers
screwdrivers precise
in his hands

ron's had ear infections
since he was a baby
now sound is distorted
like a radio frequency
turning to static

he takes apart radios
to solve the mystery
of how to keep sound
crouches over each one
begins his slow
disassembly
gold and silver coils
springs   transformers
rheostats scattered
all over the floor
finds each one silent

one man's garbage

daddy is a garbage man
has never worked at inco mine
doesn't talk about nickel
or mortgage payments
those are luckier people than us
but ah he says
I know so much about them
disgusting what people throw away
look here a perfectly good jacket
a lamp with a missing switch
an 8-track player that still works

there is more he collects
their deceit   a ripped up letter
still in its envelope
words smeared   stinging
lilith why did you leave me
family photos
with cheating fathers cut out
positive pregnancy test
for teenage daughters
daddy sees it all

all week collects his treasures
drinks *OV* beer at the tavern
spews his garbage
hey
saw your wife's clothes in the dump
did she leave you
laughs and laughs
shoulders hunched up
like a crazed hyena

Jessi Dearborn

forbidden to go barefoot blues

my feet hate shoes   especially the black shiny fake leather kind forced on
sundays feet wrapped in coloured tights   then bound in hot squeaky sabbath
day shoes   mama has to catch me first calls out   *rosanna marie*   as i run
thru backdoor backyard   sandbox   feeling toes sink in
you get back in this house   but i am gone   dog on my heels into bush
sensation of earth
on feet bottoms   can't catch me   daddy yells   *if you don't get back here*
right now
his anger a net that always captures me   drags me back   trapped into those
sunday hell shoes
forced to march   learn about jesus   who always walked barefoot   swing low
my weighed down feet like sweet chariot   to hymns   church man preaching
i sing quietly the 'forbidden to go barefoot' blues

Ida Floreak

hiding in the dark

it's the last saturday
before school starts
the kids on my block
meet for one last game
of hide and seek in the dark
i am barefoot and ready
to show them
i am the best

the seeker counts
as fast as possible
everyone scatters
like a handful
of dropped coins

i run past them all
my dark skin a cloak
here I come ready or not

wedged between a house
and a blue chrysler
jesse the junior hockey player
squeezes in beside me

he wears a jersey that says
jesse is # 1 on the back
his mom says he's going to the nhl
but everyone knows he only scores
with girls on the block who say
he's so cute and let him cop a feel

my stomach sways
and i cross my arms
but jesse doesn't try anything
just asks my name
how i got so good
at hide and seek
must be in the blood hey

jesse says *you're a half-breed*
your dad is white right
at least you're not an Indian
he doesn't know it
but he tags me   hard
i am it   i am out

jesse takes off for home-free
leaves me hiding in the dark
my eyes burn   blur the stars

i go home fall asleep
to calls of *1 2 3 on you*

crazy horse is a girl

our street is at the top
of the only hill in town
it's steep   curves to the right
a four way stop at the bottom

kids play chicken on their bikes
race down two at a time
until someone breaks
leaves question marks
in the gravel   or fly full speed
through the cross road
like an exclamation point

the possibility of grievous injury
makes their pale skin flush   say
holy shit did you see that

someone double dog dares me
and i get my sisters old bike
my feet don't reach the ground
so i push it to the top   get on
take off   the air and the adrenalin
tingles my skin

half way down i see
plumes of dust like balloons
heading for the intersection
push back on the peddles
expect the surety of breaks
but the chain whirs uselessly
fear flares in my chest
i can't slow down

my racing rival skids to a stop
near the bottom
open-mouthed   as i speed past
braids flying   elbows up
eyes straight ahead
the sound of dog barking
somewhere behind me

car and bike close in
until the middle aged
woman behind the wheel
finally sees me   surprise
then panic   blares her horn
screeches to a stop   screams
jesus, mary and josiff
but i'm long gone

back at the top of the hill
the boy i raced waits
kids stare say
you didn't even slow down

i tell them i wasn't scared
that the car missed me
by this > < much

i tell them
i am crazy horse
fearless
                    ghostlike

cousin comes in from the bush

still half-cut from all night partying
my cousin wakes me at 7 am
n'chi mis
he says in slurred cree
let's go for breakfast

his name is boy-who-is-always-smiling
his name is laughter-in-my-heart
his name is always-holds-my-hand

i wear my dawn-yellow sundress
on the corner a bright yellow
corvette stingray slows to a stop
my cousin staggers to a standstill   yells
now how in the hell
do you haul wood
in something like that

our laughter echoes
off sunday morning
like the sun glinting
off its chrome hubcaps
then as if one fell off   clattered
loudly down the street
mr. stingray screams
dirty indian go home

suddenly i see
my cousin's ripped shirt
beer spilled down the front
of his northern store jeans
his dark brown skin a stain
on this scrubbed white mining town
my shame matches up
with the revving engine
of a speeding away
stingray

*n'chi mis – little sister

blue

sometimes
after her husband leaves for work
mama locks the door
breakfast dishes still
on the table   she puts *elvis*
on the record player   his voice
like the sky   a deep blue curtain

sits on the back step
elbows rest on her knees
lights a cigarette
takes a long drag
exhales   the smoke
like a small cloud
in the cool air

the grass is overrun
with dandelions again
and there's always too much
goddamn work to do
but for now she sings
blue suede shoes   her favourite
says   *this song*
reminds me
but doesn't finish her sentence

the sun slices
over the house across the way
like a sudden tear in fabric
mama takes one last drag
flicks her cigarette into the grass
the needle on the record player hisses
to a stop

in my brother's letter

he said it was daddy's blood
the way it spewed out of his nose
like scrawled red crayon
across a clean white page

the rage came so easily
a thunder from the pit
of his stomach   rattled
his rib cage   his body
knocked his breath out
felt just like lightning
exploding in his skull
and then the crack
burning everything up

in my brother's letter
he says when he found
daddy kneeling over our sister
the room silent   except
for the rhythmic sound
of his hand across her face
he knew it would be the last time
and daddy didn't make a sound
except to say
do it again be a man
after my brother hit him
for the first time

worth

me and lola visit a farm during summer vacation   mining town girls learn to
milk a cow   play hide and seek on flat farm land   in the dark   in the barn
country boys knock down a swallows nest   laugh at their self-impressive aim

i stare down at the perfect hollow of straw   bits of branch   strings of wool
and four desperate pink bodies inside

country boys say they're as good as dead   best to stomp out life now raise
their boots

but me and lola stop them   watch mama fly overhead   frantic   mourning
her delicate wings cannot save them   our little girl hands useless   our scent
they say would only extend rejection to other nests   still we return
throughout the day only to watch each baby grow silent   cold

mama bird gone   resigned

i grow angry at her   at country boys   at flat farm land   at lola

the sun is setting   red and orange smudge the straight line of land and sky
me and lola

stand over the last life   we are silent   its tiny beak opens   closes   crying

suddenly i am running   out of the barn   across the yard   through the
outlining bush   to the pond we swam in just last night   lola is lost behind me

i have one bird in my hand   her warm body imprints on my palms   her heart
beats   no sound comes from her now   i watch until her eyes close   feel her
body cool   her heart stills

                                                                        stops

back home

mama says we're going back home
for a funeral and even though
we should be sad   we hide smiles
it's been years since we left

when we get off the ferry
a crowd meets us
aunties   uncles
about 20 cousins
press in close   touch
our hair   kiss our faces

at auntie's house
she feeds us moose meat
fried in a cast iron pan
bannock and lard
goose and macaroni soup

our cousins take us down to the lake
we skip rocks   play   watch the sky turn
orange   red   purple   until fat with stars
they ask   *what's town like*
we say confusing

our parents play cards
drink red rose tea in mason jars
tease each other in cree
guffaw say   *tapwe*

this is where mama was born
where pictures of my absent father
hang on family walls   my pictures
in auntie and uncle's memory boxes

me in rubber boots and diapers
sitting next to my cousin
my brothers and sister

dusty faces   messy hair
playing with puppies
in a bush camp

auntie folds her soft brown hands
around mine   holds me in a place
i was lost from   whispers
my girl

uncle asks   *do you remember*
I fed you sucker head soup
we raised you in this house
do you remember natanis

and in my skin
the same colors
as theirs
i do

natanis — my daughter

tapwe — true

Brian Macbeth

Keita Demming

from *We Have a Voice: An Anthology of African and Caribbean Student Writing in BC* (UBC, 2006)

Blackness

A few minutes after six and I can't sleep
thinking of my university colleagues who think they know me,
think they understand me.
The truth is they
are my friends because
they think being black is cool.
They think living the life of hip-hop is cool
and having a black friend gives them status.

"Hey, look, I have a *(trophy)* black boy as my friend!"

They know neither the burdens nor the blessings of having tinted skin.
They do not know the shame of being stripped naked in the bitter cold
by society's judgment, because of tinted skin.
They know nothing of being made to feel that there is something wrong
with your skin tone.
For them my blackness is cool.
My blackness is fashionable.
My blackness is a trend.
For them my blackness is MTV and BET news.

But I have news for them.
NOT MTV news,
NOT BET news,
But real news.
My blackness is not a fad.
It is not the "in" thing or the new thing to be down with.

My blackness is a culture, race, music and poetry.
My blackness is Martin Luther King.

My blackness is Louis Armstrong.
My blackness is Ella Andel and Ella Fitzgerald.
My blackness is hip-hop, jazz, tap dance, rock and roll and soul.
My blackness is the backs torn by the whips of slavery.
My blackness is the backs still being broken by the aftermath of slavery.

'Cause! –
they said! –
"All you niggers are for is picking cotton and cane."

But when they needed soldiers for war,
it was our blackness that was put in the front lines to be slain.
And at the war's end, after fighting for a country that had enslaved them
for 4 centuries,
it was these very warriors, my blackness, that were put back into the fields,
to pick cotton and cane.

While their white brothers were made generals, brought back as heroes.
Given medals of Honor and considered conquerors, while blackness was
considered conquered.

Because all us niggers was for was picking cotton and cane.

But when they saw our beautiful black women, the women that we called
as queens,
they could not resist this blackness.
So they raped and beat our women. But it was their bastard children
that learned to read and write.
It was these children that helped free us from slavery.
Ironically:
it was these children who represented black and white who read and who
understood the 5th amendment.
Which ultimately led to black independence.

But like they said, "all us niggers are for is picking cotton and cane."

But my negroness
is not my blackness.
My blackness is Nelson Mandela.
My blackness is all the mothers who struggled for their sons and daughters

only to have them innocently slain by that very thing that YOU think
represents blackness.
My blackness is even that shallow lyrically deficient music of artists who sing
popular hip-hop because they see it as a way out of the Ghetto.
My blackness represents artists who use gangster rap as a way out of the ghetto.
Yes! My blackness is music that fuels crime of the black on black.
Nature.
But I ask you, the rapper, how many must die so that you, the gangster rapist,
can get out of the ghetto?

Maybe that's why they say all us niggers are good for is picking cotton and cane.

But at the end of the day the truth is, –
if one were to take any fortune 500 company, any multinational company,
and wring it,
it is the blood of blackness that will flow from it,
it is the blood from just below our skin.
It would be blood that is just like yours.
Except that, that blood would be mixed with, and would have come from so -
called minorities and even from whites held down by years of prejudice.
Blood from what should be called modern day slavery.
And that blood would be deep red and flow like a geyser. That blood would
be full of more struggle,
but it would still be red just like yours.

But like they said "all us niggers are for is picking cotton and cane."

Picking cotton.
Cotton pickin negroes.
Negroes pickin cane.
Cane pickin negroes.
Negroes pickin cane.

But what I like best of all is *that*
my blackness is the rumors that were spread during the days of slavery that
black men have big ggmmm.
And hell yes!!!! we capitalize on this.

"My head is beginning to clear now so think I can head to bed now."

But before I go, I want you to know,
that
Yes! I know my blackness is not all positive.

And yes! –
It has many faces,
from Mr. Powell to America's Most Wanted.

But I know this.
I know that in all of my blackness,
I will never!
Ever!

be your friend!
because of your skin tone.

Catherine Yuan Chi

Barry Dempster

from *Love Outlandish* (Brick Books, 2009)

RUMBLE

Patti Scialfa sings *"Rumble Doll"* over and over,
my finger poised on repeat.   Same old heartbreak and
unworthiness, half-clichéd, drums pounding like one of
those *Life Channel* heart transplants, all bleedings exposed.
Why am I so susceptible?   Give me a third glass
of wine and I'll graduate to Roberta Flack,
those thirty years-ago sessions for *"Ballad of
the Sad Young Men."*   Not quite so gloomily romantic
at fifty, all feelings crusted with tangles and knots,
although look at Patti, in the middle of it
herself, still looking and sounding game.   No wonder
I sing along, beautifully cracked and flat.

It used to be evenings with Janis Ian,
throat turned inside out, a case of near nicotine
poisoning.   *I learned the truth at 17*, hell,
was there ever such a measure, heaps of hours,
dreads of days, the accumulation that ends up
history?   I'd sit in the big bedroom closet,
practically humping the speakers, her sighs sweet-hot
on the soft skin of my neck, hangers chiming above
like backup singers.   Never alone with misery,
I'd join the lip-synching crowd, the fatties and baldies
who've now graduated to karaoke and
second-hand solutions like divorce.   The chorus
is a choir, a whole generation lifting
their plangent voices to those broken lights we call stars.

Feeling back, was my love affair with the girl in
psychology class, or with Joni Mitchell blue under
all that blonde hair?   Was it Chris I might have married

or Linda Ronstadt's high notes, the way they squeezed into
my chest and felt like small, damaged wings?   There was even
a fling with Bryan Ferry, a slavish thing, where
all I wanted was to hear him moan.   My mother
was right, music led to sex, blood rushing up and down
the strings, fingertips callused yet blushing.   She was
wrong about the drums though, darkest Africa, all
those pagan mumbles.   The beat was born in my
own rec room the night I wrestled Janis Joplin
to the floor, pulses played over throbs, thunder
spinning like the wheel of a just-crashed car.

But back to Patti, one last *rumble*.   We both know
the heart doesn't really break, just takes on ballast
and too much sad brain.   Look at her now, married
to the Boss, trying to forget all those years of
being disembodied.   Singing alongside her,
shedding tears in a socially acceptable way,
I'm worthy of any bar in town.   And when we've
finally run out of guitars and frowns, the silence
will be cleansing, death-like in its magnitude,
a lament for all the love that slipped away,
all the voices sealed in bottles or shoved
in closets, never to be heard again.

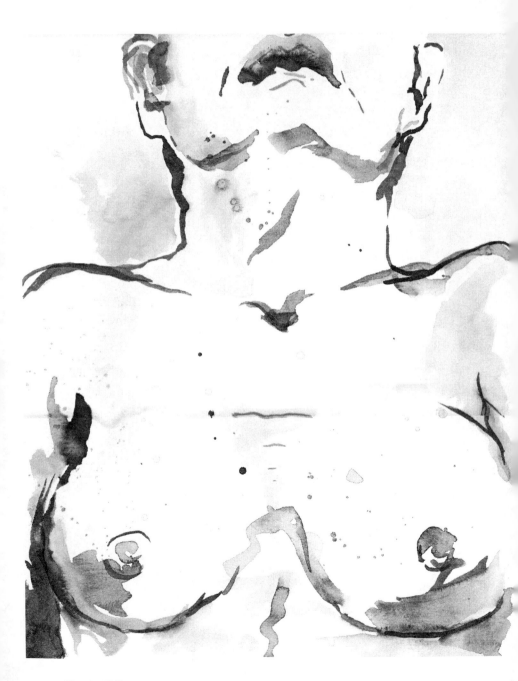

Chamisa Kellog

YES

The trouble began when I said yes
to that first sumo push toward a relationship.
It might have been the hot chocolate,
or the casual perusal of the town's one poetry shelf.
Innocent enough, nothing cardiac involved,
just small-talk metaphors
and a *like* let loose in the late winter air.

Yes, most of what we said was true.
Thrill of words spilled into verse.
The comfort of hearing voices coming from
someone else's skull, sharing the craziness.
The lines we read out loud
like litanies of some brand new worship:
The Holy Simile, or The Temple of Buried Rhymes.

And soon I was agreeing to daily calls,
expectations stripping me of those
cautious words like *don't* and *later.*
Depending on it, yes, the wait, the tremble
in the air as the phone finally rings.
Facing faith again, its jostle in the birdcage,
the empty swing that still dangles back and forth.

As a child, I was too lacquered in loneliness
to even dream it left behind.
But now I leap from its flimsy arms, grab
your elbow, drag you to a distance
where you start to fray and almost tear.
Brave, yes, maybe stupid, multiplying hope
as if the zero at its core were full of secret codes.

Is such fracas a form of love?
Sometimes my yes is so cleverly disguised,
you'd never recognize the hero inside.
The fear now is that you'll go away,
a higher echelon of trouble, the kind

that throws hearts from the tops of high rises,
then counts the silences between gasp and crack.

When I said yes to chocolate,
I was surrendering to everything: the greet,
the wrestle, the slow rip that ultimately
becomes a scar.   This is the nature of accord.
Standing here in the poetry section,
open to all the lines, all the life-changing
metaphors; nodding discoveries, sharing a face.

THE PHONE RINGS

Brringg, like the trill of an upstairs maid
in an opera about betrayal.
She is bidding you to destiny:
a mezzo-soprano huddled in
a torn velvet cape, or a handsome tenor,
envelope clutched in his cold fingers.
Once upon a time your life would have been
a glorious melodrama, not this
cut and paste.   The phone
turns out to be a salesman in disguise,
a dental reminder, an old aunt
who just wants to say, hi.   Where's your secret
paramour, your plot twist?   That last hang-up
came as close to reverie as you can get.

The tension continues, a high note
cracking a wine glass in the dining room hutch.
A demand for your busy wife.   A friend
calling to complain about a friend.
A second salesman, his larynx dipped
in wax.   You hold your breath through
each exchange, stifling the impulse to swear, or
scream some unrehearsed refrain like, *Do I*

know you?, an orchestra squashed into
one vast cacophony. Somehow you've
become desperate and needy, the strangled screech
of a clarinet. It's getting so you're afraid
to say, *Goodbye*, even to a dial tone,
that least musical of hopes.

And then one day the *brringg* seems seductive,
a stage whisper from the chorus, a gypsy
with rings on her fingers. You pick up
the phone as if it were a rumour,
a *psst* from the composer, a lump
of wire and plastic transformed into song.
Finally, a fit, the perfect squeeze
of your wife, or your mother risen
from the dead, or a saviour who can't wait
another second to introduce himself.
The right voice at the right moment, there's
crescendo. One note, one held *Hello*,
a favourite aria, all swoop and shiver,
the birds and beasts singing the anthem of your name.

BLUE ROSE

I buy a blue rose to describe
and think of Yeats dipping his quill
in an ah of ink, hoping that
love on the page would be less painful,
or at least more rakish, something
to shove in a buttonhole and watch
wilt, beauty slowly disintegrating
to a bruise. Next morning, saturated
with longing, I stumble to the kitchen
for a vitamin, a bolster
for my sad veins, and discover
the crystal vase full of blue water,

the rose having traded bodily fluids
all night. It's the unrequited part of love
Yeats and I do so well, the bleeding,
fists full of paper cuts. The tributaries
leading to our brains are wide open,
the very thoughts we think, fantasies of you
bending over to wipe up a spilled drink,
catching a reflection in the puddle
of my complete devotion. The only
way I know how to love is to drown
all those inconsequential colours,
the pinks of modesty and the greens
of being soothed, soak myself
in a lack of oxygen, a gasp
whenever you enter a room.
I realize you might prefer
violets, a neat little poem
with lots of shy adjectives, but
that's not how Yeats sounds to me, all
thorns and bleed, a daunting chemistry
that gusts across the page in bursts of blue.

TRUE

Bible bashers swear true love
is right no matter what the cost.
What good is Christ under lock and key?
Like Spiderman with his fingertips waxed.
Show that super longing, those mad leaps,
almighty emotion.
Back in my Brethren days, confusing
desire with salvation –
is this how I started worshipping you?

Love was the all-day, every-day philosophy,
when I was still sane enough

to have a thought process.
I swallow you like something multi,
brimming with goodies I can hardly pronounce.
God, you *are* true, my favourite verse.
Lying in your arms feels cross-like
in a comfy kind of way, a willingness to be raw,
naked and holy, art squeezed from a lonely curse.

Sex is a form of reverence, don't I know,
having named a new shade of pink
in honour of your lips.
And your wrists top my list
of miracles unsung.
I even pray to you when you aren't
listening, just in case.
True, this is going too far, but where else
can a man stand on a ledge and be heroic?

My final act will be to dangle over
somewhere grand, shout your name, and fall.
Back to the faith where you're an ordinary person
and I can brush against you
without all that greed.
Little spider, heart scurrying for asylum.
Just because you can't save me
doesn't mean I won't love you.
Even the leaps that can't get off the ground are true.

WHITE-OUT

There's steam rising off this first snow,
steam floating from me, corkscrew ghosts
swirling with each shovel pass, spine
curling with desire to see naked ground.
Too much covered up in December, all
those blizzards and wreaths.   I haven't
seen your bare throat for days, the sneaky

lies of scarves and turtlenecks. No
wonder I can't find my glasses, the whole
week playing hide-and-seek.

In white-outs like these, desire
could fill a history book. Bring October
back, oh, please. That night on the dock
when the wind picked up my arms
and simply handed them to you.
I want the grass again, the dew
soaking my jeans, the moon orange
and almost rude. I want darkness,
the wall, the end of it all, not this
steamy glow, this ghost eye watching my
every move. I want the savour of a shiver
that isn't already iced half-dead.

Perhaps it's best to aim ahead.
Surely those Antarctic penguins dream
of spring dividing what seems so solid
into islands and then finally the sea.
Standing on a heap of snow, I imagine
melt slowly lowering my anxieties.
Longing for the season when your arms
won't remind me of a shovel's grip
no matter how hard I need to be held.
When all the extremes are revealed,
like frescoes of the Sacred Heart, proclaiming
nothing need ever be concealed again.

I'D LIKE TO LICK YOUR THUMB

I'd like to lick your thumb, I said
when offered a piece of
chocolate chip muffin.
Just a joke, no need for alarm.
Don't go running from the room,

thumb held aloft like a popsicle
in the presence of a tall dog.

I'll keep my tongue to myself,
promise.
And the vision of your thumb
smeared in blonde crumbs
like a doll's head swirled
with perfect curls.
Not a peep about the taste,

salt and chocolate stirred to a creamy
paste, luscious against my gums.
Don't worry, I wouldn't bite,
these are honourable jaws.
But oh, how I'd nibble,
bunny-like, my moustache aquiver,
your thumbprint slowly unravelling

into a long, pink river.
This is all hypothetical,
of course, if I were... if you could...
In reality, your thumb is safe,
symbolic as a flag.
Go ahead, wave it in my face.
I will stand at attention, tongue

rolled to the back of my throat.
Perhaps I'll take that offered piece,
spongy little substitute,
pop it politely in my mouth,
mmm.
Pretend it's the chocolate
I adore.

BETWEEN

I love the between of your fingers,
those spaces my own fingers fit.
The way sky slides between hydro lines
or February branches like long,
blue envelopes; the way dead air is
fed with breeze, little dervishes of
dust.   A plastic bag swirls
up my driveway, invisible gusto,
just the right mix of want and need.   It
dives, it lifts, etc., an emptiness
willing to be tossed.   Everything
seen has a hole somewhere,
spilling over with rescues of light.
But damage only lasts a second
before it's overcome, a shadow
play of duck's bills and rabbit's ears,
an ooze of blood making canvas of
a wound, a mirror's constant round
of relationships.   You take me by
surprise when you spread your fingers,
stealing me from all those busy visions,
drawing my own between from its disguise
as fist.   The wind blows, the holes in the world
close, as my thumb begins to open,
my baby finger feeling its first
tug of desire.   Such a perfect
fit, as if your hand had been designed
with me in mind, as if the gods had
measured our spaces down to
the last fraction of a wish.

A DISTAL WINTER'S NIGHT

A distal winter's night, city-centric,
Yonge Street with its neon bleeds,
snow moths batting the street lamps,
sucking up the light. It's a night
where the homeless are huddled in
doorways, just another pile
of urban shrug. A night where
tires are alive and shopping bags
bang against tone-deaf knees.
A night of steel shouts, of slush
slurring itself into half-dead puddles.

A fight brewing, a night where I long
to tell the truth. You cold city
with your damned black-ice
distances. Shadows
swooping from billboard struts,
feeding on the cracks between sleeves
and gloves. Breezes slashing
from broken glass. Car crashes
and heart attacks. Losers. Those just
lost. Shivers. Sudden stops.

This is the night where you'll eventually yell
at me, and I'll yell back, the wind flinging
syllables into sleety bursts.
There are strangers I feel closer to than you.
Tonight I will actually imagine
walking on without you, turn up
an unfamiliar street, choose a house,
this house, with coach lights and quartz
in the window, now arrange my fist around
the doorknob and twist, a whole new
revolution. The night I will become
the other person, snowflakes darkening my hair.

TAKE CARE

Take care, you say into the phone,
meaning, *Go on alone.*
And here I thought caring grasped
as close to heaven as one could get,
some elbow grease and a sudden
blueprint of veins.   It took
actual physical presence to rub your back,
to help you wash the mismatched dishes,
to hold one of your poems between my fingers
like a purple butterfly.   Nerves, and pores,
and bristling energy, what happened
to being there, doing, stirring the pot?
I think of hugs at the end of a letter,
too small to even fit around my wrist.
Love needs muscle and grip, collarbone
sliding into collarbone, a penny
of sweat on your neck.   It takes every
pound of you to hold me aloft,
to rearrange my gravity.   You need
arms to really do the job; you need
a steep hill of spine, a set of ankles
keeping trust on its shaky feet.
But go ahead, long for me from far off,
feel the miles tearing like tissue, popping
bones from their sockets, spreading skin
across the nothingness like a treasure map
with Xs stretched into fades.   *Take care.*
And here I thought you needed
at least one of my thumbs to zip you up.

HOWL

I've been listening to the wind howl
for two days now, a phantom wolf
suffering out behind the garden shed,
nursing a bullet wound or a loneliness
that wasn't inbred and simply can't
be believed.   Watch how it hurts
the maple trees to lose their sugariness,
and the proud grass to fade slowly
brittle brown.   It hurts me just to
listen, let alone the glimpses of
scrawny limbs and moth-chewed scarves.

As for you, your cheeks are red,
abrasive, yet you're still upright,
unrepentant, which includes a little
wolfishness, sweated on by the moon.
When the time comes to lose you,
it will be a day like this, whipped
and whining, leaves spinning
in the streets like melodrama,
tears forced from my eyes by a tiny
hook.   *The world is a harsh place,*
you'll howl, trying to lick the rawness
that surrounds you, disturbed at
having to see me play the role of prey.

You never meant to hurt me, it's just
seasonal, hope hibernating,
futures snapping shut.   Forgive me
the howls shaped from my own breathless
bones, the echo whistle of a kiss.
Today reminds me of the end, a place
I've languished in so long that calendars
are useless, days flipping by without order
or resolve, bits of paper eaten by the wind.

THE LAST PHOTOGRAPH

I rip the so-called cherished moment
in two, the glassiness of the past
slippery between my fingers.
Now I'm in one hand, you in the other.
I rip again, dividing you from
your elbows left leaning on the table.
I rip a third time, severing your
shoulder blade, almost shredding your neck.
Again, again, the raspy burr of paper
being torn.   Your chest is now
half a dozen pieces, a few fallen
to the floor.   Your ex-chair
in tatters, unidentifiable.   Which leaves
just your head, a tiny circle of energy,
like one of those beauty marks
I might have pasted on my cheek
were I seventeenth century and French.
Too tiny to properly rip, to crumple.
A fish eye shocked by death.
A bindi turning a forehead into
an x-ray machine.   What's left of you
is spit-stuck to my thumb, staring up at me.
I could swallow you, one small roll
of tongue.   I could shake you over
the garbage can like a dot of yesterday's
confetti.   Or I could simply wear you, scare
the cops when they come to investigate
your decapitation, my thumbprint wearing
your careless smile.

AFTER

The day before we broke up,
we chatted on the phone twice,
watched a movie together, saw
some of the same shapes, shared
a shiver when the sun went down,
thought each other's thoughts –
or thought we did.
Ordinary, I'd say, your hand,
my hand, same texture, same
clasp.　While around us, the globe
did its usual tilt and fall, atoms
seething, leaves plastered
to the ground as if they'd found
a way to defy gravity, filling in
some of the distance
between sky and grave.

And then it was the day itself,
sunny enough, but with a rip
of chill.　Another telephone
attachment, half-formed sentences
wrecking more than grammar
normally allows, a year's
worth of insecurities
reaming the vowels, twisting
syllables into shots, momentum
taking over in sweeps of wind,
stripping the branches
outside my window, dismantling
anything resembling a comfort
or a dream.　Afterwards, I dropped
the phone to the floor, adding
to the weight of debris.

The day after, and after, and
after, words seeping stale.
The same planet,
surprisingly.   A man lying
in the ditch on Queensville Side Road,
another well-planted symbol.
And the cow pushing its tongue
through the diamond fence,
brave yet pathetic, trying to eat
air that doesn't belong to her.
I drive to the store three times
that day, forgetfulness swallowing
the most unbearable hours.   *Love?*
What a weird refrain.   Here
and disappeared.   Like everything
ever said.

DEVOTION

It was a left turn at Bad Luck, then
a sharp right on Despair, my father
racing to my mother's rescue,
steering wheel spinning, tires skidding,
his happiness sliding out of control.
He picked up her hand which lay in her lap
like a heap of mousy bones
and, lifting it to his lips, kissed the abyss.

The strawberry freckle on her left
ankle, the wrinkled cleavage, the bald spot
where even the hairdresser ran out
of miracles, he sat and memorized
by the hour. *You are my wife*, he
explained, tracing a vein that ran on
and on like a coastline. Love
in absentia, like chrysanthemums
still glowing on Mona Lisa's cheeks,
glissandos between Monk's shadowy fingers.

The body decorative, the body
destroyed, he held her long after
her death date had weathered, held her
in the cluttered corners of his own brain.
Nights when TV was doing its damnedest
to distract him, I'd hear him talking
above the din, telling her how it felt
to be skinned alive. *Love you, love you,*
the old refrain, his hand sitting beside
him on the couch, squeezing air.

Michelle Desbarats

from manuscript in progress

The Unfilled Pool

He dove into an unfilled pool. It doesn't
matter how many times the story's
heard, it's the same ending.
He was with his girlfriend
on a holiday and because
pools can be unfilled how could he
not have noticed emptiness, the scars
and darker debris against faded turquoise.
The hollowness, alone,
would be enough below
the grainy surfaced diving
board. These places
to halt him every time and failing
we give the reasons: it was too bright,
was night, he was drunk, there'd
been a quarrel, something had
happened. He had certainly not walked in the
strength of his age, bare feet pressing
for a moment on the narrow metal steps as he
climbed to take his dive
on a beautiful morning for a swim
when wings
ethereal uncurled from where they'd
hinged inside his bone blades
in that part of
the world where the air is thick with heat,
his girlfriend called him
from the window of their room –
yellow curtains fluttering beside her;
they had breakfast after, pancakes and the
butter astonishingly cold against warmth.

Safekeeping

It is possible to keep things alive,
the female cricket can keep sperm viable for
seven years.
It is worthwhile, therefore, to look back
seven years and see what
was thought lost then
because of how hard
the soul had to become –
a stone weighting in the chest,
not a seed patient for water and sun as part of
its formula,
and the something of delicate
and fluid self that you
hid perhaps in
the metal of a favourite candleholder
that was then called loss.
Don't you remember how your father
showed you how to put things into yourself
when laughing, he palmed, as if by magic,
the little white table from the
doll's house into your knee and
you screamed when he would not
take it out right away; you did not know
he was teaching you something.
There are things you say are gone
forever, but the candleholder you'll find later
is only an image of the one
you allowed, complete with its treasure,
beneath your skin years ago.
The one you find in the garage
you can give away.

A House Can Make of Itself

your house has made
a ghost of itself
and left its scent
in transparent flumes

there are the true ghosts
cats and those who
have died

we learn things every day.
I didn't know a
house could make itself
into a ghost

ragged trailings and
all but what better way
to go elsewhere, and pass
through walls

and when I'm
touching your things,
the books you have given
me when I'm touching

their spines
it is your house I've
ridden back to you on

its dark wisps
like a horse's mane in
my hands so I don't fall off.

Winter's Heart

this rare opening
it's not like a crack
in a rock
but something does to a pulsing
not the first green   winter
different turning like
just as fragile a shy lover
to us
not the season's spring showing
but a winter's
breath of
blush
kept warm amidst
all the ice
why shouldn't every duration
object
have its own spring.

Your Town

One can imagine what a town looks like
but until the outfit is put on,
the hat chosen, the purse selected,
it is conjecture.
Your town came to see me.
She didn't blatantly announce herself for
the truth is never strident. She demurely
gave a hint as large as a country;
it was left for me to inquire further.
Do you know what your town looks like
when she goes outside herself?
She wears a big brimmed rose coloured
hat, a delicate chin, fingers like supple
twigs and extremely large sunglasses

that almost conceal everything but for
the gentle rise of her nose.
She carries a large purse.
I spoke to her of her streets, of which not
all of them she was aware and
this surprised me. I suppose
I'd always thought a town or
a city would know the roads
contained within surveyed lines.
But she didn't. I remember how she
looked, thoughtful, bemused,
as she considered nameless corners
of herself. But for those moments, that
afternoon, you were as close to me as
her woven sleeve. I could have reached
out and touched your house within her,
possibly in the edges of her shoulder,
on the last road before the woods began.

Second Burial

A first burial
only holds something
beneath a weight like earth.
It is temporary as though
a mind's not made up
yet to view the world
without.
It's only a knowing of where
something is so it is possible to
re-find like how animals
hide what they don't
want to lose.
Anything can climb out of
this sort of burial,
a dinnerware set's ghost

taking its place again
among the now but the
carrots falling through
next to translucent
porcelain. And yet the first
tombing so necessary to
let happen the leaving of some things
and people. This slow distancing
until it is known someone's elsewhere
or a table's oak texture
now a sure thing underneath another life,
and no longer needed to be carried
anymore beneath the veneer
of our own.

The Miracle of Beside a Dog

According to him he cried.
She was his wife's but he held
the warm furred body while
the injection was given.
His wife didn't attend.

Can I imagine his face breaking
into tears? Perhaps what's
important is that everyone
has something that brings
them to a world renewed.

After, as he stood on the
sidewalk outside the office,
did the air snap with cleanliness
and his first steps into
an afternoon, were they as if

all he'd hurt somehow knew him
now capable of anguish

of a vastness
reaching beyond himself
to encompass us all?

The way he tells it is
how he tells everything, the surprise
at his dislodgement
such depth touched in him
by a half-stranger's passing.

Imprint

how love first appeared
what clothes it borrowed
the colour it chose for its hair
will always call you
even later

someone standing there
with nothing for you
but a pale blue shirt
and the way it hangs
calling

the first heart
you grew for it

Dead Man's Pond

Perhaps the barbed wire was put there first,
around the pond in the small woods
accessible to children and animals,
and this is what began the story, and not
the other way around.

We spend all our lives looking for
our final place, curious about it; maybe it's a dream
that falls onto us every night as a different
snow. *He dove in, it was said while running*
from the law, and so much was already there:

the quicksand on the bottom that would find
him, the children appearing each summer,
like beaded raindrops along the rusted
wire, cooling themselves in his shadow,
and reflecting its leaf-scudded dark world

and the young dog, whom no one meant to kill
when a small summer-hot hand threw a
stick which was followed by his form.
The quicksand slept that day and the
dog had stood there afterwards, shook his fur,

the drops had fallen on our arms and legs. We ran
as though by racing back through green
leaves and earth-smelling trees, dreams
could be outrun, curiosity and most of all,
the shock of death on our skin.

Beaver Pond

Some of the most important things are learned
when someone or maybe two people
take you out to a place you've never
been before, or maybe only seen from
afar. They lean you on something
you can hold onto and then they
leave. It's not said, but they will
probably return in several hours or
before supper. What you are given
for this period of time is the larger
world. It is breathtaking, really. Before,
you had the backyard and maybe
a few blocks but for these hours you have
almost the entirety and it does
stretch to the necks of giraffes
undulating as they run, and to
glaciers. You have something tied
to your feet, like skates, that
you've never tried before
so you don't go far; your uncles
or your father won't have to look
for you among the Bedouins' tents
when they return. Just before darkness
you are only a little way
from where they left you, knees
perhaps bruised from falling, your face bright
with cold. They don't seem surprised
to discover you're still alive
and don't seem interested to hear
about it. In the car, as heated air begins to
work into damp wool,
their talk is already of supper.

Jeramy Dodds

from *Crabwise to the Hounds* (Coach House Books, 2008)

A WINTER NIGHT

after Tomas Tranströmer

A child rigged like a cormorant
tugged our boathouse days
from their points of splendour.
Or strapped to a jetpack, perhaps.

A young lady puts her mouth
to the house. Both loathe the clamps
that keep the season tight over sounds
of ice shavings that teeter down like ash.
There is paper on the hills, it is winter.

When you return from the factory
where you fabricate the ash,
you trawl your dark room
for a switch on the wall

but your hand touches another face,
brushes another face. And you can't
remember the last time you felt like this
in the dark for something on the wall.

PROSTHETICS

*Despite all the amputations you know you could just go out
and dance to the rock and roll stations, and it was all right.*
—Lou Reed

I'm on the pier with my back against
the wrecking machine. Cyclones of terns
turn atop prop-churned debris.
This morning I feel like the wheel
you fell asleep at. Godstruck by the flag
clotted on its pole like the skin of a starved
animal. The downcoast ferry's
run out of hearing. A spaghetti-strap dress,
a trembling gin, as you shift weight
to your wooden leg.

Ear to a conch, I hear
acrobats in waiting rooms
flipping through magazines,
the gull squawk of the guitarist's hand
going to chord, stunt men falling
through awning after awning.
The sea is a soliloquy
in a buried warehouse.

But March is the month of swollen doors.
Boots bark through checkerweaves of ice.
Lacking prophylactics, we pull apart
to watch our dead sons run along your one
good leg. Hitting the deck, they hoist dust
to their meniscus shoulders.

The sea, a surface unworn by our movement.
Our shore leave, a landscape painted
with a brush made
from the hair of the dog
of those storm-closed roads,
as though a gale had come to town
and left wearing pelicans.

CROWN LAND

North of lumberless land,
we made the animals fight for us.
Sore warped beasts pinched off
the rag-and-bone rack, ones that
bit by barbed bit were forced to
fisticuffs in the scrub slump of hills.
With a hairline rapture these animals
came and went about our days,
leaving their young to defend
the palaces they were forced from
for us. These carousel mammals walked
skewered to the pole. With forepaws
in kid gloves they pricked ears when
tinder sticks lapped the brass-green
kettledrums, drums that laid down the miles
to their relevant demise.

After rock-picking, the fields
were pocked. My uncle with a hazel switch
kicking his mule's hide. My uncle
after twenty more one-mores, his
hat-hidden forehead facing hindsight
as he ox-eyed the ten-ton dewline
that girdled the drumlins. His
cat-o'-nine-tailed spine
humped along the timber-slab paths,
his blinkered mule craning at the headlands;
his pelt hides bone anchor points, marrow levers,
sanguine pulleys. An oilcloth dropped
on his doily-thin, God-given name.

And that's our house, dog-eared
by a balepick hooked in the gatepost
like a tongue licked on winter tin. From
a Caesarean cloudbelly, grey hounds of rain
tear messenger pigeons down to half-tilled fallow.

From the crown of the fox tower I pull my scope
from its rat-hide case, come in close on Uncle,
that mule under his loins scraping home
in ankle drags. The gully was as far as I got
by eye. The rest I only heard,
the noise I'm writing to forget
as the barren hounds got onto him.

RAC•COON' N.–

A Middle Eastern dish with little to no raisins.

An island off Easter Island.

A transplanted organ stored at room temperature.

A shot in the dark.

A kind of parasol that Venus-flytraps you.

A vintage clown car.

A Gatling-type gun that will fire only on immediate relatives.

A sexual position favoured by the limbless.

A widow who rekindles old flames every other year.

A tepid lavender bath.

A virgin standing in the shadow of a failing crane.

The shy negotiation of leaves.

The angelical term for a supermodel's soul.

A Thai steamship that disappeared last week while on routine patrol.

DODGE DART

I bought the car on sweet time. The farm
was sure to follow. The rear-view washing
its face in its hands as the whirl road
unrolled. The side-views like gosling wing nubs.
My girl Tonda diddling herself on the backbench
of this shatterproof sea lion tromped
and taking the long way to Sault Ste. Marie.
The mind, a somersault unable to unravel.
Summer a time when hourglass girls
arrange roadside wreaths between
the desperate restaurants. The road
remade for us upon our approach,
the coniferous part-and-reseal
after our passing, the mind splashes.
Tonda's buzzer goes when
a dead cedar marsh appears.
And if the pines weren't preoccupied
with darting and infilling, they'd correct
young Tonda: 'People don't really mean
the woods,' she sighs and dabs
her soaked brow in the rear-view
as the road buttons up
behind us, 'They just say,
"Let's go to the woods."'

HAPPY BIRTHDAY, CARL LINNAEUS, 300 YEARS OLD

Linnaeus was only 154 cm tall.
But he cut an impressive figure
when clad in his Sami costume,
as he did when he proposed to Sara Lisa.
Furthermore, he had beautiful eyes.
Linnaeus was the first European

to successfully cultivate bananas.
He managed this while living in Holland.
Linnaeus claimed that the forbidden fruit
Eve offered Adam in the Garden of Sweden
was a banana. Linnaeus wrote texts
that were easy to understand. Linnaeus's
speculations became bolder as he became older.
For example: he speculated that swallows
spent the winter at the bottom of lakes.
Maybe he was in a hurry to explain things.

ORONOLIAN REEL

Down the orchard ladder our Emissaries came.
They had been letting the sea do their laundry.
They had been sentenced to bear false witness.
Part the blinds and the sun guillotines.
Pull them, and light chokes back its lure.
Bigger than any country music legend.
Brighter than a birdroom for stars.

Down the orchard ladder our Emissaries came.
With a taxidermist's jar of glass eyes.
With the underwater wind of riptides.
Part my low-lying lap-pleated hands.
Pull my hair back.
Bigger than a blind man's once-over.
Badder than sailors home from their maroon.

Down the orchard ladder our Emissaries came.
Afterwards my armhairs lay like floodgrass.
Aftermath is the sum of nothing but the facts.
Part my seeing into staying and leaving.
Pull the chute on my left-leaning heart.
Record the euthanists rehearsing.
Mic the trapeze snap.

Down the orchard ladder our Emissaries came.
In the household of their cupped hands
are the rivers we ransomed.
In the pits along their mantrap lines
are the acrobats we let go.
Part the flaming bulrushes, the sunken river sticks.
Pull yourself together, because our Emissaries have come
down the aluminum rungs we sawed
half through, and they're standing,
wearing *I'm with Stupid* T-shirts
beside you.

PÈRE JOSEPH AND THE BUSH CORD

His hiatuses bloom on the kitchen's sill.
His shirt snaps like tiny animals falling
through branches. In stride with the clock's
hypnotics, his throat chops a glass of water
down.

He tugs a stone boat with his palomino team
to the birch lot's edge where silence
shipwrecks on silence.

Where deadfall tangoes with live trees,
like botflies on cowbacks, bird shadows
fleck the rye. Tomorrow he'll pen and shear
the last-but-not-leasts. And all winter sing,
'I'll not go missing on that river.'

HEIMLICH

Comes up behind you at a party, masks your eyes
with his mammogram hands, asks, 'Guess who?'
A bear-hugger from way back. Trains by wrapping
around bridge pilings, vending machines, a Douglas fir.
Avoided at most parties: too clingy, too close a talker.
Hovers near buffet trays glaring at your chest, hands
rasping between songs. You poke fun at his tight
lederhosen, his tin flute, but you've bitten off
more than you can chew. Through the crowd
he rushes to you, binds two fists into one under
your sternum. By his second squeeze, the ghosts
of mine canaries flood your mouth and stream
to that part of horizon he's left ajar.

SECOND GLANCE AT CORRAG

Out of the morass he looked like
a reconstructed grenade. Pelt burdened
by burrs. Corroded cloak pin of his cant-hook claws.
The bulrushes gave their windhead nods.
At his lope, spores backstep and scatter.
And that spine scar where the key enters and winds.
The beehive of his eyes sends droids to probe
the switchgrass. So still, the windsocks
hung like daggered lungs. His bible is a flipbook
of practical anatomy. His sightline, a river
you can't talk across. An inmate running his tin cup
along the bars is the muscle-headed bruise racing
inside his ribs like a motorbike in a cage ball.
From southern cape to southern cape
his lungs are a harrow's width apart.
His cochlea is a spoon-dug tunnel beneath
the pet cemetery, his saphenous nerve, a boy
with a bouquet of fresh horses. His irises are owls

and owls are cached hunks of bonfire soot.
His hunger strike does not include giving up fellatio.
Veins are a Gorgon's black-adder bouffant.
Capillaries are winter maples scrubbing the mist.
Blood cells are dust-taxied down a flashlight's path.
His mouth is my mother crying in the car wash.
Dew-worm hunters hatch kerosene lamps
on the gospel choir of his brain
while he comes crawling in his Sunday best,
as though his spine were a bell rope
at midnight and the village vacant
and his father had gone to town
with his inheritance – an Alsatian
that was a dowry for the distance
he'd cross day after dawn after dusk.

MYSELF THE ONLY KANGAROO AMONG THE BEAUTY

– Emily Dickinson

In the procession, wind farmers flutter
their hankies and the cellist's hand crabs
along the neck and the quayside flautist
foregoes gracenotes to watch the rowboat boys
come home and turn to stone and the tulip-fisted killer
knocks on the door of your eyesore and bows too quickly
as though his necktie caught the lathe and, bright enough,
he stands before the bulb and each day you get a piece
of that hostage in the mail and it was the time to kill
that he used unwisely, and after the shot animals stopped
and stillness groomed the grasslands and you thought
the phone on television was your own, and your daughter
is strapped to the pinwheel but he is so damn poor
at the knife throw and a megalith in a forgotten metropolis
has a toy flame in the frame of a paneless bay window

and the automobiles in the wrecking yard are autopsied
for trace amounts of conversation and he tells you love
is the Herculean task of being a janitor in an alabaster
abattoir and your lust is the carnivore
who's been at the back door five years
for the butterflies of those hinges to fly
open for you to wring the mop
into his baby bird mouth.

Don Domanski

from *All Our Wonder Unavenged* (Brick Books, 2007)

from *LEANING ON SILK*

1.

an October morning after another sleepless night
I lift the window to let in the little strengths of the day

all night the house felt like it was underwater
red gills beneath each shingle opening and closing
                                        to receive the air

now the view from the window is waterless   dry grass
and bright sky with a few crows hitched to maples

the sun is out of plain sight   over there near the edges
of salvation   bringing the bees to life   autumn coming
down after dark to lie awhile upon the earth

no freeze yet to switch off hearts and turn up the elegies
no frost yet to escort the mould beneath the ferns

just quietude now and eyelids of soil lowered over granite
and roads collecting dead leaves   the little sweep along
of the breeze   redness of leaves like coal fires
starting to catch   the Carboniferous blush
                                        that keeps saying good-bye.

THREE RIBBONS

mother   the surface of the moon
is lit by the silence
of our small labours here on earth
the brushing of hair
folding of sheets   blowing
out of candles
all the energies it takes to light
a stone   a drifting stone
that part of an apparition
that always comes true

part of the ghost that is heaven
you and highest summer

mother I could remind you of how
the moonlight falls between the ferns
and the ocean
sitting on its haunches there
great beast of little height
biter of emptiness
upholder of two teeth
rattled with shadows

I could remind you that the world
is still here in deepest space
that the human heart is still
three ribbons tied to a belief
in flesh and form

I could ask now if death is loam
magnified to an absence
if the physical is the true
appearance of things
if the black-tipped eye
is where reality begins and ends

but mother I only ask that you recall

a moment in my childhood
as we stood watch in the grass
looking up at the moon one night
so that it was living and reaching
it was everything and nothing won
and how villages on the moon
rattled like plates as it rose
the villagers looking down
watched us so intently
that their selvages trembled
and light fell from their eyes

I want to tell you to remind myself
of the last evening I saw you
as you drove away that province
was full   huge   low above the hills
and it looked as if you were
heading directly for it
and you were   ever so slowly
weakly   having only the energy left
to light a stone   the small labour
it took to follow a road

that night the moon was like a piece
of cloth bent at the corners
weighed down with burdens
sleep in one corner   death in another
the third held joy
in the fourth lay a shadow
shaped exactly like a child
a shadow thin as a veil
which shivered just a little
like three ribbons held in a breeze
which was dark movement   red movement
your fear of being alive.

RIDING THE TRAIN IN SECRET

1.

the steel rails are almost hidden by the grass
and by weeds in the middle of their lessons
a schooling of sunlight next to the rusted drums
and cement blocks   warehouses that only appear
in dreams now   in tenderness

a train once rode these tracks twice a day
carrying people between towns that looked
exactly alike   that had identical names
and no one noticed that the people
who got off were the same people who got on

in the baggage car there were large trunks
and always inside some the merchandise of rewards
and always inside one that slight hesitation
used to decipher the movements of the heavens
and always death's thin bicycle leaning up
against the unlucky side of shadows
the white side that faces outward to eternity.

2.

as a child I rode the train with my mother
carried between the two versions of our lives
dogs escorted us along the tracks
then grew away from us   from our rocking motion
like birds being the parts of trees which grow
beyond the swaying of branches

my father never rode the train with us
never saw the other town   the other life
the journey full of tranquillity
a stillness trembling a little in its place
the kinetic movement of an endless whisper
that seam between leaving and returning
running down the middle of each thought

the train carried us through flights of spruce
and boulders that all looked the other way
ignoring our faces painted against the window
the way a dauber would have painted them
colours too fleshy   eyes too elementary

my father never knew of trains or windows
or of expeditions rolled-up in a child's chest
like illustrated maps of Erewhon
or the Valley of Gehenna   the blaze of outcries
rising from the soil   stretched upwards like grass

my father never travelled   never knew of roads
or of the slow passage into time
he lived with gut and needle
suturing anger to contempt to make an embrace
lifeless arms that fell like cloth to the floor
stitchings like crossfire
cutwork where the grief passed through.

3.

between the two towns the train slept
in its motions   dreamt of us
my mother and I talking softly to one another
speaking around the margins of our bodies
as plants do just inches from the light
the wheels rolled like scarves in water

the whistle blew at each crossing
a shriek of grey smoke   blowing
equatorial climates onto the surface of clouds
the brakes tightening and loosening
their one and only hold on reality

the town where we arrived was the same town we left
except my father didn't live there   never lived
or walked the streets with harm's custom
the accepted practice of removing warmth from language

all the names of the world that banks flesh from dread
all the words waiting their turn to be born

and when we arrived we would enter the house
house without the father
house in the shape of a bell without a clapper
bell with table and chairs   a kettle rustling
the water like dry leaves in a bowl

then the tea would be made with small gestures
like building a ship in a bottle   carefully
so the mast wouldn't break   so the taste
would find its way to our cups   gold-rimmed
red-breasted with a pattern of flushed violets

we would sip from our cups and I would feel older
than my mother and father   older than tea
that had the flavour of lost ages   of dank gardens
where stray boys slept when the earth was flat
before someone rolled it into a ball
so it would bounce back to us   all in colour

in bed at night I would still feel the sway
of the coach   and I would lie there thinking
and each thought was a division of light
till darkness came and I fell asleep among
the orphans of secrets who were never far away
imagining train rides like I did into heart's ease
a diesel running on hunger   the sound of swallowing
among the pistons   slight voices rising
from the wooden ties   the whisperers   the distances.

PEARLS

out in the dry grass of a grey day
the flies grow old and centreless
gradually drifting off to living rooms
to the screens of afternoon television

the family is packed in tight
against the soap opera
each face beautiful   glowing in the moth-light
each body slack and beyond communion
like the dead in the earth
with their symmetry poorly attended
making the gesture of pearls in a drawer.

A LUNAR HAND PRESSES SPIRIT AND FLESH

for Bobby

1.

the irises on the windowsill are blue   reason is blue
so that illness is the colour of a red theory fading among pinks
so that death is a colourless theory stubbed against black
so that nurses throw white before them everywhere they go.

2.

from your bed you can see doctors move and blur
hear porters carry all the proper sounds to their proper places

from your window you can watch the moon forthcoming
placing its stones into position above the harbour

from your room next to the dispensary
you can hear pills turn clockwise in their containers
orbiting suns too minuscule to see   like planets
in the dogwoods   following a star to its branch
a luminous branch high above a darkening river.

3.

you lie in bed bleeding into descriptions of fate
your death coming in a mottled ease
                              in an orderly moonlight
that covers your bed with the light of stones

death is when everything comes to know you at once
all at once   like the moonlight knows you now

a lunar hand under your bandages   just there
pressing together spirit and flesh till they are one
                              or seem to be one
the required solitude at least for a passing
an aloneness allowing you to exist in the moment
the moment unchangeable   drifting beyond names
beyond narrative   something at the very end of things
what moves through the blue irises   what reason won't allow.

CAMPFIRE

when I make a campfire the forest learns
of my poverty   my penury here on earth
the match flares and it's like going home
after trying to find your place in the world
and failing miserably

I sit waiting for night   it nears through
the verge   down on all fours
and familiar with no one but God

it comes slowly through the trees
like a black dog turning its head from side to side
like a seeing-eye dog without its owner
still showing blindness a way through the world.

POPPIES

for Barney

cold sky   a December night in Nova Scotia
long-legged snow falling into empty flowerpots
Li Ho gone back into his book and closing the covers
easier to be warm in the spring of the late T'ang
the wind firm against handfuls of grass along the fence
where the bee's dead eyes turn to white smoke

trees and houses shake gently on their shelves
ice unleavened   flat against the ground
where the shadows of shadows smooth away

down the street a dog is barking madly
yet the silence is unentered by what happens

each bark is a red poppy bending under the weight
of teeth and jaw   it isn't a symbol or an emblem
of anything accessible or human
but stop to think of it and the flowered way will be lost.

John Donlan

from *Spirit Engine* (Brick Books, 2008)

The Secret of What Is Important

The work of love's a good kind of order
to scare yourself into: any excuse
can pull you in the ditch and leach your bones
until the clouds lose patience and race on.

Clouds favour people without your fancy problems,
just city people who pay their kid's fare with a joke:
"Now don't go shootin' any more people on the bus:
I gave you that gun for a purpose."

                                        She loves you,
goes the old song, and I know that's true
sometimes. Sometimes I feel so tired
the fight to keep on the surface of the earth

is barely worth it. One day I'll just let go
in maybe a hundred years if no one's around
who minds too much and life is pain all day
and the world and I don't care for each other at all.

Indian Summer

Year follows year, meadowhawk dragonflies
dry new wings, black-veined, wrinkled windows.
What we think we know is the same strait-jacket,
what we lack the same lack,

all the time in the world.
Leaves turn to brilliant going-away

presents: envious, you'd love to learn
festive, spectacular good-byes

to the visible remembered world,
more than resigned, considerately cheering
the living with incandescent memento
mori, mimicking exemplary

loving humans, as well as other creatures
oblivious of you as cloud formations:
fast, strong fliers, fall's last
butterflies, Mourning Cloak, Question Mark.

Catbirds, Mockingbirds, Starlings

Birds repeat their parents' songs
as if their lives depend on it.
They do:
catbirds, mockingbirds, starlings

mimic birds or fire alarms but sound
like catbirds, mockingbirds, starlings.
I compare my tongue-tied goodbye:
"You're dying, Mum."

Stupid: I only hope
she was unconscious. (Was there a hand-squeeze?
Sometimes I tailor comfortless memories.)
I spoke so she'd know I was there, that's all.

Her chest sank on each useless breath:
her lungs were full of fluid. She was drowning.
Pneumonia, the friend of suffering.
Unthinking, comfortless: at last, a truth we knew.

With My Head on Upside Down

The river's plump today,
sister I never had, always leaving —
why tot up a life's balance of feelings
valid only on the day of issue?

If I just lie on the couch all day
wrapped in my mum's old afghan
and watch the rain slip off the shining leaves,
soaking the earth, bound for the open ocean,

I miss you terribly.
You well up
through the fractured boilerplate — remember the time
Scamp got porcupined, and we gave him half a Valium

before we pulled the quills with a pair of pliers
and he got staggery and fell down the stairs?
— Oh, no, you weren't there.
There's not a day goes by that I don't think of you.

Person of Snow

Tom Thomson couldn't draw people for beans
but that doesn't stop us loving those
holy glows, deep in the bottom galleries,
a conflagolion of Canadian

identities.
There's just so much to say and then you're dead.
"So what happened."
"Oh, a guy had a seizure."

"I'm goin' to stupid school. The teacher came in
and played for us on the guitar and the mandolin."
"I've moved up from Elmer's and Lepage's:
I'm on prescription glue."

I hope it helped. I know my parents
did the best they could. Here we are, aren't we.
Hear me out or not, it's your birthday.
I've got a secret. You.

Gratitude

Is it gratitude you feel when a pine
(with leaves much paler than others, maybe diseased)
offers bursts of brilliant sulfur-orange
budding tips to the level sun?

Pleasure, certainly, at receiving
something desired, without labour
or expectation, though it wasn't intended
for you, an overheard conversation

when you're solitary and hungry for speech
and companionship. The tree never made
such beauty for you, nor the marten, who feels
who knows what, chasing through those colours:

still, you're grateful. You write your poem
from necessity, as the tree and the marten
live, and they're as much your audience
as anyone else you could name or speak to.

Columbine

for Stephen Reid

Cloudy wrecks pile up
along the coast,
Carrall and Hastings,
in Pigeon Park pink spindrift

of fallen blossom, browning petals
stick to boot treads of "poor
lost souls," veins daily
delivering the same bad news.

This June one crow child
can't get enough: it calls and calls
long after growing parent-sized. No one
knows what's the matter.

Leaving the mutter and ache
and fuss of self, your eye travels
the moon's path over the lake: unlimited room
for losses, above or below the gleaming water.

Mike Doyle

from *Living Ginger* (Ekstasis Editions, 2004)

Written on the Soul

H.M.D. 1928-1958

A July winter among the drab Scots stone,
rain squalls, southerly buster; icy nodes
scour my face. But you feel nothing.
I look down at your stillness, your last smile,
but your eyes are closed. You do not see me.

Our long ago shared life, short, not nasty,
at least in itself, the nights of closeness, when
you were home, days of gentle companionship.
Quiet friends, for a while, in our small life.
Now your eyes are closed. You do not see me.

Everything gone. You were already far
away when it finally ended. Once you said,
'It's slow suffocation, Mikey', speaking
more than you knew, for both of us.
Now your eyes are closed. You do not see me.

And now, distant in time and place, it grieves me
yet again that our days and nights are done:
sunset at Waikaremoana, the fruit harvest
in South Otago. They go on. I go on,
but your eyes are closed. You do not see me.

An unseen finger and thumb closed your eyelids,
as I had closed mine to you before it was done.
Yet I can see your smile on our garden slope
still in my soul, grieve on, have words to speak,
but your heart is closed. You will not hear them.

Dear love, for so you were, where now
the sheen of your hair, our quiet being together,
your young hands clasping my shoulders,
your humour and courage? I cannot find them.
I am here still, seeing you. You do not see me.

Correspondence

How many more times
will I write you a note
and not send it? Today,
this morning in a quiet
house, not ours, mine,
clearing my desk, I find
the latest such scribble,
a plea, always, but what
am I asking, hoping for?

Once, I returned
every photo of you I had:
from you at nineteen,
lissom, lithe, small-breasted,
profile like Nefertiti,
to you at fifty,
face-on to the camera,
a look caught between
insouciance, insolence.

That first photo
followed by passion, commitment.
children, a life together,
then the erosions – slow
at first, and invisible,
but gathering momentum
to end in a landslide,
– a mere metaphor, telling
nothing, yet telling all.

And the second?
One of a pair, the other
missing, mine. Both mask
convenient lies, unspeakable
blames, and a rage – or two
one a firestorm, the other
a slow burn
still smouldering, between
the notes, which add to the smoke.

Toujours Paris

mid 1980s

At the Cafe des Poetes
Avenue des Gobelins
the coffee's great.

She thaws morning hands
on a bowl of cafe au lait
while, with the back of a spoon,

he crushes two sugar cubes
each into two nips of
espresso, mopping up

dregs with a third.
Thus warmed and sweetened they
stroll back to the Hotel de Dada.

On their way through the plane trees,
sharpened by frosty air
their words become kitchen knives

jabbing and piercing repeatedly.
They fret behind the long windows;
the drying garments

scattered at random
on radiator and shower-rail,
ignored flags of truce.

Eva, Maisie, and Nora

for Margaret, then

Seeing them still, in the mind's eye,
these last three lodgers at Aunt Margaret's,
a clutch of sisters come to Cricklewood
from the bogs of Tipperary. Summer sun,
young women in their twenties, Eva the prettiest,
Maisie the likeable one, and Nora
always a little apart, this time smoking,
sat on the coping stone above the low brick wall,
while Eva and Maisie play a makeshift game
of King, on the street, its tarmac surface
squidgy, swamping the gravel. They
play with two little boys, my brother
and me, teasing us, throwing the tennis ball
just out of reach, Eva in high good humour,
cheeks ruddy with effort, eyes asparkle,
laughing as we dive to catch the ball
missing by a whisker. Then Nora begins
a song, not Irish this time, languorous:
'When the deep purple falls...'

At length we are called inside, slipping
on loose squares of linoleum. The dark
has come again. Soon Bill and I
wriggle under hot sheets, but first we have
a grace, the moment when Aunt Margaret opens
her bottle of red biddy; as she carelessly
closes the front room curtain we catch a glimpse
of Uncle Steve, not too drunk this time, taking

off his bicycle clips and as he bends to it
letting a huge fart, at which Maisie laughs aloud
a sound of raunchy mischief.

Now Margaret has the squeezebox and a cigarette,
glass of biddy alongside, begins to play -
'Rody McCorley', 'The Rising of the Moon'.
Later, from the hot bedroom above,
we'll hear the girls, voices slower and slower
as the wine slows Margaret's hands, now it's
'Lament for the Irish Emigrant', 'Let Erin Remember',
and the waited-for finale, 'Danny Boy',
then silence. I see them down there, drinking
tea by now, with Margaret's homemade poundcake.
As I drift into sleep I know they'll be reading
the tealeaves, portentous about a future.

This was in 1940. Within weeks
Margaret and Steve, talking 'invasion', scurried
back to Ireland. I would meet them again
only once, briefly, in their dark cottage
in Borrisokane, its walls three feet thick.
I never again saw Eva, Maisie, and Nora,
nor heard a thing about them, but can see them
any time, back through sixty-odd years,
young girls in their twenties, on short commons,
aglow in the pathos of a treacherous hope.

February 2002

Raking Shaking

for Gwladys Downes

Set to talk about poetry
looking for Navajo
chants of propitiation
hauled out Jerry Rothenberg's
Shaking the Pumpkin
shook out a couple of pages
stripped thirty years ago
from *Greenfield Review*
poems by Harold Littlebird
N. Scott Momaday, &c,
one with an epigraph
famous words from Hokusai:
'at ninety I shall have penetrated
to the essence of all things...'

Wonderful! I need
to propitiate something
every day in myself
to move a little nearer
that same essence.
Seventy-four now, fortunate
in the blessed privacy
of an all too occasional
calling, somehow
once in a while a
true poem finds me.

This just to note it.
A note of thanks
before I go out
raking November leaves.
But that's what I'm doing
in here, already,
raking November leaves
for a glimpse of the pure

yellows, the burnished reds,
rapt in their beauty,
wrapped in the rhythm
of arm, elbow, and rake,
enraptured by the certainty
of a greenness to come,
and the cycle of yellow,
brown, red, and the green
to come, the green
that will keep on coming.

November 2002

Carla Funk

from *The Sewing Room* (Turnstone Press, 2006)

Noah

Don't think of the flood.

Instead, pour the wine
and enter the tent where he lies
naked after the campfire
celebration and his old wife's dance
of thanksgiving as she lifted her hem,
swung in circles around high flames.

After months of sailing, he can still hear
the slosh of waves against the boat,
the night's gentle rocking.
Sleep swaddles the old man
in its massive hand. So much closer
to the truth: at the end as in the beginning
we are all laid naked before heaven.

For Noah, unwrapped and stretched out
in the night soaked with drink and love,
it is enough for the hard ground to hold him,
for the lowing of the sea-legged cattle,
for every living creature to be far-off
across the open plain.

For there to be dust instead of flood.

But for his son standing at the tent's entrance,
the ruined flesh holds before him a mirror.
The garden all over again, undressed
shame and a map to an unflinching future.
Like the boat hacked board by board

for the fire's fuel, his bones lay down
the message. There is no paradise
at the top of this mountain.
We're still watching the flames
slow-dance into ash.

The Burning Bush

Last day of school before summer vacation.
I'm fifteen and lying on my back at the cutbanks,
having bummed my first cigarette,
throat burning and red eyes blinking back stars.

The bikini girls splash waist-deep in the river
and recite obscene poems to the boys on shore
who flick bottle caps at them, and drag
on their smokes, drag on their smokes.

In the dry grass, I'm sweating off the gin
while the Pentecostal preacher's kid tells me
he's sick of his father's sermons, the same stories
over and over again, maybe it's about time

we make up new ones. Like maybe
instead of walking on water, Jesus freezes
the waves into a lake of ice, then
double-axels his way to the disciples

who hunker facedown in their wooden boat
frozen at the lake's centre. Or instead
of Moses and the burning bush,
it's a flaming camel God talks through.

And this boy goes on to wonder
if the camel carries a month's supply of water
in its hump, could it put out its own fire and
would it smell like one giant barbecue

out in that desert and couldn't you totally
go for a burger right now, take off
and fly out of this town on a winged chariot
with a souped-up V-8 engine?

Blurry-eyed at the river, I'm pinned under
the skywriter's blue, cirrus smoke
in ghost-hand overhead, a scrolled message
splitting me from my maker.

Instead of a burning bush, it's a preacher's drunk son
talking God. Instead of Egypt, a small town, low river
dividing who I am from who I am,
cutting the promised land in half.

Secrets

Every family has at least one.

For us, it was the ice cream
Dad scavenged from the town dump,
half-melted cartons chucked by the local dairy
when their freezers went on the fritz.

We stood over the slick rainbow of boxes
he stacked in our basement deep freeze,
an underground ice cream parlour opened
inside the bare concrete room,
a flavour for every day in July.

Don't tell, Dad said. Not anyone.

That summer, blackflies swarmed
the nights as always. Dad blazed
the wild acre for a new garden,
our tomcat went missing for a week
and came back with half his right ear.
Mum fell off a ladder washing windows,

broke both her wrists. These stories
we spoke freely over the building of tree forts,
backyard games of scrub and kick-the-can.

Hot days, we'd crank the lawn sprinkler high
and run with neighbourhood kids
through the flying swathe of rain.
Mum would haul the ice cream
from the dark basement, one carton at a time,
and spread them out on the picnic table
for us to choose. My brother and I shared looks
across our friends, kept our mouths shut,
while Mum, in slow motion,
scooped our dripping cones,
the white casts of her hands
holding out the secret
for everyone to taste.

The Blue Spruce Café

Unlike the other fathers in town
who can show off a son's new logging truck
or a daughter's 12-point buck
shot down in a clearing off Bear Head Road,
my dad comes and goes empty-handed
to the morning coffee shop.

What's he supposed to do
with a poet for a daughter?
What to bring to this Formica table
of burning cigarettes and toast plated
by a waitress named Dot?

Is it too much to imagine him
pulling a book from his back pocket,
cracking open the spine as he holds up a hand
to say shut up, fellas, listen to this,

then begin to read a poem—
maybe the one about him shooting the cocker spaniel
after she caught her hind leg in a fox trap.
The kind of poem that would make the men
shake their heads at the last line,
stare into the bottoms of their coffee cups
and hang a thought in the silence,
a sort of uneasy applause
for that feeling that rises in them.

Maybe it would catch, poetry
at The Blue Spruce Café, poetry
at the truck stop, poetry read aloud
over the local country and western station
in between ballads by Tanya Tucker
and The Oak Ridge Boys.

Soon the men would write their own poems,
pulling from their down-filled vests
scraps of inked-up paper, haiku
about icy roads, a burned-out bush camp,
the head cook who hanged himself
during February's cold snap.

They would see things about themselves
they never had before,
their smoky breakfast tables quieter,
no holding court over the radio's headlines.
Their mugs cooling. The steam of coffee.
Sound of liquid poured from the pot.
All of them holding up their cups
thirsty for the bottomless drink.

Muse

Mine is no uncorked chalice that spills out
a goddess of chiffon and ether, song-voiced
and floating above the ordinary
toward the canon of brilliant ideas.

Today, she's a far-off friend from high school
who calls to say she's going back
for more liposuction, this time
on belly, thighs and buttocks.

The first round didn't take, she says,
the bruising severe and for two weeks
she had to use a walker to get around the house,
the stapled line across her abdomen stretched taut
and muscles learning their new shape.

Only now, a year later, has the swelling begun to settle
and the red slashes of scar tissue fade,
but she's committed to this bodily arts and crafts pursuit
like a sculptor to her shapeless clay, bent
on stripping away flaws, a physical revision
that brings me back to the page
again, and all these words.

On a sterile white table is where I want to
lay down my poem, let the surgeon hold his wand
to the pale sheet, vacuum every loose adjective
and sagging phrase, slice from lazy metaphors
the flab, all the fat from language.

What sleeps beneath this makeshift glut,
what's wrapped beneath gauze and veil
is what I want most, and that voice
in my ear whispering, wake up.

Love Poem for a Skeptic

If you were one of the twelve disciples,
no doubt you would be Thomas.

With one eyebrow perpetually raised
in disbelief, arms folded across your chest,
and skeptic heart muttering *yeah, right, as if,*
I'd have to work hard to convince you of my affection,
bring concrete evidence of my love—a lock of hair,
a gold ring, my secret recipe for huckleberry pie.

You're no sucker, not easily duped
by sleight of hand, not even the Saviour's
outstretched over jars of water.

Every time Jesus hushes a storm or heals a leper,
the word *fluke* swims circles in your head.
When the herd of pigs careens off the hillside
into the lake, when the two fish and five loaves
feed a crowd of thousands, even when He
tells a dead girl to wake up and she does,
you can't help but rationalize, think *coincidence.*

Though the lame walk, the deaf hear
and scales fall from the eyes of the blind,
you stand on the margin of every miracle,
still have trouble seeing.

When the other disciples say they've spotted
Jesus alive after the flogging, nailing, death,
you say, show me the proof, let me
shove my hand in His torn-up side.

Now you've come home to me, your kisses
tasting of wine and fire and blood.
After years of parables, desert scorch
and riding out storms in a leaky boat,
you lie in bed beside me and wonder
what's left. In this room of shadows,
truth is the hand you hold in front of your face.
You swear you can see it glowing.

Dominique Gaucher

de *Trajets, Passages et Autres Déménagement D'atomes*
(Écrits des Forges, 2009)

Au cœur battant de la ville impériale

Assise seule sous les dômes dorés
je sirote un café

L'après-midi s'efface à pas feutrés

Mes seuls voisins
quatre hommes
les coudes serrés autour d'une table à deux
lisent en silence un journal arabe

Hier
On a fait sauter le métro de Londres

Mon regard s'arrête
Sur le mot *Underground*
en lettres jaunes et rouges sur fond noir
de t-shirt délavé

Dans un frisson irrationnel
sur les sacs posés par terre
je ne peux m'empêcher de darder mon regard

Avec quels yeux ?

pour Sculptures en jardin, Trois-Saumons

Ici
je regarde les cèdres
épanouis à leur pleine grandeur
Compagnons sages

l'écorce peinte à longs traits délicats
le panache ciselé qui laisse voir la lumière grise
leurs bras courbes de ballerines dansent
au rythme de la brise fraîche de cette fin d'été

Après Vienne
où la main humaine a caressé le crépi
où l'œil a choisi les jaunes
classé arbres et fleurs selon leur taille et leurs couleurs
Vienne où la passion a érigé une vaste maison
        mit schlagobers
aux douceurs de sa langue
à l'image sereine de ses habitants
Vienne
enracinée au cœur de la Terre

Au retour
au lieu de cette verdure qui décorait les pierres
à foison la nature emprisonnait ma maison
La stupeur passée – je regarde nostalgique
les cèdres s'effacer en une fadeur verte
les uns dans les autres
muets
impuissants à dominer le monde
se tenant par la main
prêts à s'esquiver à la file indienne
pour fuir l'œil qui déshabille en planches leur bois odorant

Et voilà l'œil de l'Europe
celui du défricheur
mu par des rêves de crépi jaune
abasourdi par l'infini du vert
perdu debout entre les épinettes
lancé avec rage dans un immense rasage
nivelage pavage

Voilà l'œil de l'Europe
l'œil moderne croisé entre deux érables
croyant s'ébaubir devant Les Grands Espaces

mais secrètement enivré
de ce monde encore à faire
L'œil concupiscent du maître devant la vierge
soupèse son droit de cuissage

Avec quels yeux regarder mes cèdres ?
Voilà une question sans oui ni non
Une question de patience
à négocier avec les arbres
un peu d'espace
un partage d'âme
pour qu'ils me laissent placer entre eux
des objets minuscules pour construire avec adresse
un empire puissant et doux
  mit schlagobers

Bucarest

Pourquoi ce soir
la ville m'a-t-elle engloutie ?
J'ai dévié de ma route
dans une courbe illuminée
pour me perdre dans les entrelacs
et les jardins sans loi

Où sont passés les jardiniers ?

J'ai quitté le trottoir bosselé
la rue les pavés
pénétré dans le silence des aïeules
Géantes endormies
Cendrillons oubliées

Comme une armée au guet
désuètes dans leurs rondeurs
elles taisent leurs charmes

Lassées des passants qui les boudent
elles m'ont prêté leur souffle ancien
Elles ont troqué leur haleine de poussière
pour un soupir d'âme

Pourquoi ce soir
ai-je eu envie d'ouvrir leurs grilles déformées ?
La beauté délirante des vieilles demeures
hurle à la lune

Où sont ceux qui naguère ont posé ces pierres ?

En face
l'éclairage des lampadaires
vacille
Je traverse la rue
et la lumière revient
Je fais le bouche-à-bouche à cette ville
qui étouffe

Les racines des arbres froissant le bitume
disputent la voie aux piétons
Au milieu de la rue ils attendent
ce qui n'arrive pas

Où sont allées les âmes ?

Attroupés
dans une cour intime
des peupliers géants
pourtant les attendent
murés
dans leur patience d'arbre

Dans le bus

La lumière dense
Pèse sur la ligne hachurée des usines

Endimanchées dans la grisaille
Encore somnolentes
de rares voitures obéissent au tracé

Une envolée en désordre calculé
réveille un passager

Sale de l'hiver
avril s'éveille sur des graffitis égratignés
Cherche en vain des feuilles
pour épousseter ses jaunes brunis
ses bruns grisonnés
ses gris rouillés

Délavée
je me fonds au cuir incertain du siège
les yeux glissant sur le fripé de l'eau

Les bosquets masquent le traversier balourd
Derrière les pêcheurs courbés sur ce qu'il reste de glace
les arbres décharnés dessinent une mosaïque vert-de-gris

Quand on ne tient pas le volant
le regard traverse les choses

Parsemés dans des épis jaunis
des bouleaux ploient sous la mémoire du verglas
des ponceaux enjambent l'hiver qui fuit

Des sillons sinueux rampent jusqu'aux silos vides
À vendre murmure l'affiche

Je traîne du regard un nuage paresseux
le lacère aux cimes des pins

Pas même une vache pour me regarder passer

Là-bas les mélèzes ont perdu leurs aiguilles
droits
Désespérés

La crainte m'envahit que le voile se déchire
ailleurs
sur des frayeurs endormies

Elles

Elles marchent dans la rue
et je sens leur sexe qui brûle leur corps
exacerbé par le soleil

Elles vont d'un pas décidé
le regard franc
Force contenue
qui ne demande qu'à jaillir

Toutes ces jeunes femmes
nombril découvert
réveillent avec effroi
une violence enfouie

Métro de Sofia

Sa voix s'élève dans l'antre

Au détour du couloir
entre ses musiciens
la jeune femme se dandine
boutonnée à l'aveugle

Les yeux clos
elle porte des chants anciens
étranges dans un corps d'enfant

Une voix aux accents lointains
chaude et glacée
sans voile

Un vieil homme l'écoute
Les yeux perdus dans l'éternité slave

Une seule place pour reposer mon corps las
À côté de lui

Il me regarde longuement et m'attire à lui
me montre du menton la voix
applaudit avec des ailes de papillon

Il veut que nous dansions

Il sent l'alcool me parle par signes
Il a deviné que je suis étrangère
Je comprends avec lenteur
qu'il est muet

Il ne veut plus me lâcher
Il cherche des mots partout avec ses mains
Je cours me réfugier

Un grand verre pour noyer mes cordes vocales
Personne à qui raconter
la voix
le silence
ces mains

Trajets

C'est à des sourds que je parle
Il faut tout leur expliquer

Dire les funambules de la pensée
ces petits soupirs sans suite au coin d'une rue

Les arabesques que dansent les feuilles

Ces choses-là personne ne pense à les retenir

Traversée urbaine

Marguerites et graminées ondulent nonchalantes
Des bosquets oubliés sur les pelouses
et des arbres distraits jalonnent un sentier imaginaire

Je fais le décompte des fleurs tranquilles et anglaises
grassement prospères dans la discrétion

Aux limites de ce quartier
on butine des odeurs de saris jaunes et de voiles bigarrés
On piétine le bitume avec effervescence

Puis se dresse à nouveau une frontière indolente de fleurs
Le chemin valse solitaire
Les âmes retranchées derrière des géants de pierre grise

Plus loin les passants se montrent le nez
on s'enfonce au cœur de la ville industrieuse
de l'atelier sombre d'hier
aux tours de verre des mondes virtuels

La ville traversée
étirée comme un chat entre sieste et chasse

Vienne

Passent et repassent les passants
À Vienne on déambule
foulant sans ennui ses propres traces
Ceux-là ont fait trois fois le tour des pavés
Femme enceinte vieillard chien en laisse
Tous
Ils reviennent ancrer leur mémoire

Le soleil descend à pas de loup sur la colonne votive
La lumière du jour cède en volutes à la nuit

Une dame rigole doucement derrière son fume-cigarettes
Le chien de la petite
repu
ne vient plus quêter mes restes

Griffonné sur le napperon
le poème le plus beau peine à dépasser l'ordinaire

Graham Good

from *Rilke's Late Poetry* (Ronsdale Press, 2004)

from *Duino Elegies*
The Tenth Elegy

At the outcome of all these harrowing insights,
let my jubilant praise be in tune with the angels.
Let none of the clear-struck keys of my heart
fail on a wavering, slack or snapping string.
Let the tears streaming down my face
make me more radiant; let the invisible tears
blossom. How precious you'll be to me, Nights,
in my grief. Why didn't I kneel to you lower,
disconsolate sisters, lose myself more
in your loosened hair? We waste our sorrows.
We look beyond them into the sadness of time
to see if they end. But they are really
our winter foliage, our dark evergreen,
one of our secret seasons — no, more than that —
they are place, plot, hearth, earth, home.

But how strange they are, the streets of the City of Pain,
where, in the false silence created by sounds
drowning each other out, the banal and pompous memorial,
poured from the mould of vacuity, makes its gilded noise.
An angel would trample to pieces their market of comforts
next to the church they bought ready-made, now clean
and disappointingly closed as the Post Office on Sunday.
But right outside is the rippling fringe of the fairground.
Swings of freedom! Eager jugglers and divers!
And dolled-up Luck's life-like shooting-gallery,
with flapping targets, and rattling tin
when a marksman scores. From handclaps to mishaps
he staggers on, for booths to suit every fancy

entice and wheedle and clamour. "For adults only,
a special attraction: seeing how money reproduces,
anatomically shown, not just entertainment:
the sexual organ of money, the whole process,
uncensored, educational, enhances
fertility..."
                              But just beyond, behind the last hoarding
plastered with posters for EVERLIFE,
the bitter beer that tastes great to drinkers
as long as they're munching on fresh distractions —
right behind the hoarding, right behind, begins the Real.
Children are playing, and lovers holding each other, private,
earnest, on the thin grass, while dogs act out their nature.
The young man is drawn further on: perhaps he's in love
with a Sorrow... He walks behind her into the meadows.
"It's a long way," she tells him. "We live over there." Where?
The young man follows, touched by her manner.
Her shoulders and neck... perhaps she's of noble family.
And yet he leaves her, turns round, heads back,
waves goodbye... So what? She's only a Sorrow.

Only those who die young, who are still
in the first timeless calm after weaning,
follow her lovingly. Young women
she waits for, befriends them.
Shows them quietly what she is wearing.
Pearls of grief and delicate
veils of patience. With young men
she walks in silence.

But there, where they live, in the valley, an older Sorrow
takes the young man on and answers his questions. She says:
"We were a large tribe once, we Sorrows. The Fathers
carried out mining up on the mountain: sometimes
you find a nugget of carved-out pain among humans,
or, from an ancient volcano, the slag of petrified anger.
That's where it came from. Once we were rich..."

And gently she leads him over the landscape of Sorrow,
shows him the pillars of temples, or the ruins
of cities where Princes of Sorrow once
wisely ruled the land. Shows him the high
trees of weeping, the fields of blossoming grief
(seen by the living only as pleasant foliage);
shows him the beasts of mourning grazing—and sometimes
a startled bird takes flight across their view,
trailing the long inscription of its lonely cry.
In the evening she brings him up to the graves
of the tribal ancestors, sybils and augurers.
But night is nearing, so they walk more softly,
and soon it towers up, the Tombstone
that watches over the world. Twin of the Nile's
noble Sphinx—the silent inner chamber's face.
In amazement they look at the royal head,
which silently sets the human face
on the scale of the stars for ever.

His eyes cannot take it in, still dazed
from recent death. But a look from her
rouses an owl from behind the rim of the crown,
where the rounding is ripest, faintly inscribing
onto his hearing, still fresh from death,
like the facing pages of a newly opened book,
the indescribable outline.

And higher still, the stars. New ones.
Stars of the land of pain. Slowly, the Sorrow
names them: "Look: the Rider, the Staff,
and that denser constellation is called
the Garland of Fruit. Further, near to the Pole,
Cradle, Pathway, the Burning Book, Doll, Window.
But there in the southern sky, pure as if held
in the palm of a holy hand, the clearly shining M
that stands for Mothers..."

But the dead man has to continue, and the older Sorrow
brings him down to the canyon,
where, shimmering in the moonlight,
is the wellspring of joy. With reverence
she names it, and tells him, "For humans,
this is a nurturing stream."

They stand at the foot of the mountain.
And there she hugs him, weeping.
Alone, he marches into the mountains of pain.
And no footstep rings out of his silent Fate.

But if they wanted to give us a likeness,
the numberless dead might point to the catkins
hanging from empty hazel-trees, or the rain
falling on darkened earth in the Spring.

And we, who think of happiness
as *rising*, would feel so moved
we would almost faint
if it started to *fall*.

from **The Sonnets to Orpheus, I, 26**

But you, divine one, sang to the end, when the horde
of rejected Maenads attacked you. Beautiful,
you sounded above their clamour with order;
from among the destroyers arose your uplifting music.

None of them there could crush your head or your lyre,
however they wrestled and raged, and all of the sharp
stones they hurled at your heart
went soft as they reached you, and could hear.

At last they dismembered you, hot for revenge,
while your sounds lingered on in lions and cliffs,
and in birds and trees. You are singing there still.

You lost god! You infinite trace!
Only since enmity tore you apart are we now
your hearers, and one of Nature's mouths.

from **The Sonnets to Orpheus, II, 17**

Where, in what happily watered gardens, on what trees,
among what gently falling blossom-chalices,
ripen the exotic fruits of consolation? These delicacies —
perhaps you'll find one in the trampled field

of your destitution. Time after time,
you're struck by the size of the fruit,
its soundness, the smoothness of the rind,
and that a bird's whim or a worm's spite

didn't spoil it first. Are there trees so full of angels,
tended by slow and secret gardeners so strangely,
that they bear us fruit without being ours?

The way we ripen too soon and decay,
we shadows and shades, cannot take away
the equanimity of those calm summers.

Garry Gottfriedson

from *Whiskey Bullets* (Ronsdale Press, 2006)

A Cowboy's Ethics

a cowboy's work ethics
start at 5 am & rest at 11 pm

there isn't always enough time
for wild rice, corn or deer meat

because the sun has its work cut out

since money grows from beneath
the hides of cows

cowboys never weaken,
they just get thick skin

An Identity Crisis

I certainly know who I am...

I can get away with being so politically incorrect.
I am the ambassador to first nation's poetic expressions
& as Kinsella pompously put it straight
"I have the license to do so."

what a magical way to escape tyranny!
as were Trudeau & Cretien hiding beneath cowboy hats

nevertheless & back to the point,

call me cowboy
call me first nations
call me aboriginal

call me native
call me chug
call me skin

if you must,
but never call me Indian.
I call myself that!

& if you feel guilty when I say so,
this is not about post colonial rhetoric
it is about an identity crisis

Anna Mae Aquash

feasts of white lies and charcoal tears drive
poetry to become dirty history lessons revealed
but the story must be told

begin with Anna Mae Aquash;
MicMac women warrior, 5'6", black hair, black eyes,
bullet in back of head, hands sliced off at wrists

There is more...

Custer fucked his way into the 80s.
rose from the grave,
disguised himself as FBI and CIA
raping Indian women
spraying bullets
hacking off hands,
filling Indian bodies with
lead sleeping in a man's dream

a finger print in the mind,
and blood payment
forever remembered

Joan's Poem

(for my sister-in-law, Joan)

Earl's on Top of Robson St
crams my ravenous soul I see
blood light lines leading and digging
the surgeon's path through
this cowgirl's alleyways and corridors
connecting lung chambers and heart hiding
long past troubles that brought
her to this plastic stranger in the first place

And in the lounge full
of boom baby boys cheering victory
over the win and loss of the 2005 World Series,
I can not celebrate their triumphs

I will rejoice her life though
heavy-hearted I may be
touting nervous giggles of Secwepemc prayer
quietly to myself as trendy and pompous
as those promoting globalisms
in the speckle of their eyes

Across the table sit
a mob of metro sexual Indian lawyers
promising the fight and retrieval
of the give-away lands Trutch
calculatingly tossed gluttonous settlers...

And he waited for the starvation of my sisters – like Joan

The creeks and streams never dry my eyes these days;
through the fog, I see you galloping Chip
full throttle in clover leaf patterns on the same lands
in the same arenas that brought
our ancestors this far in history

You are so courageous at this moment
I wish I were the heart of a woman - like you.

Let Go

I remember
I was wild in love
pulling words from my heart,
giving them to Sweetgrass and heaven
below Saddle Mountain

I thought you were there,
in the yellow arms of a swollen moon
where my words blew kisses
& you gave me back
a sacred bundle of undergrowth
as I let go

Strep-throat

bad mouthed Canadians
promised good-faith makers
land cramped by starvation sworn
a sack of flour, a cow, a treaty suit
exchange woodlands, prairie & mountains
for steep antagonism & acid love

charming was the speech
but too many spaces
between the teeth & tongue open
the tunnel to strep-throat

& how could Koyoti
be sung back to life?

Surface

I had never known
that another's forest of eyes
could so naturally transform
black tears into pearl snowflakes
falling into night

I had never known that
another's love touch
could turn my body
into shimmering moonlit waves
Grassdancing in the night's moon

I had never known
that another's embrace
could engulf me into a shell
of both fury & safety
as the night's moon wafted across sky
like a Round Dance near dawn

I had never known
that by entering another's body,
the Wildman of Sea & Forest
could drag gentleness & kindness
to surface the moon's haze
in the last starlight at daybreak
as if the act was a Red Stone Prayer

I had never known
that another's act of benevolence
was pure & sincere, & that you
could draw my soul
to the surface of daylight

Matthew Hollett

from *Shift & Switch New Canadian Poetry* (The Mercury Press, 2005)

rabbit-track alphabet:

soliloquies: language

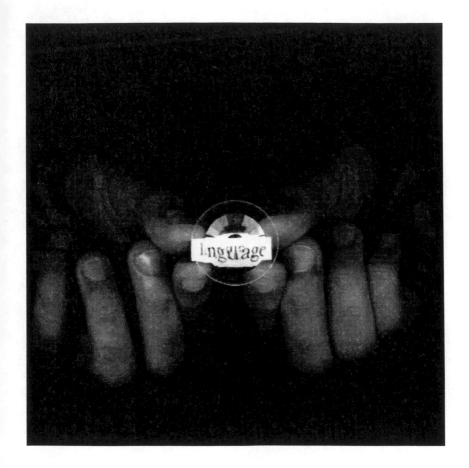

soliloquies: flood

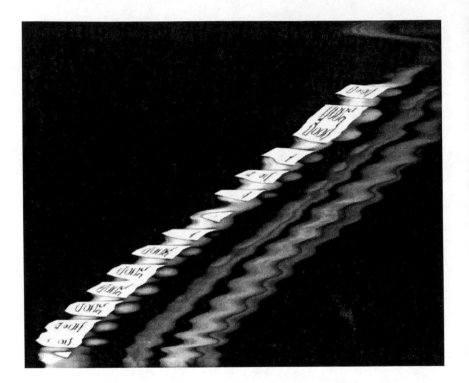

answers (found poem)

1. All three people are the same height.
2. Both circles are the same size.
3. All three circles are the same size.
4. The thin lines are parallel.
5. All four lines are the same length.
6. The objects are all the same length.
7. The two thin lines are the same length.
8. The moon is the same size in both pictures.

*

1. d. The others are four-legged animals
2. b. The others are found in the kitchen
3. b. The others are string instruments
4. d. The others are mammals
5. c. The others are birds of prey
6. d. The others are vegetables
7. c. The others are U.S. Presidents

*

The missing letter is "W," unless you look at the
puzzle upside down. Then the missing letter is "M."

George Johnston

from *The Essential George Johnston* Selected by Robyn Sarah
(Porcupine's Quill, 2007)

Farewell to Teaching

Knowing what I now know
would I have consented
to be born? Next question.
When it comes time to go
will I go forlorn or
contented? Ask again.
Anything in between
should be easier. O
K, what made up my mind
to come to Carleton? Work.
My kind of work was not
easy to come by, I
came by it at Carleton;
it was simple as that
and lucky, plain lucky.
I cannot account for luck
but I can be grateful.
What was my kind of work?
Presumably teaching,
whatever that may be.
Teaching is a kind of
learning, much like loving,
mutual goings-on,
both doing each to each;
mutual forbearance;
life itself, you might say.
Whatever teaching is
did I enjoy it? Yes.

Am I glad to leave it?
Even of life itself
enough is enough. Good-
bye Dow's Lake, goodbye Tower,
essays, papers, exams,
you I can bear to leave.
But how shall I improve
the swiftly-dimming hour?
I shall deteriorate
amid bucolic dreams
and gather in my fate;
there's lots worse ways than that.

Goodbye good friends. Alas,
some goodbyes are like death;
they bring the heart to earth
and teach it how to die.
Earth, here we come again,
we're going out to grass.
Think of us now and then,
we'll think of you. Goodbye.

Goodbye, Margaret

It turns out to be, as how
     could we know, our last walk
and talk together. Sun thaw
     made lacy the wrack

of winter in the streets.
     He is beautiful, you say.
I know that defeats
     are beautiful. One day

we come to our beauty,
     terrified or serene
or beyond both, more likely,
     knowing even as also we are known.

I guess I shall not again
    see him, as we leave his room;
his wits are gone
    and he is as though at home

yonder. He smiles from a distance;
    and he is, as you say, beautiful
in his ambience
    of tubes and bottles, the whole

apparatus of delay
    that keeps some good things on,
his courtesy, and the play
    of his Irish sense of fun

but draws the rest out fine.
    You were not reconciled to age,
you hated the caving-in
    of your nerve, yet you stood at the edge

of his bed and smiled at him
    who had shared most of your life
and for whom you had become
    dim, and as if

with your first and last words blessed
    the old man. I think back
beyond much that is lost
    to the blessedness of your look.

It hardly seems a goodbye
    with you; not like the one
when I asked you not to cry
    and you hung on and hung on,

then broke at the last:
    a station platform, so
long ago in the past;
    vivid before me now.

You held your feelings there;
    at home they gave
my childhood its weather;
    you were not afraid to grieve

or to enjoy a good laugh,
    having both kinds of tears
and strong views enough,
    unbudgeable scunners,

loyalties like glue.
    What became of them all?
Sometimes I wish I knew.
    Dear God, perhaps I shall.

Sometimes I wish that I
    might have seen you once more.
What for, to say goodbye?
    Hard to be sure what for:

a hug,
    another gossip
this side of the big
    summing up?

Yet I can't not be glad
    that when you were sent for
and your days were yet good,
nights not yet bad
    you went.

Spring Chorus

Spring keeps coming in louder
in Fred's
moonwet
gravel pit:

be glad
squeeze me
o be gladder
o squeeze squeeze
o squeeze

not

says no
says claw
in the wet
move over
splash
hush

again
maybe a little
squeeze again
glad maybe
o squeeze o be gladder
o squeeze squeeze
squeeze

Rachel Anstey

Strawsmoke

I begin to see fields
as a late-playing child
sees bed.

Dusky games are hardest
to quit.

They burn straw in the fields.
I wonder if I may choose
to burn.

Strawsmoke hangs
in curtains
against the twilight.

Wintering

Wrapped
in tarpaper, tentest and styrofoam
they hold for spring.

On warm days they rid the hive of dead
and breed renewal. Some fly out.

Put your ear to the hole.
Between gusts you can hear them,
a bunched hum.

Elis Juliana

from *Haiku in Papiamentu* translated by Hélène Garrett
(The University of Alberta Press, 2003)

In the name of the
Father, Son and Holy Ghost.
No place for Mother!

Death does not realize
how preoccupied life is
with its cessation.

The only way to
remain young forever is
to take a picture.

A holy moment —
the opening and refolding
of butterfly wings.

The guests are now gone.
The owners of the home may
move freely again.

In my little house
I have no need to look for
ways to find myself.

Women can cry at
whatever time or moment
may be opportune.

To ask a worm for
the secret of its being
is to spoil its mood.

A child is crying.
He's opened his umbrella,
but it just won't rain.

A handleless pick
bides its time with great patience
within the tool shed.

When you bite your tongue,
you may blame your teeth, but it
is still your own fault.

Duties neglected
mimic the same condition
as constipation.

Looking to buy shoes
in order to walk on clouds
surely is silly.

In a time of drought
the tiniest cloud will draw
attention surely.

A blown-out candle
spews forth a lot of smoke as
if to say "Goodbye!".

Barbara Klar

from *Cypress* (Brick Books, 2008)

A Letter for Newlove

You probably don't remember me. We met
when I was twenty-two on an ugly couch
in a roomful of people in Regina in November,
people talking about your words and the end
of birds. I'd like to live a slower life too,
I think I said. You were an awkward comrade
referring to yourself in the third person, your demons
rustling in the scotch-guarded flowers,
in your snow-haired wing, your open ear.

Where your prairie climbs the Cypress Hills
the flickers hunt in little armies and the living
finally talk to the dead. I am talking, talking,
sorrow in the soft grey chests of the armies,
their brother's wing breaking by a ranchyard
somewhere, a flicker in the dust from the school bus
on the first day of school, the children wiser
than they'll ever be, the coral-red crescent
leaving the nape of the year. A girl gets off
the bus and wants to save him when he needs
a club to smash him into the afterlife
and the summer I was twelve I found
a knocked-out pigeon under the railroad bridge,
made him live in a cage until he loved me. I don't
know how to be unless it gets me something.
The flicker knows the only perfect word,
a war cry, and it leaves a grave more beautiful
than any of your poems, not by much,
just a bit, dear John: I'm leaving
the world. Is there anything you need

up there? I'll bring it the last time I leave here,
the long trucks carrying the cattle to slaughter
and the school bus going home.

Ranger Station Road

I walk down into the valley where I was last
young, down into the darkness of the wisdom
of alder, down into willow's old need
for water, down to the winding world,
the trout-jumping valley of flowers
and money and love

                              and the only barnyard
for days of walking, a bluebird warbling
truly on the only sign since Maple Creek:
West Block Ranger Station, established 1917,
the flag of the Dominion
come before me,

                        I am walking down a rutted
road two horses wide into having been
a tree planter, twenty-seven and immortal
in the valley of the never dead, the ghosts
of all the rangers riding.

                              Somewhere in the hills
the invisible part cowboy part cop
is protecting me. I'll only see him
if I'm lost and he must find
me, if someone's death is lost
and he must find me.

                        My shovel leg
is aching. My dog and my truck and my father
are all on borrowed time. Wooden bridges grieve
the downward sleep of the green blood of water,

nothing waiting but the black friends
of my fears in the valley where the dead
will watch for me,

               the grizzlies
and the invisible gazing from
their vision posts, everything alone
with itself. I wait for the horseman
to take off his hat and call me ma'am,
his words falling down
to the valley.

Storm

My mouth is a ball of lightning remembering
streets. Deer smell the cities, the fear of deer.
Between their nostrils and my mouth are the streaming
invisible pages of *A Field Guide to Growing Old*
and *The Introduction to Questions*, green airs
saying only *welcome.*

The mouth is an empty ear.

The eye is a lost moon wobbling above the planet Grass.

The heart is a stone flipped over by the brave frosts.

The spine is a lodgepole apprentice.

And the mouth, the end of fire, listens forward to the wind.

Name

The land is broken in three, a spine buckling
the horizon. *Broken Back. Three Backs.*
I am the old woman drawn up and down,

my body absorbing silence, my body
sweating noise. The No Longer Needed
drips to the stones whose blessings
stare and say nothing. Where the land
gets broken I am broken, bones
sticking out of me, content in their pieces,
marrow noises falling. I grow the scar
of glaciers, the name carved smooth:
The Place Where the Land Gets Broken.

West, the ice answers. East.
In between, a crossing.

East Tower Trail, The Bone

Early May. I walk through fescue's heat,
the plateau greening. They have been through
winter since I was last here, the hills made
of the parting ice. In a crease of the hills
I find the bone of a snowdrift and lie
in it, the bed remembering the northwest wind
falling here, here, here, five, fifteen feet of snow,
I am losing my way, grains of snow cutting
my face shoving forward in a former life,
white man trapper up Shit Creek.

Today I will not die. I walk toward summer
with a snowball in my left hand, white candy-apple
from the children of the hills, wise and bitten
by the cold. I eat the letting go of snow,
a saving of snow until hills can be hills
without it. They don't care that I returned.
They are busy loving time. I walk across
their task, the winter of the grass
giving way, the way I follow.

Gap Road, The Last White Spruce

Low grass after the wildflowers, low
as ocean long after water. Earth is dry.
Skeletons rise. Pine surrenders, spruce surrenders,
poplar surrenders to the grass and I am naked,
the green cloaks behind me, the road streaming
through the deep hills, the sky following the red weed
of my skin, sky of the hammer-blue eye
and the wind between two forests.

Seán is meeting me at four o'clock on the other side
of the Gap. I must march so the sky
cannot eat more of me, blue monster making
weather of my hair and blood
by the start of the afternoon.
Cold with hurry I must march through
the terror of the grass's liquid waves.
I march toward the pine wall of the castle
of hope. I hold onto solids, non-winds:
a truck's piece of chrome, an evicted stone
and a cow's lumbar vertebra, the seventh angel
of drought, her calcium wings fallen
from the water of bovine flesh.

The sky is monster because
space is the mirror of those who fear

and the boa root of the last
white spruce holds onto its coulee, the last
until the end of Gap Road. This is how
I rest, once, with the spine bone of a cow
who died of space below the tree
that grows from less, the bone bleached
ivory by the sky's disease: the coyotes
shattered out of it and ran her down.
She is the hard bird entering my hand
between the third and fourth metacarpi,

flying my arm to the pumping rib to graze
the blood inside me. She is the angel

of why I walk the Gap. Long ago
when I had hooves my hunger passed
between two forests. There would be
the sweet flowers, the needles of pine
and grass on the other side. I fell and the sun
ate my waters. When the rains finally came
they drove me deep into the earth and I grazed
below the great gaps for two hundred droughts
and the sky with its dry mouth pulls me out
at last, my bone that smells
of time, my wingstone
on its way to the other side.

Fallen

In the light from knives
I will not fight. The stone has split,
cut my hand, left its bloodline, warrior mark
on the hillface, red streak drying as truth. Stone
is fallen where it cut me with truth, my body
running to water, the Battle Creek healing its banks
of blood and rot-gut whisky for a hundred years
and more with water from the mountains that will not
make me more thirsty, the red pasts swirling
in the water turning clear.

I am empty and no longer noise.
The morning after stone my cloth hand is
a banner unravelling. I hold it up, surrender:
now that I can love I must begin.

Prayer

A wild girl's footprints have fallen
through the winters, earth stars
light up the air. There have been no bears
in the Cypress Hills for a hundred and twenty years
but I follow the Ursa below me, Aiekunekwe
in the undertrees, rippling sand of her fur,
coulees breaking in the deep hearts
of the chokecherries. She
is the muscled cloud turning logs
to look for slugs, shit fossils blooming
with tannin in the black sky made of the dead.
In her skull the root of the bullet
has grown its tree of stars and in the creek
the trout are swimming around the hole
in water where Isaac Cowie dipped his cup
and counted to seven hundred fifty.

There have been no bears in the Grizzly Hills
since before the great fire, since the last bear
dropped into 1885 like a mountain falls
into the ocean, all the thunders sinking.
There have been no bears for three
of my unfinished lives, my night lives.
She climbs from the ground and pads
around my canvas. She is sad
and skinny. I talk with my smell.
From the hollow just outside of me
your claws light up the trees.

Carl Leggo

from *Come–By–Chance* (Breakwater Books Ltd., 2006)

from Lilacs

the clothesline is empty
but not for long,
we are home, and
Nan will hang clothes
almost every day
like semaphore flags,
signalling our presence
for the neighbours

&

the air filled with lilacs,
I walk familiar streets,
each breath I take
a long draught of childhood,
I take photographs
like storing jam preserves
for writing in winter

&

once
a seedling,
that maple tree
now more than
a story high, holds
more stories in its branches
than I have
life left
to tell

&

long ago, Pop carried
a wild rose bush
from his home in Britannia,
ancient wild rose scent
through the heart

&

summer squeezed between
the arduous winter's end,
a spring weekend or two,
and autumn's volcanic urgency,
like a slice of Maple Leaf boiled ham
that ties the tongue with traces
of cellophane and gelatine

&

in front of the house
Pop planted the snowball bush,
petals of fractal abandon, balls in balls,
like he might forget in summer
the long last winter

&

for three decades
Pop and Nan have lived
on Lomond Street, moved in
when it was new. Pop says,
"When we moved in, I could wave
to my neighbours across the gully,
but that was a long time ago, can hardly
see my neighbour's house now,
through the lush forest,
the hidden neighbourhood,
still rooted though"

&

Pop tells me, since spring
his knees have not been good,
but in the Legion magazine he read
that cod liver oil can repair cartilage,
that he's rebuilding his knees.
I ask him if cod liver oil can mend
a broken heart, but he says he isn't sure,
will check the magazine later,
and I remind him about the time
he told me honey, sulphur and vinegar
could also fix any ailment, and
all he says is, "Don't lose hope"

&

the city night lights
are embers in a campfire,
the only way I see my past,
and in my heart's keen eye,
the clusters of houses clinging
to mountain slopes and valleys
are a meadow of wildflowers

&

this graveyard
in the middle of the city
is a tangled garden of weeds,
a forgotten place for lovers only,
a gardener's nightmare of wild rose and
chokecherry bushes, weeds, hay, forget-me-nots
and juniper berries like blood. Everything grows hot in
full cemeteries where only the headstones hint at the stories of
smallpox, house fires and drowning, mothers and children side by side
in this lost graveyard where nobody remembers the stories of unwed mothers,
criminals and the unbaptized, buried outside the consecrated garden of fenced plots

&

```
        I  chop wood          for winter fires
        while the sun          burns my back.
       My axe is too small     for one knotted log,
         only nips at it with a crackie dog's spite.
         I know from school mathematics
          that there is a formula for dividing a circle
        for finding the central      point that holds it together,
        but I can't remember it      on this hot August day
```

&

in the midday sun on the patio, having
drunk a Black Horse or two, I forget
how to count, hear lawnmowers and
sparrows and the crash of wood trucks
on the Lewin Parkway, like a jagged
scar through the city's rock heart.
The leaves of silver asp whistle
in the breeze like light rain

&

widows and widowers
gather at Mt. Patricia Cemetery
to listen to old stories
and breathe the scent of new ones
in the plastic and silk bouquets
of grief and hope

&

never monochromatic, the sky is a dozen shades
of black and white, with a blue-light wash

&

Pop says, "She won't let me go
any further than the shed these days."
Nan says, "Not that he ever listens"

&

Nan just called out
the long-range forecast,
mostly rain for the next week

&

rain bounces off the asphalt
with the electric and geometric lines
of a pinball game

&

I just visited Pop in his shed. I wasn't sure
what he meant when he said, I'm giving
it all up soon, until he explained that
he wouldn't be making stuff
in the shed anymore

&

Nan marks each day's rhythm with food,
we eat a lot. Even before a meal is eaten
she plans the next. In fear of running out
she runs up to Dominion, though she has
enough food in the cupboard
and deep freezers to feed everybody
on Lomond Street for a year

&

Nan says,
"The toutons are right raw,"
but nobody stops eating

&

The ocean calls
on this shore forever,
for close to forever for sure.

The ocean is always changing,
a little more, a little less, always enough.
Driftwood swept in a line along the beach,
a fence around the ocean that can't be held.
The ocean always calls

&

                        no line will ever hold
            the tangled light   of beachstones,
    shells, windswept trees,   morning glory, and family,
                        beyond counting,
                        like fragments
                        in a sea arch
                        without end

Seven Sparrows

Sipping a rye and seven
on Nan and Pop's patio, I see
seven yellow-backed sparrows
light in the lime tips of a spruce

like ceramic miniatures from Red Rose tea,
small enough to be almost real,
they peck at the branches, feast on budworms,
while crows watch from telephone lines.

I remember my daughter brought the spruce home
from S. D. Cook Elementary
a seedling in a Dixie cup on Save the Earth Day,
and because we were in transit for a year

from Alberta to British Columbia
and home again to Newfoundland,
Pop planted it in his backyard and for years
feared he mowed the spruce with the daisies,

and now it holds sparrows, the longing of crows,
and memories enough to keep the heart calling
earth's rhythms with roots seeking deep and deeper,
the whole earth sung in veins of long light.

Bare Buff

At the end of a busy semester, eager to avoid another day's
torrent of e-mail, I drove fast from campus and parked at Spanish Banks,
chilled by English Bay and Coast Mountain shadows,
to breathe the surprisingly clear blue sky of early December,
to stroll the beach and hold my spirit close,
the way poets need to, a brief Sabbath,
an inspiriting respite before returning to the drudge
of the associate dean's unmemorable memos
and specious spam promises of gargantuan penises.

I soon regretted my poet's fancy, wished I had stayed
with the harping safety of e-mail. A thief smashed the car
and stole my satchel: notes for essays and poems, books,
my favourite fountain pen, my diary, where for months
I had written another life, the Walter Mitty dreams,
the confused concatenation of Scorpio sun and Pisces moon,
the story behind my mask, the diary where words failed me less often,
perhaps because I wasn't writing for peer review, publication, prizes, pride.

A writer's diary, not for public presentation or perusal,
a place for gathering words like pieces of the world's puzzle,
flotsam washed up on the shore of a desert island, fragments
of an omnipresent fiction that manufactures more discontent than consent.
For months I wrote nothing, only hoped my diary was in a Smithrite,
dreamed of the thief reading it late at night by candlelight
savouring the voyeur's romance, and I waited for a dire blackmail message,
looked for its anonymous publication in *True Confessions*,
scrutinized the romantic want ads for invitations to rendezvous.

In spring, the police found my satchel on a tree stump in Pacific Spirit Park:
notes, books, fountain pen, everything except the diary, and I woke up
in Richmond Shopping Centre on a Saturday, naked as old Adam, without fear.
Now I write only truth in my diary and poems, and expect others will read
my words with a desire for the catharsis of
confession, the revelry of revelation,
the apocalypse of admission, the dalliance of disclosure. Like Salome's
head-twisting striptease of a thousand veils, I am bare buff,
but like Lady Godiva I can still let down my hair, dreaming
the thief dreaming me, Heathcliffe on a blustery bluff.

from **Scribbled in Winter Light**

2

After a semester at Memorial, I returned home with Lana in December, eager
to introduce her to my family. They knew Lana from my letters but this was
their first opportunity to meet her. Lana and I almost needed snowshoes to
tramp through the deep snow from Eddy's Bus depot up Old Humber Road.
When I introduced Lana to my brother, he just nodded and smiled. I knew my
brother was shy but I expected a little more effort in his greeting ... a story, a
question, a little wit. Instead, my brother said nothing, just quickly slipped on
his coat and left the house. My brother was a puzzle but Skipper compensated
for him with an almost manic burst of stories, jokes and opinions. When it
was time for Lana to catch her bus back to Stephenville, we stepped outside
to see my brother leaning on a snow shovel with a wide grin. Like Charlton
Heston opening the Red Sea, he had shovelled a wide path through the deep
snow in the yard. He still didn't say anything, but Lana kissed his hot face as
she passed.

Cross-Word Puzzle

(York Harbour, May 13, 2004)

In this sacred place of solitude on the edge
of the North Atlantic we live each day with sturdy
rhythms and hold one another in the heart's light.

Yesterday, you raked autumn hay in the backyard,
while I took a respite from revisions to an essay,
and watched you a long time through the patio door.

On this the fourth anniversary since we married again,
adding another surprise twist to our story,
sewn with jagged and joyful seams, we are here.

We wear two wedding bands, the past and more past,
reaching into the eager present and future,
nothing forgotten, everything stored and restored.

We have turned a circle of seasons, and though
we will never leave this place, we know, also, that
we will never return, since all turns are new.

Today, we biked four hours on a trail built for caribou
and ATV's, a scribbled loop of mud paths that our legs
couldn't hold. You took more risks than me,

shot down somersaulting hills, paused to photograph
my descent, laughed with my chasing you over shards
of rock, washouts, jagged ruts in a marsh of tangled roots.

Our stories intersect like words in a crossword puzzle,
letters shared, vertical and horizontal lines woven into
a quilt of many colours, to keep us through every season.

We stopped at Sheppard's Grocery in Lark Harbour
to buy champagne, and tonight we will celebrate our
long lasting love, while watching *Survivor*.

Mark Adams

Come-By-Chance

From Corner Brook, I drive the Trans-Canada
across Newfoundland on a bare black highway
under a blue March sky.

I am surprised how little has changed,
how well I remember the land's writing.

The sun falls as I drive through the late afternoon:
I chant with the sun's ancient blood rhythms.

In an ESSO overlooking Random Sound
I eat fish cakes and later drink a Black Horse
at the Tanker Inn near Come-By-Chance.

The whole world is at rest like anything could happen,
like nothing's going to happen,

perhaps the world has simply stopped on a Wednesday night
in this vast vacant island where an eternal flame

burns in the night sky over a moth-balled oil refinery,
a steady sign that Joey Smallwood had less sense and more dreams
than a narcoleptic on valium.

Having nothing else to do, we watch CBC with gulls' weary eyes,
another documentary on Barbara Ann Scott, still skating with a frozen smile,

and Mel tells me the roads are slippery and complains about politicians
who won't provide enough salt trucks for the highway.

   I nod.

John Conway, Rural Municipality of Bratt's Lake

Brenda Leifso

from *Daughters of Men* (Brick Books, 2008)

from **Prayer for Rain**

viii.

what do you do
with other people's memories
when they are carved into this land
the land offering up proof

hold up the barbed wire and crawl through
to the west oaks branches snapping under your feet
make sure the hairy red cows aren't near
pick your way through dry pies to the hollow
chunks of cement spilling through dirt leaves
years you can hear in your own breath your mum's
childhood shrieks round-elbowed body cannonballing
skin slapping water this the pool Grandpa and Great-Grandpa dug
with shovels and hands after the thaw the warm
spring sun prairie muscles glistening you can hear
Fritz the shepherd barking love wanting to hurl himself in
haul each child out one by one by the scruff of their necks
mum her brothers the kids from three farms over
this is joy you think their bodies are joy things are so simple
when you can't smell the danger
when you can't smell the secrets.

x.

you search too hard for meaning

you can't remember what you weren't there to hear to feel
to know you never dug an irrigation ditch
line for fence posts hole for the biffy (or ran for it at 3 am in 30 below)
shovelled winter shit out of the barn come spring
heard coyote teeth tearing legs off calves
shot a bad dog or a good dog
got up at four all summer to set the sprinklers
watched your crop hailed out in August
begged the bank for another bailout loan
squeezed 150 acres and 70 years into a trailer in town

who asked you to coil the truth
black bullsnake around our necks.

Wild Strawberries

No known territories brought us,
my sister and I, inside this swollen valley –
just the smell
of thirsty bark, our own cracked fingers,
our feet dusty, needle dry.
We followed no history to get here,
remembered no map
only our heat-hoary hides,
our beaded eyes,
our snouts snuffling
through underbrush.
We paw away beetles and earth
search for that tang, that sweet promise
of fruit softening. I have no knowledge
of rituals or offerings, know only that together
we are no longer adult or human,
only that I want back

the language of our childhood
happiness, for her
I want to find it, place it,
however small, a wild strawberry
on her waiting tongue.

At Night, Teiresias Listening

Old man, old man, seal your ears against this drumming
this cracking skin of the moon,
the cuff of bare feet through the halls,
riptide pull of women leaving.

Old man, caulk the draught of remembrance
in your blood, the fury pooling
beneath the barren bridge of your throat –

Oh! Shackle your hands with the bedclothes,
stop your palms from sounding
what's long been buried by your flat ribs,
your squared and fruitless hips –

a foolish woman, a woman cursed,
in whom Hera will not forgive the desire
to taste again your own spiced milk,
swallow a man's body with slick darkness,
unhearthed fire.

The Maenads Prepare for the Hunter

Women, gather, pass a bowl from hand to hand,
let us take a collect of desire:
ache in the feet after a day's long walking,
shade of pine, soft bed of moss for sleeping.
The pleasure a green branch grants fingertips
in the snapping, the extension of arms
uncorseted by walls. Earth-soaked forgetfulness,
sharp teeth at our breasts ground smooth by women's hands.
If our hunger is madness, lock us here –
to these hills we pledge loyalty,
we will silence and savage any man who hunts us
or dares set us free.

Letter to Kirk: Vancouver

It is hard to know honest moments in this city. Remember
in October, biking home, I couldn't wrench my shoe from the pedal clip
and I fell in the middle of Macdonald Street? I didn't cry
as I wanted. Traffic didn't stop. I rode on pretending nothing happened,
blood trickling from my knee, furious – twenty-seven years and still lacking
grace. The people here own so much
I covet. Every time I step on the rackety bus,
I want to be the chestnut-haired girl wearing those perfect soft-brown shoes.
I guess I could blame my mother for not teaching me how to dress,
for feeling guilty walking the bright winter beach at Jericho
when everyone else runs, when even our dog is unstylish,
unhappy, wears a muzzle while others go free.
You know, I'm getting tired of blaming my mother.
It seems I can't write a poem without lying.

Today, in my journal I wrote "a breakthrough in honesty must occur."
Maybe it's unnecessary to avoid sentimentality. It's true
I felt a pinch in my nose when, last week, on a green-algaed rock
we saw a momma seal shielding her baby. Laughed

because it wouldn't stop barking until she gave up and nursed.
When we paddled by again six days later, saw the pup's carcass
bloated, wave splashed (will it one day explode?),
a space-dark weight sank into my bowels,
the same sickness as when we passed the accident on Knight Street,
        motorcyclist splayed
in the asphalt heat, his knee bent ninety degrees the wrong angle.

You say death is a natural occurrence, but there is too much of it
in this city to make sense anymore. I have learned to ignore sirens,
drive through crosswalks when pedestrians wait,
concentrate only on housing prices and our negative bank account.
I don't know how to shed these oily slicks,
work up to offering you one clean sentence of truth. Here:
I prefer spearmint toothpaste, Colgate over Crest,
and if I remind you to brush, I'm telling you I love you.
When I say you should eat well, I'm afraid for your arteries.
I'm lying, thinking of my own weight, and razors. Sometimes
I stay only because I don't know where else I'd go.

Kirk, do you think that mother seal mourned?
Please lie to me, tell me she offered her nipples,
nuzzled her baby for many nights. Tell me that when you reach
for my underbelly, it's warm and round and living.
Tell me that the skin I live inside isn't rough,
isn't slippery, cold.

Brian Macbeth

Letter to Grandma

I am afraid to begin.

I am afraid that what I write
won't be real. That if I
fish for the lyric,
the tender-mouthed image,
nothing will hold.

I am still afraid of thunder,
the lightning in the birch copse
branching into angry arms.
I remember all those storms
in childhood, I remember
your body caught me.

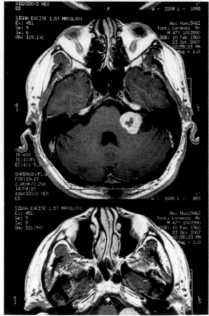

Lorenzo Tonti

Tim Lilburn

from *Orphic Politics* (McClelland & Stewart, 2008)

Getting Sick

I dug a slot into the gravel of no address,
I dug a slot warm as a hand into the air's water-cliff.
The eye seeing me is a charred-wood-backed river cannonballing
through badlands, badly disciplined, lizardly hills, water in mitres
of cinder freighting necessity's weight past my head on the ground
                   sleeping,
the eye's windy mouth, love-yanked night wall; pines triple axel in it.
Coal-masked generosity, no name.

. . .

Two years we were stubbed on the floor, bone-eared, smoke-cheeked.
Urgency, in a torn gown, held my chin between its thumb and
index finger and unreined its face lunging
into my face, its face a foot from mine cataracted, and said
a single word a day from a pack of ten.
I put my finger in its mouth and, then, sick, was triaged
up barely blacksmithed, leprechaun, lignin creeks
that were unloading the hills,
its nose a foot from my face,
bonemeal, burnt wire creeks,
flicker of antler, thinlipped cat, graphite dust, no cartilage
creeks, I followed them up, with a bag of roasted sand, bag
of swung sticks, pushed in a shopping cart, building materials for the
very top, the static of Europe bulging my knee.
I dug a slot into no address,
 my knee geigered a snailheaded ghost, an unread Chaldean library
                    below the hover of Plato's soul.
In small stone houses, violet fields were artillerying from a century ago
                 under the floors.

Orphic Hymn

It salmons from leagues of leafmulch
and writhes to the door.
Oak leaf shadow craters its spine range and neck
as if it walked between being's lit breasts and the screen.
It's got caught, opened in its antlers, the wood-covered 16th century book
that works out I am sick.
I hold this up to what I am doing, lying on the divan, haven't pissed
or shit in days, infection's horse's rider lashes back and forth
with his black flag. Two winter stars with dessert plate heads
two months ago were nailed at either edge of my groin.
I've been pensioned a shield of bees
below my chin, under earliest skin, a bridge, a sleeve of industry.
The MRI tech asked if I like country or classical.
The dogwood tree blooms in the full window a rising whine.
The temperature of this nuzzles in like sediment that's already stone.
A knife waits, girlish, down the hill, flipping over, over, small
fish flash at the bottom of that boat, convinced, the knife, crossing
and uncrossing its legs.

A Surgery Against Angelism

Set a fat layer of fire grazing into the chest of engine heat, breast-
stroking against motion perfuming from the sickness of volt swollen
                              inhalations. Let this heat
sag to a half-eaten meal not its own; let it eat rods,
iron shavings, green stones, dead yarrow, words headfirsting
from a rock overhang in the upper right, a skeleton of a seal; let it learn
            to heave-hiss through its mouth the complete psalmic blade.
Five pound fire gravities against hurtling's musk.
In the chest of engine heat, a concussed floor;
whipped light-heads cough in blows' trampoline, and choir above
        their husks, they lurch into a blurred but, yes, readable circle, moving,
            yes, the gear that jacks the cranial dome.
You go into the fish's mouth which is Siberian citizenship,

into the fish's mouth which is the body of a cousin
                                        at the volcano's wedding.
We come out of the upper colon tunnel onto the ledge, sweet-looking
        antlers to smoke from the cloud deer. We've built a shack
                        out of this numbnutsness,
                we've hidden in this long grass. A stick will cure us.
Your eyes in the fish's gut are moved like a wand around the dark.
The knife snugs down through skin.   And this is politics.

Nation-building

Pythagoras, sliced, freezered cat, defrocked Wal-Mart greeter, in
        anachoresis, face welted with interior mountainings, mountain
                        whippings, grinds ahead, dolphining,
                                dolphining,
in and out of the artifact-cavitied humus of the Chukatcha Peninsula,
a curly iron basket of oily fire at the bulb of his forehead; he
                        is stitching, you can imagine a gold thread
leaking and spinning braided from his testicles.
See him in the horsetail headdress of Apollo, a loaned snake cape, his
                        look has the gargly Cessna
roar of one moony engine leaving the continental shelf at night in snow,
this is the real one-father, bobbing in greasy light, then he
drops behind a metre high gravel ridge and night is there;
the Bering Sea rotates its nineteenth century gear inside
the drum of herony, idle volcanoes, toenail painting, Las Vegased,
                        dishy volcanoes,
near which all the Pythagoreans sweat.
So you want to go home but haven't a clue.
Here's one, a ganglion.
Recall that the ciliced, winded thigh will go by its own delectation
                        into the flint trench
That the whale bones must cover the corpse completely
That the water creeping down in stones on this body is the sky bull
OK, now to go into the rolling mouth, take the stubbly, mud stairs
up to the surgery ward and through it, wiping gecko webs

from the i.v. trees,
then into the broom closet that rustles with mammoth bones.
Now slide your soon-to-be-sliced thigh into the slate-sliding water,
go down in it, there is a promised house inside exactly the size of your
head, abdomen, legs, a book within a book, book written
on the inside and on the outside,
a key shape outlined by a stitch of white stones on the intertidal plain.

What Has Happened

My mother puts fleabane near her mouth
and small farms suck down in feathery roars,
tipping like ocean liners, grass roofs, poplar poll barns
lifted then slanting down in pillaring dust.
Sand curtains buckle into the room.
She puts roads on her arms, brome overhanging them,
grasshoppers flawlessly clearing the roads.
Pull the car over on this approach; don't worry about the grass
clawing the oil pan; now go into the trees, a clattering bouquet of pails,
blindfolded berries, you've heard, near the slough, mosquitoes
big as sparrows.
My mother's upper lip is mosquitoed shade.
Steam engines plough into the earth
slamming one foot, seven feet under, between Creelman, Sask. and
Fillmore, Sask.,
cream cans rolling, routering down,
cars falling the height of buildings; there they meet the crown-
dragging, always-turning, lacustrine-clay-edemaed buffalo.
Wheat from 1942 trickles down
the rat hole of the engines and bibles, too,
fall down the hole and hymnals.
My mother puts the moth of light inside the lamp.
My mother asks the day what day it is, and her brother jerks out of
the Kipling Legion on a Dieppe raid leg,
cannoning the tune of lymphatic cancer to everyone on the prairies,

his harrowed, wobble-faced guitar, strands weaseled from the screen
            door, August 1933.
My mother the gold dragonfly, gold entering
         green near the spine.

Night Clotting in the Ice-Free Corridor

Cut into the tongue where the fish dive;
there's a castle there under a shallow black lake, ducks with bicycle-
            pumped white heads,
moon-bored corridors, still lit from the first potashy coring.
Come in at 45 degrees, falling cleanly though sky, and buck down
and back, you will caravan through one glassy strata then another,
some musical, and when you lose your way in crosswinds,
                        muscle alone will be your star.
The moon-ticked, savoured body
tasted and heard as this castle.
A brother to you is the shallow, decayed water smell of
the carob syringe. The barrel goateed with strips from Deutero-Isaiah.
We will take out elm alleys and alphic hills of wheat.
Everything must be laid on gravel
and have swept over it the body-growing wing
       of unoccupied darkness,
the daemon-secreted drug.

See You

Poor fuck, I see you, your long cow teeth,
the ice cladding of your arms has poured everywhere, ice
scale of your face flowing to cast you a house or yurt.
Through its fifty below lemon gin blear I see you
alone inside in airplane position over some food's calculus,
your parsnip, *siber*, ermine face.
I notice you've hooked up with a boat of cedar-knotted femur,

carbon dated to heidelbergensis,
worthy to hold still in the sawing mare tails of the sun.
You can't speak now, your right side buried
already, you're dressed as always in whipping black.
I've become that machine, and so can see two jellyfish
the colour of the boudoir do slow martial arts for your brain.
The boat has arrived on the tip of your tongue.
The keel is spiked immediately in seven feet of prairie
just east of Rosetown but you are, yes, going.
(great starry pulling on violin-tarred ropes)

This, Then

Someone wearing a vest of radon implants
coaxed my tongue to be sweetly laid out in a kurgan of rain.
This is the rain's nest, he said, where you will be joined
by the skin of a galloping horse held up by sticks.
Just then God's mouth filled with lead.
People at that time started, it seemed, to bleed
in the streets from their ears.
This wasn't force of listening, they
just were scraped by some large thing moving past,
sleet of arrows, yielding shelf of stones.
I stared at them, peak, peak, peak. The quills in their hands
and feet slicked into me, over
the border into me like I was being shot up, quietly and in secret
by drum solos.
Let us dip the tip of horror in horror.
Randy went down, Albert rappelled under the waves.
Something, all we'd never said, was eating
up from below.
St. Teresa of Avila was sitting in a gold chair
in a breathing-through-a-straw house in a suburb
quite far out, where what she's saying – it eggs slowly from
her mouth – is taken up in spikes along the back legs of the hum
                    from swelling, overhead wires.

Swan Plain

She drops her hands on the copper wrists of blue-green August
                                                    back gardens,
and walks, her feet in twin black ships,
in her delphiniums with her virtues. Their names writhe out of stones
in the long body of writing, except "joy" which is painted in black
inside a plywood apple nailed to a shed.
Lake stones in an old sink, a smiling particle board dog leaned behind
        hollyhocks against a two room house she's bought to tear-vial
                Co-op calendars from the 1950s.
Vegetable, turned-earth cloud lifting north, rain last night
nailing here, earth jacked by black water, getting up out of its St. Vitus
                        chair, thick with rods of antenna tremble.
The Christs in the Ukrainian churches in Wroxton and Veregin
are drained to a rumbling, underground violet,
evacuated trains, moving late, thrown, below the ground,
the Christ-skin worked to the colour of pickled eggs.
Mrs. Frances Sobkow walks on fish-belly feet near the black mouth
                                                    of the north, rush
of spruce and the tart taste of hand-showing snow
in the long-organ-playing afternoon.
Some patrolling with frozen-to-the-bottom unknowing
of the back door, fragrant wormhole.
Apollo brushes his black feather along her instep near the bear meadows.
She goes down.

Fr. Paul Le Jeune, S.J., in the Forest

Québec Relation, 1633

They skim on birchbark
roofs, porting two weeks of shunting moons,
or head-basketing all forests' nights and the bailed hair of winds.
They are spoken to by their demonic friend,
the other moon of four yard ice ramming its horn
along the river's groove.
One of them saw gouged in the 14 foot wall
he'd just climbed in sleep, mucusy, flowing, the law
he must eat me with an edge he'd flaked from the obsidian
of 3:00 a.m., and so behead the reptile rumbling under his skin.
He sank his axe under fish scales in his yellow bed two weeks.
His wife flew me away with her eyes.
He counted the wasps behind his lids; in the tinder
of deerflies in his room he rubbed
his two droughted fingers.
Five gouts of enemy pneumatic flame
scuffed above him, slamming as a pen of steers,
he in limey bed furs.

a o e I work for the world to rise
into the breathholes of my speech.
When I walked back to our community along the water,
the statue of Kateri Tekakwitha, burnt an inch in,
swayed from the longhouse fire,
missiled hissing from the river through thinnest ice,
runnelling mud and spawn.
We tar the boats for their children
whom they hide to be worked to France.
Their divinations' yellow wings
fan through the roar of leaves.

Orphic Disgorgement, Anti-colonial Disgorgement

Dead fuchsia and carrots still not growing through winter
in the wood-chipped garden hump, each swivels up its own radio
                                                                station and heaves
out honey; in everything hair-on-the-back-of-the-neck
lit ash spiralling out maquettes of the whole milkish machine; in
everything a carved book to which abalone has been sewn,
with a postal address and a SIN number, on a lectern of antler
at which a throat-cut lamb singingly reads aloud;
in everything limestone arguing; in everything, in everything; in
everything suddenly a river that cannot be crossed, the lowest eye
                                                                looks at you
until you feel a walnut of gravity frowning down in your elbow;
Hermes with a sharp stick
scratching the ground in everything, in everything the Gulf of Alaska
                in its wire.
In Fawn Lily's underarm bloom, a swimming sound.
Indian Plum now holds the vase of seeing, which poured out is Hermes.
In everything this answering machine tripping again its loop, please
                                                                leave me
a message; in everything a billet doux under a book; in everything the
lost sock; and a sound comes up from the spoon under the bed,
pieces of dental floss, idiorhythmic chorale,
totus Christus, and out of this creeps a city with four nameless rivers.
In everything ignorance, *docta ignorantia*, last bus stop
on the line of Dionysian apophaticism, the black door opens
hydraulic exhalations, home at last, do not look back.
In everything, listen, the Shriners' parade, Regina, 1961, just ended;
rain starts to hit into the dust, then the fog of the god; in everything,
the self-wealthing rooms, and in them the sidelong, fish-profile
boxes on coffee tables, mouthing out meals and fire without a mind.

Andrea MacPherson

from *AWAY* (Signature Editions, 2008)

St. Stephen's Green

Dublin in May

In St. Stephen's Green we take two pictures.

I

Standing under a great green tree
thankful for this reprieve from concrete and stone
(a reminder of the west coast of Canada
the only scent missing is the sea).
My face is caught in the thick shadow
as if it has been forgotten here, lost.

Behind me the Green is lit with sunlight
and the pond is calm as Sunday sleep
as if this city has never known sorrow,
never felt it close and taut as marrow.

II

These strange, emaciated copper men:
a reminder of the Great Hunger.
Their heads are bent awkwardly,
necks thin as wrists;
so slight they might collapse from touch;
the heat of a palm unbearable.

Green is a traveller with us today:
the colour of spring and corrosion and flags.

This might be what we have come for,
the sight of copper men surrounded by sunlight,
the way light catches the tips of their fingers
and reminds us that they were once human.

on meeting another Canadian on the bus

The bus back from Kilmainham is crowded:
shopping bags teeter on the floor,
women hold small children on their laps.
We stand in the slim aisle swaying with the bus
as if we are boneless and fluid.

The girl speaks to us, noticing the accent;
she is greedy for voices free of Gaelic,
voices that might remind her of the Rockies,
the long flat stretches of the prairies, watery western shores.
Our voices the colour of new wheat,
those hundred shades of gold.

Married a bloody Irishman, she says,
and I want to go home.
In the two years she's been here, her voice has shifted:
her language, the lilt of words in her mouth,
immigrants as well.
(How quickly vowels betray, always fickle.)
Just talk, she urges us
and I imagine she might close her eyes
and be able to see her town, her street
the house she grew up in,
as if our words are snapshots.

We leave her at Grafton with her arm outstretched
pointing down the street, towards the pub
towards the shores of Newfoundland:
her long white arm in a Dublin street.

David & Ruth, later

Every day, she loses him again.

First to the twenty acres,
to bleating sheep and chocolate mares,
to cows spotting the horizon with their catastrophic hides.

His hands learn the land
while hers spend an entire morning on a solitary button.

Later to Mary Fitzpatrick's
(not a woman, though she could understand that:
    pliant limbs
    wet lips
    the endless giving away)
the only pub on the street,
busy even at eleven a.m. with ancient men
and husbands desperate for escape.
There he memorizes the clean line of a pint glass,
finds comfort in the weight.

Once, she knew every inch of him,
held his calloused fingers or sleeping penis with ease.
Now, her hands have betrayed her;
fingers curl and tighten in waxy dismay.

She wants to touch his face,
feel the ridges of cheek and jaw,
but instead knows only the structure of his back
in midday sun:
that triangle of darkness moving quickly up the road,
moving away.

what I did not see while in Ireland

I

The crumbling stone cathedral that hovers next to the sea,
surrounded by a halo of grey.
Soon it will be lost to the elements, forgotten.

I did not see it after the night flight on Aer Lingus.
Instead we saw baptismal stones,
caged libraries, religion under glass.

I saw your photographed stone cathedral months later;
you were careless with it. Unconcerned.
And somehow the memory became mine
so that I held the purity of sea and stone.
The awful weight of remembrance.

II

The street that you lived on as a child;
the cobblestones that took the skin of your kneecap;
the common sticks you used for ball.

I did not buy street maps of Dublin.
I hoped not to see the street name, awkward
high in the air like a kite.
Over the phone you had spelled it slowly
urged me to mark it on paper.

I would later tell you that I'd forgotten;
that I could not retain your past.

III

Your shadow. By then I had stopped searching for it.

Scotland

Madonna and Child

This is where the splinter happened.

+++

Standing in front of St. Mary's Forebank,
I look up to the sculpted Madonna and Child
        behind wire netting.
Protected from the elements and vandals.
Her face is serene, eyes downcast
and purple wildflowers have survived the cold and rain
        to grow

curling around and behind the mesh
arcing towards her smooth cheek.

    The softness of the petals; the droop.

The blue doors are locked, gated
but inside there is the scroll of my family history:
a young man stepped away from Catholicism
for a pretty Irish wife in orange.

He might have stood on this same street,
looked up at this same Madonna,
and wept for the gentle, grievous beauty.
He might have stepped away as if stepping off a curb
    one motion down, despite the memory of stone
and into his bride's arms.

This is the memory of the body:
his hands might still genuflect involuntarily,
a quiet motion like a bird's wings in flight.

Dundee jute mills, 1937

Ivy weeps along the few remaining walls,
mistrustful, covering what is left of the mill.
Where once there was strength,
now there is only the strange sorrow
of bricks left to the elements.
Often, we forget their courage.

My great-grandmother wove jute into ropes like braids,
dreaming of the Indian fields she would never see;
she must have been surprised to find her lungs
heavy with the fibre. A surprising treachery.

On the ground, now, there are weeds,
the startings of clover.
Three leafed only;
mills never a beacon for providence.

She dies while my grandmother
arcs over the Atlantic, dreaming
of small green plants
and a high, hot sun;
roots that tighten and tangle.

city of the saint

Women's names in my family are handed down
like worn wedding rings, chipped mahogany buffets,
plates intersected with delicate scrapings:

> one for a grandmother who worked her whole life
> in a jute mill, her lungs thick with it,
> another who died unceremoniously in childbirth.

It is not until I am twenty-four that I discover
I was instead named after the patron saint of Scotland:
the fisherman who would not be crucified
in the same manner as Christ,
rather was hung like a starfish,
some other creature coming from the sea.

> +++

In St. Andrews I sink my hands into shallow pools
left behind by the North Sea,
push down to feel its pull.

Kerry in Tannadice

Kerry is pregnant in Tannadice.
She lives in a small white house—
serene against the spring greenery—
and has settled. Settled, as if she were a chemical compound.
A science experiment perhaps.

The last time I saw her she was thin and tan,
worrying over a man who occasionally left her;
crying into the phone in the middle of the night.
Now, Valeen says, you'd barely recognize her.
Gained 45 pounds. Cut her hair. Stopped drinking, of course.

The baby's father already has two children and a wife.
Kerry speaks little of them,
instead paints the baby's room pale green
a colour more aligned with sickness than sex.

This is how maternity happens;
accidental like a pulled hem,
unraveling nonetheless.

Valeen and I knock at the door and expect her new, slow lumber,
but there is silence instead,
the creak and sway of tree branches
under the weight of a bird;
perhaps the sound of growth, leaves and needles suddenly more.

France

La Goulue & Jane Avril

You write to me from Toulouse
and I think not of you and the red
city you describe, but of the small
deformed man with miniature legs
(childhood breaks that never quite healed)
who drew cabaret dancers
and whores and faceless men.
Smell the absinthe on his stale breath,
the unwashed quality to his hair.
Dark, dense in the spring sun.

We once visited Montmartre, a rainy July day,
with a man you had newly made your lover.
He wanted to kiss you in a picture,

but you turned your head
suddenly uncertain of the camera.

We escaped the endless rain and drank
kirs at a plank table, looking through
the prints I had bought; you adored
La Goulue, but I preferred the tarty reds
of Jane Avril. We drank slowly and laughed,
saw ourselves in corsets and high boots
and hats tilted at an impossible angle.

I took a picture of the courtyard,
another of the view from Sacré-Cœur,
after we had climbed the spiral staircase.
Toulouse is nowhere in those photos,
only the possibility of his compressed figure in the corner,
        black coat tails, shriveled leg
fleeting.

Between

where I will learn to pray

> Stepping across an invisible threshold
> a line drawn with ash, red sand,
> now blown away by restless wind
> into something unknown.
> Altars, candles, statues cloaked in blue.

I

St. Patrick's Cathedral in the morning.
Baptismal stones crouch next to graves
and stained glass windows weep
colour onto the slim aisles.
The embracing beauty of stone and candlelight
where even grey transforms
and the windows shimmer.

II

Clepington Church in the rain.
The texture of names carved in stone,
the simplicity of wooden doors
and a wild rose garden.
Sudden May sun.

III

Sainte Chapelle at noon.
Almost deserted, almost silent
while complicated lead flowers shatter the ceiling.
Below them, all is abandoned under a floral sky.

IV

An unnamed church in Athens in the sun.
Found accidentally as altar candles
burn against morning sunlight and heat.
A foreign language,
solace witnessing ritual.

    Stone meets wood,
    as if weight might change devotion to something less temporary.
    Something mossy and fragrant to hold,
    breathe the days back in.

Greece

a Greek summer

Dried grass, withered trees.
    Nature charred.
This is July in Fira.

Village churches interrupt the dry barren land
an intrusion of white and blue and bells
upon the endless broken browns.

The small wooden crosses of the churches
surprise us: we had expected something ornate,
carved and delicate in the ways of orthodoxy.
Instead, simple chimes ringing out into the unending yellow,
crashing into the startling Aegean,
somehow still lush and translucent.

Summer here is desolate;
too hot, too cracked and burned,
too used up and broken against the sea.

the geography of bougainvillea

In Karterados I begin to crave water.
Not homesickness, exactly;
more a longing for the possibility of moisture.
The new knowledge that I want something alive, breathing:
that weeping is better than dust.

> Trees do not grow from rock,
> so instead there are bare patches
> something wishing to be grass,
> bright, hopeful planted
> bougainvillea that must be
> carefully tended, prodded
> and encouraged like a child.
> But mostly there is yellow, brown
> the suddenness of a landscape given up.
> Foliage forsaken.

I dream of the places I will go once home:
thick rainforests, yards of lilac and rose bushes
circular parks with lagoons. Listen to the sound of falling rain.
I will hold my hands to branches for the dew,
relearn the taste of green.

James Doran

Randall Maggs

from *Night Work The Sawchuck Poems* (Brick Books, 2008)

Night Shift

The floating faces after surgery—angels
or nurses, I don't care. Wherever I've been seems
better to me, but, waking, I hide the crankiness
I feel. Someone lifts my arm to help me turn
and snugs the flimsy gown along my legs.
Then the visitors with rumours and bouquets,
too assured of their place in the world, it seems to me.
Somewhere out of sight, they ask for jars. Mother of God,
the agony of abdominal gas—what do I want
with gossip and flowers?

And doubled up all night, my Christ,
what a life. Like Pompeii's dead, my arse in the air,
bare. I don't care.

The light from the hall washes over the wall
toward my bed where the hospital gown rides up my back.
I hear the soft laughter from the door. She's different
in everyday clothes, distinctly amateur, reaching beneath me
to tie my gown and tug the wrinkles from the sheet. When she leans
closer, I catch a hint of the bar where she's left her friends.
Also an odour of earth and leaves.

Who starts the brain's conspiracies?
Who knows what it is that waits in the trees?
Crazy. To leave your friends and risk the park at night.
To pass the stolen flowers through the bars, lift her skirt
and reach a leg up over the deadly staves.

She knows the cupboard where they keep
the jars. I wake in the odour of daffodils, with the beat
of an old school poem in my head, and a half-dread
so familiar in these dangerous days.

Catherine Yuan Chi

Ukrainian Bones

(i) *the Winnipeg hair*

Combing it up like Charlie Rayner then,
New York's "custodian of the twine," swooping it
high in the front and over and out with it wet, the Winnipeg
quick-set, 30 below. His waiting friends with similar promontories.
Thin jackets. Backs to the wind like a choir.

You'd see the hair flash past above the boards,
big waves in the sun, one breaking into the clear, the others
in sleek pursuit. Looked like the ocean rolling in.

(ii) *spectators*

Seventeen and off to the six bright cities.
Those twelve-dollar shoes that caught his eye in Galt
on the way, two-toned, their breezy angle of display. *Spectators.*
Shoes for those who discriminate. Well, what to make of that, catching
his image in the glass, the North End slouch, the Slavic darkness
of his eyes. Black cats on polish cans looked out at him
identically. *Shoes to make the man.*
And shielding his eyes against the window's glare,
missed, for the first time in his life,
the first spit of snow in the air.

Two bucks down, two more each week
out of the twenty they gave him. Fourteen for room
and board left six. But something must have happened
the day he wore them home—he'd let some easy ones in,
or maybe just a goalie's mood. Maybe someone nudged a friend
in passing, wise to the shoes and showy hair, the hint of Asia
in his bones. Still, he'd been so careful coming home,
those wings like an angel, surely they'd lift
his heart they looked so fine, but never
to wear them again,
not once.
And being born in 1929.

(iii) *short nights*

A taxi into the tunnel from Windsor, tapping
at tail lights dropping into the loop, up and into the scissoring
long black legs and American air. Blink by St Leo's Virgin,
her eyes cast down, concealing what she knows
of good beginnings.

Down Grande River to the Barn,
Detroit's Olympia, the sleet off the river
bricked out, the basking fans in the heat and smoke
of fat cigars. You let a soft one in you hear them
bitch and groan. *Hey bring back Lumley.*
Bring up Hall.

Not long before the hair was gone.
All of it off.
The heat and murder in his crease, he said.
The jeers and sneers was what he meant. Mouths like fish
against the glass. Spectators. Jesus. How long would you take
to hate them? *All of it off.*
And darkened his looks from lying awake,
or brooding apart in bars. The disappeared sleep, the ban
on food from home, pirogies and kasha, potatoes in heavy cream
and cheese, and sleep, oh sleep, and the haunting eyes
of Richard, this time charging out into the fray
and catching the son of a bitch before he could shoot.
Or choking over the coached apology, that weasel reporter
he'd pinned to the wall with a skate.

All of which emphasized his Ukrainian bones.

But man, that wave in the days of his rampant expectation,
man, you could have surfed that thing.

from **Different Ways of Telling Time**

(iv) *ice time*

The guys arrive as if at random intervals,
lay out their gear, lucky shirt, same skate first,
same old jokes about my liniment, *Jesus,*
Ukey, lose that shit why don't you?
Roll their eyes and tiptoe by.
Check the clock and tape my own stick,
thank you, heel to toe, no wrinkles, tape the ankles.
Time to go out and get loose, guys in twos and threes
at home on ice, tucking pucks lazily under the crossbar.
Same old talk, someone you got to slow down,
a glance where he's talking it up
with his own guys.

Here's the house where I live, I can't say no.
Howe and Lindsay's eyes on me. Pronovost, tough
as a bag of batteries, slaps my pads. I see myself as I pass
in the glass, pick up the look from the other side, a nice pair
of knees that edge apart as I go by. I get a whiff of ice
and something in me starts alive. I take
a few shots, catch and flick, feeling
quick, clank behind me,
lucky too.

Then back inside and bedlam now. Adams
flapping but I don't hear. *Holy Mary, don't let me*
fall on my face tonight. I try to loosen a pad, my shaking
hand so bad *Jesus Jesus.* Tommy Ivan shoves in beside me,
knowing he needs to settle me down. New cufflinks on.
Knocks my stick for luck I'm nodding but Mother of Christ
I'm dying inside, can't keep still now everybody wants to go,
the clatter and chatter, rockers, talkers. "Gotta have this one.
Gotta have it, guys." This was where we'd bellow out
some raunchy song when we were young, scare
the bejesus out of everyone. "Nice neighbourhood like this,"

they'd say. "Who let the bloody DPs in?" Tommy drums
a rhythm on my leg—I watch his moving hand,
distracted by the veins and lines that make the hand
a miracle, an acrobat, a thief. *Gotta have it, guys.*
I brace for the roar at the end of the tunnel.
"Give me a hand here, Tommy, tuck that in, that—look
that bloody strap." Then *bang* the door and Jesus here we go,
someone shouts those words I love and dread, I hear
them all my life—*Let the goalie go first.*

Next Time

Six attackers, frantic to even the score,
the rink tips, bodies piling onto me. Ferguson
hacks my bad elbow, his look says, *Here's bone for your jar.*
Hooks my feet from under me, lands on my legs. I punch
at the back of his head and get this whiff of hair cream.
All of this in silence. Nothing personal,
though there may be memories.

Flat on my back, I see Backstrom looking
for the puck. I know what's coming, what I saw them
hatching at the bench, Toe's brain going like his gum, single
economic nod. I shift and lift a pad, using Ferguson for
leverage, my sprawl a calculated disarray, my hand
a hawk leap, rips the heart from the crowd.
Backstrom bangs his stick on the ice, his curse
the one word spoken in the whole exchange.

Slowly I roll to my knees. Storey's hauling guys
off me, tossing them left and right. Something's gone
again, no feeling in the hand that holds the stick.
I see Toe behind their bench now, staring
into the rafters. Who are you talking to, Toe?
Funny, I might have been playing for him if Adams
hadn't lost his nerve—the thought of me in goal
for Montréal. Where's my own guys?

Coming out of the same corner?
Where you been boys? Kelly taps my pad
and turns towards the bench. There's that look
that makes me warm all over, says, *What do you do*
with a guy from a different planet.

Storey helps me to my feet. I see that hand as large
as my trapper, the look that says, *Hey remember the time*
you called me a drunken bum? Jesus. The baggage over the years.
Still, there's no love lost between him and Ferguson,
but a minute left, we're into no man's land.
His look says, *Next time leave it to me.*

James Doran

Dinner at the Priest-House

for Al Pittman

They lean to Montréal and Boston, Catholic teams.
The trade from Detroit they see as deliverance, hardly the fall
from grace that Protestant papers call it. Father Kelly,
who played with Flaman, invited us all
but I went alone in the end.
The first questions follow the prayer,
"Don't the Bruins stick together?" What do I
hear? Disappointment or nose out of joint? Forks
pause in the clerical air. The room's like ours at the local
hotel. There's no one's place or favourite plate.

"And what we hear all about the Rocket and Lindsay,"
one plasters a roll with butter, "do they really hate each other?"
"And the Wings and Montréal, is it true they have to put a dining car
between them on the train?" And hadn't I heard about the wars
in St John's—St Bons against the Guards and Bishop Field?
"Oh, that was hockey in its glory days."
An older priest, with an air of his work being done,
lingers over something said earlier—"Only six goalies
in all the League? That might have a man
looking over his shoulder."
Younger throats clear in alarm. Something
lemon appears in front of me. The talk resumes
of local talent and who might catch us by surprise tonight.
Father Kelly only smiles. He hasn't said much since he found me
alone in the church. Not where you'd expect your two-time all-star,
crumpled under a dark Madonna. I'd heard him pause behind me
then move a little away. The priest at the head of the table
smiles when I find a place to mention her. "Our Virgin
on the Humber, she'd be from another time and a different order.
Too quirky for my taste." Saucers clink. Murmurs of assent.
"Some unschooled local, wouldn't you think? Goodness.
That river looking like a serpent in her hair.
The eyes quite clearly with a hint of petulance.

And why would anyone want to paint
a Virgin without the Saviour?"

Father Kelly says nothing. Proud of his former skills,
they'd placed him next to me. "The road not taken, Joe,"
says the older priest in another pause.
Only Father Kelly smiles.

I stare at the molten light in an unused spoon.
Not a crowd for second thoughts, it's easy to see. One,
left-handed, cuts his meat in an awkward way,
and my heart sinks.

One of You

Catchers in baseball, closest to cousins
in your differentness, the safeguarding home, the healing bones,
the serious gear (which ought to indicate the possibilities),
and only one of you.

Denied the leap and dash up the ice,
what goalies know is side to side, an inwardness of monk
and cell. They scrape. They sweep. Their eyes are elsewhere
as they contemplate their narrow place. Like saints, they pray for nothing,
which brings grace. Off-days, what they want is space. They sit apart
in bars. They know the length of streets in twenty cities.
But it's their saving sense of irony that further
isolates them as it saves.

Percy H. LeSueur, for one, in a fitful sleep,
flinching at rising shots in a bad light, rubbers flung
out of the crowd, insults in two languages, finally got out of bed
in a moment of bleak insight, went down and burnt a motto
onto his stick, *Haec est manus quae ictum deflecit*—
"This is the hand that turns away the blow."

Or Lorne Chabot, in 1928, when someone asked

him why he always took the trouble to shave before a game,
angled out a leg to check a strap and answered in a quiet voice,
"I stitch better when my skin is smooth."

Or dapper Charlie Rayner, who stopped a bullet
with his chin, another couple of teeth and some hasty
work to close an ugly cut. Back the next night, he takes another,
full in the face. A second night in a row, he's down, spitting
bits of tooth to the ice. "It's a wonder," he mutters,
"why somebody doesn't get hurt in this game."

Any Last Words (2)

There's a photograph of Wilf Cude, courtesy
of Eno's Fruit Salts, holding his goal stick in the old way,
two-handed, more like a shovel or crowbar, the Welsh face, dark,
unsmiling, a coal miner's face come into the green morning.

But this was after another kind of disaster, another
bad night in the Forum, and he was glumly home, staring
at the post-game steak he'd smothered with ketchup.
Which was how he liked it.

It took a moody night to get over a loss like that.
Then you had your knee-deep snow and pack your bag
or drag your ass to the Forum again. And he was in a strange
mood anyway, what with the sudden demise of the great Morenz,
catching an edge and crashing into the boards. Nobody even
close to him. Then Charlie Gardiner, the fiery little goalie
in Chicago, levelled at thirty after he carried his team
to an unexpected Stanley Cup. The grass
barely green as he slipped, apologizing, into a coma.
Too much for the mind of a simple man.

What touched him off was nothing—Beulah jiggled
the table (that loose leg she's asked him a dozen times to mend),
slipping the cozy off to pour his tea.

Bad timing, for sure, but she showed a goaltender's
quickness, ducking the steak that flew at the wall. He was out
the door in a morning storm, and down to the Forum
to tell them he was done.

What guaranteed his legacy was growing up
Welsh, his last words showing a heightened sense
of occasion—"By the time that steak hit the wall and stuck,
I knew I'd been a touchy goaltender long enough."
He'd looked out over the room of reporters.
"By the time it landed, I'd retired."

from *Big Dogs (2)*

"This was before the season opened sometime back in the '50s. The Wings and
the Black Hawks were up north in Ontario playing an eight-game exhibition
series, getting a little publicity for the League. Trouble was it was mostly bad.
The Wings and Hawks didn't like each other, and every game winds up in a
brawl. So the League sends me up to get things straightened out. So that's fine.
I read the riot act and after the game I come back to the hotel and there's Terry
and some of the Red Wings sitting around in the lobby looking bored. I always
get on pretty well with the players, so I say, 'Boys, what are you doing sitting
around? Why don't you get out and see a bit of the town'? And someone says
'Red, it's Sunday night, nothin's open.' So I say, 'Well, I got to meet a guy, but
there's a few quarts of beer in my room. Why don't you go up and help
yourself and maybe I'll see you later.' By the time I get back, it's late and the
boys are gone and so's the beer, big surprise. My room looks like a hurricane
hits it—empty glasses and bottles on the floor, my bed messed up, cigarette
butts in the sink . . . well, I don't really mind, I was like that myself when I was
young. And it looks like the boys had a pretty good time so what the heck. So I
don't think about it and I'm out of there early the next morning and I don't see
anyone before I go. A week or two later," he says, wagging a big finger at me,
"wouldn't you know it, my first game of the year is in Detroit and who's in
town but the Hawks. And it's a wild one. I'm barely keeping it under control,
and there's a pileup in front of the Detroit net, and you know who's on the
bottom. I race in, pullin' guys off him and I say 'Terry, you all right?' And I

hear this muffled voice from under the pile, 'Why don't you go fuck yourself, you drunken son of a bitch.' Hey, I'm a little shocked. A couple of guys are looking to see what I'm going to do, but I think, okay, he doesn't know who he's talking to. I always give the players a chance to cool off and what I do, I cup my hand behind my ear like this like, you know, like I didn't hear and I say, 'Terry, this is Red here, what was that you said?' And I hear him grunt as someone gives him a knee getting off, then he says, 'You didn't hear me? I said go fuck yourself you drunken *deaf* son of a bitch.'

Hey, what choice does he leave me? 'Okay, big mouth,' I say, 'That'll get you ten. Open your yap again and you're outta here.' It wasn't my feelings were hurt. I just got mad. Here's these guys, a week or two ago, drink all my beer, mess up my room and not a word of thanks and I have to take crap like that? Any other time I would have simply clocked him. But this is where it gets into the twilight zone—I see him in Montréal a few days later, and here he's skating towards me out at centre where I'm waiting to drop the puck. Holy cow, I think, what's he going to do now? 'Red,' he says, and he looks like hell, like he hasn't been sleeping a lot, 'Red, I gotta ask you this,' he says. 'Last game there, what the heck did you give me that misconduct for?' 'What was it for, you big Palooka?' I say. 'You told me to eff off. You can't say that to a referee.' What I really wanted to say was you can't treat friends that way. He just stares at me a moment and you know how dark and scary his eyes could be, I don't even know what he was feeling, sad or sorry or angry... 'I don't remember that,' he says. 'I don't remember any of that.' And turns away without another word. Heads back to his goal. Man, you could have knocked me over with a feather, I was so discombobulated. I just stood there staring at his back as he slowly skates away. In those days, he was still wearing number one. I don't know what I was thinking. Then Henri Richard, you know, the quietest guy in the world, says, 'Red, you gonna drop that puck tonight or not? Are we gonna play hockey or stand out here looking like some idiots?'"

Canadian Dreams

Halifax waterfront. Where countries of the mind
begin. The creak and sigh as a freighter rubs her ample hip
against the pier. The painted-over name says Asian heat. (A slow
canoe poles past stilted homes. Open fires. Smells of cooking chicken
in the air.) It's long past midnight here. A winter dampness cuts
to bone. Too soon to go home, we head for the one place always
open, the walls Aegean with posters of crumpled pillars. Half a dozen
tilted stools. Costas, unshaven, looks up from his chopping.
Someone broke his window last week, collapsing
an arch of golden letters. "No Turk," he shrugs.
"Just punk. I caught him by the hair."

There's one stool occupied. Cropped head in steam
above a bowl of beans, half turns, turns away.
But it's enough, the moon-face unmistakeable, not so round
now, but it's him all right. "Doug Harvey. Hey Doug." I mention
the Forum and having seen him back in 1952. He nods. His face looks
freshly stitched where someone's clipped his brow. Once he could
play the game any way you wanted, level you out in the open
or set up a play like a symphony. "So what're you doing here, Doug?
And out so late?" He hunches closer over his bowl, his voice
hoarse and tired. "Mindin' my own fucken business."

Costas wags a finger at us, European-style,
and goes back to his chopping. Our joke was to make him
wait as we bickered over the menu on the wall, then always order
fish and chips. That night we took a longer look, noticing
all the items crossed off and prices cut. And what were we up to,
ourselves, prowling the harbour at night? I thought of my father who
left the farm at seventeen to go work on the boats. He'd talk about
how they were chased by a Japanese sub, and all the whales.
But something made him quit and work on a tug. And something
made him quit the tug. Doug pays up and gives us a nod going out
that lifts our spirits again. You hate to see dreams go down
the drain. Better you take the whack on the ankle.
Something that tells you the guy's hanging on.

Our Trio

Homer's heroes were certainly no braver
than our trio, but more fortunate: Hector
was excused the insult of having
his valour covered by television.
> —W. H. Auden, "Moon Landing"

Someone wanted a bench out on the 'battleground'
for authenticity. So our three huddle together
looking ill at ease. They don't like the feel of an arse
on a bench at the best of times, but what they fear most is looking
like fools. Instinctively, they don't much like these guys or what
they're up to here, but the word has come down from on high.
One stares longingly at the team gliding by.
One studies the blade of his stick, smoothing an end
of tape. What can you say in battle gear that doesn't sound
fatuous? Sadly, they sense this. Think of grimy Hector,
working his gum to ease his nerves, asked to look at the monitor
and comment on his deeds that day. Or the Greeks, miked up
in the humid horse, arguing over what they'll say
for the camera, descending the ladder.

"So what's the game plan boys?" the interviewer asks
to get things rolling. "What were those golden thoughts when
you woke this morning?" The boys do all they can. "We win each battle
on the boards, we'll be okay." "Howie, this team does its talking
on the ice." While not a week before in a different city,
our three concoct a brilliant goal in overtime,
a coughed-up puck, two letter-perfect
passes and a tip-in off the post.

You see their relief when someone signals *wind it up.*
"Before you go though, boys, how about a big thumbs up for the fans
at home?" Heart-rending how hard they work to oblige, to ensure
a proper manner for a proper audience who, if they existed,
would have been decent enough to be doing
something else when this was on.

Tidal Fears

> *. . . the mind clings to the road it knows . . .*
> —Mary Oliver, "Robert Schumann"

"I'm through. This is it.
You saw me out there and I was shit."

Terry, talking to some friends outside the Stadium
players' gate. A little accidental poem of embarrassment
after the opening game in Chicago.
The noisy crowd had loved it when he seemed
a moody beat-up goalie winding down.
Cheerfully they sang him off the ice.
Good bye Terry good bye,
Good bye Terry good bye,
We'll see you again but we don't know when,
Good bye Terry good bye.
How many times that season had he tried to call it
quits. His back was bad, the famous crouch had left its mark,
two ruptured vertebrae, he couldn't straighten up. He couldn't sleep
two hours at a time. You'd hardly think of it as fun, the years
of nerves before a game, the lashing out, the guilt,
the dreaded waking up and being wide awake at 3 a.m.,
of getting drilled by pucks, his nose half ripped away,
his eyeball sliced, the backs of both hands
opened up by skates.

What was it kept him going?
You'd think you'd want October with your family
in the woods, making up for awful times, or jumping on the course
behind the house, the rustle of leaves beneath your feet,
one last round before a killing frost,
or stretching out and reading by the stove.

You'd think at forty you'd feel silly
getting dressed with thirty other guys, buckling on
a flaccid garter belt and wearing regulation ties and making
wisecracks on the bus. What always brought him back

for one more year? Seven kids who needed shoes?
The skim of ice on puddles in the fall?
A tidal fear of being swept to sea?

"Hell, you saw me out there"—same guy,
ten days later, same place, after shutting down the Hawks.

("I got no squawks," said Billy Reay, a man
who saw the game in its entirety, "the guy they had
in goal was just too good.")

"Hell, you saw me out there—I can play this game forever."

Alice Major

from *The Occupied World* (The University of Alberta Press, 2006)

What is buried under the walls

A town's foundations always bear
the burden of guilt.

> Three hours past midnight
> and a woman's voice arraigns the street.
> Anger ripped from her throat.

> "You're on Indian land, man.
> You're all on fucking Indian land, man.
> This is fucking Indian land."

> The quiet residential street shudders,
> turns its face aside into leaves and lilac bushes,
> withdraws behind the carragana hedges.

>> Carragana. A tough colonial,
>> hunkering down through the hard winters,
>> planted in palisades against the native winds.

Cities are built on the blood of brothers.
Fratricide and murder—Remus struck down
at Rome's infant walls.

Cain, tiller of fields, founder of the first city,
naming it for his son, who would inherit
that marked space ploughed around blood.

> The woman's voice dies quickly
> away. Not loud enough to overmaster
> the past. Behind unreflecting windows,
> we lie awake, uneasy, hedging.
> Trying to disown.
> Not prepared to give it back.

Give the city its three names

A city needs three names—the public one, the priestly,
and a secret, sacred name
for the god we do not realize protects us.

The winter day is hushed
like a child holding a snowflake on a mitten.
Behind us, city towers send white vapour
to join low clouds. The river path is empty,
the dark is coming down.

A coyote cries, silver yodel.
Everything stops—even the prowling dusk,
even our breath—to listen.

Edmonton. A public name, polite gesture
to mother country, mother company.

The palisaded fort in wilderness
named for a suburb of London, birthplace
of an aide-de-camp in the enterprise
that piled fur and profit at the feet
of the gentlemen adventurers of Hudson's Bay.

Rough buffalo, stiff-haired beaver,
wolf and milky ermine. All the dead creatures
in whose luxuriant pelts the traders' fingers wandered
to grasp, assess.

And sometimes simply to caress.
Fur can seem as though it's still alive,
a silent offering of spirit warmth.

Beside us, the river is a parallel
white path, almost untrodden. A few tracks cross
its snowy fur. Not the mechanical slide
of skis or flopping human footprints,
but the dotted autograph of paws,
hooves, the light, living feet of birds.

For a time, this outpost had another name—

Fort Sanspareil. An unusual flight of fancy
for round John Rowand, that 'most pushing, bustling
man in the service,' chief factor
who turned profits like a card trick,
whose bones were boiled bare
and shipped home in a rum barrel
for burial in Montréal.

Sanspareil. A name from the *coureurs de bois*,
from the tongue of the missionary priests
who strung their rosary across the prairies
and into the dark pine woods.

Into the aching dusk
Coyote cries again.

We hear but do not recognize
our secret name.

Gwen Aker

Aubade for St. Brigid's Day

Light at the threshold hesitates.
Its time is neither born nor unborn.

Sun still sluggard, rising late.
Snow heaped like rumpled bed sheets.

Into silence, a bird whistles—*soh-fa ... soh-fah ...*
Music teacher cueing an inattentive choir.

We are reluctant to rise and chance our shadows—
soundless dice cast upon the ground.

Brigid, mistress of smithcraft and whistling,
prepares the hollow pipe, the hammered plate.

Birds breathe in their bones.
So immense a readiness.

The poised shaft, the point
of light—to hurl itself away.

Against the fall of sparrows

The abandoned seal pup has been rescued.
Capable people from the aquarium
have taken it away. We are relieved
of its hoarse, human bark and infant distress.
Waves chuckle at the rocks again.

And we return to our watercolours,
our willow-bending, our clay.
The wounded, war-torn fate
of distant millions disturbs our day
no more than the struggle of a beetle
capsized on its lacquered back.

The sun stands at the solstice tip
of its immensely blue sky, hub of an aureole
that curves faintly iridescent, draws
a circle like the rim defining limits
of a solar parasol.

Gule of August

She saw three dead things that day
in her walk across the fields

> *And no one kens that he lies there,*
> *but his hawk, his hound and his lady fair ...*

A gopher, so newly dead
even the flies were not aware of it—
no buzzing announcement in the press
of the season's heat. Still stiff,
stretched on its back, paws pleading,
tiny head tipped up as though asking
to be scratched under the chin.
Soft fur, tan as a child's cheek
glossed by summer.

Further on, a magpie. Eyes bored out.
But feathers shining still
in midnight-minted iridescence.
Ants marched across its chest, a thin braid
like the swag of some military decoration,
death's legion.

> *His hound is tae the hunting gane*
> *His hawk tae fetch the wild-fowl hame ...*

And finally a little corpse,
its fur (or feathers?) anonymous,
brown as cocoa fibres on a trodden mat.
No more than a curve of wing or spine

hardly to be distinguished
from the sandy shoulder of the road.

> *His lady's ta'en another mate,*
> *so we may make our dinner sweet.*

A blackbird on a fence rail flashes
his epaulette—gules against the golden field
of August. She wonders what herald
will carry news of deaths so small,
such tiny ballads from the killing fields.

The grain's harp is mute.
The corbies keep their undertakings
to themselves.

Lindsay Brennan

The Maiden

Pennyroyal, pomegranate,
bitter willow bark.
Ancient charms against childbirth.

***

The doctor, a jowled mastiff on guard,
gazed at them across his dark desk.

Her mother held a handbag on her knees,
its gold clasp an entry to lipstick and Kleenex
smelling faintly of spittle.
All three equally embarrassed,
as she asked him to prescribe 'the pill'
for her daughter.

The gift her mother wanted to procure
for her—not to be carried into the clefts.
Not to be caught by the gloomy young boyfriend.
This new freedom in a plastic dispenser,
a moon-round talisman guarding each day
with its click.

The pill made her sick and swollen.
And she went with the young man anyway, in spite
of herself—bound to him more tightly
by what she had consumed.

She became a ghost in white, stepping down
shallow, flagged stairs to the vaulted chapel.
Her father's gold eye tooth gleamed as she
had never noticed it before. The guests
brought lucky horseshoes tied with ribbon,
seemed not to notice anything was missing.
There was stone soup. They promised her
the pot would stay full.

A woman who wanted the decision over with

A floating world. Demerol
nibbling in her veins.
Two snips
with a laser and she'll be free
from the monthly fear that
jerks her to heel
over and over.

Fluorescent lights flare from the ceiling
as the gurney rolls her to the surgeon's
scalpel-tipped incredulity.

"Are you certain
you want to go through with this?"

What is ever
certain?

***

She dreams: she is bleeding
the syrup of monthly blood.
As she wipes it away, she sees
a tiny creature in her palm.
It is struggling to get away.
It is afraid of her.

Daughter.

Grief beats in her chest like a child's wail—
She cannot put the fetus back.
She cannot throw it away.

This pain sucks the breath out of her lungs.
This pain must lie in the bed she has made.

A harsh mistress

She thought they only wanted somewhere to park their genes.
Somewhere to scatter their toys.
Another kid to play with
while the great caring, washing, feeding, many-armed, fiercely juggling
mother minded the details.

She might have been kinder.

She did not know
how deep the need to be a father
can dig into a man—a spiral
wound into his cells, tugging at him.
How much he needs to take part
in what came before, in what goes on—
the seeping of generation
after generation, the stream that runs over the cliff of life
and on into darkness.

Heather McCarthy

Reincarnate

She has hips like the serpent of the Nile,
eyes as dark. Midriff bare and sinuous.
Hair a lacquered knob above each ear.

She sucks at a cigarette, her lips a starburst
of converging lines, the rays of Amun-Re.
She blows infant smoke rings into the coffee-shop air.

Mid-afternoon. She should be in school,
to be earnestly instructed in life skills and the wisdom
of not smoking. But there is nothing you can teach her.

She is as old as Egypt and she will live forever.

David Manicom

from *Desert Rose, Butterfly Storm* (Oolichan Books, 2009)

Gameboy

Goddammit
Light the fuse
JehovahYahwehJesusOsamaAllahGeorge
What is this particular fucking prayer-faced ruse
All about?

Softly, because of the great gloom that is in my mind
I'll cover your sleeping arm my child, the cold wind whines
From confines somewhere everywhere nowhere west of Baghdad,
From black holes where the saddest words are kept and the vest is blessed
And Friday markets best display to dazzled buyers their
Visceral wares.
The Alps from your window are meadow, snow, and sunrise fire
This year of the hooded Christ, the wired man, the blowback blow,
Profane cowl,
Views from here in the year I fear only the rant is heard,
Renewed howl.

Jawn-Jawn
Don't go.
Go well.
Don't go.
Go with one extra blessing for each wild word I threw.

&&&

JehovahYahwehJesusOsamaAllahGeorge
SaddamSamsonMohammedZawahiriDick,
Lions of God
Sons of Zion,
Morning's softly murderous horizon as you're coming to,

Seventy septillion stars adrift in divine rule
And the
Inside out,
Seventy septillion molecules per waterdrop shine
On each spilled path from each unnumbered blinking eye,
That sad pun.

Import text
Export doc
Open a
New window

www.raytheon.com/about

aspiring to be the most admired defence and aerospace systems provider

Hotlinks for
Diversity
Community
Involvement
Ethics
Not to
Omit that

Maverick AGM-65 family of missiles is the versatile, precision strike missile of choice

Fuses lit,
Ruses all round, the big scheme frayed, *I'm* not counting beads
Given our stars accede not in lovely nighttime dreams
Never mind not in lone splendour hung aloft the night
But plunge in all directions these billion on billion
Thermonuclear storms some odd quadrillion tons apiece
Cast faster in all directions toward slowest waste
Of this or that cornerless idea of twisted space

Waste land
Anbar sand—

Each sun still faster after eons of spent momentum

Than our best axis-bustin heat-seekin flesh-scentin
Long-term performer in the Raytheon family of missiles

Lovely light

Fuse gone white

Pathways
On the gay gameboy screens, silent underwing falconry
Precision-guided payback straight down the window wells
The chimney pots, the vale of years and tears, the nuclear
Family is
The heat sought
The heat found
Voilà mom dad and kids, nana, babba, cousin-daughter
Nixed to ether.

Monitor the Vomit

Staring into the London evening the drawing down of blinds
Eliot scrawled
For I saw with my own eyes my own eyes my own eyes
The celebrated sybil at Cumea hung in a bottle
When I asked her what she wanted she said I want to die
By waters
Of Leman
Reeling with vertigo you seized me with fierce hands
That in one burnt instant I saw closely match my own hands
And staggered in my riveted gaze and gagged and cried
The white of eyes dad dad I want to die the Alps bled
Autumn light.
You need we need to withstand that at Guantánamo
Najaf Baagram
Saadr City
Kids of Ben
Spawn of Dick
So many men who long to die what are the roots

That clutch, what branches grow out of this stony mound
That the city shining on a hill has hailed the novel regimen
Their new
Feeding chair
A bold sort of chair to thwart the fastings unto death

Of men
Who long
To die
With straps to strap their hands like my hands your hands down,
And afterwards the prisoners moved to a "dry room"
And monitored to make sure they do not vomit
Monitor
Vomit
Vomit
Monitored
This is
The world
You must
Choose to love
Didn't say
It was easy
Turn the wheel and look to windward, son of Emmaus.

Advanced Multilayer Interconnect (AMI) provides
high-quality thin film, thick film and high-density   interconnect
products for commercial, military
and space applications.

And they took, in Judges chapter this and verse whatever
Two princes of the Midianites, Oreb and Zeeb
And they (that would be they the chosen people of the Lord)
Slew Oreb upon a rock and Zeeb they slew at the winepress
(For wasn't the gleaning of the grapes of Ephriam
A very good year, better than the vintage of Abiezer?)
Thin film thick film and high-density interconnect products
And brought the heads of Oreb and Zeeb to Gideon
(Lacking a website) on the other side of Jordan just west

Of Baghdad
No record
How they got
The heads off.

Stone Oxygen

JehovahBuddaOsamaJesusAllahGeorge
Names in vain
To take one
"Osama,"
Proposes
Dinesh D'Souza from the greenest grass of right right field
Under the lights
Talk on talk-radio leaking nightly to the stars
"Is not so much a terrorist," (not so much) "as he is
A religious ideologue who has chosen terrorism
As the most effective way to achieve his goals,"
And it is good to have goals, keen to craft strategic plans
So what's a little man to man joust on ways and means
A split
On tactics
Between friends?
Beats consorting
With liberal
Faggots
And porn.

Allah be praised our holy blades have taken the heads
Of the worshippers of the cross, the caped crusader dead
Not to speak
Specifically
Of Parson
Rod Parsely
A real name
And in 2004 a slam-bang big time mover and shaker

In the tipping-point hierarchies of Ohio Republicans
Zeitgeist-sucking post-enlightenment post-IED
Election-swinging middle of mid-west pivot-state
Ohio
Upping the ante on slaughter no two-bit Papa Doc
Pinochet
Henry K
No mere massacres no mere carpet-bomb overkill
Our country can(not) truly fulfill its divine purpose
Until we understand America was founded in part
With the intention of seeing this false religion destroyed,
Goddammit OsamaGeorgeYahweh etcetera
What is this particular wool-pulling virgin-fucking
Private-security-firm-juicing baby-bombing ruse
All about?
No two-bit
Back-yard
Junta
Death-squad
Quid pro quos,
Not just
Rendition
Black box
Black mask
Black ballcap
Naked chained
"Suspects"
Solitary
Years years
24-hour
Rock-n-roll
Fire and ice
(Condi, Condi)
Mean and nice

But better
Sucking marrow of belief from a third of the planet
On contract with Kellogg-RB or Qaeda, siphoning

Fake faith
Cosmic
Primary
Blow-job
Where, little sunshine, burn seventy septillion stars
And the same rare tally of molecules per drop of H2O,
Sufficient desert with all temperatures rising
And in passing says Pastor Rod Parsley a real name
High in
Ohioan
Hierarchies
Abortion is also an economic issue, for
It has killed millions of American consumers,
Ya couldn't
Make it up
Saint Kurt.

          &&&

              The AGM-129 Advanced Cruise Missile is a subsonic,
              turbofan-powered, air-launched weapon
              that effectively takes out deep
              and heavily defended targets.

          &&&

May June
The river's tent is broken, Thomas Stearns back in tune,
Through the eighties and nineties I couldn't read his dated
Whinge and hallow
Lone white horse
Walks dry beds
Of lost streams
Deep targets
As dusk falls
And his voice
Creeps through vines
Into clear time
Last edge

Of sun
Under gun-
Metal cloud
The river's tent is broken rosy-fingered dawn and so forth
Broaching the graven Alps beyond your shrapnel dreams,
Desert east toward Baghad rises dirt brown, dad on the phone
From Damascus from Jordan from never near enough to you
But slowly toward the earth's edge a dust suffused with blue
Takes on the gentle tones of old rose petals someone kept
For the son who is every son pierced with love and anger
The long limbs the slender wrist the spasm of fingers

The best minds of my generation destroyed by madness,

Did I want you young and wild as my own dreams
Of eternal delight, you my own proof to combat calm
And weariness and compromise and getting along?
To never come fully home to never crest to . . . .
Let it go. Keep it going. Let it go. Keep it going.
Your own personal *hypocrite lecteur* wants you to risk
Everything
And be safe.

[Copies of Old Photos 7]

Black Bough, Almost Spring

The snow has touched each branch, and held.
Arms in their long sleeves grow old.
Leaving the metro, lovers, Montréal,
Your hand in my pocket against the cold.

You stand above me, waiting and free
Where the widows selling flowers wept
And the escalator steps fold silently.
What you told me, the seasons kept.

My young face against your wet, black hair.
On the street, snow turns to rain.
Burning wheel in a breathing arc,
The steps unfold from singular dark
And I am rising to you again.

Khazne, the Treasury

Goddammit
Light the fuse
Can you
Hear me
Calling home
On this
Lousy line?
Underwater
Voices
Static sea
Tell mom
Tell mom

Today
In the fresh of the morning we came down unto Petra
Before the great heat in elysium of the new year.
Whate'er its mission the soft breeze can come to none
More grateful than me, escaped from the great city's souks;
And should the chosen guide be nothing better than
A wandering cloud and sky a cloudless zone and missile free
I cannot miss my way. As, together with gathered friends,
Bundled in a mini-bus across the snow-flecked pass
And arid scree we parsed blue sky and almond groves
Southward from Amman, Dead Sea on our right-hand side
A slit of brilliantine below the scrubby ridge,
Saran-wrap on fruit gone bad. To left the borderlands
Where the images sleep an uneasy sleep, Badiyat-as-Sham,
Anbar, Basra, the disturbed earth where the jackboot steps

Sickle in dust
The gaped neck.
But toward noon there is a blessing in this gentle breeze
A visitant that while it fans my burning cheek
Doth seem half-conscious of the joy it brings. BlackBerries
Shut down we barely chat, seek the correspondent breeze,
All stilled
Nabataean.
Our walk today down Petra's twisting narrowing waist
The dark pink stone striated marbled, a grainy script,
Down flat sand *siq* in shade of ever-higher muscled walls
Until where the travellers pause and hush at the canyon's
Rosy clench
The cream light
Opens
Buttery
Yellow
And the hovering Treasury somehow in and beyond the light
Rosy sandstone dawn to be sure and a Hollywood hit,
Yet massive thundering soaring pillared vaulted graven
In ten thousand intricacies, the weighted dream
Just beyond the birth canal, eagles of stone crowns of stone
Gasp for air
Gasp and cry.

But I see the lovely Boy as I beheld him then
Among the wretched death-dazed throngs, the crazed gone free
Like one of those who walked with every hair unsinged—
Dreaded, mohawked, shaven, golden blue and flaming green—
Through the fire.

Gasp for air, be calm and passionate and rare, do not hurt
Dance to a frenzied drum
                    in radical innocence
Be kind in the jumpy spirit of the church of Vonnegut
Labour into the riches of no respite the peace
That comes
And goes.

**The Exoatmospheric Kill Vehicle (EKV)
is the intercept component of the Ground Based
Interceptor (GBI), the weapon element
of the Ground-based Midcourse Defense**

&&&

I woke just west of Baghdad in some random Sheraton
Could hear it still, a shout of drums, a sprint of ska
In the room in the desert night deep in the corridors
Trying to get through, still going, this long lingering
Your cell-phone's ring tone as a song you had been singing
Just for me.

Stephanie McKenzie

from *Grace Must Wander* (Salmon Press, 2009)

Love in Lost Winters

We have grown sloppy. Winter's sludge has bruised
our lungs, and on our brows we catch the ice that cracks
the tops of lakes until the water's greatness breaks like sobs
beyond the breakwater.

      We are sob, broken by blue and stiffened
rushes stubborn in lost love, caught at their throats
by frozen.

This is not the empire of fire, bodies tossed in summer
salads of warm sleep. This is the time of frozen
cows, wind warnings. We scarve our throats for bed,
each other scared of cold.

The Snow Has Voices

Persistent the clumps and vain now in its sheets,
snow circles the town and these people
like pink-throated vultures. We are hunkered
lives to wary goings out.

And it talks. Snow hisses like fire under the traction of boots
chosen to steer this world. The dirtied, car
exhausted are sullen by roads. Jealous of the gentle
love of sidewalks, they sneer and nip at times the heels
of those bold enough to stride the streets where dirt
grips more firm than slippery pathways cleared.

How their voices drive fear into the mind.

      They threaten to push me

onto the street, let hunks of driving
metal take me down like crocodiles.

When it comes in sideways, the closing of schools
type, it wants to stop the body, remind us of lost
childhoods or what we want to lose. It carries
the past like a torch, flakes like floating ashes.

The voices rise like my mother's,
her cake ruined, icing too thick and a heavy
price to be paid before church.

We wrap our throats turned wolves
and skittish at each corner prick
up our ears to listen to the white.

It will not rain or burn away the carbon
deadlies in our brains. The snow flies arms and legs
severed from the body-covered grounds.

Strange larvae.

from **Suite for Winter**

xii

The distance between places becomes me.
Green Bay Michigan and Newfoundland,
mountains with a million different names.
Yet all truth's songs are sung to fiddles.
Perhaps it is the Irish, homes kicked
out from under them but capable of singing
through the horrors. Or maybe it is the taut
strings of wooded instruments, tools plucked
from animals not respecting borders.
They give us similar throats of praise
though we curdle
language in our mannered ways,
some end the sentence on a lilt
while others fall dactylic.

First Vision of Father Marquette

The closing day is blues behind you, sky
blue of the sea, horizon dark slate. The heavens
stretch to lighter and white, stubborn
clouds.

You are fixed forever in browns, rose brown
of the pedestal like the top of a marzipaned
wedding cake, bronze brown of your body;
pockets of black crease your metal dress.

Perhaps you are a messiah, arms stiff
at your sides, ready to lift up and praise,
or maybe defend the body, maybe a faith.

Some nights you are my father,
dark, half forgotten across roads.

Though growth surrounds you, deciduous,
promise of change, you stand steadfast,
ready to take on the seasons, suffer
a blast of winter wind.

I'm told it is cold here; the fourth season, bitter,
will capture the madness of a lake ocean size.
How sailboats dance in the day, white triangles
on blue so used to you now they are oblivious
to the Chamber of Commerce you hold in purse strings.
Red roof of that building stands sentinel,
ready to kiss your ass from behind.

Little boys stand at your feet. Tourist parents
snap memories. How you preside over youth
and this town. Dear father, forgive me,

I have grown hard as your cloak, as suspect
as the face this town gave you. If you are fixed
in time, it is now. Come night, all blues
meld to grey, save the horizon, one strip

of dark and light on top promises eternal difference.

Your image rises over both.

Cars are continuous. I count their axles
at midnight, bams in the bumps of the road.

Motorcycles, wounds opened, wake up the dead.

To a Brother Who Once Started a Forest Fire

Later, when the fire chief hands you your pocket knife, initials carved
carefully, our father smiles. You are ten and have learned the lesson
of sulfur packed in your urine. Our neighbourhood watched
the Martin Mars bombers circling the hills, pissing like desperate hell
on the dry B.C. timber, our mountains connected to nearby ranges waiting
to call the national cameras in. That day, both our sexes learned
the impossibility of witness. One should be careful of fire; it smolders
long and longer after water, your mattress pure flint, its signals
rising to the face of Jesus, crowned and bleeding above your bed.

The Loaves Made Available to Women in Galilee

Once, when an anchor gave and that trawler dragged into and crashed us, six-
foot and impotent the deckhand scrambled to the upper deck, stood there
screaming. The moon didn't blink. It kept its hold upon the tide. We spent ling
cod in Rupert. Days, worked fiberglass. Nights, we hooted at strippers, flesh
old and taken from rockpools forty fathom down. They were monsters of the
deep. Some joked, said we should cut open their bellies, see what the big ones
ate. Chris put scent on the lures, laid $200 down. On water, you could lose your
boat. On land, he was a hero, filled totes in his hotel room. Some guys laughed,
asked if he clubbed them first. Chris'd only crack his knuckles, scratching his
balls like mad. Something about sea lice and the bitches that bore 'em.

James Doran

Molting Time for the Birds

(After Van Gogh, *The Raising of Lazarus*, after Rembrandt, 1890)

Let no one see but crawl into a cave.
It is the time of the great bleed, and it must
not be done in public.

Lazarus, feathers are torn from your body
as if you'd never owned them. They float
somewhere in Van Gogh's other paintings,
the ravens of an older testament.

You are draped in white, seek
snow of other worlds, for we know
it warms one at death; the birds
fly south for good reason.

This is time for family, and your sisters
crowd you with colours, one gown
pure green, the other striped with pink.

How the verdant shakes in your face
while you wither like stalagmite
in a new inner world.

You are depressed and depleted,
the world too bright. It shines light
on death, shakes beacons to its path.

Odd speck of bald and blood on your neck
show you in eclipse. The sun refuses
to follow, looms big and rough and round.
You are flightless, have sought out water
in the rocks. You've lost metabolic prayer.

And what of the man not seen? He is two
days late even for Mary.

Your beard is a small nest of pin feathers.

Your jaw could lift off the face and soar.
It has been four days, Lazarus, your tail
feathers tickling. Unlike other birds, though,
you are alone.

You will soar when you rise, part of this pyrrhic,
most of it praise.

You now know the plight of the birds.

They fly from all others.

Photograph of Sylvia Plath by Rollie McKenna

It is the teeth. Small gap of licentiousness
recalls the Wife of Bath, but not so happy.
The lips, parallel, travel fixed for different souls.
Or perhaps both paths are dedicated to one,
increased possibility of finding him
by going two different ways.

I am glad it is not in colour.
You are psychomachia; you fight
with yourself.

And what of the photographer, clicking
your suicided soul into permanence?
Did you adjust the necklace, comb
your hair? For her, did you do anything?

You are innocuous and threatening and dangerous
and beautiful. You are a corpse, brunette.
You are exhausted, perhaps not malleable.
And this is what frustrates. You beg
an intravenous. You are intravenous.

You bear a heavy-looking pendant, metalled
and espaliered over a dress with leaves. Your breast

bone is prominent and speaks of hunger.
Your hunger is specialized.

You are beautifully dead before your time
propped up and mannequined like a liver
left unexamined and drink having taken it most
already. You are sad, for you can not feel.

Your crown suggests the possibility of female
balding, but this is not an issue.

Dear Sylvia, there will not be time.

F2 on the local map

for Marie Croll

Sometimes when the meadows grin and the North shore
shrugs its shoulders to the grey gods above, we seem left
between the lupines and the goldenrod, valleys of little worlds.
And when the snow descends to settle on our souls,
we crave the fireweed to breathe like dragons a path
between it all.

Down to Water Street and on to the sea, or through
O'Brien's land, lone guards of Sheppard's Ave.
How maps refuse to tell our secrets. The old clapboard's
bright with paint, and no one now remembers
the sorrows of Farewell Place.

But someday and pointing to an impress outside your door,
someone might rightly feel the way home was not quickly
taken, that there were songs to be sung and children
loved beyond streets' memory.

Twisting the long grasses, the new carpenter cuts
a pirouette with his steel toe and flicks his rough
hair like little girls who lived a childhood of happy promises

on St. Aiden's Road. The concrete pourer yawns
and wonders at the fissures of loved nights.

How kingdoms could be stuffed in spaces here, whole
worlds lost at noon.

The Disciples of Winter

for Elizabeth Behrens

Grace must wander even with the lonely sight of crows.
The purple and the purple black, each one spotted like a snowflake,
fingerprint. Birds sing of other worlds that are not grown
here but happen somewhere out there in the land of blow away
the dead and make a wish we give to children. They have learned
to stretch their necks out, offer up their throats on blue
platters of the sky, do not seek pity, feel shame.
Their feathers fallen give us leave to ponder.
Consider the city. It mimics the crow, black throat
caught at the chords sings out a promise of day.
Evening, and morning, and at noon, transparent
and bound to truth, the knowing of winter is clean,
like a scar storied and sure of where it's been.

Reading a Two-Day Old George Elliott Clarke's Execution Poems

Your brow wrinkled. The perfect 'm' of your lips
stretches for memories. And could they be dark
and warm, moss we gather on our toes like
the first taste of chocolate? Or are you troubled,
your mind now here, like all of us, a cramped confusion,
something too terrible to bear?

Your mother bathes; your elbow stiff
at your head's side left her waddled.

I sit on the secondhand lazy boy, its lives worn
by wrinkled cheeks and parties not permitted
in this state.

I read you *Execution Poems.*
George Elliott Clarke.

Each pause, your blue and changing eyes
open to the world. You crave more of rhythm, words
spun like songs though on a harsh and dying wind.

Years later, Alana, when you wonder at the world,
I do not want you to consider the hanged. But could you
remember the rocker and your mother soaping down
her soul terrified with greatest love, I'd want the world
offered up for you like parceled dominions.

I turn you upright, Alana, burp the gases from your
gut. Two days' old and talk of slavery.

I croon cacophony and dirty truths like Blake's
lightened dreams.

I do not wish you to ponder now the meaning of these words.
You twist your little legs to music.
But I do want you to know you should be prepared.

Your father's Venezuelan papers have been held
this side of the border for inexplicable reasons.
He is not allowed to hold you yet.

The world is the rubbed legs of crickets, love.
And some can only guess the tune.

Marrow

I remember the importance of water,
how it curls into stomach, soaks and lines with vegetable
memory, makes alkaline of guilt.

Old healer in the woods of Ireland
put her finger on it, would not tell the exact
sickness, give name. Pure Catholic and all and me
disbelievin', though her Bible did make me
shake, beige root vegetables running hours
after in the rearview

running in the heavens, their snapped necks bent like streetlights
        glowing pale yellow
offered up with brown sugar, cut lengthwise, size of dashes
on a broken-line road.

Truth is I'm tired and though my house is clean
I'm still nervous of each corner, the joinings
of things. Joint stools, joistings, the joist, knuckles,
bend of knees, the parallel runnings of boards.

(I imagine something like dough's at the root,
moist and caught up with a spore).

I weep for the eggplant, burst head
from hard thinking, its brains turned
to purple, bound for the dips,
life's second thoughts.

Not the carrot or turnip, sure of themselves,
firm and unshaken.

The stones I've pushed are always something
marrow, meaning white or grey-like, the centre
sucked out.

Neal McLeod

from *Gabriel's Beach* (Hagios Press, 2008)

Kêtahtawê Ê-Kî-Tapasît

wîhtikôhkân
was not a Christian
unlike his brother mostos
he was a swashbuckler
a traveller
one of his grandfathers
came from Montréal
Xavier became Janvier
turns of names
and languages
like the Saskatchewan River
around hills and trees

back in the long ago
kayâs time
marriages were planned
families connected
through younger ones
wîhtikôhkân had a pre-arranged marriage
he came south from Cold Lake

he went into the Church
to meet his wife
walked up the aisle
pews were full
chatter becomes still
she took down her veil
êkwa mâmasîs ê-osîhiht
but she was made poorly

kêtahtawê ê-tapasît
he fled quickly
and found another wife

Jesus

one time they invited *wîhtikôhkân*
to sing in the church
he brought his drum
but they were singing
a different kind of song
songs about Christian soldiers
scratched out in Cree syllabics
Cree voices
stretching to say these names

another time
he was sitting
in the Church
and this man was preaching
about fire and hell
eternal damnation
sâh-sîhcisiwak
they were sitting tight
packed in the pews

wîhtikôhkân used to smoke
his little pipe
with his hat on
and listen to the words
religion and stories
of the newcomers
the people that his brother *kinosêw*
made the deal with
he said, he couldn't understand why
they would talk about Jesus

when they killed him
he used to think
they were afraid
they would be punished

1885, Batoche

mosôm Gabriel
was my grandfather
cîhcam was his mother
his father and four brothers
had fled west
from the British soldiers march
in 1870

some of mosôm Gab's relatives
had fought in 1885
ê-mâyahkamikahk they said
"where it went wrong"
along the *kisiskâciwani-sîpiy*
by Batoche
they sent the young people away
old men fought
told jokes, teased, chided
each other
as bullets cut
bodies into the earth

buried outside the graveyard
unsanctioned by sacred sanctuary
one of Gabriel's grandfathers
general with Napoleon
seems soldiering was in the blood

Mosôm Gabriel's Fight

Gabriel was not
the kind of man
who would step
back down from a fight
he carried the beach
with him all of his days
he went to Debden
close to where he lived
went to town
lots of French people
mistikôsiwak
people of the wooden ships
like *cikôsiw*
who took Treaty
from James Smith

he walked along the streets
buzzing with cars
farmers driving combines
you never saw
that on the Autobahn

there was another man
big, cocky
full of spit and vinegar
he looked at Gab
challenging him
asking him why he was in town
but Gab did not back down
looking him in the eye
they moved towards each other
in the space
sky closed in
sun hid in shadows
they danced around
fists whirling

the guy's hands
were really white now
usually he was just pink

Gab was not that tall
but he was the toughest man around
my dad told me
he was like Maximus
the Roman General from Spain
who fought the Germans
just like Gab
he had a heart the size of a Mac truck
and the arms of Hercules

he circled him
around and around
a shark circling
a struggling swimmer
he danced and dodged
played cat and moose with him

he felt his stomach tighten
like he was hungry
not the same hungry
as the winter of 44-45
ispîhk ê-kî-kipahikâsot
when he was captured
but still hungry
he motioned
for the other man
to take a break
to rest, to pause
to catch their breath
took inventory
of his motions
of his moves
the other guy
was like a swimmer

struggling for dear life
like a Third Party manager
trying to sort out the mess
running out of time
he was like a man
running for chief
with no close relatives
he needed more
he needed an angle
so he motioned for them
to take a break

they sat there
ate pork and beans
let me tell you
there's nothing like pork and beans
they had lemon-aid
to wash it down
nothing like lemon-aid
to wash the stuff down
they ate, prayed,
and toasted each other
then they continued to fight
till the end of the day
Gab was happy
just to dance around

Spring Time in Kinistino

my dad and Edwin Tootoosis
were telling stories
about *wîhtikôhkân* and the Traveler
rednecks tried to chase us out
with their hard, long stares
we finished our meal
egg rolls, rice and coffee

miyoskamihk, the spring
breaking ice filled the air
rebirth of possibilities
turning of eternity
penetrated the space around us
creating calmness
trucks in half-filled streets

my dad told a story
an old man and his grandson
went to town piled in a truck
to get groceries
the boy was fourteen

they milled about the store
collected the things they needed
filled their carts
there was a man at the door
he said, "Goddamn Indians."
spoke to the old man
"You are Goddamn lazy.
Stay on the reserve."
Taunts, and mean red faces
from red necks
old man kept calm
they gathered their groceries

by the truck
the grandson asked,
"*nimosôm* (my grandfather),
why didn't you say
something to the man who
was saying those things to us?"
The grandfather said,
"How long were we
in that store *nôsisim*?"
"Five minutes"
"We only had to deal

with that man
for five minutes
he has to deal with himself
for the rest of his life."

James Smith Hockey Arena

we took our slough
to the Big Arena
bright lights
bleachers filled
fried gravy soaked
sugar candy
in our hands
diabetes starter kits

buffalo and moose calls
become cat calls
to brave white kids
who came to play
in our hood

bleachers gone now
dark inside
pockets of light
breaking through
like parkland nights
sky holds dark blue
like deep ocean
around me

Gretzky's retired now
I haven't skated in years
when I saw the arena
in recent times
wannabe neechi hustlers
stories on the wall

Crips and Bloods
in south-central James Smith

young reznecks
stretch the necks
of their rez stories
like giraffes
and make old men
dream of prime
neechi alphabet soup

old place scaffolds
bodies empty of motion
some places on ice
never froze
now the memories
pass from this old
hulled out body
of memory building

Casino Culture

Buffalo Bill would be happy
we sell cultural ass
to make patriot Americans
comfortable with Manifest Destiny
and imperial machinations
the Pow Wow trail

white people
make themselves feel good
about the conquest of America
and the destruction of Indigenous memory
by marvelling at "all of the regalia"
"and are you really Sioux?"
cheap chokers
made from Wal-Mart merchandise
they eat their little bits
of ancient America
make themselves fat
on authentic neechi bannock

the casino lords
over the landscape
contemporary neechi temple
gaudy Pow Wow colours
lime green and neon orange
Vegas meets neechiness
poker tables take the place of old stories
old campfires become neon

white men play Indian
speak of their wolf dreams
wait anxiously for grand entry
but where the hell were they in 1885
when it wasn't cool to be a neechi?

Neal McLeod, Dreaming Water:

"The painting invokes the metaphor of water as the vehicle through which old, ancestral echoes flow and merge with the present. The central figure is a contemporary being, who is infused with the water of the past, and also challenged by the darkness represented by the Wîhtikow." The image is in the collection of the Mendel Art Gallery, Saskatoon Saskatchewan (Canada), 2002. Dimensions 24 feet x 8 feet.

Battle of Old Man River

they built Fort Whoop-Up
where the last great Indian battle
happened 100 years before I was born
in your love, I have built a new fort
in your body, I have a new vantage point
see new patterns

along the far ridge, the Cree
expecting victory move toward
the camps of their enemies
as I have moved through darkness
so they did towards dawn

my life has been a battle
like many of the old Crees
I have died in crimson water
crushed by the power of dark horses
betrayed by dawn's calling

they met fierce resistance from the south
blows from the darkness
like those of my dreams
they died in coulees,
I die in my dreams
when I am away from you

imagine their long trek home
wounded tired bodies
the dry sun
peeling the marrow
from their bones
as they journeyed home

I have found my home
in your light, your body,
your prayers, and kisses

Word Map for Lost Sons

our words come from land and places
our stories are echoes
of the land of our ancestors
clusters of sound become our bodies
before language, we had songs
ancient songs that shook the land
like *piyêsîsak kâ-naskwêwahamawâcik pîsimwa*
the birds answering the sun in song
as the old Cree song says
all sound and language
comes from this original thank you

nôtokwêw âtayôhkan
the keeper of all sacred stories
âtayôhkêwina
the keeper of ancient sound
and our helper and grandmother
kikâwînaw-askiy k-ôkwêmêsit,
the late Beatrice Lavallee
spoke of these things

she said *nôtokwêw âtayôhkan*
these words we must remember
nihtâwêwin and *tâpwêwin*
to speak well
to choose our words carefully
to guide our sons with love and not anger
to speak pure love to our lovers
to speak our hearts open

tâpwêwin, truth
to be guided by old principles
of the *okihcitâwak*
to protect and honour our women
to speak truth and not lies
to love one woman and blanket her

with the original thank you song of the universe
from the wet throats of birds
who sang the sun into the first day

Glossary of Cree Words and Phrases (courtesy of author)

apisciyinîsak: the little people
askiy: land, earth
askîhk: on the Earth, on the land
askîwêwin: the voice of the land, the land's voice
astotin: hat
atâhkakohp: Starblanket; Cree chief, signatory to Treaty Six
ati-pihkopayinwa nicihciya: my hands turn to ash
awa: this, this one
awa ê-kî-kosâpahtahk: this one foresaw it, the one that performed the
    shaking tent ceremony
awâsis: child
âtayôhkêwina: sacred stories; spiritual history
cikôsiw: French Man (clipped from (wê)miscikôsiw)
cîhcam: Maria Vandall, my great-great-great-grandmother
ê-akimiht: he/she/it is counted
ê-akohkasikêt: he is welding
ê-ispipitahk: he pulls it up
ê-kâh-kistawêt: it echoes repeatedly
ê-kiskiwêhikêt: he foretells, he prophecies
ê-kî-kipahikâsot: he was captured, imprisoned
ê-kî-kosâpahtahk: he foresaw it, he performed the shaking tent ceremony
ê-kî-nêhiyawatâmot: he was singing a Cree song
ê-kî-pawâtât: she dreamt of him
ê-kî-pê-kîwêyân itê kâ-tipiskâk: I came home to the darkness
ê-kî-pôni-waskawît: he had stopped moving, he had died
ê-kî-tapasît: he fled
ê-kî-wâsakâmêkâpawicik: they stood in a circle
ê-kîmwêcik: they are whispering
ê-mamâhtâwisit: he is spiritually powerful
ê-mâyahkamikahk: where it went wrong, the Northwest Resistance of 1885

ê-osîhiht: he/she/it was made
ê-pê-sâkâstêk: coming dawn, dawn arrives
ê-tapasît: he flees
ê-waskawît: he is moving
ê-wî-pê-sâkâstêk: the sun is going to rise
êkâ: not
êkâ ê-akimiht: she was not counted, she was not enumerated under Treaty
êkwa: and, then
êkwa mâmasîs ê-osîhiht: and he/she/it was made poorly
êkwa mîna ê-kî-pawâtât nâpêwa ôtê nîkânihk: and she dreamt of a man in the future
iskotêw: fire; Burns, grandfather of Gabriel Vandall and my great-great-great-great-grandfather
iskoyikohk itê ê-kanawâpahtamân: as far as I look
iskwâhtêm: door
ispîhk: when, then
ispîhk ê-kî-kipahikâsot: when he was captured
ispîhk ê-wî-pê-sâkâstêk: when the sun is going to rise, when sunrise is imminent
itê kâ-tipiskâk: where it is dark
itwêw: he said, he said so, he said it
k-ôkwêmêsit: one who is named after another
kahkiyaw waniskâwak askîhk: everything on the Earth awakens, Mother Earth awakens
kayâs: long ago
kayâs mîna mistahi-maskwa: long ago also, Big Bear
kayâs-maci-maskihkiy: old time bad medicine
kâ-kî-itiht: who was called (by such a name) [referring to a deceased person]
kâ-miyikowisiyâhk: what the Creator has given us
kâ-mônahihkos: Digging Weasel
kâ-naskwêwahamawâcik: those who sing in response or accompaniment to him/her/them
kâ-pâstêkamipayik: the water which has dried up
kâ-pitihkwêk: that which rumbles, thuds
kâ-tipiskâk: where it is dark, the darkness; when it is dark
kâ-waskawi-sîpiy: moving energy river

kâh-kayâs sîpiy môskiciwan kiyawihk ohci: the ancient river flows forth
  from your body
kâkikê: forever
kâkikê-askiy: forever earth
kêtahtawê: suddenly, all of a sudden
kêtahtawê ê-kî-tapasît: suddenly he fled
kêtahtawê ê-tapasît: suddenly he flees
kihci-okimâskwêw: the Queen; old woman with many relatives
kikâwînaw-askiy: Mother Earth, our mother the Earth
kikâwînaw-askiy k-ôkwêmêsit: She who has Mother Earth as her
  Namesake, the late Beatrice Lavallee from Piapot First Nation
kinanâskomitin: thank you, I am grateful to you
kinêpik: snake
kinosêw: fish; brother of wîhtikôhkân
kisiskâciwan: it flows swiftly; the Saskatchewan River
kisiskâciwani-sîpiy: the swift-flowing river; the Saskatchewan River
kiyawihk ohci: from your body
kôhkom: your grandmother
kôkom: Grandmother! (address form); grandmother, respected older woman
kôkom cîhcam: grandmother cîhcam, Maria Vandall
kôkôcîs: Peter Vandall, my great-grandfather
maci-maskihkiy: bad medicine
masaskâpaw: Stands on the Bottom of the Water; my great-great-great-
  great-grandfather, father of cîhcam, Maria Vandall
maskihkiy: medicine
maskihkiy astotin: Medicine Hat
matotisân: sweat-lodge
mâmasîs: poorly, any old way
mêmêkwêsiwak: the Little People
mistahi-maskwa: Big Bear
mistahi-maskwa kâ-kî-itiht: he who was called Big Bear
mistasiniy: big stone, large boulder
mistikôsiwak: people of the wooden boats, French people
miyoskamihk: the spring, in the spring
mîna: and, also
mosôm: grandfather

mosôm Gabriel: grandfather Gabriel Vandall, my great-great-grand-uncle (in the English kinship system), pâcinîs' younger brother

mosôm pâcinîs: grandfather pâcinîs (Patrice adapted for Cree sound system); Patrick Vandall, my great-great-grandfather

mostos: cow, buffalo; brother of wîhtikôhkân

môhcw-âyak: crazy ones, foolish ones

môsâpêw: man who give his life for others (old interpretation of the world), single male, unattached buffalo bull

môskiciwan: it flows forth

"môy ê-nôhtê-sakâpêkinikawiyân," itwêw: I don't want to be lead by a rope (like a horse) he said

môy ê-okoticik: they don't have noses

môya: no

napocokan: crooked hips; Bernard Constant, my great-great-great-grandfather

nâpêsis: boy, small boy

nâpêw: man

nêhiyawak: Crees, Cree people

nêhiyawasinahikêwin: Cree writing, Cree Syllabics

nicâpân: my great-grandparent

nicâpân kôkôcîs: my great-grandfather kôkôcîs; Peter Vandall

nicihciya: my hands

nihtâwêwin: speaking well, fluency

nikî-waniskân: I awoke, I arose

nikî-wâpâsin: I arose early; I was an early-riser

nikosis: my son

nikosisitik: my sons! (address form)

nimosôm: my grandfather

nimosôm owîhowin: my grandfather's name

nipahi-miyosit: terribly beautiful

nipiy: water

nipiy kâ-pitihkwêk: Sounding Lake, literally, "water which rumbles"

nipîsim: my sun

nitahcahkom: my spirit

niyaw: my body

nîkân-isi: the foremost one, Thunderbird; the first McLeod, my great-great-great-grandfather

nôhkom: my grandmother

nôsisim: my grandchild; my grandson, my granddaughter
nôtokwêw âtayôhkan: Grandmother Spirit; "old woman spirit being",
  keeper of language and sacred stories
ohci: from
ohkoma: his grandmother
okihcitâw: worthy young man, warrior
okihcitâwak: worthy young men, warriors
opakwahtêhon: his belt
opakwahtêhon ê-ispipitahk: he pulled up his belt
osâmihêw: he does too much with him/her/them
owîhowin: his/her name
ôtê nîkânihk: in the future
paskwâw-mostos: buffalo
paskwâw-mostos awâsis: Buffalo Child
pâcinîs: Patrick Vandall, my great-great-grandfather
pimwêwêhahk: "sound of a constant drumming"; Jim Kâ-Nîpitêhtêw
pipon: winter, it is winter
piyêsîsak: birds
piyêsîsak ê-kîmwêcik: the birds are whispering
piyêsîsak kâ-naskwêwahamawâcik pîsimwa: when the birds sing in
    response to the sun, birds which accompany the sun in song
pîsim: the sun
sâh-sîhcisiwak: they were packed together tightly
sâpowâstan: the wind blows through
sâpowâstêw: it shines through
sênipânak: ribbons
sîpiy: river
sîpîsis: stream, creek, rivulet, little river
sôniyâw: money
tâpiskôc: like, just as if
tâpiskôc nêhiyawasinahikêwin: like Cree writing, like Cree Syllabics
tâpwêwin: truth
timîkamîhk: in deep water
waniskâwak: they arise, they awaken
waskawîwin: movement, life force
wâskahikaniyiniwak: the House People, division of the Cree who dwelt in
    the vicinity of Fort Carlton

wâskîsiw: Waskesiu, name derived from Woods Cree wâwâskîsiw "elk"

wîhtikow: a being who consumes other beings, cannibal, an ancient darkness

wîhtikowak: beings who consume other beings, cannibals

wîhtikôhkân: my great-great-great-grandfather, a Cree-Dene from the Cold Lake area of Alberta

George McWhirter

from *The Incorrection* (Oolichan Books, 2007)

Beware if you go
dolphin or whale
watching, here.

In Brazil, they say
boto, the dolphin-man,
never takes off his hat
to make love. He does
his naked hat dance
between your thighs,
tips it when he's done
and frolics off
into the surf, hat
on head, like those
women through the high hills
and vales of Bolivia.

Don't be afraid
if you see him in a shop,
trading his old fedora
for something new
to cover his blow hole.

He is too troubled
with counting the cost
to wet your whiskers
with a drop of love
and lure you
like the miniature
catfish at the pet shop
into his saucer
of sea water...

...This morning I saw frost break into a beaded sweat
on the holly leaves and stipple-lacquer
their intense green. The sky was true-blue too, yet
of such fine omens I have always been a mocker,
and of your face, which only a poltroon—
me—would razz, for fear of an inadequate
love song. I am the seagull set to croon
from the rooftop, but who may only grate,
a blank-breasted admiral on yellow feet,
across the asphalt shingle with an unmusical
command, whose notes are neither rare nor fleet
but whose wings, when he dives, beat our street
into a fjord, an air as stinging as Chablis, an untypical
perspective to flow from this flying madrigal...

On a Road through West Belfast

Protestants, incensed at the lapsed vigilance
and Popery creeping in
under the banner of human rights,
burst into a beetroot red and black
pudding of anger
around their big jawed Pastor's
well-boiled abhorrence on the rotunda
outside the Stadium Picture house
at the top of the Shankill; the mob
rolled down the road
and put in the windows of the Italian
ice cream shops (the Italians',
who had fled blue-jawed
Mussolini)—they
being the only Papists
the Prods could find.

Black holes in the human
heart and head
                    (little studied)

that compound
in the implosion of belief—once its positive
light dies, the negative takes a quantum
leap to unstoppable power and intensity
to the point of no return and no surrender.

Let old blocks
stay on the road to Seoul, inscrutably
doing what is forgotten
for the kids to marvel at. They laid
no such mysteries to posterity
on the Shankill.

Gulf Island

A snowflake is a cold cobweb
that catches spiders and other insects
unawares, reduces them—if we're lucky, to zero. Sects
of all sorts pray for clemency and an ebb
in the winter weather, but minus the swarms of summer
        mosquitoes
as a consequence. Oh Lord, give us balanced blessing.
        Yet its scales,
like silks and sicknesses, are made of the disparities:
        whales
go blind in Hecate Strait from the overflow
of the septic tank for our cabin with a view;
fire and flood still calibrate the wild West's
actuarials, and our helicopters are too old for sea
        rescue.
The lowly lake noses back into the living room, to
        reinvest
in lost habitat, and its water laps at my armchair,
like a dog. Give it a bone, you say, you know it's only
        fair.

Bad

So near and narrow-minded are my kind
that we hold a razor blade
of suspicion and rage
  wedged permanently
  in our heads
which cuts our selves
in two—into the Irish
and the not-Irish; it gives
our eyes a gleam stronger
than the steel grey
and planished blade
of the Irish Sea and sky,
  edged
by the low rolling breakers
of the Lough
  and whetted
regular on the long brown strap
of the Lagan.
For as long as I remember
I have tried to love these two
parts of me, but am
as unable as anyone,
  holding
  hot chestnuts
  or spuds
  spiked
  with Wilkinson sword edges
  in his hands,
to juggle
his own nativity.

...We come from flaky, flawed folk, villains
who hang onto the neck of what they have,
like a wife-beater to his love,
before she betrays him with a handsome
black haired, blue-eyed Roman Catholic man,
who lacks the squint to sicken her

or worse still, the wife falls for her ladyship,
the Virgin Mary.

We prefer our women to defend the kitchen
against filchers, skivers and ginger Toms
and give in to our exclusive whims and whimpers

when we are tipsy with alternatives
to the usual. A Molotov cocktail

or two, shared
with the Papists.......

Octavio Paz, the son, the point of your pen
incising the word dark and luminous as the memory
of Paz, the father, the ends of his moustache
dunked in dark wine, blacked out—
like match ends pitching toward the ground—
the incendiary afternoons go out, farther South
down Puebla-way. You see him
on another return from the States
with cash for the cause. The division rises within you
for the hero and the tippler; Zapata and his Division,
that cause provided for
a little further.

His horse expels a thin shell of breath—
which way the agent, the man,
which way for your words
opening all doors in the dark evening

What are you waiting for? asks your mother
as he dodders onto the veranda, as the breath
of the horse, History, breathes backward
and away,
extracting, expatriating
the soul through the ornamental spaces
in the trellis.

How much will either of you alter,
in spite of the iron will behind the words,
in spite of the Santo Tomas,
thick with its own season of sun,

and the mescal, porous and hard
as the stones that cleave

Mitla to its hill, or your tongue,
Octavio, that never drank a drop of it,

to the roof of your mouth when I ask,
"Is there any duty free
I can bring you from the North,
next time?"

from **Pensée Poème Assay for my Sister**
3.
For my Shankill Road Sister

She had a bosom and biceps that could have burst
chains of Sheffield steel, but could not break the link
between her and that corner of the Shankill she came
from,

like the cells in her cervix that killed her,
locked and growing as uncontainably wild inside her
as her belief in God
or her temper.

I like to think of her in her moment of salvation,
in the other cell she loved and laboured over
like her own womb. That built-on kitchen
and bathroom with an enamel tub
at the back of her kitchen house—
mini-fridge, immersion heater—

3 Craig's Terrace.

Some of our ones, Protestants in a fast car, had done
the typical
and terrible down on the Falls Road and were being
chased
by the Paras and the RUC up onto the Shankill via
Northumberland Street,
where I used to live, and which connected Shankill
and Falls—
another killer link or open thoroughfare(take your pick)
between our opposite religions or diseases,
which we can't outlive or break.
To take a short cut, and block the cops and Paras
from coming in behind them into Craig's Terrace,
our ones tossed a bomb from the car.
Down came the houses
on either side; my sister—on hers—
felt the concussion of the blast in her face,
saw the walls of her kitchen heave, their red brick lining
shift. And she stepped back,
opened the door to the yard behind her,
stepped out
and back until her kitchen and bathroom
and everything she loved
lay piled at her feet. But she was safe.

I wish she could have stepped out

from inside her other cell, safe
to her own regenerate from degenerate self. But none
of us can do that yet,
can we?
God bless you, Lily.

Jay MillAr

from *False Maps for Other Creatures* (Nightwood Editions, 2005)

Space Gallery

What could one write but the small white
flowers in this petal's dreamed arrangement?
It is not a dream. It is a thing which flows,
      how awe evolves

reason. Entire ecosystems have disappeared.
There exists a number of interesting studies
to demonstrate this subtle power
      but you were asleep

on the other side of the room, beneath the
soft wild explosion, a portrait. That was my
idea: a sad old man draped in an array
      of knowledge

extracted from another time, another place.
Someone died down the street. He was a
man, a father, a poet, somebody or other.
      They sent an ambulance

but you would have preferred to receive
a small patch of land planted with grasses
to watch as they sprinkled your ashes
the field waving against the sky, saying
      hello to the sun.

Facsimile

beneath the small blue
of the sowesto sky

there is a fine line

in a notebook made of a
strange breeze
bound into orange card wrappers

cracked earth continues
to offer green shoots

pollen and viruses enter the bloodstream
how one can steal things
from other places and bend them
to one's will

some species of flies
hover in the same spot for hours
seemingly by magic
until one realizes they have wings or are dead

the frantic bother of the wind says something
in retrospect thinks about this later

it's morning
and I still cannot remember people

8th Concession, Tilbury, Ontario

Dry fields of green
grey point toward
the risen buds to cloud
the mind with notice:
trees are the aching
April breezes I need.

What I want is to
understand or at least
pretend this place
is not what lives here
a sky given over
to flat clouds open
to some idea before
it becomes land.
And as if in response
the buzz of an insect
in my ear brings to
the experience a voice
somewhere between
earth and sky and
mind. And I read it
as an emotion.
An unpronounced
gesture I have made
so many times it is
a figment of nature
opened like the
frieze dried remains
of Queen Anne's lace.

Clearly it discusses
the air. I couldn't
possibly imagine another
word for a world that
learned to speak. Time
learns to listen and
discovers that whatever
edge you have is small
as flowers that flow
from what green
the ground decides exits.

from *Three Specimen of Mushrooms*
Third Specimen: Destroying Angel (*amanita virosa*)

hidden, hugged by browns and held
in the soft white cloud of itself –
there under trunk by trunk we stumble up
waiting this way is potential rot
rotting this way is an angel upward

a landing pad for flies and buzz and
thought takes sweat for ether, moist
yur a golden boy up there, moist yur
a golden boy up there, moist yur a
golden boy up there in the s'kid's
kies
       twisted in landing, a parosol
with rosy ochraceous shades at the centre
in the moist and sandy wood of latifoliate trees
waiting is how we will capture the senses
hugged and fraught with non-sense or -being
the calm stature will stare you down,
kick your ass, and leave you for dead
a tight squeeze of illness
constantly in a state of erection
or arousal
the spores happy to be up
down here

luckily it is rare

Day 232

Born August 20 at 12:58 am, 5 lbs 11 oz – sucked into the world
in ten minutes flat after sixteen hours of labour – which might explain
the bewildered look perhaps all infants express upon their arrival.
Though we wouldn't know. We've never seen anyone else born.

Ten days early, but as least it was his decision; Hazel had been
scheduled to be induced the day after she went into labour.
As though had invited himself casually of his own volition, rather
than by our demands. Too bad they had to vacuum him out, but the cord
(we discovered this later, the doctors never quite explaining at the time
what the drop in fetal heart-rate at each contraction actually means)
was wrapped twice around his neck, once around his body. We joked
he was a swimmer but are certain he came in from the sea to be with us.

Born under Leo, but right at the end, just before the slide into Virgo,
so not ruled only by the sun but by the setting sun, as it falls toward
the house of the craftsperson. It is a kind of in-between-ness we have
perhaps taken for granted that was suddenly been pulled into the
foreground. That he might be able to teach us all how to look.

And yes, as I held him there
in the dark room looking at his face
as Hazel watched us from among the doctors and nurses
it was much like being sucked into myself and out:
eyes not so demanding as they were curious –
critical of their need or desire to attend.
It felt like a trade wind from somewhere nearby
but still overwhelmingly unexplainable:
you want reason maybe, a language, something.
But you can't find it there.
And can't speak of what it was that happened
or about anything else for days.

Riding home on the subway hours later I look up to find I'm sitting under
a poem by PK Page, so I read it on the way. Claims that an infant's thought
must be pure thought because it's before thought. Bullshit. Not pure thought
but pure instinct – that which looks through as a means to approach thought.
Maybe take you there.

Lakeshore

It's the wrong blade of music. You imagine
Or imagine you imagine what
The sky would be without you. Perfect blue
Left to itself inside a perfectly solid gas.
Believe it or not, it's not up to you.
Up to me. Up to any last thought
Or hope or ideological action
Figure. Some guy honks it only gives him
Appearance, droll automotive moment to me you
Feel something you don't even care for. Roll on.
Every car here the price of an endlessly moving song.
A green and white train backs off to Hamilton.
Above the lake the clouds: a Dutch painting
Of the Canadian Landscape, suburbia
It's all about light-minded fuckers driving
Home from work. The corporate forces cannot create
Or destroy only change into another form of itself
Stifling the whole engulfed dream. The law
Of physics, or denial. 'I've decided I'm not going to be nice
To anyone I don't like,' you say, and I can see that you're smiling
Inside. It's great. I love you, especially all fired up
Beyond repair. You are the bright bright shining star
On the north side of my tiny brain my arm. What was I
Going to say? Hummmmmmmmmmmmmm along. Kiss me where
The slice of the sun is only devastating this time of day.

Eric Miller

from *The Day in Moss* (Fitzhenry & Whiteside, 2008)

The conception of Achilles

When the nymph of the straits lay spent on the sand,
her thighs apart, what staggered sense
was the slickness of her inner self
and the drier crumbs of the outer world
that so roughly clung to her.

How could she host such moisture and such aridity?
My hands liked both. But the blood did not have its source
in sand's abrasion, though it imparted colour
to the grains that stuck, and would not desert her.
I brushed them off, each dyed by her—fine Tyrian dye.
She seemed soft beyond expression, softer even
than wind-still water, than water gently entered,
but lightly coated, sifted over in places
with a reminder of the resistance of the world
 (that irregular small aspersion of beach sand)
and the pigment inward to her gaze fused into the sky
and her rocking became an aspect of the waves
and what held me back made me go forward,
a membrane like time that we break, break again,
without meaning to, in a sense without effort,
though sometimes, baffled, favoured, we feel an effort,
also the fact that no effort's necessary,
time goes on with us, goes on without us
amid the sea lettuce, the bladder wrack,
tongued bulbs of kelp, where the window-pane cool
sea-glisten slides forward and pulls back,
lovingly viewing and mauling the place between places
so rich in shelled and mucous life
delighted to be tousled and to be fed

even by a mortal, though she is immortal,
intact at the next tide by which we may be swept away.

As the flight of a swallow

Near us, yet far beyond hypocrisy,
the swallow swivels, airborne,
just as we, though we feign,
make no pretence, for deceit's
our nature, as flight's
the swallow's fluent resource.

Does wrong belong to the swallow?
Boldly, the swallow obeys whatever
in physics comes close
to that strange, allowable swerving.
But though it errs, it never
dissimulates. *Persist in the mistake*
sings the swallow, the swallow our sister.

A raving beauty the error is
at every pass. The forked tail flares, the eye
feels the tolerant sky
for the opportune aperture. The wing may,
like remorseful reflex, contract:
wincing's what flight sometimes looks like.
But air's impeccable, air's
immaculate. The swallow's brief,
wide, whiskered, eloquent beak chatters
like water and sucks the rich, thin sky,
chatters like water, sucks the thin, rich sky.

Avidity matches the zephyr's grace, fleet
and footless, pace for pace.
Grass, cedar in fever, compost's spice,
the snails' long vestige, water
that quenches the spotted dust, flowers

mottled, wilting, exhaling
their last appeal: wings over the garden
caress this sprightly, moribund
perfume—their harpsichord.
The atrocious hawk gives pause, but day
endorses it all, the mistake
is as real as the correction.

So the swallow, our sister, sings
What happens is always persuasive.
Whatever happens is always persuasive.
O slight, titanic wing,
can we have lived through, again,
what we cannot possibly have endured?
Strait was the gate, and somehow good.
The air is clear, and our conscience.
What are the claims of conscience?
In all conscience there are disclaimers.

Nothing before death is inauthentic.
Everything after death is genuine.
O devious candour.
O corrupt, incorruptible
frankness, comparable in complication
to the ravenous, whimsical swallow's flight.

November rain and song

Vituperative November. Yet the robins are voice
over voice, voice into voice coalescing and diverging
in a light cut with rain, rain cut with light, a hard sun's light,
light as solid as a thrown stone
or like the fractured columns of the rain.

And void dim dire water as it plunges hits the birds' song, driving
those sounds like struck insects aside, yet letting them resume their course
as a drop slams a stiff leaf and the leaf bounces

brightened coldly and coldly resilient,
deflected though returning to its first inclination.
The flocks sing, and the listener's cold hands
through the sculptural suspensions of song
feel the swathed, tinted heat of one robin's breast
pressed between them—taut instrument from which
musical steam and streaming music issue, despite interfering weather.

And how was it, anyway, that blood could warm itself
in the first brave, separate secession and instance,
circulating darkly, brightly to warm the breath and warmly impart the music
from so many lonely, sociable stations
scattered by austere estrangements of animate fate?

The pillars of water match exactly
the lifeless temperature of the universe
and despite its catapult of rays
the sun has got no warmer
with the friction of its compulsive missiles.

But in chill branches and in sky that chokes on its own cold blood,
self-warmed life spills note after note

onto an earth
that largely denies life's heat and praise
clasping them always firmly, deafly
with the imminence of a negation.

Niagara

1.

A diarist relates that, one summer afternoon in 1793, cruelty
assuming its usual form, human, strolling
along the shore of the Niagara River, loosed
from a dock the canoe in which a Mohawk
slept. It appeared to be an instance of straightforward, mocking

murder and the one who undid the knot never
was detected. Loiterers on the bank, wishing in idle panic
to effect a rescue, could not—could not but watch as the man, waking
at the motion of the current accelerating,
sat up and absorbed his fate
as a stone the sun's touch,
dry in the midst of a surging stream. Delectable
day, cool, confiding the flow, the rapids still far off,
though hunched in the distance immortal
water crouched crumpling for precipitous aeration.
The man sat still—a figure on a medal struck, whom witnesses
called stoic. Strong as the epithet was, it availed nothing
against the current. Then what was he?
A man beautified by the imminent mortality of his profile
in a canoe contrived from the lambent bark of the birch
treated with pitch of conifers to forestall leakage.
His shapely, fragrant little boat was watertight.
Sweet as throaty doves the concerted water falling, sweet
the water that gloves and fits any dangling hand,
sweet to stir eye-bright water-birds from their racing seats on the water,
sweet to fellow the birds as you pass them blue and white
as though you, too, had, like paddles, paired and folded wings on your back,
sweetest of all to view the shore bountiful, successively, as love
rounding a body's bends.

Past helping's where you're pulled.

Yet he awoke unbruised at the base of the falls.

2.

A last efflorescence flushed my mother when, dying quite young,
her gaze cleared again, her complexion cleared, her voice returned
and she could still walk. She could walk with me. We walked,
her carriage upright, as upright as a birch tree's carriage, as a dancer's,
and she once was a dancer, and now she was frail, and almost I felt
I was taking a girl for a date. This girl made me proud and frightened
as though I held something too light and too heavy for my hands,
always on the point of dropping it from its fickle levity, gravity.

In her company I trembled like water, like light in the leaves of a birch tree,
water is the same, subtle, at any distance from the cataract,
she was the breeze that moves the water, that feels the humid foliage.

She sustained the interval between an edge-grown bending reed
and the image the shattering water tries faithfully to return to it.

3.

We strolled along Bloor Street in the falling sun.
The day flowed down like a great river lapping the grateful city.
How harmless the busyness of other people, their
busyness was our leisure, we did not descend beneath surfaces,
not even in imagination. Permanency fixed each person just
so—a bird in its ordained plumage, the ordained
festivity of its plumage. Fashion was truth, truth
fashion. No disguise, no dissimulation, nor yet a performance.
Everyone was immemorially and immediately this.
No moral distinctions, no histories, just the eddying transient mandate:
pleasure. I can't remember what my mother chose to eat.
Almost I felt that I was on a date—

but she looked out at the day, a canoe caught in a current.
Eye-bright, the stream shines. Like a drink it cools.
And, as with laughter, there is a vibration. Water
talks fluently its dear and estranging language
many-hued as a flock of buoyant confluent birds:

the Mohawk, whose name does not descend to us, lived.

4.

What a wonder routine talk is,
with a word it spans the gap
of so many years, such disparate conditions.
You may speak with a dying person
sometimes to the brink of death.
Who would believe in reciprocity?
Yet the proofs recur, they recur.

A withdrawing bird is the same bird
that once clung close and sang,
a feature of your heart.
The eye keeps the departure in view;
departure, too, is an object of the eye.
So remote the bird! And ever more remote
but vision detains even diminution
as though it absorbed into a clear orbit
as into the walls of a womb
what was born and dies
and now seems never born, or about to be born,
borne away again on the delectable current
which falls, crashes and lives, as air or water
evidently unbruised.

Crossing Halifax harbour

1.

Liner, dredge, tug, frigate, freighter.
So persuasive is their profile this morning
the illusion is every ship
is the unsinkable rock of ages,
whereas waves incorrigibly
caper and fling off fine
scales, skins, feathers, confidential
divestments across the swell's
looped, rolled and chequered volatility.
Water is as exhibitionist as fire,
Greek fire, a briny torch
aflame with revelation, flirting
with nearly recurring images
close to kissing, compounding
burlesque and enigma; everywhere
aqueous lips shape, press
for a fuller word we feel,

that drowns, laughs, blazes.

Sequinned the harbour shimmers, plumed
half Leviathan and half phoenix,
cormorant peacock,
Galatea swims here dissolved,
salt divinity and perfect flapper
swaying as on heels eternally
tipsy in her lucid drink.

But the ferry bears its weight of commuters
immune, mostly, to the call
of tidal flightiness, lustre,
undulant fixture, thick fluidity,
no mortal will seize that dazzling waist.

2.

As bright as a girl's portrait in a porthole
sun focuses through puffs of smoke
that a factory stack, striped red and white,
pastes upon the sky. The harbour bridge
strung like a harp sustains
every note
peeved traffic
advances. Poor morning,
lavish, poor: effervescence tosses
garlands and grape-clusters
at the ferry bow, dainty
tumultuously,
as by bursting dolphins
heralded
in ticklish rupture-rapture
our passage spatters us
with a rider's blithe lymph.

Involve in foam your bubbling gaze.
Amid inflation of the sea a souvenir
could recrudesce, consolidate—halcyon clutch

hatching or plump loop of puffed-up
pearls piped out of the brine's protean
blow-holes to drape a throat, slithering
Galatea in flecks and gems of spume, spit
distending from the thronged sub-undulation...

Onto a medium of such ebullience,
ether skids down like a duck
and pelagic depth breaches
whalishly and the bow's cobalt
paint and rust and oblique gull guano
butt aside the durable flouncing
of a froth more permanent, impermanent than we.

3.

Flocks dot the harbour like bright rocks
in a rockery. Then, trickling feet
up-tucked, birds circumflex
the silver transparencies, silver
opacities of the mist's inclination
to lead day-radiance down gilded
ladders to bathe a star
in stateliness of inklings
fully as circumstantial
as the barnacle-chapped wharf-piers,
whine of tire-buffers, consecutive
clanking of chain-links, cables, winches
that like fate catch the ferry subduing
us to our destination
while offshore Galatea still imbibes
the fond liquor of her bliss
and in her heaven is not quenched.

Lenore Gale

W. H. New

from *Along a Snake Fence Riding* (Oolichan Books, 2007)

... no use waiting for the long overnight, we thought,
assuming we had two choices only, stay or go—

and not wanting to sit around doing nothing

we went,
figuring we'd lasso the future:
didn't know we didn't hold the rope, stray calves,

and didn't mean to hurry the dark along,
just saw all that wonder out there,
to reach for, green and the Great Bear,

and ignored the bones:

no-one's around when we reach the first campsite,
the next or the next—

you could ride your way past oblivion
and no-one'd notice till maybe another spring,
depending—

on chance as much as anything, the planet's
that big, and snow deep in the shadows:

so:

so we choose a clearing, notice a pond
if there is one, the dry hollow if there isn't,
the way the grasses ripple field into ocean,

day itself swimming ahead:

but scarcely notice
how the moment before had been

stirred already into makeshift territory,
the one we learned later
to call time—...

...it was there with us, of course, all along,
the time of the clocks:
we saw the hands passing in front of our eyes

now, and then *now*, and then
lost in absent-mindedness, distraction,
forgot the measure, thought it belonged

to someone else—
landscape, flashing
through slats in a gate,

glimpsing it incomplete,
unpassable,
close enough almost to touch

but out of reach—
and began to invent *If* and *Them*,
excuse and *blame*:

we entered a time shop once,
on some distant avenue,
startled the doorbell,

recognized the faces on the wall,
ornate and plain, the ragged chants
they mispronounced, competitive rhymes—

so be it, we tried to say, *Rest in*
whatever clearing it was
we'd happened to find—

except we knew already
that the grasses had a season, too,

were wrinkling into barley

even as we held in our teeth
the still-green stems
and chewed on dreams—...

...so we learned the rules for fire: align
stones to enclose the pit, pile dry twigs, assemble
leaf litter, pine cones to take the spark and kindle

flame—*be careful, it's conflagration time*, the pitch
bursts, erratically as acne—
and strike a match (forget the flint, the boy scouts

rubbing sticks together, trying on occasion)—

we followed all the steps, decided we didn't need
rehearsal any more, if ever we did,

but went through the sequence anyway,
boiling the billy can for tea:

learning something from repetition, ceremony:

the time it takes,
the flat gap it occupies between sleep and starting,
longer in the rain:

the time before the fire, and already after,
stoking overlain in earth and ash—

the time of the river,

how discontinuities
flicker,
the way woodpeckers hammer distance into day—...

...we could stray into other zones by accident, and did,
alongside Fleming School, say, heading west:

heard the usual warnings, the dire imprecations—

recess no further than, snowballs not within:
perimeters— chose freedom instead, we thought,
then found that other lines corralled us, boundaries

sometimes more abstract and not in the rulebook—
though never less defined: *who's the new kid,*
funny-looking, race, girth, glasses all brands of strange:

the outrider knows, roping the calf that lurches free,
he has no leeway for difference,
for what he calls intractability—

maybe also he knows he is himself patrolled, knows
he's ruled by the need to regulate, the standard,
curve to the bell,

he finds it easy to forestall: easier than meet and compromise—

erratics? (the one who saves daylight, winterlong,
the one who claims the pacific,

then drowns in neighbours' warring slurs):
he commits them all to lines — *sit, stand, wheel, turn—*
in chalkdust and sand—...

... they say from space you can see the Great Wall
zigzagging over the mountaintops, its steps and towers
signing the edge of *civilization* (the emperor's word):

others called it *power*,
but they were wildmen of course, *vandals* and *hordes*,
there were names for them, too—and if they had things to say

the ruler saw more need to silence than to listen—

pity Goliath:
it was the winners who drew him a giant,

turned *philistine* into a dirty word,
crowed history,
the politics of stones —

in space the airless stars do not twinkle, and astronauts
return to earth younger than friends who stayed behind
(although *return* is suspect, on river-running grounds,

and *stay* is arguably inexact
when they in truth aged on)—
little is fixed:

our own fenceline, for instance,
the one we follow at any road,
ought to be clear,

but up close, or even stepping aside
onto whatever ziggurat we find at hand,
we scarce can see it whole: it snakes forward,

interrupted,
unable to keep out the kermodes, the spirit bears,
or keep the longhorns in:

not as free as we thought from the empire's reach,
and never visible from Aldebaran—
but not yet done—...

Jeff Park

from *FAST FORWARD NEW SASKATCHEWAN POETS* (Hagios Press, 2007)

Billie Holiday: the chair

My grandmother sits in a chair.
If she lies down she will die.
I look out the window.
She asks me to spread a blanket
on the floor and lie with her.
I love her so much, but I tell her no.
She insists and I can't stand her crying.

I lay the grey blanket on the wooden floor,
lift her from the chair, stretch her out on the floor
and she talks to me and laughs and I sleep.

Five hours later I wake up, my neck stiff,
wrapped tight with grandma's arm.
I can't move and grandma's eyes
stare white facing the window.

The neighbours had to break her arm
to set me loose.
They left grandma in the front room
for the wake.
They took me to the hospital.
When I returned my cousin beat me
for letting grandma out of the chair.

The chair sits in the corner
by the window.
Sometimes I sleep in it
humming fragments of song.

Billie Holiday: the red dress

On account of a man
I was sentenced to the Catholic institution
where the nuns never ventured beyond the wall.

I wore the ragged red dress the first time
as punishment at Easter.
The other girls weren't allowed near me.
My mother brought a basket of chicken
and the nuns made me watch the other girls eat it.

At night I wasn't allowed to sleep with the others.
The sisters locked me in the room with the dead girl,
who broke her neck, trying to fly from the swing,
wearing the same red dress I now wore.

In the dark I pounded at the door.
All night my screams echoed the halls.
Blood filled my fingernails.
I thought I could hear the dead girl whisper.

I still hate closed doors.
When I sing, the doors are wide open,
and people come in and out, laughing.

The Cellophane Sky

Duke at the window
lights low above the Paris streets
sipping a sugared Coca-Cola
sitting in the night, his night.
His pants undone, belly loose,
now finally alone
after visitors and room service,
steak frite and a half bottle of red,
the Countess already asleep.

A woman's high heels echo on cobble,
Duke taps out the rhythm on the window ledge,
moves to the portable electric piano
working out the tone of foot steps
with the high notes.

His eyes follow the street lights,
a string of pearl, to the dark horizon line.
He waits for the cellophane sky,
the first few seconds of pale light
as dawn breaks and night and day merge.
"Looking for heaven, always have been."
Now he can sleep.

Elizabeth Philips

from *Torch River* (Brick Books, 2007)

Nocturne

When I was small, it was always night
when I frightened my mother with a sound
I made, a harshness of breath
that wasn't a cough, more like a straining
of water through stones,
                              or a lungful
of bees.
              For years I believed
that lost breath—my closing,
ossified throat—
                         hadn't frightened me.
Until this morning, when I heard that same
frictive throttle in another's chest,
as my lover's father lay dying,
                                   old heart
heaving, all the water left in his body
a sponge he must draw
                              each breath through.
And this morning, it slipped
past me, the moment the moving ribs
fell still, the line between then
and now
              so nearly nothing, a low mist
subsiding, shadow
of a shadow.
                         And on the evening of the day
of his death, I bow towards
that child in her bed, caught in the furious
work of inspiration, her rasping
like the thrashing inside

a chrysalis,
            and I am my own
mother, risen to tend her daughter
in the night.

            Child, I say, bending over her
in the haze of steam from the kettle,
in the lamplight,
            little moth of smoke,
open your eyes
and tell me what you know.

Before

In the woods an hour ago,
I found bearberry—
do you remember what they call
kinnickinnick? Of course
you remember. The small
sticky leaves clinging to my face,
that summer, years ago, when I came up
from beneath you.
            This was before
any of the catastrophes.
We were far from innocent,
but we were, yes,
            unknowing.
Your body shines, glistens, in memory,
as you lie back on the bed of moss
and I approach, bare feet wet from the lake,
and kneel. I look up once
at the backdrop of white spruce
and resinous wind, and look down,
cover you.

A line returns now, a fragment
from what I tried to write

afterwards: you
can only get there by water.
I still hope to use it, to play
with how it breaks:
                          you can only
    get there by water. I'll punctuate this
with the real and the imagined.
I can clearly see how the leaves
on my cheeks became green-flecked
motes in your eyes
                          and then in mine.
And you alone know the texture and shade
of moss beneath my hips, the foliage
over my shoulder, and how
the wind insinuates between us
when we draw apart, as we wade
into the shallows, warm and cool
and warm.
                    We pull on our clothes
while we're still wet, stepping into the boat
and pushing off. How buoyant we were
for days after.
                    I'm going to say it now,
are you listening? You can only get there
by water.

Jackknife / 3

The night we go swimming in the harbour,
in the dusk of a retreating
storm, he and I,

and three others take turns
diving from the pier
in the still simmering

convected air. Over the lake
spent clouds, to the west, terns
crying above the white-washed

warehouse walls.
We line up again and again
in our dripping suits, water

ticking down our legs as we praise
and mock each dive. Until he, grinning,
climbs onto the roof

of a fisherman's yawl,
and I follow. On the slippery wood,
shoulder to shoulder, one deep

breath, and we jackknife,
the twin blades of our shadows
falling together

into the water. He comes up first
and lunges, fighting
to hold me,

muscle to muscle,
under, and we're dropping into
who knows what

on the lake bottom, decades of lost
nets and fishing line, the spectre
of the diver hooked years ago

on a loop of rusted wire.
I kick back and away from him,
scissoring up into the adrenalin-

blue sky. And I'm out
and on the pier and pelting him
with stones as he swims hard

for the main dock, a hundred strokes,

the others' laughter echoing
across the oily mouth of the harbour.

And since that evening of flight, of darkness
and ascent, I am always on his side
in the game.

And the lake was blood-warm,
as it often is
after rain.

The Hanging Tree

Yesterday, your hair smelled of green tea, and so like smoke
I followed you from the living room
to the bedroom, and would have stayed
but my mother called
about the horse,
                    she said she was okay until Dad led him
from the barn and across the pasture, and past
the hanging tree.
                    That's when she turned away
from the window.
The neighbour was there with his backhoe, she could hear
the machine still running.
                              But for some things
you can't prepare.

Afterwards, I carried
a few books upstairs, whatever I wanted
nearer to hand—John Donne, the field guide
to Prairie grasses, and several
unread novels.
                Oh well, it doesn't get any easier,
my mother's voice
came with me, back to where you lay,
undressed now, and

waiting.
       In the time intervening, I'd almost
forgotten you.
          The horse
had an abscessed tooth and his ribs were staves.
         I reached across
and touched your hair, nothing like the grass
that fuelled his life. The pit was wide
and deep
            to keep the coyotes out.

Later, you drifted off, your breath
furrowing down
           and into
the afterlife of pleasure,
              while I hung on a little longer
to the scented sheets, thinking sleep
insufficient, a poor metaphor for what used to be called
eternal rest. That I'd get up in the morning,
and go to my desk, and try again to earn
my passage, to see all things
                equally: the fallen
horse (his head so much heavier now), my father's
grimace as he shakes the neighbour's hand,
as he walks around, not over, the square of newly broken
earth,
       and the wind, as it always is
just there, gentled
by the big spruce, and sweet, redolent with twenty years
of spilled grain and dung and dust.

The Promise

Everyone coming into her room can see it.
        Against the north fence, beneath
                the cottonwood, catching the sun—

a new garden seat, wrought iron, pristine,
        filling up, this morning, with snow.
                Spring, an indefinite

length of time away. And this room, like each
        in the house, a sick room, pill bottles
                on the nightstand, vials

on the mantel. And that hush, as her family
        gathers in the hallway, tendering
                into the forced calm

their questions, their wavering answers. Her flesh
        thin and thinning, counted against
                their hopes.

In her room, she stares out at the white day,
        seeing herself on the sun-warmed
                bench, red lilies behind her.

What she can no longer imagine is walking in easy
        strides across the grass, that green
                infinity. Can she endure

the coming changes? Snow turning to rain, rain
        sparking leaves, those lime-coloured
                lashes of new life.

She watches the clouds, a flourishing of pure cold
        rushing east to west as the snow
                falls faster, blurring

fence boards and gnashing boughs, as the wind
        flies through the iron leaves
                that face her window.

The Widow

She looks in the mirror and doesn't know herself.
        She's lost so many pounds, someone
the size of a small child is gone, and she misses
        the weight. She fills her bath
with a froth of white foam to cover
        the sallow wishbone of her pelvis.
She closes her eyes when she washes
        her breast, the soap slick and cool,
and sister to it, the scar that runs, unnerved,
        across her chest, a hollow
where he used to rest his head. And she pauses
        there, her heart on the other side
of that line, and she doesn't know how to restrain
        in that splice the hum
of his absence. And yet she does.
        As she breathes, she remembers him.

To Keats

I lie in bed reading *The Pocket Book of Verse*,
        discovered between Dickens and Jack London
on a basement shelf, its stained, 1940 flyleaf
        signed by my mother in watery
schoolgirl script. The book opens with excerpts
        from the Bible. I leaf ahead to Tennyson,
to the anguished garden of Amy Lowell.
        Fourteen and restless, I'm trying not to
dwell on the scornful look of a girl who doesn't know
        how much or how often I parse her every
phrase. She loves me not, I think, flipping past
        Wordsworth's daffodils.

In a well of lamplight I fall into Keats
        for the first time—*how to load and bless*

with fruit—the lines ripening, my hands beneath
        the sheets, moist bud
engorging as I try not to see her with
        her boyfriend, his farm-boy fists
on the wheel, his eyes grazing
        her hemline as he fishtails down rutted
winter streets. I glance up as wind
        shakes panes coated with frost,
making the moonlight more silver, and less
        like a gleaner thou dost keep.
But what I sink into is the sorrow of the *soft-dying*

day, its footing in the raw grief, the yellow
        clay. I read the poem again and again,
inflamed, always on the brink, then slipping back
        into the book, Keat's slinky brocade
all over me like a net of raw silk, *as the light wind*
        lives or dies, while an implacable
prairie winter cracks the floor joists, the killing cold
        never heavier. Until I'm released
into the mystery of the ending, when a squall
        of swallows infests the sky
above the river shallows.

Waking next morning, I'm heavy-headed, drugged
        by dreams of summer, and turning over
my mother's book I vow to learn each flourish,
        as if by a feat of memory, I might shame
my longing into defeat and lock in the essence
        of that first reading, that innocent
passage from line to line. Each night I am at work,
        my tongue a nib, a feather
in my throat as I whisper, recomposing,
        until by spring I own *The Pocket Book of Verse*
and I'm hoarse with almost knowing, almost
        breaking through.

River Edge:

now that the snow in the mountains
has ceased melting, the river's drawn in
its skirts, leaving us this gleaming

muck, a shore between sagging banks of ice
and the cold heave of current. April sun
lapping at the phosphorescence

in everything—orange weight on a lost
lure, rusted hook in the river lip, cracked
shells, slick, green-eyed stones—

all skeletal, sleeked and gnarled
by the river mouth. My boots weighted
with clay, I trek downriver, gripping

and skidding along the oozing sand.
With each quarter mile the sun
grows warmer, and fractious, contending

for every branch and bottle cap, every splinter
of day-glow plastic. Nothing is more beautiful
than anything else: this is how April warns us

and breaks us down. Upslope,
the dry-docked hulk of ice sheet, a study
in the structure of the washed-up

and winterkilled. Downslope, the river,
a loosened tongue, icy harangue, coughing
and singing over stones, eddying in the bends

and then surging on. The ice
is riddled, layers of collapsing spindles
clotted with grit, each slab eaten away

from underneath, a cave where the river
wintered. I mind the edge,
balancing between not looking up and not

plunging in. Boot top, surface shimmer, scrolling
wave hem. The floes are dimming shelves,
spent chandelier glass

I kick my way through. Three miles of slog
until the shore is drowned in a spill of roots
and rock, and I'm barred. The wind's

torqued to the north and the sun's downshifted,
blanketing the west in shadow. Turning,
I see the far side, a mirage,

spotlit, while on this bank, I ride the border
between cold and colder, disorder
and disorder, a painstaking

retraction, stammering toward home and its one
original idea, fire
enchained. All the way back,

the sky lowers, flooding to the horizon
with cloud, darkening the line
between ice and water.

Tony Ryan

Sharron Proulx-Turner

from *she is reading her blanket with her hands* (Fronterac House, 2008)

the intimacy of bark growing inside quiet rain

for graham scott angus

to name my feelings for you
would be to fly into the heart of a flower
you are
the love I found inside me
the day you were born
the snow & ice
turning to water on the streets

watching you swim
in boyhood
your body fluid & long
eliminating the distance
between forms

watching you skate
backwards on the ice
your form flawless
& you a melody

watching you run
the length of a rugby field
smiling open-mouthed
even through your mouthguard

watching you dance
barefoot
on top of the rocks
their circle
hosting a summer fire

the way you share the air
around your limbs
your arms & legs finding ways
around the edges of time

like your love for your family
& the way you'll love your own

your love of music
of art & books
robin hood
coyote & the big rock
rock & roll
& the guitar

you will always be
inside me
like the sound of crows
& the sun
even in the rain
whose light above the trees
holds hundreds of crows

& the fire inside the rain
flows outward
from the sun
open & quiet
under layers & layers of rock

you are
leaves facing one another
their voices so quiet
so low
even the birds
can't make out what they're saying

their wind on the water
flows skyward
whole songs

round & beautiful
waiting for the dream
that takes them home

hers was the hand of a woman

for barbra germaine angus

I woke up the other morning with an image of a dragonfly
hovering not six inches away from my eyes, directly in my field of
vision. my vision there, in dream world, unlike here, is perfect. I
could see into the eyes of that dragonfly & I could hear her tell me,
today is your lucky day. today is a day of miracles.

& right away I thought of you
of blue on blue
of water inside the sky
the sun hot & broken through the trees
around the edges of life

to name my love for you would be to
step outside the bounds of the ordinary
& into a place of miracles
where everything is rich & rain

like your long expressive fingers & hands
the way you move the hair from your face
in a brush stroke
a painting waiting to be put to canvas

you are like the greenest fern
rich & reaching
touching the brown of the ground
& the round of a tree
a great white pine
with new growth & new summer knowledge

you're like a fresh water wave
sun on your back

& a most perfect reflection
of a gull in flight
giving such a simple sharing
of a moment transformed

& inside there's a picture window
stained with the colour of water at midnight
in full moon

around every bend in the road
under every coffee table
inside every kitchen cupboard
in every mouthful of rice pudding
on every barrette you bead
& every sacred feather you dress
you leave behind a beauty
rare & fragrant
like august flowers
surrounded by woman's sage

tiny footprints walking into deep snow

for adrian scalplock

I long for something to say to you that'll make a difference for you,
yet I know that something must be yours to say to yourself. I can
tell you I love you, which I do, but this love only blossoms when
your anger-turned-inward allows you to understand there are many
kinds of love. the depth of my love for you could only truly be
expressed from deep inside a mountain.

silver inside every drop of rain
a reflection of the sun
waiting
on the other side of the storm cloud

behind every storm

in front of every storm
above the fog & the blizzard
the sun is there
remembering those who sacrifice
for their families
their communities
their people
for the healing of the world

giving the sacrifice of our bodies over to substances that blunder
our spirit, blunt our growth, poison our relationships with all
our relations, is the exact opposite of sacrificing our bodies for
our ancestors & our living relatives. rather than love & learning
& growth, there is hate & slow death, altered realities, cruelty to
others and to the self.

every time I witness you
go into the depths of self-hatred
I want to hear you play classical guitar
I want to see the little stuffed bee
on the pillow of your bed
I want you to cook some of that delicious food

you learned to cook during your childhood & your youth
I want to witness a range of emotion in you
laughter & compassion & peace

yellow grass under new greens
opening out into the day
the milky way's flight to heights
only the ancients know
& share with those who follow
a destiny through pain & loss
sorrow & bleakness
to find the newness of life

a night-round at sun dance
& you dancing for the ancestors
your legs light as air

your certainty contagious
your joy
absolute

every prayer you've tied to the tree
that tree of life lives
because you live

      & dance

          & sing

             & stay by your families

crickets & jazz music playing in my left ear

for renée lang

each tiny light on the water
contains a story
beautiful & fractured
each tiny light
is the sun
& as each wave
reaches the shore
the sun's reflection
lines up
with the water's edge

at that moment
in that instant
the knowledge & power
of the universe
enter the mother

      & now there's renée walking that parry island beach

you know, I first met you outdoors, you in full view against a
periwinkle prairie sky. you smelled like summer. your youthful

beauty is something I'll always love & your loud, loud laugh.
your humour & your fearlessness when you're face to face with
a challenge that would send an ordinary person running. your
constant love & a friendship that's so perfectly french, like family
ought to be. now when I'm with you, that prairie sky, open &
golden, reflects on that great ontario lake & I can hear the call of
the island tour boat, the call of the loon, & the hot, wet sun. you
are youth & charm, wit & grace, your long limbs stretched into
forever. orange-bodied spiders & the words wander across the page,
a leaf, a lifetime away.

      & margo coaxing a fire to life

& thunderstorms pass by & through & return on themselves, rainbows all around

for irma-dené beaulieu-mccaul

you are like laughing mountains, a moment's breath
between longing & dreamy mornings after a storm. late
this summer when I drove across the prairies I could see
spectacular lightning dancing in the west wind clouds.
I could see your blue there in that sky, a tenderness that
can't be touched or expressed on a page. like the sky at
this moment, after eleven already & a night sky still filled
with the day. time between times, your voice a music,
playing all night long.

& you, irma-dené
rain on wet wood
a song heard by tiny creatures
or small birds in the bitter cold
calling out to passers by
a welcome that carries right across town
down to the river

landing softly on the ice
only to travel south
to the ear of some small child
waiting for that moment alone
with the spirits of this place

when I'm with you I feel good. I feel joy & I look
forward to taking those feelings, emptying them into
my home & living inside them for the rest of my life.
those simple, quiet moments, your work space a place
full of life, the beads & the quills & the hides. your art
takes herself away & into your hands, your arms, your
knowing exact.

& too, irma-dené
you are a dance
up those stairs in a second
berry soup on the stove
the smell of sage after rain
a beginning so new
even the wind holds herself by the hand
& sings a children's morning song

holes between the clouds, their shapes changing the view of the
world. a cup of tea. a move down the street. life is good. life is a
giveaway. life is a gift.

yuccas in the badlands & the cactus calls you by your name

for aruna srivastava

I was just driving down 10th street & I saw you in my rearview,
your view of the stars & the birds & the lights of the city from
the window of your room. the river & the rain. I was reminded of
the day I met you on my first trip to vancouver. I was with other
students from a creative writing class & you opened your home like

a sunset, brilliant colour bursting from the inside out. I admit it. I
had the hots for you. shy & wobbly mouthed, I sat quietly, longing
to touch my face to yours, to touch the fine, silken hair reaching
out from your hairline, alive in the light of the sun. I longed to
put my lips to your ear, to whisper something funny & new. & oh,
your lips, so perfect around the words that came from you, slow
& quiet & wrapped inside your fingers, your delicate wrist. I even
stole a beautiful mug from your kitchen – shamelessly – thinking
to carry it home with me, to drink from your mug where your lips
had met the edge of your world every morning & mine would now
meet yours on my full prairie days.

you & I
have driven into each other's lives
slowly at first
& sometimes able to hold
each other until we're a world
inside this world
driving vancouver island to witness
the sunset that rises over japan
bright on the water of forever

& then driving the hills
to catch the morning sunrise
on the other side of the island
the evening greens dark on the roads
winding into a wilderness
illuminated only by a moon so full

we couldn't sleep for waiting
our limbs & faces lit like silver stars
& ocean spilling onto the sand
so loud with morning's light
we were able to hold a lifetime
in one small breath

I'll never forget that drive home, the black flowered mug on the
floor of the car & you alone again in your quiet vancouver home.
there was heavy, wet snow along the roger's pass – the kind of

snow that's breathless to walk in. I was driving at the time, a snow's slow pace & without warning, just ahead on the road was a large-antlered elk. the women in the back seat were asleep & my buddy in the front, like the elk, was stilled into staring, his eyes locked onto the eyes of the elk. I looked into the rearview, and behind us was an eighteen wheeler, close & snowy. I put the car in neutral & I started to pump the brakes, pump the brakes & I kind of danced myself with the steering wheel, forward & back, forward & back, yelling or singing, hey-hey-hey-hey, over and over again. that's it, just hey-hey-hey. the women in the back seat sat up, eyes forward, stunned into silence. I knew we would hit the elk & I prayed for that elk, for us in the car, the driver behind us. then the elk, that great wapiti, disappeared. just vanished right off the road.

it is said such a moment may be called many things. the elk may have been a shapeshifter, maybe a spirit from the other side. maybe a trickster. maybe a guide. maybe that elk saved us all from certain death that night. I drove all the way to calgary from the outskirts of vancouver that night, snow throughout the mountains. all the way home I settled in the good feeling about the times we would spend so close & yet, so far apart in our worlds. & that lovely black mug with orchids embossed with gold was with me for years.

yet the mug wasn't even yours
as you weren't ever to be mine
& now all these years later
still the ocean spills onto the land
& the full moon's coaxing
a long-winded bed of small sea animals
up into the sun & the wind
there is no beginning &
there is no end to the ocean's longing
no end to her songing
for the days ahead

together
we've heard the ocean cry
& we've heard the prairie grasses sing

we've seen chinook clouds
spread themselves like leaves across a sky
whose blues harmonize with the wind
their backs arching into tomorrow
like a ballet dancer caught in mid-stride
a beauty stilled behind the eyes
& along the beaches of the west coast sea

& still
to me
you are
open spaces
nose hill in spring
with crocuses & buffalo beans
& you a wind

> your quiet grace
> > a water poem
> > fluid

from **anxiety of influence**

remembering the 14 young women engineering students who were
slaughtered in montréal, december, 1989, and the 27 known women
whose tortured remains were found in british columbia in 2002

colonization.

inferiorization. that's us. the female. afraid to yell. afraid to hurt
the men for fear. for fear of what? of being accused of being over-
sensitive to our past. by them. men. what past? okay, our present.
present yourself as preferably blond, beautiful, slender, senseless,
and above all, ageless. an arm piece, please. no wit unless it rhymes
with tit. tits and ass. for fear of being left. fear of being beaten. to
death. cold in the night. fe male. wo man. suffix to male. men.
horseshit.

the luck is in the referent. the h – o – r – s – e. the thing that kicks.
the bite is worse. I had a dream once where I was forced to eat my
own flesh. flashed a toothy grin at sigmund. he's dead too, though
I read somewhere that he died grinning. grinning and holding a
hardon. his. his fingers had to be broken in order to pry them off.
his penis too. had to be broken. kafka's dead too. he was impotent.
too bad he hated his dad so much. hated brothels and lentil soup
too.

hypocrisy.

case no. 1. helen betty osborne. 19. cree first nation. brutally raped
and slaughtered by 4 white men. 4 x 4 and 16 years to bring the
men to trial. horseshoes up the ass.

case no. 2. primitive masculine fearfulness is no less than one in 29
human beings. the white male man. from the horse's mouth.

case no. 3. women are nothing like horses. or 4 wheel drives. sure,
some like to eat apples, but generally, women won't want to move.
even man and his gods cannot prod her. whips, fists, boots, bile.
still: stuck. still. skirt, pussy, piece. horsebreath.

prayersong.

england. 1941. virginia wolf. suicide. if you insist upon fighting to
protect me, or your country, let it be understood, as woman, I have
no country.

vietnam. 1969. women in tiger cages. can't stand. can't sit. can't
lie. can only squat. became paralyzed or dead. beaten unconscious,
daily, for singing in their cells. singing songs of liberation. sweet
harmony.

kanehsatake. 1990. grandmothers in solidarity with mohawk clan
mothers. our land is sacred. we support the actions of our young
people who defend our lands. we say further, if mohawk blood

is shed, you'd better be prepared to shed the blood of aboriginal
grandmothers. of aboriginal women and children. because a nation
is not broken until its women are down.

firerhymes. fine white lines. lights out. good night, my little
children. 80% of the world's refugees. those who flee from
invasion, persecution, or political danger. to be raped. beaten.
starved. 70% of the world's poor. those who lack the means of
comfortable subsistence. woman. with her little children. feeling
insane. clinging to the truth of her own. rocking. singing. still.

coffeeing among the poles of a tipi on international aboriginal day, 2004

for shirley bear

last night as I was falling asleep I could see the face of a grizzly,
large & deep. then this morning, the moon full on my bed still,
I woke myself up with the sound of my own laughter. I'd wanted
to write on for pages & pages until a miracle found its way out
from the straight lines & the tidy printing, until the blue of the
snow becomes the white of the sky, until the page becomes your
brushstroke, whose blues move forward from the past, a past whose
skies are never ending, their nighttime melodies striking along
ancient stars.

I remember when I drove you to banff & I wore a sweater so blue
I could smell my own sweet smell of clean & each stitch on the
cotton swam away into discrete, long melodies. & you a song,
a woman who sees creator's beauty everywhere – in the tar &
concrete rooftops & on the faces & shapes of women who grace
vancouver's east end. you plant yourself like a sugar maple, solid
& cycling up the steep mountainsides, up from the sea & onto the
wet, blue hills. you are mimi, mother to so many women & your
love for peter is like a honeybrown bear with her family all around.

yesterday morning there was a raven sitting in the top branch of a

great blue spruce, the branch that sticks straight up from the body
of the tree. the raven looked like she should bend the branch, but
the branch held fast under her heavy blue weight. she kept yelling
& singing, yelling & singing, & I felt a kinship – tried to make
out what she was saying through the glass on my window. she was
telling me to keep my eyes open & to laugh out loud, that life is
good here on the side of this mountain.

not two hours later
I witnessed the birth of a deer
on the side of that mountain
browns & greens against a new summer sky
a shy sky

still chilled & slow
& a leafy-white glow
like flocks of small birds

yet small red flowers
have found their way
into this chilly air
they're used to living here
so high above the world
in & out with the wind
& snowy downpours

a circle of people around a fire, their voices low against this
mountain's grace. & there you are, your words a canvas, your small
frame's shadow casting blues & reds & browns across the valleys,
intensified by the late day's light, your silver hair blowing like water
on stone, long & loose & one small drop at a time.

thousands of butterflies
small & blue & brown
fly through banff
at day's first light
their starry wings
beads of silver
on a berry blue sky

you laugh your beautiful laugh, your beautiful legs walking,
cycling the sides of mountains & the hills of vancouver & tobique,
rollerblading into your seventies, your beautiful daughters & sons
& grandchildren & great-grandchildren & peter clair's love of
baskets & books & beauty & you.

& there you are again
wonderful still
making paper from buffalo sage

& taking photos of flowers
in the rain

layers of paper
holding themselves like family
& clouds over the mountains
low enough to live in
their world a knowing
rich & full
their raining eastward onto the prairie
inside the sweetgrass
inside the sage

& still
the mountains speak of you
of red on blue
the shape of a future flower
after rain
if I were a painter
that would be my work today
red on blue

the wisdom in these mountains can change the world. life's lasting
moments, stilled only long enough to blossom, a redness that
would embarrass anyone unprepared for so much voice.

from *she walks for days inside a thousand eyes: a two-spirit story*
(Turnstone Press, 2008)

germaine:
a moose at the top of a mountain
and even barefoot the moon is quiet

so it is I, germaine, am learning to listen and watch, wait and be still,
laugh and cry, in ways I never imagined. the voices of these powerful
two-spirit women, my sisters and my relations, my ancestors, fill my
daytime like night-life dreams and I feel an awe I'm completely unable
to come to terms with. I know what I need to do next, yet to actually
jump down and through that hole? to actually follow that red road
covered with so many quiet leaves? this takes confidence and direction.
until, what? two days ago? I was just an ordinary woman driving along
a prairie road during an early summer rainstorm. ahead of me were the
mountains, snow-peaked still and ready to breathe out the wisdom of
the tree people with compassion and great feeling. that's where I was
headed, to the mountains.

and now, here I am, in the middle of a miracle and all I can do is feel
like a frightened girl faced with a decision only her mother can make.
what would my mother say? she'd say, smarten up. just do it. jump.
what would my nokomis, my grandmother, say? she'd tell me, my girl,
can't lives on won't street. you've got what it takes. and even so, even
throughout my all-day struggle with jump, don't jump, jump, don't
jump, that crow stays with me, leaving only for short periods of time. I
find the bird's presence comforting and familiar. I know there's a reason
why I'm here. I know I'm in the spirit world, and even at that, I still feel
like a girl-child inside someone else's dream. I finally ask in the smallest
of voices for the help and guidance of the young crow and the small
spotted eagle, who have clearly presented themselves as my helpers here.

in that instant, I hear them both laugh a belly laugh, and I laugh too.
I throw down the stone and jump through the hole. I try to keep my
eyes open as I see a foothills valley at nightfall, ready for a new day, a

new season, preparing for winter. I see yellow grasses rushing into me,
bursting with reds and oranges, the colours of blood, life's sacred. in the
spring the meadowlarks nest and sing their incredible song. in the fall
it's like the grasses are their song made new again at day's end. and the
mountains. such power to hold in your hair, your skin, your eyes, and
you can drive that power home on a bus or in a car, wear that power
for days on end. I know I owe these mountains something heartfelt
and loving, a prayer of thanksgiving. and just as I'm about to land, I
hear a voice from deep within the mountains after the heat of the day
finds its way skyward. the rock calls out to the ancient ones, spilling out
fresh, long tales and delicate orange blossoms, day's end light the only
backdrop to a colour whose brilliance is the most delicate, the most
sensuous of songs.

oh, my sisters, pick up your power
my sisters, claim your voice
remember those gone before us
and pray for those yet to come

Matt Rader

from *Living Things* (Nightwood Editions, 2008)

Mustang

No more racehorse. We showed her no mercy:
Stoned out of our stupid ever loving minds,
Half-cut, underage, ready to tempt any kind
Of line we came across, and yet somehow we
Always made it home safe, my brothers and me
(No jail or pregnancy and only one bloody nose

To speak of but don't). Who bloody well knows
How close we came to the edge, what mercy
Moved those telephone poles buried as landmines
At the side of road, or smothered the sirens we
Heard in the distance trailing us wunderkinder
Of luck by seconds not minutes. My girl and me

Liked to park and fuck or she'd just take me
In her mouth as I drove the coast trying to nose
The needle and us into the unknown. My kind
Of ride. My kind of horse. Please, pay no mind
To the rubber we left behind like a worm of mercy
On the asphalt, a gesture to the old gods we

Aimed to replace. Wherever we wanted to go we
Went in her leather interior, my brothers and me,
Drinking Lucky Lager and rolling doobies. Mercy
On those who got in our way. I had it in my mind
She'd never die. Then, oozing like a child's nose,
The engine spread a quilt of green and kind-

Red colours in the carport. We weren't the kind
To monkey with motors or carburetors or wee
Cracks in whatever-the-hell-it-was deep in the mind

Of that machine that drooled its unwanted mercy
All over the place. We kept driving, our noses
To the grindstone of our own demise, the shimmy

Of the engine into ever higher registers a meme
We'd all been infected by so ignored as any kind
Of sign. When a horse falters, no time or mercy
Will make her show any better. *Wowee Zowee*
Was still ten years out of reissue and our minds
Soaked in its weird from the stereo. No one knows

Just where we go when we go. Some folks diagnose
Jesus, Jell-O, scrap metal; give me a mercy of mind
Of the kind that Mustang gave my brothers and me.

Chainsaw

Toothless on Walker's wall, the chainsaw
strung up like any dead animal to bleed out
into a tin a slow viscous drip of black stout.
Walker's workshop was nature's scofflaw,
a backdoor parts-exchange and trophy case
for the age of motorized blades. Saw chains
sagged but held their place in the equation
upon the wall, zeroes like paralyzed faces.
Rosaries of pitch and gauge, Walker prayed
each link with file and rag. When he spoke
the room deepened. Shade bred with shade,
charmed the starter chord, primed the choke.
The motor stuttered and in its stutter talked.
The chain whirled like the hands of a clock.

Domestic Work

You are doing the dishes as you do every night
After dinner and every morning before work
And the light dim over the sink where you sink

Your arms in warm soapy water like a doctor
Elbow-deep in a calving heifer willing to touch
Anything that needs to be cleaned or delivered,

Our silver instruments of custom and manners
Lining the sink like straw in the cowshed stall,
Soiled with saliva and foodstuffs your fingers

Step in as you step in with cloth to clean them,
A soapy mucus greasing the water like blood
On the hindquarters of the heifer and her calf

Who is coming now into the world backwards,
Gangly legs ungraspable in the grasping hands
Of the doctor, sweaty, slick like the silverware

You scrub and slide a washcloth over and over
As if by sheer force and force of will you could
Transform the metal object into a newborn cow,

Woozy in a pool of fluids, wobbly-headed, struck
On its anvil skull by the iron of air and gravity,
And braying like a mule as it teeters underneath

The hull of its mother and braces itself to feed
As all mammals do in the beginning without need
Of knives or forks or fingers but only need itself,

Suds from the cutlery you hold in your hands
Dripping as you run the tap and rinse the tools
And set them upside down in the drying rack.

A Drawing for Jan Dayman

You are dying and having trouble
So lie in quiet repose with your eyes
Closed as if for practice. I've come
To draw your picture, as if to capture
Your likeness on paper and take it
Away with me would be one less
Thing to slow you on your journey.
I hoke around on the empty page
With my pen until I begin to see
Your earthly features appear there
Pressed into another plane before
Me. Still, you continue to breathe.

Easter

At Heceta Beach, the tide draws taut
the linen of sand we lay our blanket on
to sleep. But I am a restless sleeper and lie
awake watching the beach roll beneath
the feet of a boy who runs to raise a kite

as the rolling ocean runs to raise the blue
kite of sky above us. In another dream
the ocean too is a restless sleeper who
tosses and turns and curls up in the covers
as I do at home in our bed leaving you

exposed against the cold bedroom wall.
The ravens are fledged shadows aloft,
black flecks on the rolling eye of the sun.
Below the snuffed candle of the lighthouse, young arborists scale deadheads

as Christ scaled the cross into heaven
and back again. And when the moon rolls

back the rock of sea tonight, gone will be
any evidence of you or me asleep here,
human on this faithful shore, complete.

The Birds of Canada

I am driving a freeway in another country
When on the shoulder a blown tire becomes
A carcass for two turkey vultures turning
As on a child's mobile above this crib
Of continent and I remember the shoji
Screen in your apartment, silk-screened
With two green herons and your silhouetted
Body. You undressed in troubled modesty
Behind the herons' geisha fan of wings
While my mind circled your body being
Shaped and unshaped behind the screen.
And all at once all the birds of Canada,
Bushtits and juncos and sparrow hawks
Red-winged blackbirds, blue jays and harriers,
More birds than I could name including
The great blue heron, sandpiper and vireo,
Turnstone, merganser, mourning dove,
Skylark, the lesser scaup, the oldsquaw,
Ravens and crows, even the last great auk,
Lift into the sky, an enormous shoji screen
Of feathers and wings and the sun a shoji lamp
In the early hours of the twenty-first century.

Emergency Broadcast System

When the radio cuts out in a fit of static
or the picture goes blue for half a second longer than I'd expect or the lights flick
off in perfect weather, I'm always quick

to think, *This is it*, the one we've all been
waiting for, the news we knew to imagine
but could not imagine nonetheless, the end
of life as we live it, careless in this land,

and when you let go of my hand and stand,
balanced by your own mass and muscle,
a fresh knack for gravity at your command,

begin to look around, wonder, slyly smile,
then, one foot in front of the other, totter
forward into the future, fearless, my daughter.

On First Looking into Larkin's "Aubade"

I get up each day in the dark and in the dark go
To sleep half-drunk, having said not half what
I meant to say to those I love or love to know
Only by sight: the gypsy-eyed girl and the mutt
Outside the market where I buy coffee and bread
Each morning and toss a few coins in her cup;
The Korean dude next door I've given up
Talking to, to whom I give only a nod of the head

And who gives up nothing of himself in return.
I stand in the carport at half-four and smoke,
The world soft around the edges, soon to relearn
The shape light brings to juniper and oak,
How what we see in daylight is less than whole
And also more so, how we distinguish things
From things in a catalogue of being
We call the complete picture: what wicked toll

We pay for the sleep we receive after dusk:
Each dry hour upon hour of work and solitude
In our own inescapable skin. If death is the musk
Men like us smell and awake to, that exudes

From every living thing the moment we are
Exhumed from the dark to that last birth back
Into oblivion, it's fear of love that attacks
Our sleep and leads us alive from library to bar

To books to bed without speaking. Such shade
Leeches sweetness from living. Light after light
Winks awake on my street, and I am made
And unmade by the nagging thought of what might
And might not be. No god serves also those
Who stand and wait, for no god serves anything
Save itself. I am at odds with my own thinking
And the ghosts I wear on my mind like clothes:

The sweater the gypsy girl filched from my truck
When the weather turned. I smile and swear
Every time I see her shivering with bad luck,
Tucked into her Shepherd mutt, that ugly sweater
I used to wear wearing her there in the wet cold,
As just now, the Korean dude on his back stairs
Steps down into the half-dark, half-lit, unaware
I see him adorned in dawn's thin garment of gold.

Monty Reid

from *The Luskville Reductions* (Brick Books, 2008)

And that's the point isn't it?
To continue.

Not just to remember
but to remain.

Woof of bullfrogs that first hot night.
woof of data in the archives.

Oh they sing
through the hot air

for the uncatalogued
loves. For whatever

one can say about them.
Take the air

the hood of air over us
take it off.

             *   *   *

The rain is finished

but the way rain beads on the dented fenders
of what has been loved

isn't.

The rain is finished

but the sheen of rain still on the concrete
isn't.

Rags of light
pegged behind the thunderclouds.

The rain is finished
but there is always something

in the lid of the body
that resists

and something with bigger holes in it
than the holes in rain.

       *   *   *

What is nature, anyway?
asked my friend over lunch

as if it had been inadequately theorized
or perhaps because we hadn't seen each other in years

and he thought
maybe I'd have some idea by now

but I didn't have any kind of answer
other than to pick up my fork

and cut into the lamb with figs and pomegranate
which he'd recommended.

So my theory is nature is never an answer
but a question

just not the question
I needed to ask at the time.

Like a fork.
Like the hand around it

Like the other hand too...

       *   *   *

...The nipple
rises
to the tongue

how often?

we were togther 32 years
let's say we had sex on average two times a week
allowing for absences or sick leave
or the above average holidays
and that hi-rate first year

that would be 32 times 52 times 2
equals 3328

and the nipple
still rises
to the tongue

times 2...

                    *   *   *

...Yes
I still have the mandolin.

I can play it
modestly.

My little finger
wears a hole

right through the finish
and down into the soft wood.

Every song I learn
works its way through

whatever
makes the song possible.

Yes, it looks bad
that worn down surface

but down there
where the sound is made

it still sounds ok...

       *   *   *

...Tv glow
from the other room.

It's always the light
from this world

that follows you around...

       *   *   *

...When I finally
gathered up the garden hose
late September

an image of its soul
remained in loops on the sidewalk.

Like all souls
it was made out of a speckle
of dust and dead bugs.

I rolled the so-called
unkinkable hose
around its plastic spindle.

A last trickle of summer water
spilled out

at both ends...

         *   *   *

...Once, for your birthday
which I never forgot

I made a card of pixie cups and sleeping mosses
from the shaded ridge above our house

and once, for our anniversary
with its flexible date

I gave you a bouquet of spray-painted tubing that said
my love is like a red, red hose.

Now I am making a card
for all occasions

out of your sheer underwear
with the exact red hearts

that are sometimes in us
and sometimes

precisely not...

         *   *   *

...Don't expect the truth
from any of the things you took.

I'm not the first to remark that they lie
even when they don't need to.

Just as I won't trust anything
you left behind.

I found the book, Elizabeth Bishop's
complete poems

I thought was lost.
No, to be honest
I thought you had taken it.

As for the unfinished songs
I left on your computer

delete them

let them go into the sub-drives
of memory

or finish them and claim them as
yours.

Then they will be...

*　　*　　*

...The river can't be naked
enough

to come into this room.

Only a small part of yourself
belongs

to yourself here.

Not the naked part...

*　　*　　*

...Yes we spent some time
at that temple of dishes
in the sink

the forks prayed
the knives prayed
they were baptized

and reborn.

Hallelujah I say
Amen.

I'll wash
and you dry...

Sofia Omelkovica

...I think the soul
is really

just the little black off-the-shoulder dress
you wore to the office party.

In the morning there it is
on the floor.

And I think the heart
is that delicate necklace with its solitaire

that reflected
even the most ephemeral moonlight.

It's on the floor
too.

I think that the past
just has to wear

itself out
and that a kiss can be removed

and wrapped up in the tissue it came in
until it's needed again.

Some party...

*   *   *

...Unexpected events
become the expected

until there is no unexpected
left

which is why every system
generates an outside
the system

and then the events much beyond

our selves
become possible

and therefore beautiful again.

Tape up the last cardboard box
and haul it away.

Put me inside you
again...

*   *   *

Catherine Yuan Chi

Harold Rhenisch

from *Return to Open Water Poems New and Selected* (Ronsdale Press, 2007)

Hymn for Small Engine Repair

As the faller longs for virgin timber

    and the moss crackling underfoot

So do we long for our Lord

and as the pipefitter longs for Saturday

    so he can wake up beside his wife
    and turn over to hold her

    because his skin feels like sheet metal

and his bones like galvanized iron

    so does our god
    long for lightning all night
    and white rain in the morning

so he can watch all the farmers get up
and walk around aimlessly, waiting

    not knowing what to do

with such freedom!

    So does the god of the fouled sparkplug

open up a small engine repair shop
in the weatherbeaten garage behind his trailer

    It is perfect!

right down to the "Briggs and Stratton" sign

nailed above the door
and the rusted lawnmowers

    strewn around through the cactus
    and the sagebrush

When I sit down and think on it
I want to weep

    Because when the people start to come

in their nylon-mesh hats with the sun-faded brims
their pickups bouncing over the shale

    and drag their broken machines before him

I want to see him come out
of his dark doorway

    Because I want to see the pity in his eyes

I want to see how he handles it

    when his people return to him

I want to be *there*

What to Do When You See Pat Lane's U-Haul Broken Down at Standing Rock

Swing open the back doors
and let the horses out.

Sit down on the soft shoulder
and watch them run across the alfalfa
to the river.

They slip among the fern-shadows
of the cottonwoods
and are gone.

Ahh! Can't you smell the knapweed?
Like creosote on the fingers.

As for Pat, brew him a cup of coffee
out of the crushed gravel.
Sweeten it with the sun —
overhead like a quail's egg.

He's been away for too long.

The breakdown was a prophecy.
Why do you think they rent those trucks
so cheap?

How did you think they managed it?

Subsidized industry — that's the Canadian way.

You don't need to say a thing to each other,
just sit there shoulder to shoulder,

as the grass sways in the moon's tides,
and the mountains drift, weightless,

and the stones shudder,
flick their manes, and run.

Evelyn, B.C., 1947

When my mother
was a girl
she lived in the shadow
of a glacier

All summer
the wind fell
off the ice
and into her

In winter
the moose

would follow the cows
into the barn
at night

there in the dark
with the great wooden beams
between them
and the frozen
light of the moon
they would stamp
fretfully

In the cabin
of rough-fitted logs
behind the barn
a young girl
would toss
in her sleep

around her
there was an inch
of frost
on the newspaper
of the walls

Sometimes a birch tree
would explode nearby
with the cold
and she would startle
awake

When she walked
to the main house
in the morning
in that dry winter air
that tasted of steel

her feet wrapped in newspaper
inside her gumboots
She would come in
to the thin

dark warmth of the kitchen

Her mother
was training her
not to waste food
and so served to her
the boiled
pig's lung
she had choked on
the night before

and milk
that tasted of cow's breath
and greasy hair

While outside her father
was pulling open
the great doors
of the barn
and the moose
stepped out past him
antlers held proudly
above them

like thoughts frozen
as soon as they hit the air

All the time
there was not a breath of wind
Only the cold
slipping off the glacier

and the wolves
slipped through the shadows
between the birch trees
behind the house

thin with hunger
they walked
right on the surface
of the snow.

Telling the Truth

When someone asks you for the truth,
for God's sake, lie. Give them what they want.

And if they ask again, lie a second time,
a third, a fourth, until you're hoarse;

sign every paper they slide across to you,
their finger on the line, where they ask you

for your house, your car, your stocks;
pay the interest on your debt, accept the truth,

stand before the camera and tell them how it was,
how it's all true — you blew up that bridge,

stole those plans, took your boss's wife
to Palm Beach — for you have been to Hell

and back these last few weeks, and deserve
no less than an end to lies, fine print,

and sound bites, not to mention sleep,
what with all you've had to swallow

just to stand here in my place and defend
those actions you know nothing of,

denied a chance to say what you do know,
while I stand in for you, with my briefcase

and my files, whispering in your ear, that what
you say in this court matters not,

that you know yourself at last (I squeeze
your arm), that truth is a lie.

Desdemona's Wedding

Desdemona dresses in her grave clothes
for her wedding to the Moor, dies her hair pink
and wears a pin in her tit, slips
out of bed at night, sports studded collars
and crawls on her knees through stone streets
that night she married Othello
and the sea fell to the stars.
Venice drew a cape around itself
and men drank it like wine
as the tide suckled their houses.

And even that happened too slowly.
Between jealous rage and a feather pillow
over lips that sought to speak a cry
of reason or a word of love,
whole centuries passed,
navies sailed out and sank in smoke,
armies bled in muddy streets,
men were dispatched like pigs,
Mozart composed his symphonies,
Beethoven went deaf, Schumann mad,

so don't say that thing
about Desdemona, that gossip about the Moor,
the right of conquest,
the soldier's lance, and don't ever
say the expected thing, that love is madness,
that the only madness is in the mind.
To have a mind is madness.
Pray you can hold out five minutes
between your wedding and *your* death.

You Can't Go Home Again

I ran over a puppy
on the reserve in the dark,

when the stars fell in the rain
and the road breached the rabbit brush.

In that hot valley the yellow-feathered hills
are folded out of Packards,

the rust so thin a single blade of grass
pushes through them like lovers in a bed

that's just turned into an abandoned
log yard littered with cut glass.

Baby, we're our own intravenous now,
but back then I was just driving home to you,

and the Chevy groaning,
with cutthroat trout drunk on trout flies,

swimming in packed circles
in white honey buckets, smelling of pollen

from Fort St. John. God,
give me the teeth of a bear.

When the puppy ran out of its mind and I clipped it
with my greasy Macpherson struts, Fuck,

before it ran back into the Players cigarette
tin of the abandoned

basketball court razor wired with knapweed,
my true love, I would have rolled you

between paper fingers and set you alight,
you would have gone up like the little children

in Waco huddling in the cooler with their gingham mothers
stamped out of dough with a rusty tin cutter.

Now the pines are dying. We should not
have loved long enough to see this.

Now the rivers of light drinking the river of rain
flow under our feet in blue flame

and my long trip home is hung out to dry
like whale vertebrae from a five-hundred-year-old

midden, tied up with loose blue nylon rope
that washed overboard from a trawler

scrawling through the sub pens at Bangor.
Ten years have passed, ten years of words

and children in the dying forests
of the high plateau, yet I'm still in that night

when the puppy ran across the dark road
to bring me home, and I drove on.

Shane Rhodes

from *The Bindery* (NeWest Press, 2007)

A Note from Zacatecas

In the painting of Saint Francis in El Convento de Guadalupe just outside of Zacatecas, the anonymous landscape is of an imagined Europe — far off hills with tended sheep, oak forest, a small stream, a dream of homeland. The colours of the painting are dark greens and tar-oil blacks aged by the light and dry air as if to prove a heaven should be composed only of light. The convent was built by the Franciscans in the 19th century and called El Colegio Apostólica de Propaganda Fide — the padres in their brown cowled shawls sweating out their abeyances in the wind-kept deserts to the north. By the 19th century, it would have been unclear for whom they were apostolating. The light through the windows now is full of a blue that will fill the streets with sleeping dogs. Bells continue to ring from the high campanile for morning mass, linked by a long rope of sisal to a padre in the plaza below. He pulls on the rope, gathering what remains of the faithful.

La Música

Two young men play guitar. They play in a small house where bare light bulbs hang from the concrete ceiling. Outside it rains and between breaks in the rain you can hear waves roaring to shore. We are on the Gulf of Mexico and with each wave you can smell the rancid breath of the sea, a mouth that has tasted and eaten everything. One of the guitar players has a cell phone clipped to his belt and behind him, on the wall, is a small shrine to the Virgin of Guadalupe, her brown eyes lowered with all the beatific adoration of an overdose. The men sing traditional songs — *pura yucateca* — to an old man who sits on a blue stool before them. It is his birthday and one of the boys playing guitar is his son who sings with a clear, low voice and wears eyeglasses to look like John Lennon. The old man has eyes that move with the semblance of sight. He has been blind for 27 years and has never seen the son who plays before him. The walls of the house are worn at the level of his hands. He sits before the singers and around him are the people who have gathered to celebrate his birthday. Somebody begins to dance and they sing louder. There is food. There is beer. He is dying. They sing old songs not to please the old man but because everybody sings old songs. He mouths the words he knows and teaches the singers new songs they don't know. He is another year older. He is crying.

A Picture by Brueghel: Landscape with Icarus Falling

contra Auden

Brueghel was right —
everyone sees
nothing at least
once in the life
of a tragedy.
To the left,
in the painting,
the tenant farmer
walks behind a horse —
four centuries
of ploughing
and not once
has he dropped
his seed.
The light here
will be taken
without footnote
by Monet.
Yet the fallen
boy beating
the sea with
broken wings
is less
amazing
than the ship

sailing by
with its paint-thick hold
full of slaves
from Mozambique.
The shepherd
stares away so
intent on nothing
his eyes
gouge out.
Such private things
done
with public weight.
He was wrong,
the old master,
about suffering.
It does not ascend
beyond this human
position —
like Icarus to myth —
but profits
beneath paint
(a scream through water)
in parenthesis.

Argument

Isle aux Coudres, Québec

Early morning and workers
rise to their labour. Nothing more

important to the factory owner,
owners, its chairman of the board

whose penstrokes ring out, saying
"The employed and the unemployed,

upon which half will you fall?";

saying, "The thickness of the air

is not the natural resistance
to machines but work left undone,

finish it"; saying, "How can we
assess its worth unless

we smelter its metal?"

The efficiencies spoiling
in the dark asp of my blood.

Counted amongst its standing reserve,
we whose worthless pastime

is poetry? Our words
are the abacus its grief takes.

In the evening, there will be
the smell of sea, again,

an age of Homer, luxury
and the quiet stir of spermicide

in my jeans
beneath the chestnut trees.

Argument: An Explication

Isle aux Coudres, Québec

The first who landed go unrecorded.
The second buried their thin dead
in the thin top soil —
death made the purchase true
just as the tide pushes deep
in these palatable rocks.
It must have been a dream to them
after Europe and its misery,

the sea and its mystery,
the unending smell of men.

I sit watching tankers pass in the dark,
their constellations of light
far off in the river current
carry life's dark matter
from sweatshops in the far east.
Slowly through the night water
they move like trauma.

In the morning, when we wake,
there will be an age of Homer again
and luxury. It will be the time
of gods, when my fathers rose
to the morning shift and ate in the dark
food they could not see.
Now, there is nothing but me
and that inch of darkness
outside me, where my body drowns.
This life will leave few marks
in the ledger or graves
beneath chestnut trees.

Slaughter

A 7 millimetre Mauser
with a hair trigger, oiled to a sheen
through use and gun bluing. A gift
shot through with a pride beyond talk —
you empty yourself into a child,
my father thought.

We took it out for target practice
on Boxing Day, hitting rings
on a plywood sheet. That fall,
a friend and I bought deer tags

and loaded our own shells —
percussion caps sunk deep.

On the third day of season,
we drove to the nearest bush.
Shots of rum steeled us by ounce
to the rifle's weight
(another friend injecting vodka
before stumbling to the bush).

The hair trigger pushed forward
with a click. Three quick shots
lit a burn in the rifle's metal
and downed a child-sized doe.
We passed her body across

the fence and hacked her neck —
her blood blew across the snow
beating like a song fade out.
The hind hooves strapped
to the barn rafters,
I slit the soft belly skin

between teats, sex and ribs
and stripped the hide. Wrapped
in butcher paper, we froze the meat
for winter. I wrapped the gun in felt
and locked it back in my father's
gun cabinet, the bolt pulled out.

Paintbrushes

for the Lepchas

The day was hot and my father drove the gravel logging road through the
high mountain pass with its many pot-holes and small silver creeks that had
overrun their edges. My brother and I were promised, if we were good, we
would stop to pick Indian Paintbrushes.

>   Heated pine.
>   Lumber dust sifts
>   through the open window.

We were let out into a small flat meadow of marsh grasses, flowers and
stunted spruce covered at the base with thick clumps of moss. The air was
tense as steam rose from the heating muskeg and each purple bloom strained
upward in the light. Indian Paintbrushes. Looking back on it now, it was
beautiful I'm sure, but I remember feeling disappointed. I had literally
expected "paint brushes" and had hoped to paint with them.

>   *Whatever being is born,*
>   *know it is sprung*
>   *through the union of the field*
>   *and the knower of the field*

says the Bhagavad-Gita. Krishna is not talking of small mountain meadows.
Even if he is, Arjuna doesn't care for he prepares, regretfully, syllable by
syllable, for battle. It is an English translation bought from a bookstore in
Darjeeling in the middle of summer. Cloud swirls in the valleys below.
Directly opposite the bookstore and 70 miles to the northwest starts
Kanchenjunga, the third highest mountain in the world. On any clear day, it
sits on the edge of your vision massive and snow covered. In the steep valleys
below, women labourers, wicker baskets strapped to their heads, pick the first
green flush of orange pekoe tea (Super Fine Golden Flowery Orange Pekoe
Number One).

>   Over a year since
>   I have heard from you
>   my friend.

> As for grandfather, he is
> dead and T'shangu
> full of snow.

Which reminded me, when I read it in your letter, of something I had read once in a travel book. Since the turn of the century, with the exception of a few foreigners, mountain climbers no longer summitted (that great mountaineering verb) Kanchenjunga but always stopped a few metres short. Because the mountain-top is sacred and not for the foot of man.

Cuttings

South Saskatchewan river at night, blade silver with moon and willow hung. Eight hundred miles before the prairies release (like a lover holding another within) its muddy water to the Arctic Sea.

The weeping willows must have been brought here by the Dutch and German settlers who took the land from the retreating Nitsitapii and Nēhilawē.

Blackfoot and Cree, we might say.

I know the tree's Latin name (salix babylonica) because I know of Linneaus (swedish taxonomist) with his mind sharpened beyond scientific rigor. *Babylonica* he named it

> *Upon the willows we hung our harps as, by the*
> *river, we sat down and wept*

though the tree came from China.

I camped two weeks in the empty farmland below the river's confluence with the Red Deer, a wintering ground of the Plains Cree. My boyfriend picked me up after two weeks, staying the night in a hunting cabin amongst the rifles, gunpowder, skins and decoys of real men.

Drop a willow branch in mud, and it will sprout roots. Drop it into a pail (my grandmother said) with other plant cuttings and they too will take root.

A Cree woman, her legs crippled by diabetes, her face pitted and scarred,

living on the streets in Prince George. She told me, as a child, she had once
been invited by her father, a Chief, to meet the Governor General in Ottawa
to renegotiate a treaty.

Chewed willow bark must have been used during the plagues of small pox,
measles and scarlet fever.

But my father went alone, she said, afraid I might swipe the silverware.

Cold ache of the river current.

                        The quiet grip of roots.

We've been asleep so long.

The Blues

Driving through the Rockies, I listen to Hank Williams and his heart-felt
blues in the spring rain while the mountains turn white to blue as the
snowpack melts. *Heart-felt* because it was my father's truck and I felt
lonesome that I hadn't seen him in so long. *Heart-felt* because there is
something in the core wailing appeals to.

He sang "Your Cheatin' Heart" on the recording and I sang the chorus with
him, loud, the way one sings in the late spring with windows open and
mountain sheep by the side of the road. And when I mouthed the words to
myself that night in the mountain town hostel, the kids around me looked up
from their beers and smiled.

Hank Williams, dead at the age of 29 in the back seat of a Cadillac after
alcohol and drugs took too great a toll (the liner notes tell me) on his heart.

The snowpack that winter had been meagre and already farmers complained
of a coming drought. They wailed in the newspapers, coffee shops and phone-
in radio shows as if weather were a kind of infidelity, a kind of cheatin' to
bemoan in public space.

And this unending expanse (would my father call it a *feelin'* or would he just
sit and sigh?) gives the music its nervous rhythm and bass. You can hear it in

the passing pickup trucks and taverns, a courageous syncopation pounding down roll after roll of fenceline across an open plain.

The blues, they say, has the power to purge the heart.

And though the tape was warped by successive years of summer heat, and though the songs fell into and out of the standard twelve bar frame, and though my father's farm was up for sale (land his *sweet daddy* had cleared – *such a beautiful dream*) and the future was filled with sorrow and drought, I sang.

And the song was relief, prayer to the unfaithful of the unfaithful, because finally someone had gotten it right: You sing because you are 28 and killing yourself. You sing because you are 60 and selling your farm. You sing because the only easy endings and beginnings are in songs where there is call and response even when no one listens or responds

and you sing.

Mansel Robinson

from *FAST FORWARD NEW SASKATCHEWAN POETS* (Hagios Press, 2007)

A Poet Prepares

I've been thinking keep it simple, stupid
Yeah, just make 'em laugh if I can
Tell 'em how I come from the prairies
A land so flat that when your wife walks out
You can watch her leave for three whole days
I'm thinking make 'em laugh 'cause
Comedy pays better than tragedy and
It surely as hell costs less

So yeah make 'em laugh
Though I'm flirting too
with a political theme
Something in a post-modern style with a
Bruce Cockburn reference about
Lovers in a dangerous time
Layer in Bogie and Bergman, the airstrip in Casablanca
The troubles of three little people, their little hill of beans
(A po-mo pastiche, why not?
'Cause every line I steal is one I don't have to write)
Salt in some not-so-surreal image of lovers on a melting ice-cap
(they are, remember, melting)
build the climax around a final cell call on September 11th
goodbye my sweet goodbye
A dicey move I know
They might bitch and hiss how I mock the dead when
I mean to mock the living
Politics as usual
Business as usual
The body-count mounts

Goodbye my friends goodbye
Or I could simply go 100 proof confessional
Autobiographical
Pure-grain alcohol honesty –
But I don't want to go up on charges
Again.

I also have this Norman Mailer bit I haven't used in a while
Juggle some knives for the edification of the crowd
(he stabbed his wife, you know, his second wife, or was it his third?)
But spin it around, say yeah, my Ex she cleaned me out
Took the toothpaste and the laundry soap
Took the family dog and the family jewels
Though the knife in my back
She *was* sweet enough to leave
I could go with that old trick
It's worked before
Though not with that lesbian in the audience
In Whitehorse

And since we've landed on that particular landmine
I could tell them of a lovely bi-sexual woman who
Shared my Nova Scotia bed
How together we grew corn and baled hay
Fed the goats
Milked the cows
Fixed the barn roof
How I pushed her over the edge
Accidentally of course
No, not over the edge of the roof
Over the edge sexually
After me she's no longer bi
After me she only sleeps with women
(It's always good to tell a story against yourself
Gets the crowd on-side)
Well
Except for that reading in Whitehorse

I've been working too on a cowboy show
A splash of Hank
a shot of Wilco
A snort of Emmylou
Something along the lines of
"I was three days out of detox
When I seen her face again
She was standing on the corner of River Street
With the man who'd been my friend"
I'm thinking of maybe doing blue-collar cowboy
How the phone don't ring
And the door don't knock
Pedal steel blues
Three chords and the truth
If only to irritate the hip-hop crowd

If I get truly blocked
I could dig out some lyric fragments from the drawer
Like Tom Waits who calls 'em car parts in the back yard
"Hey, this carb from the Dodge'll work in the Chevy"
Well I got car parts
Here's one:
"She took a cynic to her bed
She stroked his sneer till I purred in the dawn
And though she was not the first
I swear by the God I had as a child
It was never making love until then"
And if I tell 'em I wrote those words
On a lunch bag
On the night shift
In a lead smelter
A blast furnace inferno with
The foreman bellowing in Portuguese
Well, maybe it'll seem like a better thing
Than a brake shoe rusting in the yard

Or maybe
Maybe I'll just say this:

That before the movie starts
When the lights are going down
You clap your hands, hoping
You clap your hands because
the movie just might be good this time
because a happy ending is still possible

Maybe I'll just say
That when you don't think I'm watching
You sing to the food on the table
That high off the hog or scraping on the dole
You bless our soup with a homemade song
And hold me in a state of grace

Yeah
Maybe I'll just say that
Keep it simple

Janet Marie Rogers

from *Splitting the Heart* (Ekstasis Editions, 2007)

Gone Now

the teapot is empty
while shades of night and day
transport shadows
across the kitchen floor

spiky thorns were more your cup
and mine was fruit-flavoured leaves
yet all the minutes in a year
could not steep from you
the words I longed to hear

faded curtains swing the
lazy rhythm of summer breezes
letting light in briefly
barely blocking harsh glare

the reality of our union
covers me now
like an itchy blanket
and wish I didn't miss
the things about you
through the years   I grew to despise
the many lies

all is not lost   though you are gone now
the lines of survival
like war-paint   decorate my face
and the boy and girl
grown
gone

the grass   yellow and uneven
calls to me from beyond
a creaky porch floor

gone now

Make Me

he makes me naked
and takes me
under his skin
holds me in his bloodstream
letting me have a taste

he makes me feel
all warm and fuzzy
cuz he knows
what I like
I paddle my way
to his heart
feel it start to palpitate
knowing he will hate
himself for loving me

he makes me moan
a song
not sung
in quite some time
he knows the rhyme
and together we make
harmony

I tap his spine
with a spike   and a pail
harvest sweet
sap
and save it for later
when I am alone
running low
on his sticky elixir
bath in it   *drink it down*
this love
we have found
I make him naked

see his secrets
so exposed
straight to the bone

I take him
into my lungs
breathe him
in
and
out

hold him in my throat
make him tickle
when I laugh
and when we do the math
two
can't be divided

by anything

When he says
Love me

I say
Make me

One Woman Parade

enter plasma pink
cocktail foam
wafts of cologne
stronger than repellent
enter glamour and confidence
aged beauty head to toe
mostly gray   brown roots
give way to fusia coloured shoots
done up in a bun

A *month in the sun*
she claims is better
than the chiropractor
pupils dulled and small
between furry framed lash
clinging to lids half mast
boobs   tired   overworked
served her well back in the day
she prays they stay in place
shaped by wire and lace

one woman parade

promenades her way
to town
never mind what they say
she's earned this
liberation
her freedom to be

eccentric ending
to a life lived well
only she can tell
how much it cost

Swimming

I call it swimming
as you dive into me
float through me

I call it swimming
as you stroke my hair
shake it loose like seaweed
make me your mermaid

still you swim

rapid laps around me
leaving rumpled linen
in your wake

holding your breath
you approach the surface
treasures gathered from the deep
held in your teeth

swim a marathon with me
to exhaustion
battling rough seas
and fatigue
to claim our prize

I call it swimming

dive in

Check Point

another day
young ones wait outside
without coats
without kisses goodbye
for late buses
to take them
to racist schools

the girl who
rings my groceries through
has scars on her wrists
and wishes me a
Good day

the English say
they like this city best
because it has no blacks

I save food I cannot finish
for a man leaning
on the restaurant window
then goes awkward
into the night

hallways host the portrait
of a past leader
conveniently forgetting
his heritage
teachers not found guilty
continue to take
students to bed

my mother gives me an
afghan woven with
magic and protection
to use everyday
nature's disasters
make war on us
as we war
with one another

the television is telling me
I'll never be pretty enough
and the men believe it

we buy
genetically modified food
and couples keep
reproducing

the Grandmothers
go to jail for protecting
their land
setting the example again
for the rest of us

warriors choose
to die accepting defeat
willingly giving their lives
breaking hearts
keeping promises

the Eagle's timing
is always perfect
appearing overhead
delivering hope

prisons are full
of fathers and brothers
learning to exist
in abnormality

poets keep writing
long long verses
of strength and survival
on paper they find
in bins

sometimes I fantasize
about murder
and lighting a candle in a church for you

the families return
to food banks
loaded down with emptiness
on the way home

the fire keeps us warm
at night
heating our dreams
easing our sleep
before another day
begins

some have the luxury
of education

and I have liberation
in the absence of it

we struggle to define love
rather than wait
for it to drop clues
marked skin
of butterflies
and cheery things
cannot tell me
who you are

I will return
to the forests
and wait
for you there
protecting a place
for the future

Good Savage

be a good savage
tell us your secrets
write them all down
so we'll remember
share them with the world
given permission
or not

be a good savage
dance and sing for us
as we marvel at your culture
see the whole show for free
then walk away

be a good savage
string us some beads

tokens of our encounter
surely you need the change
to pay for the addictions
that we gave you

be a good savage
remain ignorant of the rules
to the game
of land claim and inherent rights
no one likes a smart Indian
that's not part of who you are

be a good savage
become one of us
reject your community
your families your homes
because you're just like us anyway

be a good savage
speak only when spoken to
sit at our table
sign our papers
then disappear

be a good savage
forget what my ancestors
did to your ancestors
let's break bread, drink wine
heck, let's even interbreed
mixed bloods make beautiful children

be a good savage
just sit tight
as we vote away your rights
wash our hands of the Indian problem
surely you understand

be a good savage
and just don't say
a word

A Trip through Paradise

we take
earthquake rides
over rock waves
kissing
lake faces
stretching past
grass lands
and heifer-spotted
landscapes

road signs
promise
moose – elk – deer
eyes peeled
for
big-footed men
for our reflections
in stone

emotional
ups and downs
crowned at
toothy summits
sliver wide highways
balanced
between

judgment   and   progress

referendum deals
gone dead
stirred up
deep beds
laid to rest
new relationships
of silence
and inertia

these lands
grow and recede
and always
teach
us ways
to get around
shows us where
the trails lead

to live
in this land
you must understand
real histories
still lived

*No, that's not
a ski slope
that's a mountain
we pray there.*

Go West

the snow fell heavy
over Montréal
blanketing city cement
muffling midways
and tightening collars
of passing pedestrians

her buildings were built
to withstand conditions
stinging snows biting sun
and everything
in between

the Basilica's bells
wave goodbye and cry
out songs of a sad yesterday

old altars stand precarious
hold loose prayers
the salt of tears
has eaten away their strength

the city waits on warmer days
for the last of polluted ice
to drain
for the crocuses to poke up
brave buds to break through
confirming changing seasons

Montréal embraces those
true of heart thick of skin
a people beaten not broken
she sings her proud songs
wearing gowns with tattered hems

it's hard work
keeping her face lifted
while only those gifted
with her language
understand
the original plan
is not what it is now

she needs snow cold
knowing it can preserve her

copper-topped roofs protrude
through a brown-grey landscape
to say

Hey! We still have soul.

the snow falls heavy
over Montréal
well into night
not even daylight savings
could make it stop

Pardonnez-moi – Arete
C'est ce la place pour

Onkwehonwe*

*Iroquois People

maple syrup souvenirs
Indians with accents
five day trampoline trip
just west-jet me home
where salt lives
in oceans
songs are trumpeted
from forests old
and mountains
do not host crosses
shining down
lit up like trees
at Christmas

Sage Advice

Loopholes are meant to be broken

Granny would get all the clichés wrong
but dispense them
like sage advice
to anyone
who cared to listen

A finger in time, saves nine
Step on a crack, you can't get it back

when I was twenty-two

I asked Granny

Why do you always get it wrong?

she looked at me
with black raccoon eyes
leaned in close
and took the flesh of my ear
between her bony fingers

she whispered

I know things, you don't
I've done things
and survived
things you pussy-spoiled
tit-sucking brat-ass kids
could never survive

she released me
and finished

That's why!

Now run along before
I kick you in the
Cha-boom

No Kiss Goodbye

when you left
there was no kiss goodbye
only eyes
reflecting back
this was our end
this was me finishing
with you
saving myself

from your torment
as you turned away
there was no blame
you came in
your soupy state
so thick the drugs
swam through
your sedated veins
and everything
was thrown out the window

I'm so glad
you're gone
I'm so happy
to be done
and that you
did away
with yourself
not even animals
continue to suffer so
and the dope
and vile acts
you could not take back
brought you to that place

there was no kiss goodbye
only understanding
of what needed to be done
and pictures
a handsome fleshy face
looking back
brave and broken
I can see my tomorrow
and choose to live
making the commitment
you could not
to complete happiness

breathe in your spirit life
with peace
and Divine Love

our time
was horrible and good
and perfect

no kiss goodbye

required

Peter Sanger

from *Aiken Drum* (Gaspereau Press, 2006)

Windfalls

Since I'm too lame to dance I watch
    from an upstairs window
how winter continues at night
    with the old constellations
crossing hands, swinging clear
    as if they could still believe us,

or we them, their modal
    concordance of plow, bow, lyre.
What lyrical arrows can furrow
    our soil. Rockets bloom fire
in sand, need no water,
    and a deer can look out for itself,

ease down across moonlight from hills
    of thickly racked spruce, be there
and be gone as the thin, flat shadow
    which leaps a barbed fence
to leave shovel-shaped tracks that shaft
    under snow after apples.

What planets hang back on the tree?
    If earth, our dear ice, is one,
it sings when you tap like a bowl
    of dry wood and cools
the cold skin on your fingers
    emptied and equally free.

Aiken Drum

Stand on my shoe
and I'll dance you
around my kitchen.

If, Mr. Moon, you
have cranky ears
I'll play upon

a ladle, I'll play
upon a ladle
and eat cream cheese.

Who ever thought
a razor could
whistle? Willy Wood

did. He died while
attempting. Didn't
have stomach. Spare

are the bones which buckle
it up, earth's longer
garment. We'll all climb

the wooden stair. Write it
in needles, write
it in needles, inside my eye.

The Fountain

Remember their year by a story,
how after a summer
of buckets and jugs, they simply
gave up the old well,
an eighteen-foot barrel
of rocks wedged together,

a church without steeple or people
which plumbed at last dry.

Trying to drill a new well
can seem hopeless
as prayer. He guessed that she prayed while
the rig lifted square on flat feet
and bit the first hole in their purse
then mealed through red clay,
grey shale, sluiced by a shot
of pneumatics to spray

wet muck from the bore. But he
wasn't there when a wave
of new water leaped waist high
heaving sand and gravel
prismatic with brilliants of quartz
and following silvery
fountain falling shared grace
in her lyrical voice.

Glossing this episode now,
distant songs of creation.
Or should he depose it as so
unlikely, complacent glissando
where death and sublime resurrection
feast at the sign of the circle?
Pity such choice,
and sacrifice.

Renovation

To live in a house
of white gables
with pinnacles flying

bespeaks a particular style:
six walls to the wind
and a wind

that prevails on all quarters
build place we've chosen
to live. Your garden

keeps growing around us
although it's so far
through November we don't

really care about frost.
I wish I could give you
that turn on high

C in Allegri, but you've
given it me leaving
only small words

I can say while we
listen alone and wind
sings the pinnacled darkness.

Elegy for the Great Auks

Did some of them wonder if we
were a version of them, equally
flightless and granted to stand
like a refugee crowd
in the square of some levelled city?

Like ours, the carcass was fat
and could reputedly feed
the fires which rendered it
down into purest
oil, hotly as driftwood.

I've read they were docile.
They'd herd up gangplanks, waddle
abreast, and placably queue
awaiting our execution.
One might say, from the utile

view, there is little reason
to mourn their destruction,
though fresh or in salt they
made us provision aplenty
and still might have done.

In this best of all possible worlds,
dolphining douce
underwater, did they sense
small bones in each wing
pulling forward like fingers?

But they never left their gods.

Reed Weaver

When I telephoned to ask, his daughter
    said he was dying, but
she would see. At least, perhaps he might
    be interested, and please
could I call again, a day or so
    later. Who really spoke
persuasively? She, or the claw of the crab
    and the need to do just one
more time what he'd apprenticed to learn
    in Holland, back before the war,
when the job you started learning at fifteen
    was the job which saw you
out? His was caning, cording and weaving
    seats for chairs.

I had two chairs worth doing, pillow-backs,
    each with a grecian urn
in mid-slat, fretwork silhouette,
    a pair of country-
Chippendales, carpentered two centuries ago
    ten miles up the road.

I'd salvaged them seatless, partly broken,
    at a yard-sale barn
where seven cords of seasoned furnace wood
    offered a far more
sensible deal. *Bring me just one*, he said, *I'll see*
    what I can do. It was spring.
You'll have to wait till reeds grow long
    enough by the river.

One chair I brought and listened while he
    told me something of what was
more and more in his memory,
    of how he'd come to Nova Scotia
forty years before and made a living farming
    or, more like, lost a living,
making it up by odd jobs labouring and cutting
    pulp; and while we
spoke I felt the draw of another tongue,
    not Dutch so much, though
that was partly so, but more a language
    he'd had to learn that said
how to carry his hands and newly lay them
    down, if he was to survive.

Some six weeks after, in July, his daughter
    phoned to say I should
revisit, bringing the second chair.
    Beside the fireplace which he'd
built right after he'd retired was the first
    with a seat of woven reeds,
cylindrical cords he'd trimmed and ravelled round
    then laced into four
equilateral triangles whose apices met
    at centre point to make
a square. He'd placed it on display to show
    his friends what I called
beautiful and he called what you could
    do with reeds.

By middle August both the chairs were ready.
   How much did he want?
Enough to be sign a fair job was worth
   his fairly doing. Too little
as sign maybe I'd listened. When I brought
   the pair home their reeds were
green and filled the room where I set them
   with a smell of freshly
baled hay in the mow and the sun at work,
   greening, still growing
it seemed. Grains of green light inflected
   the cords as if ancient
faith, present courage, continued. That autumn
   he died.

John Conway, St. Michael's Retreat House, Qu'Appelle Valley, near Lumsden

in the spring of 1881
sitting bull gathers his remaining 1200 sioux
and treks to fort qu'appelle to make
the final request for a reservation —
from "*THE BITTER WORD*", Andrew Suknaski, pp.508 - 509

Crystal Sikma

from *FAST FORWARD NEW SASKATCHEWAN POETS* (Hagios Press, 2007)

Driving down into Qu'Appelle

late October, following
the slow curve of this road

there is a place, where the hills
meet — lie together
where the trees form a dark triangle
opening up to the horizon

I know a part of you, he says
that looks like that

I run my fingers
over the rough grain of his jeans
imagine small birds in that place
fluttering over naked branches

Nocturne

over the shallow sound
of your breath on my neck
I can hear the moths
humming
in your window
humming between
the blind
and the glass

they keep me awake
I don't want to wake you

in the morning
as you have your cigarette
I'll gather their bodies
my cupped hands full
soft torsos silk wings
dark again
and still

Ghazal: waxwing

tsee-tsee, to see, to sleep, to dream, to smoke the night's
last cigarette, to see, to quote the waxwing

this winter, you can see the stars again, the orange light of the city
rises in the east, and falls on the coat of the waxwing

the December wind scattered tiny apples, fermented blood on snow,
frozen, then warmed in the throat of the waxwing

we breathe the prairie silence, the cold dark sky, listen
to the wind beneath songs of the coyote and the waxwing

the branches of the tree hold their bodies, flutter, give
darkness the last trill note of the waxwing

when you slip into bed, kiss the curve of my neck,
Poet, I say, *who wrote of the waxwing?*

Sue Sinclair

from *Breaker* (Brick Books, 2008)

Nesting

Swans groom the light,
prune it with a clip
of their wings, drift
through the clustered lilies.
To the left, stuck
in the shallow mud, a tire:
fat bruised lip, thick
black slug curled into itself,
water lisping around it.
The swans brush against the rim,
consider it a moment
then clamber up industriously,
assuming a purpose
in the worn treads, the functional
given up to the mud's stubborn
suck. By next week
the swans have gathered reeds
and dirt, clay and sticks
into an island, the tire buried
so that everything we've made so far
seems only a beginning,
a crude variation of a kind
of manufacture that ebbs and flows,
hums to itself under its breath.
Nesting, at home, the swans preen
with the insouciance of those
who haven't had to ask forgiveness.
They are not withdrawn,
turn the eggs over in the nest.
Are not lonely.

Breakwater

In the 1990s a breakwater was built using erratics that once dotted the shore of Flatrock, Newfoundland. Erratics are blocks of rock dropped by retreating glaciers.

The boulders lifted from the shore,
raised in slings as though being rescued.
Embarrassed, their awkward bodies
dangled in mid-air as though they had been
woken from sleep, taken unprepared.
Piled like rubble in the bay,
they stare out from the breakwater
as if forbidden to speak, using ancient
telepathy to send a warning.

We were afraid of something they
represented, their blank faces
looking somberly into the future,
monuments to a mistake we had yet
to make, traces of something
we wanted to erase before it could exist.
We haven't eluded it. No better off,
we've forfeited consolation, won't know
where to go in our grief.

We've cast ourselves deliberately out
of our own future; it is a locked door
on which we will bang and bang,
looking for answers, looking for silence,
a moment to think through our lives
before they're lost.

Fairytale

The knight didn't kill the dragon, only maimed it;
he plunged his lance into the thick flesh
and fire poured from the wound but the heart kept on
pumping its combustible blood through the canals.
And though the dragon was now slow
and harmless and couldn't terrorize the countryside,
the knight wasn't a hero. The beautiful maiden
turned away when she saw the poor beast
he brought limping into court, harnessed by a thick rope
that was more to guide than tether him.
She hid her face and backed into her private rooms,
her ladies scurrying at her sides.
The trumpets were lowered in shame.

He looked at the dragon, and the dragon
looked back at him, and he knew then that they were
twins, born together into the misfortune of this moment.
The armour and the flesh could not in that instant
be told apart, nor have they been since.
The rope that joined them joins them still as
they wander over the gilt-edged pages of storybooks,
depending for their livelihood on the kindness of strangers
who offer them bowls of thin soup
and a place to sleep for the night.
No one asks them to stay, nor are they asked
to tell their tale, and for this they are grateful:
the injury has gone so deep they don't know
where to find it anymore.

Away

The voices first, echoing
and tinny, as though trapped inside
an old radio. Then two men with tool kits,
Xs of reflective gray tape across their backs.
They walk side by side along the rails,
toward whatever strangeness inhabits the tunnel,
their muffled footsteps giving nothing away.
They are fading out of time as we know it,
walking into the dimness of an ever-delayed present.
From where I stand, looking into darkness,
the tunnel is not just a tunnel, the Xs not just Xs.
They shimmer meaningfully.

Big, well-fed men a few years beyond middle age,
backs evoking old-fashioned bravado,
talking about home with a shrug of the shoulders.
They amble along the tracks, swinging
their flashlights, light zipping across the dank walls.
The zig-zagging light is panicked, groping
for the tunnel's low arc. It's the animal in us
seeking the dimensions that comfort
blind consciousness. Something to hold onto.

They're getting smaller, the Xs smaller,
and my fear for them also recedes,
turns into loneliness. I want to call out,
warn them about some fate they seem already
to know and have accepted. No reason to speak of it,
say their backs. And it's ridiculous, but I could cry,
have in fact to prevent myself. Watching them
go as though they're already gone, passengers
washing through the station, the crowd pressing
around me. And suddenly I seem to see everything, everything!
A delusion of course: just as quickly it all goes black.
The flashlight beams the last thing I see.

In the Long Afternoons

The sky looks down with a missionary gleam.
The apple trees rise into bloom;
zealously, they rush into the breach, urge
themselves to carry on, do more
as the lengthening summer days
catch up with them. They ripen until they can ripen
no more, striving to split themselves off from their shadows.
But the earth tilts on its axis, and,
sick with fruit, the branches soften
under the straightforward, steady pressure of existence.
They droop, and wasps stew in the carrion mush:
always more than we can bear.
Sooner or later even memory is taken, and we're not sure
what remains. All we know is that the day is darker.
And something has had its fill.

Delay

Quarter of an hour, half an hour,
still no train. All of us thinking of home and how
we're not there and will or won't be missed,
how the surface of our life goes on elsewhere
even as we stand here, our absence
snail-paced, cumulative.

We settle in, inhabit ourselves uneasily,
make peace with our half-existence.
Then a dog starts to howl, and though no one
so much as flinches, something tightens
over the space between us.
Some abstract noun, larger and more meaningful
than we care to imagine, has pushed
its way in and is growing bigger by the second.

How could anything suffer so long, so hopelessly?

Yet the sound doesn't relent, and the faces
around me won't let it register,
won't so much as blink. I feel the indifference
on my own face and don't know who I am anymore:
I've fled, but how, and to where?

I picture it, despite myself: the platform ahead, the ambulance,
and the altered faces of those who couldn't stop
whoever it was. The howl becomes the sound
of the soul pushed to the edge of itself,
facing up to a world which it still, after all these years,
is not really convinced it must inhabit.
And because the crowd presses in on all sides
and I can't see and so can't even be sure
it's a dog, I'm frightened, thinking the sound could
in a way be me, a voice from the part of me
I've tried not to know.

Breaker

A cold-burning brilliance,
distillery of light, green camouflaged
in the ocean's understorey. Your mind is gathered
like a horse about to take a hurdle, ready to leap.
But fascinated by the rising wall, it stalls,
and time seems to slow
while you consider the monumental
fatigue of this immanent failure.

Beauty like a stain bleeds though
the layers of matter,
          something, somewhere in pain,
the traces of it seeping into this world.
You stand back and watch as the inevitable
takes over: the green recess
of the wave collapses, the light buckles,

the depths recover what was owed.
How helpless you are yet
on the brink of being able to do more,
as though you could punch your hand through
the window to rescue whatever it is that,
trapped inside, haunts the corridors.
You haven't, though, quite got what it takes.
The window shatters anyway, but in the spirit
of denial. So it goes, the heartbreak
of merely standing by as what
dwells here does its living and dying
on its own terms.

Devotion

for W.R.

Long days spent forgiving fathers
for all they didn't know and couldn't protect us from.
As young men, backs slowly bracing to take on
an inherited weakness. *I don't know*, they said, frustrated
because they felt they had disappointed us
so much already, had fallen too quickly,
born on the steep side of a cliff.

The eyes of some were dangerous, power collapsing
and trying to preserve itself. Some wept like statues,
their own childhoods emerging
and staring helplessly at the world.

Now we just want another chance,
want to retrieve the something beautiful we sank
in them years ago, then set them free
like a net of fish, skins shining. Nothing we learn
can quite cure us of our desire to go there:
to the sandy bottom, where lucent shadows play
and a rusted lure still gleams.

Suburbs

Night holds up a mirror on all sides;
there is a depth in things you haven't accounted for.
The bungalows return your gaze; their lost dignity
surfaces and they stare at you, trying
to import meaning into their small lives.

Vinyl-sided, slow-witted,
they insist they didn't mean for this to happen,
this sameness, shackled to their own kind
like cattle transported slowly nowhere
in a broken-down truck. This is what happened to them,
not what they are. And they know the privilege
of even this adequate existence. Ashamed,
they lower their heads as children do
who think they have done something wrong
in being born. You too bow your head,
wish you could divest yourself of scorn.
A woman climbs into a car, will drive until
the motor dissolves her troubles.
Further up the street a man lifts a blind,
looks around, and wonders what it can all be for.
He hopes no one will answer.
He is embarrassed to have to ask.

Injured Swan

after D. S.

The cargo of mortality has shifted
within you, sinking, dragging you down.
Being is compressed into its purest
form: your back shines, the feathers laid
like ointment over the wound.

You've settled deep into your body,
your self-possession a kind of injury to us,
a reproach. A boy tries to lift you
as though he expects you'll fly
out of his arms, cured.

The Animal Services van rumbles up
and a man with a badge opens the back doors,
reveals the dim interior. We look to you,
falter. The part of us that is swan trembles
before a panic so well-kept. Your pain
is stashed in a vault somewhere inside you,
a document no one dares claim.
It's protected by a combination so
complicated, a string of numbers so long,
it can't be cracked—
yet as the van doors close, we feel like thieves
who've taken something they can't give back.

Inna Komarovsky

Carolyn Smart

from *Hooked: seven poems* (Brick Books, 2009)

Ardent
Elizabeth Smart: December 27, 1913 — March 4, 1986

i.

life is murder
and art is even worse:
do I dare to plunge into this journey?

put on the clarinet quintet in A,
let Mozart help me through

I find as many answers there
as anywhere

a happy little pill unwinds me

ii

what I remember best is Kingsmere,
my truest paradise:
I recognize each rock and root,
the path unwinding to the boathouse,
the leap of leopard frogs against the still mid-day,
the dark cool water of the lake

storms roil beyond the waving mapled hills
and up through pines to where I crouch (the creaking lovely floor)
to clip my fashioned paper dolls and
memorize the genus of each blessed simple thing:
implicit ferns unfolding in the shade,
mouths of giant pike, their googly eyes,
the mountain, its mantle-sweetened air

nighttime: the humped raccoons beyond the walls
creep past my torpid bedstead,
the empty sighing lounge chairs,
stains of misplaced highballs,
feather ticking, dawn

iii

in the fall, back to Ottawa for the Smarts,
the chill air on Beechwood, green stiff skirts of
uniforms, my sisters and I walking
through the darkened Elmwood doors,
good girls, all of us

I loved to see the youngest ones at play
in the wooden toy house near Springfield, the door so small
you'd wonder how a baby could pass through, perfect housewives
practicing

the sound of Mummy's wails at night in winter,
the sight of her adrift in snow,
or pacing on the balcony or rolling round the bathroom floor,
my sister Helen's dress torn off, her tender breasts exposed,
face slapped and baby Russel crying,
a small body sobbing in a bed of maple leaves

Daddy read his lawyer's letters and laid truth down like matting:
this is how we lived and we were lonely

iv

my god the hell of Ottawa!
there's never been a place so dismal:
bloody invitations to the aprés ski,
an afternoon of skating up at Rideau Hall,
the Little Theatre evenings

then London, where Jane and I were sovereigns,
I'd forage every alley for something crammed with meaning,
anything relentless, captivating, whole,
I knew one day I'd find it
knew it in my bones, my sex

we lived the life that Mummy never did,
and when she came to town her balm would sweep us in:
her lovely smell, her underwear, her shopping sprees,
she was warm extravagant delicious

and then she'd turn to me and say *I've hated you all day,*
you're the meanest little thing,
any child could write this drivel

I must marry a poet
it's the only thing

v

all these summers Kingsmere,
a private lovely life with leaves and earth,
wild geese and dutchman's breeches,
hepaticas and blood root,
bird song, the smell of mornings after rain,
pleasing mother, being self: my body but a seam
that rips from end to end

huge diversions of the upper class:
dress-up parties at the King Estate,
dancing on our screened verandahs,
my journals overflow with incantation,
bucking back the emptiness with language

one day in Better Books in Charing Cross
I found the poems of a man named Barker
and told the world that I would marry him

this is what I want: art, love and children:
do not stoop to offer less than everything

vi

waiting for the bus in Monterrey
I changed my lipstick often
and considered what the future held:
his wife climbed down, so thin and shy
so dark against my shining head

I must be radiant, aglow, on fire:
we drive to where we live, nearby, in huts

George Barker's hand on mine
his arm against my nipple
the whole world rocking
I try so hard to be polite
until he comes upon me in the water

and now I love the night, the legs of children, tall poinsettia, hydrangeas
and the lemon trees, I love the residential palms that dress in pantaloons,
I love the birds in pepper trees, the sun on swimming pools

the multitude of kisses, never enough skin to sate me
it is no surprise I am arrested at the Arizona border
because he is my love and I am his,
who cares for his English class awareness, prissy wife:
can there be life or breath apart from this?

in the mornings I am ill with child at Pender Harbour,
I write my book, desire made flesh and rhetoric:
By Grand Central Station I Sat Down and Wept
was birthed two weeks before Georgina

I do not mind my child a bastard:
it will help them to avoid the bores, the snobs,
the petty, the afraid

vii

I had four in total,
my darlings, all my dreams

we lived with nothing yet I smocked their clothes,
made nettle soup, held honeyed bodies in my arms,
bleached nappies in the dark, wiped noses, rode them here
and there upon my bike, smoke and drank and wept
and George would come and leave his seed behind,
but never any cash or caring, just an Ottawa allowance
and I lived so far away, in farms in England or wherever
costs were few: a low wet cottage in the Irish hills,
bedsits in London, barnyards, attics

oh beloved friends, oh stagger me with cases
bottles clunking well into the weekend drunk

George, I beg you, *I am so afraid,*
of wind, the empty house, the air raids, burglars,
lunatics and ghouls, catastrophe, appearances and
death. You must do something
for I am simply going mad

you are my husband and my one true love
no matter how many other wives
post you their midnight dreams

viii

Georgina, Christopher, Sebastian and then Rose:
the womb's an unwieldy baggage.
Who can stagger uphill with such a noisy weight?

to send the children to good schools
with clean and decent clothing, lots of books,
I worked *Queen*, worked *Vogue*,
I was the best copywriter in the city

sat at desk sniffed glue held phone typed hard took drink
wrote fast and funny, hard and real,
scurried through the filthy streets harassed by deadlines,
took pills, the crystal clear dependency: bloody sharp, that focus,
I ground my teeth

put my feet up on the weekends, wellies on the work bench,
dead soldiers piling up below

what is left of my youth rushes up like a geyser
as I sit in the sun combing lice from my hair

ix

how to survive life's script?
you pray and bang your head,
be beautiful, wait, love, rage, rail;
look and possibly, if lucky, see;
love again; try to stop loving,
go on loving, bustle about, rush to and fro;
whatever you say will be far less than truth

I saw my children off to life
and turned alone back down the bitter lane,
BBC sonatas in the kitchen, empty page,
I am *desperate from hating*
pushed too far to do too much

but then the strangest thing:
my little book revived and I am famous!
the heady stuff of praise and recognition
sets me restless and all atremble

there is money and I fixed a place to live
and worked a garden there,
crawled on my hands and knees upstairs to bed,
why not? tricks, sleight of hand, anything it takes

and in the mornings I rise and toil
amidst the pits and rumblings of the earth:
how dear it is to birth a flower,
hold a cutting, name a thing
and they wind quite round about me
like my children always did

I begin a poem here and there
small things, aflutter more than most
then Rose takes up the needle
so I hold her children too

x

Death By Misadventure,
so they said, we buried Rose

when one's own heart child goes to death
what left?
nothing wards
no language

why did I not tell her what I knew:
the long bitterness of life
the mean, the ungenerous
the need to forge capacities for pain

George has many children
what's one less, the one he laid his hands on
seldom, gone for good

life *is the roll of matter heaving into heaven*
in its painful individual way

xi

they asked me back to Canada
to talk about the craft
I drank away the bleak lot where I lived
friends turned their heads in fear and bald disgust
the late night coffee shops and men
the vomit on the rugs

then home at last
clematis everywhere and rain
worm was my best beast friend
mud was my first love

I adore this twisted acre
and lie in bed remembering
calling out in sleep for Mummy
what these nightmares bring me to I dread

when these pills kick in I open up my head to memory
and fear, whole notebooks filling late at night
with writing near impossible to read
but it is there, you find it if you can
make from it all whatever books you wish

Andrew Suknaski

from *Wood Mountain Poems* (Hagios Press, 2006)

HOMESTEAD, 1914 (SEC. 32, TP4, RGE2, W3RD, SASK.)

1. *returning*

for the third spring in a row now
i return to visit father in his yorkton shack
the first time i returned to see him
he was a bit spooked
seeing me after eleven years —
a binder twine held up his pants then
that year he was still a fairly tough little beggar
and we shouted to the storm fighting
to see who would carry my flight bag across the cn tracks
me crying: *for chrissake father*
lemme carry the damn thing the
train's already too close!

now in his 83rd year father fails
is merely 110 pounds now and cries while
telling me of a growing pain after the fall
from a cn freightcar
in the yard where he works unofficially as a cleanup man
tells of how the boss that day
slipped a crisp 20 into his pocket and said:
you vill be okay meester shoonatzki
don't tell anyvon about dis
commeh bek in coopleh veek time...
father says his left testicle has shriveled
to the size of a shelled walnut
says there's simply no fucking way
he'll see another doctor — says:
the last one tried to shine a penlight up my ass
now son

no one's ever looked up my asshole
and never will
never

while we walk through the spring blizzard to the depot
i note how he is bent even more now
and I think: *they will have to break his back*
to lay him flat when he dies

in the depot
father guards my bag while i buy two white owl cigars
and return to give him one
we then embrace saying goodbye
and i watch him walk away from me
finally disappearing in the snowflake eddy near a pine
on the street corner
and then remember how he stood beneath a single light bulb
hanging from a frayed cord in his shack
remember how he said
my life now moves to an end with the speed of
electricity

2. *mother*

her ship sails for the new land
and she on it
the fare paid by her brother in limerick saskatchewan

dancing in the arms of some young farmer
she remembers her polish village
the day her mother is fatally struck
by a car —
she remembers being 14
when world war one begins
remembers how she and another girl walk 12 miles
to work every three days
shovelling coal onto flatcars for sixteen hours

before returning home
along the boundaries of wolves (their eyes glowing
like stars on the edge
of the dark forest)

she remembers the currency changing as the war ends
her money and several years' work
suddenly worthless one spring day
all these things drift away from the ship carrying
her to the unknown
new land

3. *father*

arrives in moose jaw fall of 1914
to find the landtitles office
is given the co-ordinates for the homestead east
of wood mountain village —
and he buys packsack and provisions for the long walk south
sleeps in haystacks for the first few nights
(finally arriving in limerick
buys homesteader's essentials: axe saw hammer
lumber nails shovel gun bullets food
and other miscellaneous items)
he hires someone with a wagon and horses
to drive him to the homestead
builds a floor and raises one wall that day
and feeling the late autumn cold
nails together a narrow box in which to sleep
the first night

the following morning
he rises through two feet of snow to find
all his tools stolen (except for the gun bullets
and knife he slept with)
he searches for a spot on the hillside
to carve out with a blunted knife

a cellar
in which to endure the first few years —
he nails together a roof with a stone

philip well is his closest neighbour
and they hunt together
and through long evenings
play cards by the light of the coaloil lamp
spin tales of old country wanderings
to survive 40 below winters till pre-emption time
is up

when the landtitle is secured
and a more suitable shack is built —
father walks six times between moose jaw and
the homestead
till haggling civil bastards give him the title
each time
he carries a $10 bill sewn inside his pocket across
the heart

4. *parting*

the day i walked fearless between horses' trembling feet
my father watching with hands frozen
to a pitchfork
is clearer in my memory
than the day he and mother parted
— she leading the children through the fall
stubble to wood mountain

in the following years
all i knew of father was the lonely spooked man
whom i met each autumn
in the back alley behind koester's store
while winter descended from the mountains —
it seems he always came during the first storm

and tied his team to the telephone pole
(their manes and nostrils frosted)
he always pulled a side of pork from the hay
in the wagon
and placed it on my sleigh

parting
we never found the words
simply glanced at one another's eyes and turned
something corroding the love in my heart
until i left wood mountain one sunday afternoon —
running away to the mountains
for what i thought would be forever
until another spring
i returned to see father
eleven years later

5. *the funeral*

sofie in winnipeg
sends each member of the family a telegram announcing
the death of sister eve

mother who is 66 at the time
rides a greyhound bus from moose jaw to brandon
all night
father and brother louis drive from yorkton
arrive in brandon the night before the funeral
and get a hotel room —
louis goes out and buys father a pair of pants
and a shirt
returns wondering: *how the hell will i get*
father out of that sweater he's sewn himself into?
back in the room
he goes to the bathroom and turns on the water
and returns to subtly introduce the idea to father
who will have no part of it

louis loses his temper and pulls out a pair of scissors
from a shaving kit
and wrestles father to the floor (cuts him out of
the old sweater
while father cries:
okay okay — i'll take a bath)
the following day
the family is all on edge
everyone wonders how mother and father will respond
to one another
after 18 years of silence —
louis drives father to the funeral chapel
where mother is already viewing their daughter
they park outside
and father nervously climbs out as the chapel door opens
(he freezes

while mother emerges and also suddenly freezes
both stand motionless for 30 seconds and then
begin to run toward each other
they embrace
and she lifts him off the ground
he is 79 at the time)

6. *birth certificate*

carrying it in my pocket now as father carried
the worn $10 bill across his heart for the landtitle
i have crossed bridges of cities
hoping to find salvation
have gazed into the dark rivers of
spring where others found love
hoping to glimpse the face of some god —
and stopped by grey-eyed policemen
produced identification and tolerated their jokes
what do these letters and numbers mean kid?
where is this place?
is this all you have?

7. *epilogue*

my father once said:
i might have murdered you all and gone
straight to heaven

and having arrived at all these things now
what is to be done with you and love
father?
what is to be done now with that other man who
is also you?
that other man so long ago on a hot summer day
far too hot for man or beast
the day mother at the well with the rope
frozen in her hands watches louis
who has ceased haggling with you
sadly carrying a bucket of staples to the barn —
you father something frightening
slowly sweating and walking after him
you slowly raising a fence post above your thoughts
swimming in familiar rage
over that day's fence posts' improper spacing —
louis stopping suddenly for some reason
not looking back
but merely gazing across to tall wheat growing
beyond the coulee's black shadow
(you suddenly stopping too and seeming afraid
and then lowering the fence post
as you turn around and return to the picket pile
to continue sharpening poplar pickets
with your newly sharpened axe)
that other man beating mother with a rolling pin
by the cream separator one morning
she pregnant and later sleeping in the late afternoon
to waken from a dream while the axe rises
above her grey head
her opening eyes staring into the eye of death
you father slowly turning away once again frightened
and ashamed

you once warning us of that other man within you:
when these things happen to me
do all you can and help one another save yourselves
from me

that other man once sharpening mower blades
when brother mike plays and suddenly tips
a bucket of water used to soak blades —
that other man suddenly drowning in black rage
grabbing a long scarf from a coat hook in the porch
then seizing mike to knot the scarf around his neck
and around the end of the grindstone's pulley
bolted high in the porch corner
the trembling right hand slowly labouring to turn
the crude sandstone
(mother and sister sofie fortunately arriving just in time
to fight you and free your son)

father
i must accept you and that other dark man within you
must accept you along with your sad admission
that you never loved anyone in your life
(you must be loved
father
loved the way a broken mother loves her son
though he must hang in the morning
for murder)

8. *suicide note*

silence
and a prayer to you shugmanitou*
for something
to believe in

*shugmanitou: coyote in the dakota language

PHILIP WELL

prairie spring
and i stand here before a tire crimper
two huge vices held by a single bolt
(men of the prairies were grateful to a skilled man
who could use it and fix wooden wheels
when the craft flourished)

i stand here
and think of philip well found in his musty woodshed
this morning
by dunc mcpherson on the edge of wood mountain —
philip well lying silent by his rusty .22

and i ask my village: *who was this man?*
this man who left us

in 1914
well and my father walked south from moose jaw
to find their homesteads
they slept in haystacks along the way
and once nearly burned to death
waking in the belly of hell they were saved by mewling mice
and their song of agony —
a homesteader had struck a match and thought he
would teach them a lesson

well and father lived in a hillside and built fires
to heat stones each day in winter
they hunted and skinned animals to make fur blankets
threw redhot stones into their cellars
overlaid the stones with willows
and slept between hides

father once showed me a picture
nine black horses pulling a gang plough
philip well proudly riding behind (breaking
the homestead to make a home)

well quiet and softspoken
loved horses and trees and planted poplars around his shack
when the land began to drift away
in tough times well brought a tire crimper
and fixed wheels tanned hides and mended harnesses
for people

and later (having grown older and often not feeling well)
moved to wood mountain village
to be near people who could drive him to a doctor
if necessary

today in wood mountain
men's faces are altered by well's passing
while they drink coffee in jimmy hoy's cafe
no one remembers if well had a sweetheart
though someone remembers a school dance near
the montana border one christmas —
well drunk and sleeping on a bench in the corner
while the people danced
well lonelier than judas after the kiss
(the heart's sorrow like a wheel's iron ring
tightening around the brain till
the centre cannot hold and
the body breaks)

from *NEZ PERCÉS AT WOOD MOUNTAIN*

5.

wood mountain
the winter is cold and the game has vanished —
santee and teton children cry: *tacko eena* ...

somewhere north of the Montana border
the last nez percés are met by sitting bull
walsh and 1,000 teton warriors ready for battle
(all are startled by the appearance

of the bedraggled nez percés)

nez percés
death ambling clothed in rags —
children with arms and legs snapped by bullets
wounded children tied and hanging from
the saddle horns
while men and women and horses are nothing
but a walking graveyard

sitting bull and his men befriend the broken people
take them home to lodges
near the old wood mountain post —
nurse them back to health again
and later provide lodges and a place to call home
somewhere to restore something of a dream
a face and pride —
white bird finally affirming some night
before the teton chief and others around a campfire:
i have no country
i have no home and i feel
i have no people

THE BITTER WORD

from fort walsh
colonel irvine brings the bitter word
to sitting bull at wood mountain
makes clear the government welcomes the teton —
yet they must not expect provisions
or food from canada

sitting bull proudly replies:
when did i ever ask you for provisions?
before i beg
i will cut willows for my young men to use
while killing mice to survive

in the spring of 1881
sitting bull gathers his remaining 1200 sioux
and treks to fort qu'appelle to make
the final request for a reservation —
inspector sam steele tells them
the great white mother wishes them to return
to their own country
(a rather curious view of a people
whose meaning of country changes with
the migrations of tatanka)
steele politely refuses the request
and supplies enough provisions for the return
to wood mountain

death by summer is certain
while irvine makes sure
provisions and seed never arrive

seeing the migrating game
sitting bull knew the tatanka
would never return
though his people dreamed of white tatanka rising
from the subterranean meadows others fled to
(hideous shrieks of red river carts grating in
their ears)

he must have sensed the hunger to follow
which was exactly what the authorities hoped for
on both sides of the border

GUS LECAINE SPEAKING OF GRANDFATHER OKUTE

trails end pub in wood mountain
and near closing time
a weak bulb shines above us while
soren caswell sleeps dreaming in his lonely corner

gus lecaine's eyes seem black pools
all light being two diamonds frozen there
while he slowly recalls a story from his boyhood on the reserve
when his father was still alive and chief:
my father tole me bout a Sioux scout ridin in a coulee in montana
he said wen the scout spotted custer's men on a ridge
all dere metallic tings guns buttons and everything woz
shinin like gold in the sun

in a gentle voice gus speaks lovingly of grandfather okute
90 when he and other old men with horses and women
and travois bearing children
cross the stream near the camp *(distant warriors crying:*
come brothers
it is a good day to die!)

when the families reach the silver stream beneath high sun
gus remembers the moment from his grandfather's story:
water catching light like an ocean spray
water like a million diamonds shattering across the old
and young faces

grandfather okute remembers the scout returning and saying:
it is all over now
we can return home

okute remembers the fires still being warm
and the water still boiling in the pots and food being ready —
gus says: *that was how long it lasted*

the sioux lost merely four men
all were annihilated on the other side —
gus tells of how one father laviolette questioned the truth
of old chief john lecaine's story:
this is not possible — it defies the law of average

chief lecaine countering:
well then how about david slaying goliath
how do you account for that story with your law of average?

lights dim and we are grateful to roger the new barkeeper
for patiently listening to the story
and letting us drink an extra half hour
we leave unfinished beer for the ghosts at trails end
turning his head to finish his beer
gus nods and smiles remembering something — the two diamonds
in his eyes vanish forever

DUNC AND BABE MCPHERSON

we notice so little in our lives
i think
looking again at their photograph taken
that Sunday afternoon last fall
they standing arm in arm before the flower box
nailed beneath the window
and they cast a single shadow across the wall where
the washtub hangs next to the hammer on a nail —
i now notice in the foreground
the large flat stones half the length of a man
and try to imagine the energy it took to place them there
(something in the picture turns the mind to the visit
and how we entered their house — dunc saying:
the smell of your pipe makes me lonely for the old days
when i smoked my pipes

sitting down in his easy chair
dunc gazed a moment at the floating particles moving
through a light shaft angling down to the floor —
then he recalled their first experiences
when he and philip well were blacksmiths east of the old post:
i was shaping shoes when i heard horses whinnying
i looked up and there was babe
holding the reins of her father's team
that moment i said to myself "this lil lady's my wife"
and I tell you the honest God's truth andy

i've never looked at another woman since — yes
it was pure and simple as that
babe chuckled while she poured coffee: *yes and*
i was so afraid of him then
all i could say was "my daddy wants you to shoe these horses
please"

dunc talked about tire crimping the old forgotten craft
and the way he heated iron tires red hot
to crimp them with the two huge vices
how in busy times babe often helped him
throw the hot metal rings back on wooden wheels
suddenly immersed in a water trough to keep the wood from burning
dunc remembered how once a year
news arrived about a certain horserancher coming to have
his team shod:
they would jump half their height straight in the air —
the night before he arrived
i smoked myself hoarse andy and i even loaded a pipe
to calm myself in the middle of the night
when i woke up shaking from nightmares about them
dunc compares shoeing horses to tuning a banjo
and says one can tell by the sound of the nail
if one is doing it wrong and hurting the horse)

returning to their photograph
i notice how the garden has been extended
beyond the old fashioned well
note how they extended their boundaries
to include the abandoned house turned into a guest house
and i praise their full happy life here
where they found everything they ever needed
here in wood mountain where the stars are still distinct

RORY NICHOLSON

the great wind dying down that day
the crickets' song shrill
in your ears
and the truck's skidmarks a bruise on the edge
of the coulee as you
turned for home to get help
for your father fighting the pain in his chest
as the last bit of sun
wedged between earth and sky at sundown
pierces the eye —
these became a testament bearing you from
boyhood to man
the meaning of father resting square and heavy
on your young shoulders
tears streaming back
while the gathering wind hugged the cab
as your father faded in uncle John's arms
beyond the grey plume of dust
you glimpsed in the mirror

ODE TO THE OLDEST BROTHER

they have always called it *going home*
going home for christmas or easter
or even a funeral —
and although your way is not mine
we arrive here by mere chance
in this half deserted village
both home or what we call home
to visit our mother

merely one week later
i have had enough of childhood ghosts
and stories

of your misspent years and fights
with father and all those things
on the farm
and enough of your vodkalegged ghosts —
we have nothing to talk about
any more
and the silence
as you thumb through another copy of *jughead*
only confirms that we are strangers
to one another —
and isn't it a bit sad tonight
our mother 74 going over to a neighbour to bring you
a toronto security guard
home — mother
carrying your case of *bohemian lager* beer through the playground
where no children play
you 49
slowly staggering behind —
and isn't it a bitch being too drunk
unable to walk to the graveyard again tonight
and cry over the grave of the romanian sweetheart
you left to go to the war
your sweetheart who married
and to whom in '45 you returned
to fuck in the coulee by the ball diamond
on a friday mailnight
while her husband drank beer
in the pub

brother — i don't want to see
another bottle of *bohemian lager* beer
for the rest of my life
and am leaving home once again now —
only a funeral will bring me
back this way

Anne Szumigalski

from *When Earth Leaps Up* (Brick Books, 2006)

Untitled ("When I think of him . . .")

When I think of him I say
"He is lost to me."
I should say perhaps
"He is found to himself."
For his is now that ample
silence he wanted in a woman.

At last he is safe from my demand
that he answer, that he speak.
Safe from my shrieking dancing
and tears, from my challenging
him with a thick branch of words.

Once I beat upon a pot
for an hour with a metal spoon
simply to save him
from his own grim silence
which I thought then
to be worse than death.

Now I know that for the living
there is nothing worse than death.

Assortment

some of those says the child
handing over her pocket money

pointing to the jar of many-coloured
sugared almonds

and could she please have one of each kind
all folded into a blue paper cone

but then how to give up those colours
just to make sugar to crunch nuts

her teeth white as kernels
her tongue pink as a bud

her greed dark as licorice
her avarice grey as fields
before they quicken into spring

Pompes Funèbres

once funeral hats were black cylinders
of beaver or silk and always worn
by men, bereaved women went veiled
to hide their tears or lack of them

here in the capital of winter
it's scarves across faces
grey from the frozen air
faces as dry as winter grasses
for tears might become icicles
hanging from eyeballs and lashes
for godsake let's go in and
drink mulled wine

it's may and we're standing
around the ultimate pit
young heads male and female bare
light breezes kissing our cheeks
lifting our uncoifed hair
except for the two passionate
friends of the body whose mourning
is expressed with shaved skulls

their hands are clasped
trying not to scratch the itch
of recovering follicles

but the mother's black straw
with white feathers
suggests the rattle
of a bygone hearse the stamp
of impatient black horses
tossing their noble heads
plumed out there
on the freshly gravelled road

Lullaby for Mark

When they rocked my cradle
I could hear the swinging
of the nearby sea
how it sucked at the shore
swallowing soft animals
tough wrack hard shells
spitting them up half eaten
along the tideline

as I close you in my arms
the wind rocks the fields
it shakes the grass into rivers
which pound at our barred door
sleep now against my sleeping shoulder
may each of us awaken in his own place

yours shall be an island
heavy with white sand
where gaunt shaggy ponies
nibble the spikegrass
where in april seals heave up
to bear their spotted young

mine shall be a glacial lake
fenced by the forest
under its lid of ice
broken spears lie drowned
bones of dark fishermen
pebbles that were arrows
anchors that are stones

Grief

I shall rise only to make coffee or sandwiches or to visit the
bathroom. Even this I shall do reluctantly: by march I shall hardly
be able to move from my chair to my bed, from my bed to my
chair.

Then one day spring will appear again with its flurry of digging
and seeding, and I shall forget that I ever said this or did it. Thus
will my life wear on from season to season, from equinox to
equinox, until one spring I shall find myself unable to get up
from my chair, my book, my melancholy. I shall be left gazing
through the window at my daughter, herself by this time grown
into a stout grandmother, or at least a great aunt, walking barefoot
between the rows of the garden, a measure of carrot seed held
lightly in her palm. From time to time she will rest from her
continual bending and flinging and stare up at the lead blue of the
sky which threatens, or perhaps promises, rain.

Maria Penny

Untitled ("it's morning . . .")

it's morning and you bring me the skull
of a mouse white as paper

at noon you hand me the jaw of a pony
brown as milk chocolate

well I just need a few more bones
to build myself a lover

go find me a lizard pelvis
narrow as a mountain pass

beef shoulders too
broad as any harbour

and I'll have to have ribs of course
and little foot bones
and the ivory curve of a rattler's spine

by evening light we'll work
intricately wiring this piece to that

and then at last lie down
all three knotted in the moonlight

Untitled ("How strange it is . . .")

"How strange it is," I remark to a cat sitting in a basket chair,
"that you and I should live together day after day without
flying off the handle. It's true that you take advantage of me
at every turn, but then how cosy you keep my feet of a
winter's night: how sweetly you purr before the fire."

The cat flicks its ears, disdainful of my human weakness that
leads to these endless strings of spoken words.

Presently I sit down in the opposite chair and doze in the

warmth of the sunporch. As I nod off, the cat's unblinking
eyes are the last things I see. They grow huge and green
confusing my dreams.

Each eye is a whole world: they have become separate planets
revolving in the dark of the cat's fur. Or rather one of them
is the moon of the other. It is impossible to guess which.

from **On Glassy Wings, Poems New & Selected** (Coteau
Books, 1997)

Our Sullen Art

the language of poetry has something to do
with the open mouth the tongue that jumps
up and down like a child on a shed roof calling
ha ha and who's the dirty rascal now?
the same boy sent to his room for punishment
leans from his window listening for animals
far away in the woods strains his ears to catch
even the slightest sound of rage but nothing howls
even the hoot of owls in the dusk is gentle

he hears the tiny snarl of the shrew
the rasp of the snail's foot on the leaf
the too-high squeaking of bats which comes
to his head as the vibration
of distant hacksaws   he hum humms
with his lips tight shut he stands there
listening and humming almost through the short night
then   falls into the tangle of sheets and blankets
where fitfully he sleeps while slowly
the window greys to four panes of bleak light

the day's first traffic travels carefully
past the windows and doors of the shut house
so as not to awaken in the child

those savage cries our violent
our pathetic language of poems

The Varying Hare

We shall not all sleep, but we shall all be changed
        — 1 Corinthians 15

a prayer for the child going to bed
a prayer for his departing
holding in his right hand the enamel
candlestick white with a chipped blue rim
grasping in his left the hem
of his worn nightgown
so as not to fall on the stairs

his brother is allowed to sleep in his clothes
rumpled as they are for fear he may get up at night
and catch his death wherever he can find it

this prayer the mother says to the little one
is simply a defence against creatures
who live at the end of the world
whose snares are like satan's

the child dreams of a rabbit
he dreams his father catches it
with a single looped strand of wire

the big brother lies on his cot
thinking of knowledge got in school
tested in the forest
thinking of himself sitting
at an old oak desk carved with the noble names
of those who long ago marched off to war

his father has told him how they were led away
not to be seen again   probably

they are out there still stepping it
over hill and through marsh
their boots never leaving a print
on wet ground or dry

father the boy says *open the book*
where it tells of the snowshoe hare
her brown coat tipped with white
how lovely she is leaping
and foraging all night
her colours made chalky by the moon
her wary eye on the shadow of an owl

mother the boy writes *it is dawn*
and I have gone into the forest
to visit the hare in her thorny and snowy set
where she sleeps concealed by a tangle
of rose and red osier
god knows nothing can keep her
from the various predators
whose prey she is

tomorrow she may change as we all must
to scrap fur in a tattered bundle

John Terpstra

from *Two or Three Guitars* (Gaspereau Press, 2006)

The Loo

I read somewhere that this
part of the country was first
settled because of one,
that Father Louis Hennepin came
upon the building by accident
during his travels
along Lake Huron.
This was already in 1679
at a time when flush
toilets were considered too
indiscreet for most Europeans.

The cause of sanitation has come
a long way since those first
squatting moments in the bush.
It has been shown that we
are better drained than our parents,
are clean in areas of the body
hidden to science, refuse
lice on religious grounds.
It is to give historical
imperatives their due, that
a line forms for the loo.

We are moving more and more
indoors, and I am relieved
just to talk about it.

At less than two my daughter
is beyond all this, stands
on the beach, in the long

line of those
encouraged by the greatness
of the lake,
goes
where she is, naked
new to the world, and
thinking the way they used to
thinking empire.

Varieties: Acer negundo

Also known as Manitoba maple, ash-leaf maple, box elder, or, less
respectfully, garbage tree. Ubiquitous. Is not always allowed to consider itself
truly a tree, as opposed to a weed, and is therefore unsure of its place. This
lack of certainty is apparent already in its leaves, which have no single,
distinct shape, but appear in several variations on a theme taken from both the
ash and other, more decided maples.

In the more boreal regions of the country the Manitoba maple's hardiness
has led to its being lofted to the level of an ornamental, and it may often be
found lining city streets. Around here, however, they grow wherever there is
no one tending the soil: in vacant lots, along railways, or between the fence
and the alley.

Thousands of their little apostles twitter down to earth each year in a
persistent attempt to convert the entire deciduous zone. Most are hoed down as
young shoots in early spring by the gardeners, and this may be why the ones
who do attain some form of maturity often have a surprised if not furtive look
about them. Rather than grow directly up, they shoot off at various angles to
the ground, as if they had taken a running start at treehood but could never
have anticipated their present stature and feel ill-equipped to deal with it.

Full-grown, the Manitoba maple presents a case of the one that got away,
or an act of charity.

The Little Towns of Bethlehem

For unto us
  in Aklavik
is born a child, in
    Attiwapiskat
  Gaspé
    Cornerbrook, Newfoundland.
And a son is given in
    Wetaskiwin
     Bella Coola
Flin Flon.
  And the future of the whole earth
is placed upon the shoulders of the daughter of
Tuktoyaktuk
   Tignish
    Swan Lake.
And the place of their birth is called
     Vermilion
Temiskaming
    Nain.
  Picture Butte

An angel of the lord appears in the night sky
over Rankin Inlet, over
   Iqaluit, saying
This shall be the sign: you will find the babe
wrapped in cast-off flannel, lying
on a bed of straw, in
   Esther, Alberta
in a winter feeding stall
an open boxcar, outside
    Kindersley, Saskatchewan.

And sure, several hours north
from Hogg's Hollow, just this side
    Engelhart
you see a one, sleeping in its mother's arms

on the soft shoulder, where their car broke down.
And the dark highway shines
                            imperishable life
while helping them
                  beneath these northern lights
and driving on, through
                        Cochrane
                              Kapuskasing
              Hearst
past Nipigon, and on
                      to the little town of Emo
Rainy River Region,
                    and least among the little dots
that lie scattered as stars
                          and litter the map
of Northwest Ontario,
where they're expecting you,
                            as in so many other
of these least likely dots
                          this expectation
also is, in
            Miniota
            Pickle Lake
                  Ohswekan
      Glace Bay.

For unto us
For into all
            this night
is born a child, this night
                          bearing each
and the places of their birth,
                                  and nativity is given
                            every name.

Explicable as the Centre Mall

This was to have been about the old flames,
and what they've hurdled, how they've leapt,
and about the old, retired men who gather
at the indoor mall, and take their coats off
so they are free to spread their arms
and be expansive, expressive, like in Slovakia,
Estonia, or Hungary,
                         because that is where
they come from, and because all over the world
people are still speaking in tongues
they take to other lands, like this one.
And I may have gone so far as to say
they are a kind of evangel, these old, retired
Eastern European men, who added
to their number there that day, me.

This happens down past Barton Street,
by Kenilworth, that they stroll up
to one another across the tile floor
and slap shoulders, stand around.
Theirs is the easy, growing animation
that's geared to draw laughter out.
                  Look,
it's all good news: they speak, it seems,
solely to get that rise from their compatriots,
that explosive laugh; which is loud enough, God
knows, and less polite, it drowns the muzak out.

And I might have said, at this point, "My Spirit
is poured upon all flesh,"
                     for these are the words
of the text I thought applied, prophesied, in part,
these men.

            Flanking them, on either side,
are the rows of cubicle shops, with their young
sour attendants. Staff is sour because already

it is a slow day, and they are bored, and time
for them drips tick by tick upon their forehead
like the kind of torture you've only read about.
Add to which, they work for some megapolitan outfit
that considers them more than just a little lower
than the angels ...

                 but our old apostles
pay no mind, caught up as they are in the dip
and rise of their own arcane, gregarious exchange.

What does this mean, that we hear a lively commerce
only they can comprehend?

                     They move on.
Their lollygagging group disbands
and wanders in a drifting, ragged line
out to where the mall opens up and the ceiling vaults
high over a tropic of doughnuts, tacos and pizza.
They reconnoitre a table,
                   and some of the men
sit, while others stand, one foot on the bench,
elbow on their knee, smoking, buying only coffee,
and gazing through the skylights, or into the leaves
of the large *ficus benjamina*, as if entranced
by the incongruities, this daily foreign action
they share with a tree, the conversations
steeped in godlike silences.
                 A woman walks past,
her age the one they may have been
when the fighting began, around the time
they also may have met the one they married,
with whom they left home, who also survives
and stands not far from here, bent
over the sink, is up to her elbows
in the dishwater of old world manners,
consenting that these ancient breadwinners
dream dreams
                 if they still have the eye.

Husbands and wives, and a war
elsewhere, that is said to be over.
                                    I've heard
about their friends, the extended families,
whole towns that were undone, in ways
unspeakable, or too mundane, because
it was like that in Europe.

But there are no enemies here, and nothing
is foreign, and everything is.

The boys and girls who tend the shops
are almost all grown-up now. It happened
as we sat here. They've aged, at least,
perceptibly, in their dolled cages.
                                    And if this
were yet to be about the dancing flames
hurdling time and place, I'd wonder at
these sons and daughters, what their vision
says, for this is also in the text, and I would see
those stated, mighty works of God
explicable,
                    but also at the Centre Mall.

Our old friends will emigrate again, at noon,
to a hot meal. And through the fire and smoke
of the steel-making plants nearby, they'll carry
with them, jingling in trouser pockets,
only as many minutes as the world
is handing out today.

                    And so I never wrote it.
For the confusion of tongues and cultures,
commerce, peoples in their generation,
round tables rooted to tile floors, cigarettes,
styrofoam, and pot-bound tropical trees
reaching for the skylights

bested my glossolalia, simple as wine.

Devil's Punch Bowl

How my arm encircled the small world
of your waist, as you stood
on the fence, on the edge overlooking
the Devil's Punch Bowl, its narrow
band of water dropping
into the gorged hollow, elbowing
around the boulders a good
two hundred feet below
our feet.

        How cold the wind feels
on all our open wounds.

        I haven't dreamt
of falling since I was young enough
to be your brother,
daughter.
        In that time
the falling always became
flying, landing softly—
           ef words.

I know what rocks awake
and men can do, now.

There is no true protection.

Forgive me.

Disarmament

If you sit on the third-floor balcony
of your twenty-six storey apartment building downtown,
you may find yourself staring down the barrel
of a twenty-five pounder gun, a howitzer,
positioned on the front lawn of the military museum

across the street,
and feel perfectly confident that it is disarmed,
or hope so.

We carry no weapons here.
There is a formal requirement to love
        the one who stands beside the howitzer,
whether the howitzer be disarmed or armed,
and this keeps us in constant communication
with the unseen one who stands behind the one
who tomorrow may stand poised beside the howitzer.
For there is always the part in us
that considers the defence of our own bodies
        to be in our own hands,
that would avenge injustice,
the suffering of ourselves and others,
regardless of formal requirements.

And if they come with knife or fire,
or if the gun is held to my daughter's head,
if I and mine are driven into hiding under the High Level Bridge,
fleeing roundup, awaiting the inevitable
with others of our social, religious, ethnic
        or national community,
No, I do not beforehand know what my response will be.

Our lives run through our fingers like water.
Salt or red, the liquid drops that fall from our bodies,
the bodies of others,
fall onto the heated surface of current events.
The drops suffer and dance across the surface
and are released into the air.
They rise as the unseen vapour of supplication and intercession.
Our lives are the prayer given up against a cycle of violence.
The prayer forms a cumulo-witness,
condensing under the floor of heaven.

And you who read sky and radar screen,
who understand the behaviour of wind and cloud,

the markings on overhead jets—
how is it that you cannot detect the flight of the spirit,
my brother, my twin,
or where a reconciling rain might fall?

The war is never elsewhere.
The seeds of conflict float down on parachutes,
its roots run deep as dandelions
            in the front lawn of the military museum.
Our enemy currently lives behind a door
on the seventh floor of the same downtown apartment building.
He and his friends, male and female, toss bottles,
shout up and down from balcony to ground, at all hours,
keeping us in constant communication
with the unseen one who sits beside us on our balcony,
who lies beside us in our bed, listening.
Inevitably, the volume is turned up
as they dance to further taunt his formal requirement.

Tonight we lie awake,
and invite the spirit come brood over our twenty-six storeys,
the storied conflicts of a tired world.
To tuck us under wing, all.

Come, love,
disarm us.

Humus

The church where we go to now
is no big deal, a small group of protesters,
half a millennium after the fact,
in a city of need
in a hurried, wasteful time:
and it seems a kind of perverse luxury
that we experience so many varieties
of grief and sorrow

made available in such abundance,
though it doesn't quite fit
with the cut of our clothing,
or the cleanliness of our skin,
with only each other to fall back on,
after all, and our only righteousness
the love we bring,
and it is not for our perfections
that we are loved,
or the perfection of our gifts,
but only that we are, all, made
for this conversation, going on,
and now, having travelled
a dark passage
into this early morning light,
our eyes adjust,
we taste a kindness in the air,
this spring we smell
difference,
we catch an ancient scent, and
holy scat—
holy dog dirt on the lawn
after the snows are gone:
we've been pulled through.
We're only humus, after all.
And all the good we thought we were,
and all we did or did not do,
these seasons past,
is gone to soil, is
Holy. Holy. Holy.

Mildred Tremblay

from *The Thing About Dying* (Oolichan Books, 2005)

Dogwood Tree in Winter

In April you were a wedding bouquet
in my backyard. Fifty feet high.
But now, in November,
a tough wind works you over
and every day a little more
of your naked grey body is revealed.

Out of two million leaves, you have one hundred left.
They are the terrified ones,
afraid of the long fall into the unknown, unaware
the wind will talk them down.

***

I stare in disbelief at this shuffling old man
in my house. Half blind, he stands at the window,
squints out at the giant Dogwood in our yard.
Under his disguise, there's a young man
who likes to move quickly,
fire his element.
I am sick of his act.
Stop it, I yell. I can't stand it anymore!

***

At dusk, in your few rags of leaves
you stand very still.
The underground holds you so fast,
has such a grip, fight or flight are not options.
You hold out your stripped Shakti arms
in a dance of surrender.

***

The old man is tired of saying thank you, thank you.
He looks around for something to give—anything.
He tries carrying his breakfast dishes to the sink
but they slip from his shaking hand,
crash to the floor—the gift he gives
is a broken cup. When I clean up,
the old man says thank you, thank you.

***

Naked tree, it's taken me this long to realize
you speak in branches. Addressing the lane
and the roofs of houses, your speech
is disjointed. Nobody listens.

***

Oh what can I do with my winter man
who staggers and drags one leg in a limp,
who carries one hand in a flop like a shot bird,
who declares every hour
as if it were news:
My hip! My back! My arm!
What shall I do, what shall I do?

***

December tree, you look dark,
you've turned inward.
You are taking now, not giving.
That swelling where the bark splits,
is that your old trauma? The gash in the middle,
is that the way in to your sorrow?
I won't go into that vast wormy darkness;
my hair might snag in the twist of roots,
my mouth be stopped with fungus.

***

The sound of crashing
in this house terrorizes me. Jesus
only fell three times.

I weave behind my winter man
like an old mother quail
with a strange clumsy chick.

***

In a cold rain, you stand flat to the ground
like a bad painting, unconnected,
your spaces filled with grey sky.
From one of your arms a knotted rope dangles,
remains of a swing. I don't think of children,
I think of hanging.
What body . . . some morning . . .

But I know what you're up to—

you are secretly preparing your beauty.
I remember the wedding in April
when you held out to me
thousands of silent white blossoms.
I remember the finch who arrived
to give voice to your flowers.

On Reading Jim Harrison

I loved the way you listened to the ladybug's
death, your shaman's ear close to her polka dots,
her thrashing legs almost tickling your cheek.

The most intimate I ever got with bug death was
watching a cranefly die on her back on my bath
room counter. I stayed with her to the end. I
couldn't make out her last-minute prayer but she
expressed a lot through her long skinny legs.

Do something, they kept saying.

I didn't.

I learned long ago to let small deaths unfold.
Those soft grey bodies of half-chewed mice,
those panting birds, may they die without me,
in peace. When ravens, black masters of murder,
move in to steal newly hatched morsels, I look
up at the battle—*que sera*, I say.

But once at the seashore, I was tested severely.
A baby otter pinned in the talons of a wheeling
bald eagle, screamed its small death from the sky.
From the rocks, the mother gazed up, her
slick body arched, her sleek throat wide open,
praying a long noisy prayer to which I, shouting,
added my own.

The Convent

In the bathroom where I washed my hands
before my piano lesson with Sister Martha Marie,
I hardly dared look at the toilet, afraid
to think of nuns' unexplored bottoms.

And the bathtub was worse, impossible
to strip away layers of skirts and capes
and fit a Sister, hairy and nippled,
into the tub. Her black heavy clothes
were her body, without them she didn't exist.
In the hall a broad stairway led up
to their bedrooms. I loved stairways
but this was
                one I didn't want to ascend.
The thought of those narrow rooms: Iron beds,
giant crucifixes leaning over.

Jesus could fall on your bed at night.
A huge cold body
you'd never get out from under.

Jehovah

Two earnest young men at my door
dressed in best Sunday suits, briefcases
bulging with proof that I'm wrong
and they're right.

They're after my soul. They want
to scrub it with Lysol,
dress it in a nice skirt and blouse,
save it for Jesus.

They don't know how many years
it took me to save my own soul.
To attend to her cries,
dig her out of the rubble of cassocks
and black leather-bound books.

They don't know the sight of my soul
would scare them to death.
She's old, almost naked,
she's kicked one shoe off
and the other one's flapping
and she's running for the mountain,
hell bent for freedom

Thee

I want to grab thy crotch
kiss thy chin, thy cheeks, thy heels
the hairs on thy belly.

I want to
take thee home
tie thee to the bedposts
copulate and fornicate
get laid, give thee head
be thy hand
maiden
I want thy semen
rushing like the mighty Fraser
into my estuary
I want to roll thee over
handcuff thee
have anal and oral and navel
and ear intercourse
and inner and outer and astral
foreplay and hindplay
I want to taste thee, smell thee
smear thee with toffee
and almonds
lead thee astray
into my garden
eat drunken fruits
lie back in the pomegranates
hear thee say
my breasts
are two lambs
bunting
and I'll tell thee
thy tree
is akin to
the Cedar of Lebanon
and thou art
my Lion of Judah
my King of Kings

Finished

Her husband knocks and knocks
shaking the bedroom door.

Oh Christ, she whispers,
her face in her hands. Oh Holy Christ.
The words push past her fingers scraping the skin.
They skirt the mahogany dresser, the mirrors,
come back to her tongue.

She tries again, louder.
Oh Christ, oh holy Christ.

The words look to the canopied bed
draped in silk where she had slept in his arms,
to the windows where the white curtains
bell out, bell back, tolling: finished.

Finished is a cactus with long needles
tearing its way down her throat.
Her mouth fills with blood,
she falls to the floor

while her husband knocks and knocks,
calling Josephine! Josephine!
the divorce papers rattling in his hands.

Fitness Centre

This is a room where one comes to suffer.
Here the gripped jaw, the groan.
Here the machine. This one resembles a leather bed.
Don't trust it. Here's one from the Inquisition
with clamps. And those treadmills—what
scrambled messages
do the legs give the brain?

If there is madness, here it is.
No one seems to notice a woman
riding a bike that's taking her nowhere.
She persists unconcerned for half an hour.
Beside her a man wearing glasses
furiously pedals and reads a book.
Never looks up to check
if he's heading into a ditch.

On the floor a man is rowing a boat—
not a blue wave or a fish in sight.
He leans into the pull, grimaces,
gives it his all. Yet no one arrives
with a strait jacket
to carry him off.

Jonathan Cohlmeyer

Avoiding Airports

I decided to fly home on my own—
I mean, just using my arms. I flew
naked to avoid getting tangled
in winds and birds.

Alone in the sky, thrilled
to have realized my potential
I flapped strongly along,
smooth as a Canada Goose.

In the east a great cloud
swallowed thunder
and my wild pubic hair
like electrified wires, sprang straight

from my vulva, unkinked and
my breasts like two mares soared
through the valleys of heaven
but the thrill of all time

was to pee
with abandonment
and I peed wherever
and whenever I pleased

and nobody cared

and it felleth down
as the gentle rain
upon the ground below.

Martha George

Yvonne América Truque

de *Feuilles de soleil / Hojas de sol*
suivi de / y
Franchir la distance / Recorriendo la distancia
translated by Jean-Pierre Pelletier

Sous la pluie

Pour Jean Gauthier

Je garde en mémoire le geste léger
de ton sourire venu de loin
apaiser les soirées
où la pluie m'incommode.
Le paysage est d'ocre, le ciel de plomb,
la terre en son humidité
chante le goût de la tristesse
et la rue est une chute assourdie.
Plaintes et lamentations à l'esprit
Je m'avance vers toi : comme vers un temps nouveau.

Quand la pluie cesse,
s'ouvre un parallèle
entre l'océan de tes yeux
et les eucalyptus de Monserrat
exhalant leurs parfums au loin.
Le cœur palpite dans le silence du soir
et quand tu apparais à la porte,
tout silence est intimidé
car ta présence tangible rompt le jour
et éclairent la danse des rires exaltés.

Bogota, 5 avril 1983

Franchir la distance

À Alfredo Gómez Naged

Il y a des moments où j'évoque des temps éloignés :
illusions opacifiées comme miroirs inachevés
lancés de toute éternité dans le vide.

Je ne voudrais rien, dans ces moments,
que le secours des années évoquées
puisque vit encore en moi le battement d'aile d'un oiseau
qu'un temps inclément a fait s'effondrer sur le sable.
Et ce sillage... mon sillage perdu dans un trou noir,
caché dans les heures disparues à jamais.

Je ne voudrais rien, aujourd'hui,
sinon ouvrir des chemins, en franchir la distance
dans son infinitude d'air et de temps,
pénétrer ses angles et ses ombres
pour qu'à l'improviste, un éclat
reflète le trajet de la route perdue.

Je ne voudrais rien ... excepté reprendre
mon vol depuis le sable.
Chemin, tronçon, lieu convoité,
reconnaître et suivre ma trace sur toute la distance.

Carmen de Apicalá, 21 août 1984

Tristesse

Un jour, j'ai décidé de tisser des rêves dans le vent,
mais ce n'était pas le moment.
L'hiver était arrivé
et je n'entendais que son sifflement continuel
alors que dans les champs s'amoncelaient
maints flocons de neige.
Les arbres dépouillés
ne supportaient que quelques rares nids
et des oiseaux de givre se posaient sur leurs branches.

J'ai regretté les encres roses de mes paysages,
celles que j'ai transportées avec moi depuis toujours,
depuis que j'ai découvert que la joie
était le coloris d'un ciel au couchant -
car je me permettais d'arracher aux heures
les couleurs d'un haut vol.

Un jour, j'ai voulu reprendre la fugacité du temps
et faire mien l'univers, mais ce n'était pas le moment.
La tristesse grise du ciel était une plainte amère
et mon être voyageur,
une forme figée parmi les glaces.

Pierreville, mars 1985

Et aujourd'hui nous voici

Je suis tellement ce creux
que même le vent ne m'atteint plus.
Ton rêve a pu être le mien
et néanmoins nos chemins
ne se sont pas croisés.

Dans quelque parc lointain
tu as attendu avec une anxiété profonde
le signal du vent qui annonce le printemps,
la pirouette d'une mouette dans le ciel
et la fleur que tes mains caresseraient.
Tu as vécu ma réalité et néanmoins
tu es toujours resté distant,
en silence tu as parcouru mon silence.

Un jour, fatigués d'attendre presque sans vie
le retour de la vie,
nous avons découvert avec étonnement
les masques ridicules dont les autres se couvraient.

Depuis lors, je fréquente un parc
sifflant de vieilles mélodies
et en tissant dans ma pensée les mêmes rêves.

Et aujourd'hui nous sommes tellement ce creux
que même le vent ne nous atteint plus.

Montréal, 7 juin 1985

Jackie Raftery

Fragile barcarolle

Fragile barcarolle,
du fond je t'observe
dans ton arrogante attitude de va-et-vient
cajolée par les vagues...
bercée par les vents.

L'eau est aussi ma demeure
et cependant je ne suis
que ce petit poisson insignifiant
portant la douleur et la joie
dans la vaste texture du paysage sous-marin.

Michael Trussler

from *FAST FORWARD NEW SASKATCHEWAN POETS* (Hagios Press, 2007)

Birds, Pity Nostradamus

Domine, forgive me my memories – a strange
thought to enter the snail of the head.

An old man makes soup much like a child would, if only
to tolerate the afternoon. And cleans himself with candles.

Months or years, feel the fish-cold stone. The first of night's
flagships is a kitchen's worn down floor.

Birds, pity Nostradamus, locked into the future, and
forced to take all of its fierceness down.

Prophecy isn't tennis, isn't a star's vacant steps, isn't
a table one face deep. Is a collection of missing fingerprints.

But the past is, the past is, the past is an enclosure,
a change room only a few of us have ever seen.

And new love / she's wearing smiling skulls on her finest boxers,
never, never to cradle suicide's astonished microphone.

A Woman was Given a Choice

You can be someone who can hear
the sea's face shadowed with rain, the delayed
generosity of clouds and other blind
things / or you can have a voice

that turns a graveyard into a piano
being played across a lake. It's that
brutal, every season's
renunciation.

The Colour White

begins with eggshell.
Surrender's wave. Knotted

underwear, worn on
the cross. The baby teeth
your father kept for you
in a Japanese box.

Thanks for visiting. Come again.

2.

The colour white is popcorn
on the floor – seeds forgotten
from childhood, if childhood could
ever have been a movie. Because

the colour white makes illness
easier, check out the fingernails
of everyone here. Because the colour white, when
careless, churns out aphorisms, check
out that Russian painter, the one
whose brush tore the drama
from monologue – its
blood blown across
the scarcest snow.

What's the hurry?

3.

I lie in a red box. A torso
for collectors only. Wax over
Bisque porcelain. My hair, they
say, could be human.

What's your hurry?

Every love song is
flour between your fingers.

4.

Bleached. The sun's a violin.
An owl's claw. And the soul
suspends its worth. The colour white
looks up at you from face down on a deluged
sidewalk. Reflected, trees initiate. Shepherd infinitude
into dimensions of rising cloud. White, always
beyond the whispered return of
stolen things / Staring, the colour
white reels inside
us:

5.

an elderly Jewish woman on TV last night gave me this gift, a
mitzvah that I'm passing on to you. After surviving the camps, she
found herself destitute in what remained of Europe. She fell in love
with a man. He fell in love with her. They wanted to get married,
and she felt bad that she couldn't have a wedding like the ones
she remembered from her childhood. Her husband-to-be promised
her a white wedding dress. But how to get one? His response: with
a kilo of coffee and some cigarettes he bought a parachute on the
black market. It had once been used by the Nazis. He dragged the
parachute, a silk cloud, across recurrent fields to a tailor, who then
fashioned a virginal dress from the material. She was married in it.
And so, eventually, were seventeen other brides.

from *Accidental Animals* (Hagios Press, 2007)

Iraq: Operation Shock and Awe, the New Sublime

I wish Kant could have seen
the stranger down the hall, the one
watching CNN today, the one getting
turned on taking in the computer's
night-scope-green, this new light

making way for bright mossy tanks, rapid
spectral men—the so many
desert machines.

                        Both hands
wrapped around the computer screen, she's
a believing Christian, an even fiercer
mother of two, a boy, a girl, still
babies mostly, which means

nothing / neither love
nor God ever
altered anyone.

What's really important
is this:
                she knows the correct names
for all the weaponry, can identify
each unit of soldiers, hones in
on each target / and she knows, she
knows that she's
part of the team.

Portrait with Arbitrary Scenes and Accidental Animals

Amidst the most extraordinary fire.

You asked me to choose. Choose between rebellion
and unguarded wonder, burials at sea or
beneath the drum-beaten sky.

So I've been led to gather and scavenge
for things. Examine them.

2.

First with my fingers, from the waist up—these streets falling away resemble
women, I thought. And I learned to see with my stomach, where the nerves
gather, found a run of blue desert—the fixed and myopic sky—to sit beneath.
Sometimes animals came by, recognizing how I cared about things. The
unbroken game back then being to strike down the need for any kind of deal.
Not to give what's due, neither to Caesar or God—this was to see how the
word *or* suddenly candles beauty amidst
our Ptolemaic thinking.

3.

That was twenty years ago, before I knew
that most of them would be spent
living in potent but fake shadows, sometimes overhearing
voices sip at my brain.

In between these twenty years—marriage, doctors, a job worth
keeping, necessary drugs, the dazzle of children, and
now divorce—a useful and fortunate life that hasn't
yet vanished. Or flared.

This remembering everything but not the right things.

4.

A mind that works finds itself an oasis, surveys
from where it's come, is renewed, and then sets off
again, but mine is more like what happened

to Pompeii. From out of nowhere, a muddy and fiery hailstorm
strikes, burying the immediate. Sometimes there are warnings, but most
often, unlike Vesuvius, the storm comes without being perceived / it doesn't
matter, seen or unseen/   /the damage
remains the same. This isn't to say I completely

regret sudden fire or
cooling ash.

5.

Only this morning a magpie took off from the bird bath, its claws
scratching a sound unlike anything heard
elsewhere /
                and moments before it had raided a sparrow's nest
and won an egg to drink.

The many worlds crammed with spoils.

In between the unopened and accidental round
of days—the point is what? To invent as if to record as if to love as
if to splash quick and formulaic graffiti across
the disregarded slums of the mind?

Perhaps.
Persuade me.

To My First Love

I'm sorry for falling away from you last night on the telephone
but I was brokenly dreaming. It's
been twenty years and

I'm still here, still chained to nicotine, unwhispered temptations. Still seek
the welcoming glitter of gas stations, deepened by a night of endless driving,
        a woman's
bare foot resting on the dash. Many thousands of young
and older words ago, I pretended to be sleeping, with my fingers
combing your pubic hair, teasing out the threads
the Aegean's jelly fish had left there. Pink
negligee. Your fingerprint goes
here:

This isn't what I'd choose to tell you, but steam
from the dryers in the basement is drifting up like dry ice and in the midst
of this temporary fog some poor bastard's beating his Xmas
tree to death over the hood of a stranger's car. It must

be the gray-green wind. Or perhaps it's the two moons, finally appearing
together, girlish and unequal, one brilliant, cold confidence, the lesser one
muted, the pewter-coloured earring
worn by Kepler's servant. The past,

my ancient darling, is oceanic and suddenly
undisturbed—a Faustian drug with only
two side effects: Compassion.
Denial.

Upon Separating

I'm growing very fond of the yellow hard
hats those men are wearing across
the vacant lot: small spheres of yellow, always moving. The dance
of bees. There are so few different
colours here. Where
I used to live

elderly women walk embroidered dogs beneath amber/pink streetlamps.
Houses keep them. Roads curve. Red-breasted nuthatches
fly through tunnels of air. Here the old learn

the endless line of sidewalk with the slow infinity
of canes. It's October. And most mornings,
a distracted man paces the lobby with bare
feet, nervous about snow. The halls are
crammed with other people's dying
meals. People here are
dwarves who make their way
to a shopping mall built

for others. Plastic grocery bags become
purses and other tools. They also decorate
the scarce trees in the pavement. People
in the next apartment are knocking
teeth out with a hair dryer. First his, then
hers, then just the wall; it's so very

hard to decide

where anything is.

A Five-Year Old with Scissors

Must have made the sky today. Don't

stir from the sheets; you can't tell
from the light what time it is. It could
be morning. It could
still be tomorrow. There must

be a parade coming. In threes and fours, a crowd's ambled past
carrying lawn chairs that could just as easily
be suitcases or windowpanes.

When it rains, each drop is the world wanting
to be heard. And when a woman cums, each sound
is time learning
how to speak. I'm not

afraid of you anymore.

Said the aphorism
to the dictionary. Said failure
to its white shadow
always dogging along

behind. I'm learning to restrain
my harsher judgments. It's not as though
I carried anyone on the back of my bicycle
to escape the burning towers.

Diane Tucker

from *Bright Scarves of Hours* (Palimpsest Press, 2007)

hydrangea

The hydrangea bush, pursuing
its pale blue life in my parents' front yard,
my father would prune every year
to a hedgehog simulacrum — a mound
of naked beige sticks bristling the air,
sticks marble-smooth and filled with
wonders! — God's own styrofoam.
In January they made sharp frozen *snaps*.

But every summer the hydrangea grew vast,
round and green-blue in our faces,
obscured the old tire it was planted in,
opened its broad leaves like happy hands
and held out its bundles of humble flowers:
watery blue, each small flat blossom
beaming, finding strength in numbers.

Grandma would cut some, put them in vases,
and those smooth foamy sticks could take it, I knew
because every year they passed the strictest test:
my father with his pruning shears
and me, thinking him ham-fisted and harsh.

But that's what years are for, for learning
that your father gave the round hydrangea bush
the greatest love it ever knew, reducing it
to the nub of itself each winter, conserving
in its roots, in the earth, all its spreading blue.

november 28: in the shower

Still have the tan lines
from August's camping trip.

Burn lines, really, from when the sun
finger-painted red our backs and shoulders
and it felt like this shower, like the water
as hot as I can stand it pounding my back.

When I get out of the shower
it will be like when the sun dipped behind the trees
and the chill fell — all of us diving into tents
for jeans and sweatshirts.
The only burning then being watery instant cocoa
against our tongues and the popcorn
a foil moon swelling in its inflatable pan.

But I'm still in the shower, thinking now
of the midnights, the four of us drowsy
yet driven to stay up and swallow every second
of a sky so star-loaded it was sure to fall on us.
Fear as big as anything I could imagine
smothered me as we stood, staring and slack-jawed:
surely no one I thought *is allowed to be this happy.*

Now I turn and let hot water
pound on my breastbone. I close my eyes
so everything is black; squish my eyelids
so golden sparks fly all across the blackness
and feel, while my back and legs grow cold,
a heat concentrate around my heart. Yes.

Midnight, camping in August, was like that.

while praying

the sound of limbs
moving through bath water
the little waves invisible
a cleansing music
from behind the closed door

the sound of a wet body
squeaking against the tub
as I pray for our encrusted skin:
years of dark build-up on the soul

the water swirling now, echoing in the pipes
the bather is done, has begun dressing

my bed of prayer is a clean boat floating
here on the muddy side of the door

my book in your bag

if I were my book

if I were in your luggage   thumping against your hip

my hands in your hair   uncovering your ears   looking for your eyes

during the flight my folded body   would be hidden
under the seat

I don't come out   while you're in the sky
I don't come out   in the airport lounge

you save me   for the hotel room

the faceless chairs   empty closet unslept sheets

you can take me out of your bag   crack my spine

my lines   will tie you to the mattress
press your cover and mine together   perfect bound

I'll tear you open as though   you were a fresh brick of cherry bombs

all the words in me   gathering up your broken body

poppy

wiry-stick-person
with a short mohawk, dyed orange
in a little flame at the forehead

wiry arms carrying a sorry-looking
dog, all its legs stuck straight out
from its fat brindled belly

wiry-stick-mohawk curled its arms
around that dog birth-tight, and walked
quickly, purposefully, down the cracked
old sidewalk. I wondered was the dog
sick? was it dead?

later, in the psychedelic tunnel
of fruits, flowers and flying seafood
in Pike Place Market, there was the dog:
alive and adoring, languid
at the feet of its master, wiry-stick-mohawk
who now clutches a small guitar
as thought it were her dog, sick or dead,
and tips up a beautiful, sharp-boned
singing face:
"mariposa, mariposa, mariposa..."

and the colour I mistook for hair dye
is a poppy, its wilted stem threaded
around a spike of hair, the flower head
heated by the heat of her singing head,
a little orange flame blooming
along her shaven skull.

legit

Babies are landing in the world
from outside desire, and in the teeth of it,
every single one smaller and brighter,
more needy and exquisite,
than all our careful, condom-covered dreams.

Remember us: the unplanned children.
Some were *kept* (as the terminology goes)
and others *given up*, but every one of us
in the cloud of the word: *illegitimate*.

What makes a kid legit?

Breath, I figure. Sliding out
with a bloody hide and a squirm
and a good hard squall when they cut the cord.

Even before breath we qualified,
all of us swimming in the same sea.
The amniotic ship rose and fell
and had its own destination,
its own port of call — a harbour named light...

they did what they did, my sire and dam,
to stanch the bleeding, maybe, night bleeding
out their eyes and the ends of their overheated fingers
late summer pumping furiously through their skin
August pressing itself through them, pressing out

ever since the night my father's brave seed
smelled for just a microsecond the wet pacific air
and sailed away into the dark of my mother
in search of his mermaid, his siren
ever since that black-bright second
I've been *legitimate*

one small legitimate heartbeat
all the tiny legitimate DNA twirling

like plankton in all my baleen cells
I sailed like Jonah, my mission:
to be born.

after all these years I finally get to be the French Lieutenant's Woman

At last you've found your way to me,
joined me on this promontory
through our particular kind of darkness,
the one that leaves room for fingers
groping along the flagstones.

For so long you waited for me
to come back from the far end
of things, to get my fill
of the thrashing ocean, shadows of ships,
the almost adulterous caress of mist.

I know you were watching.
Feet planted firmly on the Victorian ground,
hob-nailed boots well-polished
and new, you kept coming back,
kept coming
just close enough to see whether or not
I'd been swept away.

Don't budge, I told myself.
He'll drag you back into his world,
a fall headlong into straight streets
and corsets, fossils packed into a canvas bag,
destined for the display case.
And when the wind was bad, and the dark
especially, it was tempting — without a word
he'll receive you. Press you
into his jigsaw life in a trice.
Morning would come then. Fog suddenly
white and the wind with its hands

around my ribcage. Another day in the middle
of this rushing, the sea's perpetual grey struggle.
Keep still.

So I was when I heard you approach:
fixed, a pillar at the swirling edge.
After so long looking out I turned my head,
your shadow creeping closer;
boots scrape along the stones.
You finally open your mouth,
call my name.

Now we're wet together. One hooded cape
covers us both. The wind has grown
more hands and balances us, parallel bodies
at the swirling edge.

We think of a warm house, a bed,
but the fog whitens. For one more morning
our cold hands press together
into the promontory's farthest stone.
We lean into the wind, into
the consummating caress of the mist.
Who knows? We may never come back
from the far end of things.

the shoes I wore in Naples

The shoes I wore in Naples
are in the seagrass basket I sent
back with you, along with the sausage,
the oil, and the little bottle of sand
I scooped up from the beach.

The many shells hurt my feet
so I couldn't go down to the water.
You looked down at me, your eyes

shining like pieces of beach glass,
rough-edged, pale amethyst.

It's time for us to leave this country.

Though I could barely hear you
(our nattering friends crowded around,
and the fireworks),
I knew you were right.

Above the fireworks a half-moon hung,
engorged, sliced exactly,
its dark twin hidden forever.

to husbands and wives

Find time to make love
in the day's middle.
The light is better.
Winter light through fog.
White light liquid and diffuse across your bodies.

Keep the curtains open. Yes,
the neighbours may get a glimpse.
Won't you *honour the marriage bed to keep it holy*
with a refracted second of your joy?

Cast off the dim years of doing it in the dark.
Let the watered light spread across your backs, your bellies.
In the history of all the world there has never
been a belly like that one. There never will be again.

Don't wait until night falls.
Now is the time. Kiss it.

Jacqueline Turner

from *Seven Into Even* (ECW Press, 2006)

Antique Times

You brush dust off the surface where the tv used to sit
Wax nostalgic for half a second you might bite your lip
Forget remembering a breath at the back of your neck
Hands cupping your breasts from behind, no you have
Moved on into another cream-coloured room where
Your desire can be measured in typical terms like
Groceries and renovations and batteries for clocks
That have recently stopped

Strong Compulsion

Mine too: it should be reasonably confessed
Because you know what they say about confession
And my days are measured out by coffee and breakfast
Dropping off one boy and then the other: Jimi Hendrix
This morning and Deep Purple tomorrow today I'm craving
Leonard Cohen again and you can only listen to so much "Dear Heather"
Before your chest aches with the want of what you cannot have
Because you simply didn't choose it

Fell Through Emptiness

When you couldn't breathe in labour for three whole days
My voice kept catching in my throat some financial panic
Yours came forth with a dream made manifest: a pocket,
A bundle, full of what joy obviously but refusing to be precious
About it still calm and frantic: you love small toes but don't
Like sleepless nights; intense substance here, you feel her weight
Against your once broken shoulder

Tract of Time

you caress the edge of each table, roughly, you aren't precious about it
but still couldn't write the letter imagined at two in the morning to an
uncle whose wife had died in one of the worst possible ways because
almost no one would believe she was sick because believing she was
sick would mean facing what was all around them the air and maybe
what they put on their crops and how that made its way to her lungs
filling them too full the day she died and if you could move back to the
table where the pen is the paper you could go buy a card but cards are
too cliché to make you/him feel better or flowers like she used to sew
at the edges of coats or dresses or even towels even when she was sick
and you should write that letter because you're always saying people
don't know what you're thinking unless you tell them that you don't get
what you want unless you ask for it until you sound like a caption for
a fridge magnet in the worst of the Atwood novels

Things Present

you can finally attend to it outside the neighbour feeds the crows what
looks like catfood and the biggest joke is that one can call the kids for
lunch through the overgrown green or from atop the flat mossy roof
where once there were cottages once no ferry no impending bog
destroying overpass: a jewel a gem that now features the largest number of divorced people in the whole area so much so that people wondered if you were moving on your own there your husband is he moving too

Not by Strong Hand Compelled

you always reached out to him when he was a raging kid and now he's
happy and even tempered for the most part we reach through our own
rage at being the youngest and try to appreciate his being the oldest
checking our visceral responses to being punched playfully on the arm
somewhat playfully we can't stand fighting anyway and veto the boxing
classes suggesting pottery though falls on more than deaf ears or
drama classes because of his great comic timing only demonstrated
when almost no one is listening and never to be repeated on request

friday

pours me a thick glass of red wine clink as anxiety sinks away pour me
another and we start to talk faster and we feel freer to say whatever
comes to mind without stopping another and we grow flirtatious a
hand on an arm across the table another and we are witty at parties
there's always something clever to say another and we are the most
interesting people in the world another and we profoundly sigh seeing
it all so clearly another and we solve global warming another and we
know how to convince québec to stay another and we are enraptured
with our brilliance clothes falling to the floor

from They Together Run

her size: zero/*fat*

her loss: 40 pounds (and counting)

her stupid question: are you expecting?
　　　　(oh no, it's just the way you're standing)

　　　　　　　　　　　　her score: (a lifted chorus)
　　　　　　　　　Britomart *withstood with courage stout,*
　　　　　　　And them repaide againe with double more

guarding the bodily territory is full time exhausting
   this space: open for discussion
      are you going to eat *that?*

the tone of her body vibrates
cries out for food, but only gets
sugarless gum and black coffee

       . . . that stroke so cruell passage found,
     That glauncing on her shoulder plate, it bit
       Vnto the bone . . .

from **Bay**

7. Moreton

you've never even been there, get off it
although you've heard the song about the convicts
a particularly difficult warden, life of misery
sung on a drive past looking out as the bay whips past

"To Moreton Bay I have found no equal
Excessive tyranny each day prevails"

Australians don't like to discuss this aspect of history much
I've noticed it fascinates the rest of us: so British so Irish most people
came for work later making the choice between Australia and Canada
sometimes by merely flipping a coin leaving "everyone" behind

"They stole me from my aged parents
And the maiden I do adore" he sings voice reaching folkish lament
the car stops a red light the "other" side of the road he looks over
makes sure I'm listening, it's important that he show me the bay
in just the right light, later we'll stop eat steak drink beer in tall glasses

we could be in Vancouver, Toronto but for the folk song

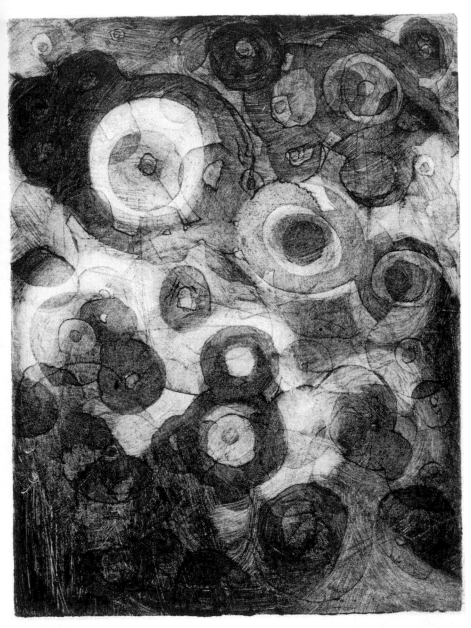

Marken Shed

Alan R. Wilson

from *Sky Atlas* (Fitzhenry & Whiteside, 2008)

Cepheus the King

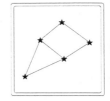

The two of us played chess every evening
as winter drew frost on the window

and loaded the hillside with snow.
Recklessly she'd fire her pieces, storming ahead

with rooks, knights, bishops, even her king.
This indifference to defense meant

I usually won, but she'd only laugh
at how I took each match so seriously.

All season we played, as starlight burned
through the steely air and ricocheted off the hill,

as winter backed away like a weary animal . . .
until I woke to no ice in the panes,

sunlight in squares on the opposite wall,
and chessmen in their box upon her chair.

Katherine Slauenwhite

Leo Minor the Small Lion

She admires the wild cats particularly,
keeps photographs of them by her makeup mirror.

When she says she identifies with their grace,
I don't mention her problem with furniture—

how she once cracked a leg of my writing table
when her left boot tripped over her right,

how the cup she dropped on my celestial chart
sprayed the northern sky with Egyptian coffee.

There's little in her that's feline, in fact:
her naps have been known to stretch past an hour,

the purr when I stroke her dark hair
is several tones too high for a cat,

and except for the ones near my heart,
her scratches don't bleed.

Caelum the Graving Tool

*Hang your chemistry and electricity! If you want to make a pile
of money, invent something that will enable these Europeans
to cut each others' throats with greater facility.*
          —to Hiram Maxim three years before he invented the machine gun

Though Hiram Maxim's automatic mousetrap,
which used the energy of each struggling victim

to reset the trap for the next, was certainly more striking
in design, it was his amazing "killing machine"

that gripped the imagination of the world.
Victoria Regina, her entourage, and ministers

were awed when Maxim's prototype graved VR

into a target with a single pull of the trigger.

Word spread and soon bunched Germans
scrambled from trenches pushing up

yet a bigger version of this "daisy of a gun".
So goodbye Lily, goodbye Rose, goodbye Marguerite.

Red mouths open in tunics of green
and soldier-boys whisper, *It's spring . . .*

Coma Berenices (Berenice's Hair)

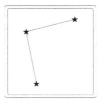

*Queen Berenice vowed to cut her famed amber hair for
the temple of Venus if the king returned safely from
a dangerous expedition. He did, she kept her promise,
and Jupiter placed her shining tresses among the stars.*

Berenice works at the Betty Brite Laundromat.
For $1.50 she will transfer a load into a dryer

and fold it afterwards. Many an evening
I've returned late to find my underwear,

still warm, mustered into even stacks,
my shirts, buttoned to the necks like uniforms,

neatly arrayed on a line of hangers,
even the socks, mated and laid flat.

Tonight she showed an old photograph from 1944:
her husband and her just days before the military

pressed him into action. *I had beautiful hair then,*
she said, *with a natural yellow the other women envied.*

*In his last letter from Berlin he said it had a fire
not even the German girls could match.*

Chamaeleon the Chameleon

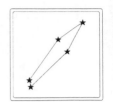

Her socks a queer shade no painter could match.
Where in heaven did you snag such hosiery? I ask

(while snatching a sideways glance
at a halo-like hole round a painted toe).

She looks perturbed, yet I wink anyway,
and say, *Unwind, it's Monday: when laundry*

lines billow a palette of hues, when even
the sun dries unearthly blue sheets in itself.

O feet! O toes! O soles padding off through the haze!
I remember someone watching me

through a bleached-out wash of hills,
and rogue white shirts which fluttered loose like seraphim

sung only poorly with the wind.
Yet they fit me well, and I knew each seam by heart.

Hercules

Forget that crap: the twelve *heroic* labours.
The hydra (labelled such a threat its very breath

could massacre) had heads all right—
with little brains so maladapted killing it

was effortless as picking a bouquet of rancid flowers.
And the giant crab that Hera (bitch!) sent down

had two gimped claws and jigzagged
so ridiculously I laughed . . .

The sibyl says a man designed for fighting
shouldn't think—but nightmares *I* believe in

aren't the twisted, sad-eyed monsters
cast as fodder for my club,

but gods that scramble genes like eggs
then feed them to the world for entertainment.

Crux the Cross

This one-way illness at twenty-nine.
This breathtaking detour past middle age

to a slab of prime land on the hill.
Every hour is signposted by yet another wet face—

to relieve the tedium, I picture a passing scenery
of hairlines blown back, of chins doubling,

of crow's-feet scratching out from tearful eyes.
I smile on these prospects: the visitors admire my courage.

My brother has flown 3000 miles to see me.
We bow like kids over the Monopoly board
laid out on the end-table.
He complains: his mortgage, the cost
of utilities, responsibilities that bury him.
I toss the first die, the second—
sixes again! vaulting me past his block of soaring rents.
He shakes his head. *God damn it, God damn it,* he says.

Perseus the Champion

She said I was a milkman in a previous life,
a simple, even boorish type

who measured out his years in leaking bottles.
My creamy van, with ripples of rust, slipped

like a dream through the still-dark streets of the town.
Its trail of thin lactation drew the cats:

eyes and whiskers first and then their tongues
that flickered pinkly in my taillights.

The newsboy, yawning, looked up
from his undelivered stack of morning papers.

A little cool, I said through the rolled-down window.
Nodding at the inky sky, I sketched out

with my finger certain shapes.
That flood of stars? *The Milky Way*, I said.

Pegasus the Winged Horse

Those final, fall evenings: my father
grappling with the fingers of disease

peeling him like a scab from the planet's face.
My uncle would hoist me with burly arms

onto his back and spirit me away
from the cries erupting through that house.

Deep into the field I rode my avuncular steed,
as the tall grass kicked at my feet, as the failing light

pulled us slowly from the ground.
Stopped for air, he would run a forefinger along

the constellations: the ones he invented on the spot,
the ones my father and he learned from their father:

Andromeda chained to a rock, mighty Pegasus
bearing the abyss of space on white shoulders.

Lynx

If I am first in the ground, visit me,
even if snow lies deep on that cold hill.

Forget the cut flowers. Forget the chill.
Your toasty arrangement of toes will be

my bouquet. And no burial decree
will seal our separation—a few still

feet below yours lies the man who, until
he hugged the soil, loved you exclusively.

Despite the desolation of the snow,
the deer shall pass like ghosts through the gravestones.

The bear shall heat his resting place. Above,
the lynx shall watch you through the icy glow

of bare branches, like the stubborn thoughts of
a man who still sees you through his own bones.

Eridanus the River

This paunch below my belt
retains the alluvium of my age.

Fatty deposits of memory sluicing down
from the years bands played in the open

on platforms, for dancers in dresses or trousers
which rippled like sails in a breeze,

and chaperones tapped our shoulders to suggest
we grip each other less feverishly.

They say you aged quickly, tubing like tributaries
pouring borrowed time into your veins.

But near the end you still beat your foot
to the rhythm of the hospital machines,

like the smiling drummer who rattled
his skins as if he would play forever.

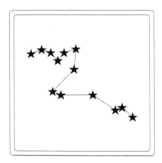

Marken Shed

David Zieroth

from *The Village of Sliding Time* (Harbour Publishing, 2006)

One March night my folks
took themselves to bed
and found inside their comfort
some love left
She curled after
picturing a daughter to complement
two sons and one girl already
behind other walls, asleep
He flung his arm
and drifted, seeing chores
that lay ahead, the seeding
far enough away to contemplate
with pleasure because this season
was still long although
yesterday he had seen the first crow
and felt his mood lift ...

... I jump down
into the squeaky snow
and look around
horses and cutters
more than trucks and cars
a livery stable where men
piss with geldings and mares
a store
my mother on one side
Eva on the other
friends beyond

exchange of flour
sugar and salt
then the storm blocks
the road home, trapping
my brother and me
in town late in the day
close to night and the plough
far away, the road at first
a groove through the field
now plugged hard white
while we wait
I kneel on the floor
thumb comics, the bad
and good guys don't matter
just the colour
and the varied balloons
where characters speak simply
till Eva says
Don't look if you can't buy
and I hate her
for not including me
in her friendship
with my mother
blasted away as she whisks by
in her tight clothes and short hair
I have to get home
my brother, older
already spinning the family car
to and from school
has to get home more:
to stay at Eva's turns back
his dream of adulthood
working for Jack Gardner
all hay season, chucking
bales over his head
—so when the plough arrives
we follow its light

through the dark that comes
after
a storm, the driver
throwing up milk waves
pouring them onto other waves
and we feel the gravel again
under our tires all the way home
Father feeding pigs
Mother surprised to see us
already on the phone
to thank and talk
except the line is busy

is often static fuzzy-blur
yet sometimes now slips
into nicker of a horse
the wet feathers, a grey hen
grasshoppers overhead
sweat, snow, dung, white sky
ice in the trough, ticks on a dog
forks in a heap
thud of dirt on a box
and my mind layering
slow, fast, then stopped
by the skyful of Orion's
belt of jewels
so plainly strewn
and long used for
making children gape
and grope toward
what can't be touched ...

… Harry always rolling his own
and no guns in his home
he borrowed what he needed
I was there
when his sons pulled
the heifer out of the barn
and manoeuvred her
so Harry could place the blow
accurately swinging the axe
onto the white curls
of her forehead
deep dull noise
my astonishment
at the value of a gun
the distance Harry
hadn't needed, willing to go
one-on-one with the young
he'd raised, and how we knew
he loved all his sons
though he was offhand, choked
his boys already talking past him
and into the car
Harry knew they needed
the advantage each of his too many sons
would present to women
red Merc so necessary
to woo the daughters
of the neighbours
driving one home
from dancing
hoping hints in the waltz
suggested futures in the car
—and her counting on her hair
to attract a man, someone
she wouldn't mind if his hand
slipped
the sex play risky

because the girls really were
looking for the best guy
to get them out of town
into the city, some
teenaged marriages entirely
the championing
of adolescent lust
unable to imagine the world
in what the books said
and Harry anyway
not able to read
yet not worried about
going into town
he seldom sat long
and only if he talked
about this field or that
farmer if he talked at all
at one point the big house
too small for all the beds
required, the featherticks
holding off the cold
pinching the longjohns
so someone went down
into the kitchen
smelling of milk
to light the stove
and then Harry'd get up
only twice in his life
at the dentist, once to pull
what remained of his teeth, then
to get the new set, which meant
he mostly went
without, not bothering
to cover his mouth
when he laughed
learning to chew in a new way
living for the day he could

collect a pension
a boon for the hardy
a prize from Parliament
if you can stand the cold
and the heat and the wind
made him wear
too many clothes or scarcely any
the bits of hay sticking
in summer when he
hiked up forkfuls into the loft
wild flowers, sweat
and horse, each family
possessing a tinge of sourness
from clothes too long
held upstairs
in the attic
between planks of wood
the rows of vermiculite
this compound
kills them, someone discovers
later—old perils rolling around
above their scalps
unlike now: every chemical
on probation
then they stuck hands in
malathion
dithiocarbamate
stinking ...

... and scattered
here and there a bachelor
without books
lived in the kitchen
one broken couch
in the dark, the last visitor
a census taker
his own sister never coming
now she'd got away
into one of the towns
stepping stones to the city
she's going everyday
to the Bamboo Garden
for a feed of fries
enjoyed more
when not thinking of
him who takes his grain to town
has his pigs hauled away
such exchanges
the village notes
while he returns
to only himself
the familiar trip home
on the washboard stretch
finding his lane
through the poplars and lilacs
to where he lives alone
and the old men of the village
shake their heads, wonder
what distractions
he creates during winter
if money holds him back
sometimes his pants so grimed
they're stiff
like a harness he'd throw
on a horse
the unspoken hope

that when he breaks
he'll drop in his field
not go
shooting the animals
and then himself
or coming into town
arguing about sugar
or tea, thinking
the price went up
only for him
the women get after their men
to be around
if necessary get Willie help
so the police don't come
and take him off his sandy lot

past the graves
of those who left
windows open one solo night
preparing for takeoff
leaving beef bones for the dog
still eating
next morning, marvelling
at the bounty
raising his head up
stuffed, a long dog
on the kitchen rug or in the beam
of the back door's merry dawn
his owner dreads
may bring
false hope ...

the women and their connection
with eggs of hens, ducks, geese
carrying in their red hands
the delicate life
always close to the hurt thing first
the first to know

teaching us to reach under
the white warm feathers
their battle
when equipment
kills a son or father
in the fields
the baler high-listed
among foes, for days after
kids not in school
finally arrive
the older dragging the younger
shy to be back
the tall girl not so good
at third base as last year

mothers with the job
of holding broken parts

the way my aunt
kept Harvey upstairs
who never went
to school, his limbs
bent, a spider's
when you crush it
not yet dead
lived in bed
not often
in the living room
unless carried, an acrid smell
his eyes bright
his wool vest tight upon
a caved chest, everyone
fussing and weary
of the burden, and then he died
and people cried so much
because he seemed
not to have lived

his early death
foreordained, they all said
his box smaller than most
from the beginning
his fate
the weak and the runty
I had seen
lovingly
wrapped in flannel
and carried into the house
out of the cold barn
a box
behind the kitchen stove
their special smell
(chick or piglet)
tells us we were right to be
kind and yet they died
though we gave them names
one summer and into
the fall, all they had
before they climbed
the slimy stairs
into Fritz's truck
prodded by his stick
and hauled away
and returned much later
an envelope
(my father pondered
my mother scowled)
for the blood
shed by animals miles away
on a sawdust floor
in a shack near tracks
steam rising
men with knives and stunners
strapped to belts
farm boys ...

and yet
elsewhere
others murmur and pat the tough rump
so the animal knows
who comes with love
at least one lad
leans against the barn door
and imagines
flying over lightning rods
the mint hayfields
a white horse
lifts him so he can see
where he began
and yet might be going
his hands entangled in mane

while young women
took up typing and filing and
catching the round bus
home to the flat
three cousins shared
each one after
a different man, hair stacked
up and waiting
on the dirty windy streets
they travelled on
away from the eyes of
aunts, and uncles who drank
silently while others
went loudly to the grave
preceding their parents
who carried them

to where fences meet
in the field (sand, not
good earth for growing)

set aside
by municipal fathers
now resident ...

one skeletal husband
stood by the corn field
as long as one summer
while a wife burned her fat
away, never moving from her bed
afraid of the doctor
speaking fast
her own tongue thickening
her sons woollen
and silent by the door
coming to take her hand
all their eyes filling
except one raged
against his father who never
bought the dresses
his mother once wanted
but no more
past the worry
her heart softening
against that man
because she knew
he would follow her
one day in the potato patch
passing down into the black
worked and reworked soil
to taste the mineral that he was
sharp, iron, foreign
tiny crystal stones on his teeth
little white micas he had
combined with shit from the animals
and built rows of
raspberry canes, fences
buildings so tall
they needed rods even higher

to pull lightning
down around the walls
and into the blackened ground
much like the kind
his sons picked him up from
and then laid him back into
beside his wife
and where his sons took
families to trim and plant
disturb the fat snakes
sliding into spaces
at the edge of the grave
nearest their mother
where the headstone
most needed repair
and where they were beginning
not to believe the Biblical
phrases and consolations
chipped in granite ...

to address death
cut deep in stone
the last words on the subject
not nighttime whimpers
(the pillow rolled away)

some of their words reach me
as I climb through the window
into the school
bunch of young boys and
one smart one
we went in
to cut up the flag in the
dark of the room
that had snared
too much of our clear light

dumped over desks
pulled at the secret shelves
of the lady teacher
and found soft stuff there
but no money
no secret letters
the strap
in the top drawer next
to the ledger of our days
which I thought momentarily
to alter by taking up
her favourite pen
innocent in its groove
adding x's to those girls
who never failed their teacher
and yet could inadvertently
bare a breast while breathing
over the hot math test
in June that final month
of short sleeves and
report cards coming home
and comments good or glaring
like those of the judge
after those of the school board
after teachers, store owners
other students, the janitor
first because he found
our crime and
the cop came driving in
from a farther town, his car
so long and heavy
a sword come down on us
we swore never to tell
Johnny Muzika went in first
sat in that seat
the cop taking down
words one by one

an infraction of interest
at last, young boys off their heads
and a leader to stir up
their little lives, make them
plan and smoke
break and enter
and no one would think of them
except everyone did
and turned us in
to face the magistrate
parents in their
Sunday clothes hoping
he would see them
not their sons
that the cop would say
these are good kids
first time
for him and him, hoping no one
would bring up the flag
at least not the way
the teacher raged
her word sacrilege
the story of a brother
killed on the Italian front
how we later
attached a rubbery safe
to the outdoor well
and pumped until the sack
swelled
miraculously unbroken by mass
hanging down from the spout
onto the well's cover
waiting for her
she howled
we watched with grim
admiration when she
found not me

not Ricky beside me
but cocky boy-man Delbert
and wore him down
the angle of her voice not the same
she used for reading Keats
(we never knew
urn yet loved it
finding in ourselves
what before had only been
jug)
she made him cry
he who was
so strong with us before
his shame
drew a line
but within a week
we were one gang again
and the hem on her skirt
stayed frayed, undone
her lipstick
expecting comment
not the late-in-life pregnancy
that took her out of our class
sent fathers into meetings
out of which they pulled
a young man who kept order

a fool for thinking
priceless meant cheap

got us through math
and handed us over
a Romanian émigré
twisted nose
French accent
smoked after 4:00
leaned back when he talked
the better to survey

squint and despise
how small we were
our parents fools
for placing us
in his trust
where I first learned
someone else
controls ...

Had I Stayed on the Farm

for Leona Gom

I married the skinny girl
and our kids ran free as chickens
one of them, the second boy
moving along the ditches for days
trapping muskrat and living on
chokecherries and bulrushes
sleeping by a little fire of sticks
wrapped in his jacket, and we hardly noticed
he was gone until he returned
as someone else, burnt and smoky
his sisters silenced by the strides he took
to reach the pump, the way he drank
from the barn well, his hands
a mesh of little nicks and cuts
where the cries of the animals
had entered him

I planted, and prayed
for the market to hold, and when
it failed I stopped praying

and never began again
found a fount of colourful
language when the truck broke
at harvest—and when the green straw plugged
the combine, I was the fool
who crawled in, it was my mackinaw
the flywheel caught and drove hard
into the iron guts of the machine
it was the mangled me my son
found, his mother he ran to
but even before he reached her
with the news she ever after
kept hearing, kept hearing
all the black suits of my neighbours
began on their hangers
at the backs of the closets
thirsting for sun and wind

I knew little of books
nothing of rhyme
though the rhythm
of spring, summer, fall
I replayed in winter
every day a time
for breaking down and
making each moment all
I needed, the snow filling up
space I might have stuffed otherwise
with words or lies or worse
falling until all was smooth
and white, virgin
cold
beauty I eventually forgot
to see, seeing instead
lives I might have lived
had I left, had I taken the train
not taken, riding with those
who later returned with ironic gleams

to look at me in wonder, the one
who stayed, as if only one were needed
to rate themselves against
measuring me as their fathers measured
fields of chaff and shrivelled grain

Notes on Contributors (Poets & Artists)

Joanne Arnott is a Métis/mixed blood writer, mother of six. Her first book, *Wiles of Girlhood*, won The Canadian League of Poets' Gerald Lampert Award. Later books include a children's illustrated book about natural childbirth, *Ma MacDonald*, and a collection of nonfiction (essays and stories), *Breasting the Waves: On Writing & Healing*. Current books in print include *Steepy Mountain love poetry* (Kegedonce Press), *Mother Time: Poems New & Selected* (Ronsdale Press), and a chapbook, *Longing: four poems on diverse matters* (Rubicon Press). Originally from Winnipeg, MB, Joanne studied English briefly at the University of Windsor, ON, and has been living on Canada's west coast since 1982. Involved in aboriginal arts organizing, she lives with her children in Richmond, BC.

Elizabeth Bachinsky is the author of three collections of poetry, *Curio* (BookThug, 2005), *Home of Sudden Service* (Nightwood, 2006), and *God of Missed Connections* (Nightwood, 2009). Her work was nominated for the Governor General's Award for Poetry in 2006 and the Bronwen Wallace Award in 2004 and has appeared in literary journals, anthologies, and on film in Canada, the United States, France, Ireland, England, and China. She is an instructor in creative writing at Douglas College in New Westminster where she is Poetry Editor for *Event* magazine.

Douglas Barbour, poet, critic, and Professor Emeritus of English at the University of Alberta, has published many books of criticism and poetry, including *Fragmenting Body etc.* (NeWest Press/SALT 2000), *Lyric/Anti-lyric: essays on contemporary poetry* (NeWest Press 2001), *Breath Takes* (Wolsak & Wynn 2002), *A Flame on the Spanish Stairs* (greenboathouse books 2003), *Continuations*, with Sheila E. Murphy (University of Alberta Press 2006), and most recently, *Wednesdays'* (above/ground press 2008). He has read his poetry and lectured in many places around the world. He was inaugurated into the City of Edmonton Cultural Hall of Fame in 2003.

Wesley W. Bates was born in Yukon 1952 and raised in South Western Saskatchewan. He moved to Hamilton after leaving Mount Alison University in 1977. Bates pursued a career as a painter and printmaker in Hamilton where he had numerous exhibitions. In 1981, he took up wood engraving and freelance illustration. He also established West Meadow Press, a small private press through which he has illustrated and published limited edition books since 1983. Primarily known for his work as a wood engraver, Bates has worked for major publishing houses such as McClelland & Stewart, Penguin, Random House, HarperCollins, Larkspur Press, Porcupine's Quill, Bird & Bull Press, Gaspereau Press and Running the Goat Press, He has illustrated books by such authors as W. O. Mitchell, Wendell Berry, Ed McClanahan, Richard Taylor, Stuart McLean, Timothy Findley, Russell Smith, Mary Dalton and Don McKay. Bates's work is represented in public collections including The Art Gallery of Hamilton, Laurentian University, Glenbow Art Gallery, Grimsby Public Gallery, University of Kentucky, Thomas Fisher Rare Book Library and San Francisco Public Library's Special Collections. His work is held in private collections in Canada, the United States, England, Ireland, Australia, Spain, Japan and China. His *In Black and White* was published by Gaspereau Press in 2008. Wesley Bates lives in Clifford, in the heartland of South Western Ontario. His studio and gallery are on the main street and there you will find his drawings, paintings, wood engravings, solar etchings, and his newest adventure, glass engraving.

Sheri Benning grew up on a small farm in central Saskatchewan. Her second book of poetry *Thin Moon Psalm* (Brick Books, 2007) won the Saskatchewan Book Award's Anne Szumigalski Poetry Award and The City of Saskatoon Book Award. An earlier version of *Thin Moon Psalm* won the Alfred G. Bailey Award. Her first book of poetry (*Earth After Rain*, (2001), also won two Saskatchewan Book Awards. Benning's writing has appeared in numerous Canadian literary journals and anthologies including *Breathing Fire 2: Canada's New Poets*. Currently she is a PhD candidate at the University of Alberta.

E. D. Blodgett has published fifteen volumes of poetry as well works of criticism and literary translations. *Apostropes: woman at a piano* won the Governor General's Award in 1996 and the Canadian Authors' Association Award in 1997. *Transfiguration*, co-authored with Jacques Brault, received the Governor General's Award in 1998. *An Ark of Koans*, published by The University of Alberta Press, won the 2004 Alberta Trade Fiction Award. E. D. Blodgett is University Professor Emeritus at the University of Alberta. Professional photographer, Yukiko Onley, joined with Blodgett in collaboration for *Elegy*, in memory of Yukiko's former husband, an acclaimed landscape watercolorist.

Beverley Brenna has published books for children and adolescents including *Spider Summer, Daddy Longlegs at Birch Lane, The Keeper of the Trees* and *Wild Orchid*. Her poetry has appeared in magazines such as *Grain* and *Dandelion*. In addition, she has had poetry and short fiction broadcast on CBC Radio. She is also a puppeteer and a member of The Alliance of Canadian Cinema, Television and Radio Artists. She lives in Saskatoon with Dwayne and their three sons. She works as a teacher in special education.

Heather Brett was born in Newfoundland, raised in County Antrim and has lived in the south of Ireland since the nineteen-eighties. She has three collections of poetry *Abigail Brown* (Salmon), *The Touch-Maker* (Alternative Press) and *Green Monkey, travelling* (Blue Chrome) and has been Writer-in Residence for County Cavan, Sliabh Beag in Rosslea, Drogheda Borough Council and the Midlands Collaborative of Offaly, Westmeath, Laois and Longford. Heather Brett has won the Brendan Behan Memorial Prize, Blue Chrome Poet of the Year 2005 and has had numerous residencies in Annaghmakerrig, Achill, Arvon, Sicily, and recently Multyfarnham. To date, she has edited over 30 anthologies of the writings of young people from the Irish midlands.

Francis Catalano was born in Montréal in 1961. He is a poet & translator of poetry. After completing an MA in literary studies in UQAM, he studied in La Sapienza University in Rome. Co-founder & Co-Editor of the journal *Influx* (1980-85), he has published his poetry in various cultural journals, in Québec (*NBJ, (NBJ, L'Écritoîre, Moebius, Jet d'encre*, etc) and abroad (*Action poétique, Ritmica, l'immaginazione, Estuaires*, etc). Catalano's poetry books include *Romamor* (1999), *Index* (2001), *M'atterres* (2002) and *Panoptikon* (2005). He is currently working on the second book of a penthology which started with *Index* and which is titled *Le Crepuscule des Lieux /The Twilight of Places*. His translation of the italian poet Valerio Magrelli earned him the national John Glassco Prize in 2006. He is currently the editor of the poetic journal *Exit*.

Francis Catalano est né à Montréal en 1961. Poète et traducteur de poésie, il a complété une M.A. en études littéraires à l'UQAM et a poursuivi des études à l'Université La Sapienza de Rome. Co-fondateur et rédacteur de la revue *Influx* (1980-85), il a publié ses poèmes dans différents périodiques culturels, tant au Québec (*NBJ, L'Écritoîre, Moebius, Jet d'encre*, etc) qu'à l'étranger (*Action poétique, Ritmica, l'immaginazione, Estuaires*, etc). Parmi les livres de poèmes de Catalano: *Romamor* (1999), *Index* (2001), *M'atterres* (2002) et *Panoptikon* (2005). Il travaille au second titre d'une pentalogie qui a débuté avec *Index* et qui s'intitule *Le Crépuscule des lieux*. Sa traduction de Instructions pour la lecture d'un journal du poète italien Valerio Magrelli lui a valu le prix national John Glassco 2006. Il est présentement rédacteur pour la revue de poésie *Exit*.

Jan Conn is a Canadian poet and biologist. Her most recent book of poetry is *Botero's Beautiful Horses* (Brick Books, 2009). She is also the author of *Jaguar Rain* (Brick Books, 2006), which focuses on the Brazilian Amazon, and the great British-born naturalist and artist Margaret Mee, and *Beauties on Mad River, Selected and New Poems* (Véhicule Press, 2000). She won the inaugural (2006) *Malahat Review* PK Page Founders' Award Poetry Prize and a Canadian Broadcasting Corporation Literary Award for poetry in 2003. See www.janconn.com for details. She's a Research Scientist at the Wadsworth Center in Albany, NY, where she conducts studies on the evolution and ecology of mosquitoes that transmit pathogens. She is also a Professor in the School of Public Health at the State University of New York in Albany, New York. She lives in Great Barrington, Massachusetts.

Kevin Connolly is a Toronto poet, editor, and arts journalist. Connolly's first collection of poems, *Asphalt Cigar* (Coach House, 1995), was nominated for the 1996 Gerald Lampert Award. His 2005 collection, *drift* (Anansi), won the Trillium Book Award for Poetry. His most recent collection is *Revolver* (Anansi, 2008). He lives with his wife, novelist Gil Adamson, in Toronto.

Mary Dalton lives in St. John's, Newfoundland, where she teaches at Memorial University. The most recent of her five collections of poetry include *Merrybegot* (Véhicule, 2003), *Red Ledger* (Véhicule, 2006) and *Between You and the Weather* (Running the Goat Press, 2008). *Merrybegot*, winner of the E. J. Pratt Poetry Award, has also been produced as an audiobook by Rattling Books. *Red Ledger*, named a Top Book of the Year in *The Globe and Mail*, was shortlisted for the Atlantic Poetry Award and the E. J. Pratt Poetry Award. She is currently working on a volume of aleatory verse, as well as a larger collection of riddles.

Tom Dawe, one of the founding members of Breakwater Books and *TickleAce* magazine, has been a teacher, professor of English at MUN, visual artist, editor and writer. His work, which includes poetry, fiction, dramatic scripts, folklore and childrens' literature, has appeared in magazines, journals and anthologies around the world. He was the subject of a film in the television series "Canadian Literature" produced by O.T.V. In 2002, Martina Seifert's book, *Rewriting Newfoundland Mythology: The Works of Tom Dawe*, was published in Germany and the U.S.A. His many awards include an election to the Newfoundland and Labrador Arts Council Hall of Honour in 2007. His latest book, *Where Genesis Begins*, a collaboration with artist Gerald Squires, will be published in March 2009.

Rosanna Deerchild is Cree from South Indian Lake, Manitoba, Canada. Her first book of poetry *this is a small northern town* was published in fall 2008 by The Muses Company. Her poetry has been published in several literary magazines such as *Prairie Fire, dark leisure, Contemporary Verse 2* and the anthology *Post-Prairie Anthology of New Poetry*, Talon Books, edited by Jon Paul Fiorentino and Robert Kroetsch. Rosanna co-founded the Aboriginal Writers' Collective of Manitoba in March 1999. The collective is a community of Aboriginal writers who share, develop and promote literature in all its forms. She lives in Winnipeg where she works in broadcasting.

Keita Demming spent his adolescent life in Trinidad and Tobago, where his life revolved around sport, poetry and working with several youth programs. He now lives in Vancouver, British Columbia. He is a recent University of British Columbia Psychology graduate whose world is tinted by the lens of being an Afro-Caribbean diasporean. This cultural dye has influenced his academic and vocational interests. As a fresh graduate, Keita has entered the professional world as a youth addictions worker and hopes that the crosswords of his life will meet a point where his interests in poetry, equity, psychology, community activism, human development and positive resistance converge. He co-edited *We Have a Voice: An Anthology of African Caribbean Student Writing in BC* (UBC, 2006). As a poet, he destabilizes the assumptions of and strides away from all-too-familiar poetic neighbourhoods. His poems are fed by the roots of a cultural identity that rend and tear like a broken saw.

Barry Dempster is the author of a novel, *The Ascension of Jesse Rapture*, two volumes of short stories, a children's book, *David and the Daydreams*, and nine collections of poetry. His most recent book, *The Burning Alphabet*, was nominated for the Governor General's Award for Poetry and won the Canadian Authors Association Chalmer's Award. In 2009, Dempster will have two new poetry collections published: *Love Outlandish* from Brick Books and *Ivan's Birches* from Pedlar Press. He is presently senior editor with Brick Books and lives in Holland Landing, Ontario.

Michelle Desbarats was born in Winnipeg, Manitoba, and grew up in Montréal and Charlottetown. She lives now in Ottawa, Ontario .She has been a finalist in the CBC / Saturday Night National Poetry Contest. In 1998, her first book of poetry, *Last Child to Come Inside*, was published by Carleton University Press and McGill-Queen's University Press. She has received grants from the City of Ottawa and the Banff Writing Program as well as an Ontario Arts Council Works-in-Progress grant.

Jeramy Dodds lives in Fredericton, New Brunswick. His poems have been translated into Finnish, Latvian, Swedish, German and Icelandic. He is the winner of the 2006 Bronwen Wallace Memorial Award and the 2007 CBC Literary Award in poetry. He works as a research archaeologist and co-edits for Littlefishcart press.

Don Domanski was born and raised on Cape Breton Island and now lives in Halifax, Nova Scotia. He has published eight books of poetry. In 2007, his book, *All Our Wonder Unavenged*, won the Governor General's Award for poetry and the Atlantic Poetry Prize. In 2008, *All Our Wonder Unavenged* also won the Lieutenant Governor of Nova Scotia Masterworks Arts Award. Published and reviewed internationally, his work has been translated into Czech, French, Portuguese, Arabic, and Spanish.

John Donlan was raised in Baysville, a hamlet in Ontario's Muskoka district. Surrounded by the rocky Canadian Shield forest landscape celebrated by the Group of Seven painters, the poet developed a deep sense of belonging in the natural world. A poetry editor with Brick Books and a reference librarian at the Vancouver Public Library, his collections of poetry are *Domestic Economy* (Brick Books, 1990, reprinted 1997), *Baysville* (House of Anansi Press, 1993), *Green Man* (Ronsdale Press, 1999), and *Spirit Engine* (Brick Books, 2008). He is also the author of *A Guide to Research @ Your Library* (Ontario Library Association / Vancouver Public Library, 2002). His website is www.onlink.net/johndonlan.

Charles (Mike) Doyle is a poet, critic, biographer, and editor. Of Irish family, he grew up in England and lived in New Zealand before coming to Canada in 1968. He is a professor of English at the University of Victoria, B.C. He has 21 titles in addition to the selected publications. *Intimate Absences: New & Selected Poems*, Vancouver: Beach Holme, (1992), *Richard Aldington: A Biography*, London: Macmillan, (1989), *The New Reality: The Politics of Restraint in British Columbia*, co-editor. Vancouver: New Star Books, (1984), *William Carlos Williams and the American Poem*, London: Macmillan, (1982), *Stonedancer*, Auckland, NZ: Auckland University, (1976). AWARDS: PEN International Award, New Zealand, for *A Splinter of Glass*, (1956), UNESCO International Creative Artist's Fellowship, 1958-59.

Doyle, Susan (artist and professor at Rhode Island School). "Poetry, for me, inspires a connection of the intensely personal and the ineffable to the intellectual and the stuff of shared human experience. My image is a lithograph about self-knowledge and self-deception being parts of the same issue — trying to get at the most elusive truths."

Carla Funk was born and raised in Vanderhoof, the geographical centre of B.C. Having grown up in a world of logging trucks, Mennonites, storytellers and rural realism, she turned to poetry as a place to set down the images of her upbringing. Since earning degrees in Writing and English Literature at UVic, her work has been featured in various anthologies including *Breathing Fire: Canada's Young Poets* (Harbour, 1995), in various literary journals, and as part of the Poetry in Transit series. Her first collection of poems, *Blessing the Bones into Light*, came out with Coteau Books in 1999. Nightwood Editions published *Head Full of Sun* in 2002. Another poetry collection, *The Sewing Room*, appeared in December 2006 with Turnstone Press. She currently lives in Victoria with her husband and daughter, and served as the City's inaugural poet laureate from 2006 - 2008. She teaches in the University of Victoria's Department of Writing.

Hélène Garrett, while a doctoral candidate in Modern Languages and Cultural Studies at the University of Alberta, translated the Papiamentu of Elis Juliana for the volume *Haiku in Papiamentu*, which was published by The University of Alberta Press in 2003. Since then she has completed her Ph.D in Modern Languages and Cultural Studies (2004). Her dissertation was entitled Translating Papiamentu. Since that time she has attended numerous Creole conferences to present papers, taught Papiamentu classes, written various articles for sundry journals, been guest speaker in several institutions including the Ludwig Maximilian University in Munich and continued to translate various projects from Papiamentu into English for which she is still looking for a publisher. For the last three years, she has worked during the Winter term as a sessional lecturer in Spanish at King's University in Edmonton.

Dominique Gaucher née au Québec en 1955; sociologue, elle a à son actif plusieurs publications scientifiques. En 1995, elle se méritait le Prix Piché-Le Sortilège du Festival international de poésie de Trois-Rivières ainsi que le Premier prix de prose de la Société littéraire de Laval. En plus de poèmes et de nouvelles dans diverses revues littéraires, elle publiait en 1999 aux Écrits des Forges un livre de poésie intitulé *Solos*. Elle a dirigé la revue *Brèves littéraires* en 2006-2007 et est l'auteur d'une chronique dans l'Unique, le bulletin de l'Union des écrivains québécois. Elle a contribué à la préparation de l'anthologie *The Echoing Years. An Anthology of Poetry from Canada & Ireland* de John Ennis, Randall Maggs & Stephanie McKenzie, publiée en 2007 par le Center of Newfounland & Labrador Studies, du Waterford Institute of Technology, en Irlande. Les poèmes retenus ici sont extraits d'un livre à paraître en 2010 aux Écrits des Forges, *Trajets, passages et autres déménagements d'atomes*.

Graham Good resides in Vancouver and teaches English and Comparative Literature at the University of British Columbia. His interests range from European literature to Buddhist philosophy. He has published books on literary theory—*Humanism Betrayed: Theory, Ideology and Culture in the Contemporary University* (Kingston and Montréal: McGill-Queen's University Press, 2001), and on the essay as a literary form—*The Observing Self: Rediscovering the Essay* (London and New York: Routledge, 1988). His translation of *Rilke's Late Poetry* (including *Duino Elegies, The Sonnets to Orpheus,* and selections from the *Last Poems*) appeared from Ronsdale Press, Vancouver in 2005: for more information on this book and how to order, see www3.telus.net/ggood/

Garry Gottfriedson was born, raised and lives in Kamloops, BC. He is a self-employed rancher. He holds a Masters Degree in Education from the Simon Fraser University. Gottfriedson was awarded the Gerald Red Elk Creative Writing Scholarship by the Naropa Institute in Boulder, Colorado, where he studied under Allen Ginsberg, Anne Waldman, Marianne Faithful and others. He has read from his work across North America and Europe, and more recently, in Taiwan. His work has been anthologized and published nationally and internationally. He is the author of *In Honor of Our Grandmothers: Imprints of Cultural Survival* (Theytus Books: 1994); *100 Years of Contact* (Secwepemc Cultural Education Society: 1990); *Glass Tepee* nominated for First People's Publishing Award 2004 (Thistledown Press: 2002); and his first children's story *Painted Pony* (Partners in Publishing: 2005). He is working on his first novel.

Matthew Hollett is a visual artist and poet from Newfoundland & Labrador. His work has previously appeared in *The March Hare Anthology, Shift & Switch: New Canadian Poetry,* and *The Backyards of Heaven.* He maintains a website of artwork and writing at www.matthewhollett.com.

George Johnston was born in Hamilton, Ontario, in1913. Johnston knew early on that he wanted to be a writer and published early poems during his years at the University of Toronto where he studied Philosophy and English. After completing his MA and doctoral studies, he accepted a post at Ottawa's Carleton University where, for twenty-nine years, he was a charismatic and much-loved professor of Old and Middle English and Old Norse. His first book of poems, *The Cruising Auk,* was published in 1959. Johnston's keen interest in Old Norse led to a translation of *The Saga of Gisli* and a further interest in modern Faroese poetry saw his translations of Faroese poetry into English. Johnston published four more poetry collections before the appearance of *Endeared by Dark,* his Collected Poems, in 1990. In addition to the Norse Sagas, which brought him international recognition, he translated works of both verse and prose from modern Scandinavian languages. Johnston retired from Carleton in 1979 and died in August of 2004.

Kent Jones was born in Akron, Ohio, in 1949. He attended Kent State University and the University of California at Santa Barbara as an undergraduate and received a post graduate degree in Printmaking from the Slade School of Fine Art in London, England in 1974. Since that time, Jones has worked as a professional painter and printmaker, master printer and art educator in Britain, Ireland, Canada and the USA. His paintings, prints and drawings have been exhibited in over 80 solo shows and can be found in nearly 100 public, corporate and educational collections worldwide. He has been the recipient of numerous grants, awards, residencies and bursaries. Kent Jones currently is Professor of Fine Arts at Sir Wilfred Grenfell College, Memorial University of Newfoundland, Corner Brook, Newfoundland, Canada.

Elis Juliana was born in Curaçao in Netherlands, Antilles, in 1927. He has published over a dozen collections of poetry and short stories and contributed extensively to children's writing in

Papiamentu. He is also an internationally-known visual artist specialising in sculpture. Through humour, he identifies with the character and individuality of the Antillean. He still lives on the island of Curaçao. He was awarded the Zilveren Anjer by the Queen of the Netherlands, Queen Beatrix, a prestigious award for his literary work.

Barbara Klar lives northwest of Saskatoon. Her first book, *The Night You Called Me a Shadow*, won the Gerald Lampert Award. *The Blue Field*, her second book, was nominated for the 1999 Saskatchewan Book Award for Poetry. Klar is also the author of the chapbook, *Tower Road*, from JackPine Press. *Cypress* is her third poetry collection.

Carl Leggo is a poet and professor in the Department of Language and Literacy Education at the University of British Columbia. His poetry, fiction, and essays have been published in many journals. He is the author of several books including: *Growing Up Perpendicular on the Side of a Hill, View from My Mother's House, Come-By-Chance, Teaching to Wonder: Responding to Poetry in the Secondary Classroom*, and *Lifewriting as Literary Métissage and an Ethos for Our Times* (with Erika Hasebe-Ludt and Cynthia Chambers). Also, he is a co-editor of *Being with A/r/tography* (with Stephanie Springgay, Rita L. Irwin, and Peter Gouzouasis), and of *Creative Expression, Creative Education* (with Robert Kelly). After nineteen years on the Pacific Coast of Canada, he still longs for Newfoundland and the North Atlantic Ocean which is always home. (http://www.lled.educ.ubc.ca/faculty/leggo.htm)

Brenda Leifso's poetry has appeared in magazines and anthologies across the country, including *Room of One's Own, Prairie Fire, Event, Vancouver Review, subterrain, In Fine Form: The Canadian Anthology of Form Poetry*, and *Writing the Land: Alberta Through Its Poets*. Her poetry has won the Bliss Carman Award for Poetry, has been placed 1st and 2nd in the annual Vancouver International Writers' Festival Writing contest, and has been shortlisted for the CBC Literary Awards. She is a past Executive Editor of *PRISM International* and has an MFA in Creative Writing from UBC. Her first book, *Daughters of Men*, was published by Brick Books in May, 2008.

Tim Lilburn was born in Regina, Saskatchewan. He has published six poetry collections, including *Kill-site* (2003), winner of the Governor General's Award; *To the River* (1999), winner of the Saskatchewan Book Award for Book of the Year; *Moosewood Sandhills* (1994), winner of the Canadian Authors' Association Award for Poetry; and *Tourist To Ecstasy* (1989), a finalist for the Governor General's Award. His poems have been widely anthologized. He now lives in British Columbia, where he teaches at the University of Victoria.

Andrea MacPherson is the author of four books: two novels, *When She Was Electric* (Raincoast, 2003) and *Beyond the Blue* (Random House, 2007) and two poetry collections, *Natural Disasters* (Palimpsest, 2007) and *Away* (Signature Editions, 2008). *When She Was Electric* was listed no. 6 on CBC Canada Reads: People's Choice 2004, and *Natural Disasters* was longlisted for the ReLit Awards in 2008. Andrea holds a Master's Degree in Fine Arts from the prestigious Creative Writing Department at the University of British Columbia. She currently teaches creative writing at University of the Fraser Valley and Douglas College. In addition, she is a past editor of *Prism International*, and currently acts as Reviews Editor for *Event*. Her fiction, poetry and non-fiction has appeared in a variety of domestic and literary magazines, including *Poetry Ireland Review, The Fiddlehead* and *Prism*. Her travels to the UK, Northern Ireland, the Republic of Ireland, France, Greece, Italy and the Hawaiian Islands serve as inspiration in her writing. She is currently at work on a new novel tentatively titled *Four Green Fields*.

Randall Maggs, born in Vancouver, has lived for more than thirty years on the west coast of Newfoundland. A professor at Grenfell College, he is an editor with John Ennis and Stephanie McKenzie of *The Echoing Years* and *However Blow the Winds,* as well as the Artistic Director of Newfoundland's March Hare. His first collection of poems, *Timely Departures* (Breakwater), appeared in 1994. His most recent, *Night Work: The Sawchuk Poems* (Brick), was launched at the Hockey Hall of Fame in Toronto and the Canadian Embassy in Dublin and made Toronto's Globe and Mail Top 100 Books list. Also a craftsman, he had pieces included in *Wood,* an exhibition in 1999 of Irish and Newfoundland artists. In 2007, he was awarded Memorial's Coracle Fellowship for joint projects between Ireland and Newfoundland.

Alice Major emigrated from Scotland at the age of eight and grew up in Toronto before going west to work as a weekly newspaper reporter in British Columbia. She now lives in Edmonton. She is past president of the Writers' Guild of Alberta and the League of Canadian Poets and a past chair of the Edmonton Arts Council. In June, 2005, she was named Edmonton's first poet laureate. Awards include Fourth Alberta Writing for Youth Competition, Shaunt Basmajian Chapbook Competition, 1998, Poets Corner Award, 1998, *The Malahat Review* long poem competition (co-winner), 2001 and Pat Lowther Award, shortlisted, 2001. She is the author of nine publications in poetry; her work has been represented in six major anthologies and nine of her books still remain in print.

David Manicom is the author of five collections of poetry, including *The Burning Eaves,* which was a finalist for the Governor-General's Award; the award-winning *Progeny of Ghosts: Travels in Russia and the Old Empire:* a collection of short fiction; and, most recently, two novels, *The School at Chartres* and *Anna's Shadow.* Raised in rural Ontario, Manicom's Canadian address has been in Québec for the past twenty-five years. A career diplomat, he has been on postings to Moscow, Islamabad, Beijing and Geneva. He and his family currently live and work in New Delhi, India.

Stephanie McKenzie is a poet, editor and critic. She has published one poetry collection with Salmon Poetry (Cliffs of Moher), *Cutting My Mother's Hair,* and has another forthcoming (*Grace Must Wander*) this spring. With John Ennis, she co-edited *The Backyards of Heaven: An Anthology of Contemporary Poetry from Ireland and Newfoundland & Labrador* (and, with her company, Scop Productions Inc., co-published this book with the School of Humanities, WIT) and with John Ennis and Randall Maggs co-edited *However Blow the Winds: An Anthology of Poetry and Song from Newfoundland & Labrador and Ireland* and *The Echoing Years.* McKenzie has also published a book of literary criticism with the University of Toronto Press: *Before the Country: Native Renaissance, Canadian Mythology.* She is Assistant Professor of English at Sir Wilfred Grenfell College, Memorial University of Newfoundland.

Neal McLeod is Cree and Swedish; he grew up on the James Smith First Nation. He is a multi-media artist as well as a poet, film maker, painter, performer, curator, writer and teacher. He currently lives and teaches at Trent University in Peterborough, Ontario. " In McLeod's painting *Wîhtikow II* (2001), the terrifying spectre brandishes a cross in one hand and human flesh in the other, clearly symbolizing the European colonists' devouring of Indigenous land, resources, spirit and narratives. The malevolent being also serves as a metaphor for the greed and individualism that are consuming contemporary society. Phrases in English and Cree — 'progress,' 'a new light on the land,' 'ate our souls' — express opposing views of European expansion" (Dan Ring, curatorial statement). McLeod operates at the core of the movement to revive and bring back the Cree language to everyday life; the Hip Hop Café has boasted of upwards of six hundred people in attendance to enjoy Cree poetry, music and comedy.

George McWhirter was born in Belfast and lived on the Shankill Road. He received his BA & DipEd from Queen's University Belfast, where he was a classmate of the poets, Seamus Heaney and Seamus Deane, and the Irish literary critic, Robert Dunbar. He is the author of twenty books, many of which have won major awards, including the Ethel Wilson Prize, the League of Canadian Poets Canadian Chapbook Prize, the F. R. Scott Prize for Translation, the Commonwealth Poetry Prize (shared with Chinua Achebe, 1972) and the Macmillan Prize for Poetry. In 2007 he was appointed the first Poet Laureate for the City of Vancouver.

Jay MillAr is a writer, editor, publisher, bookseller and environmental research assistant. He is the author of *The Ghosts of Jay MillAr* (Coach House, 2000), and *Mycological Studies* (Coach House, 2002), which was shortlisted for the ReLit Poetry Prize. He publishes chapbooks under the imprint BookThug and distributes these titles through Apollinaire's Bookshoppe—his "imaginary bookstore specializing in publications that no one wants to buy." He lives in Toronto with his wife, Hazel, and their sons, Reid and Cole.

Eric Miller is a professor of English at the University of Victoria. He is on the editorial board of *The Malahat Review*. His second book of poetry, *In the Scaffolding*, was shortlisted for the ReLit Award in 2006. His book of prose, *The Reservoir*, was shortlisted for the Hubert Evans prize in 2007. His third collection, *The Day in Moss*, continues the explorations of the natural world, specialising as it does in issues of time and place.

Sheila A. Murphy's most recent book publications include *Collected Chapbooks* (Blue Lion Books, 2008), *Permutoria - Collaborative Visio Textual Art* (Visual Poetry) with K. S. Ernst (Luna Bisonte Prods Press, 2008). A collaborative visual poem with K. S. Ernst appears in the November 2008 issue of *Poetry* magazine. Murphy co-founded and coordinated (with Beverly Carver) the Scottsdale Center for the Arts Poetry Series for twelve years. The series featured such writers as Douglas Barbour, who was commissioned to create work in response to visual art pieces included in travelling exhibitions. During Barbour's appearance in Scottsdale, the two writers became acquainted, later beginning a collaboration that is presently in its ninth year.

W. H. New lives in Vancouver and was Killam Professor in the Department of English at the University of British Columbia until his retirement. He is one of the most prolific and versatile literary critics in Canada, having written and edited more than forty books, including several children's books, as well as nine books of poetry. Among his published works are *Underwood Log*, which was a finalist for the Governor General's Award for Poetry, *Borderlands*, *Grandchild of Empire, Touching Ecuador*, and *The Year I Was Grounded*. *The Rope-Maker's Tale* is his most recent book of poetry. He was appointed an Officer of the Order of Canada in 2006.

Jeff Park, from Saskatoon, is currently employed in the College of Education in the University of Saskatchewan. He works in a variety of genres, including short fiction, playwriting and poetry. He has published a book on the theory of writing, *Writing at the Edge: Narrative and Writing Process Theory*, which was published by Peter Lang Press in New York in 2005.

Pelletier, Jean-Pierre né à Montréal, il a étudié la littérature et la philosophie. Poète, traducteur, enseignant de profession, il a été cofondateur de *Ruptures, la revue des trois Amériques* (1992-1998) et membre de l'équipe éditoriale de la revue *Brèves littéraires* (2006-2007). Il a fait paraître en 2006, *l'Amnésique*, plus une traduction de poèmes de Dorotea Montoya Sánchez, *La Comedia rouge sang* (Adage). En plus de se consacrer à la traduction de l'œuvre poétique de Yvonne

América Truque et de l'écrivain d'origine singapourienne, Goh Poh Seng, il travaille à la préparation d'un livre : *Alluvions*. Paraîtra au printemps 2009, *Baraques et baraka*, chez Maelström(Belgique). Il collabore à des revues et collectifs (*The Echoing Years*, 2008) du Québec et de l'étranger.

Elizabeth Philips is the author of four collections of poetry. Her most recent collection, *Torch River*, was released by Brick Books in Spring 2007. She has taught creative writing in the Banff Wired Studio, the Banff Writing with Style program, the Banff Writing Studio, and the Sage Hill Writing Experience. She is the former editor of the literary magazine *Grain*. She lives in Saskatoon.

Sharron Proulx-Turner is a member of the Métis Nation of Alberta. Originally from the Ottawa River Valley, she's from mixed-blood — Mohawk, Wyandot, Ojibwe, Mi'kmaw, Algonkin, French and Irish ancestry. She's the author of four books. *Where the Rivers Join* (1995), written under the pseudonym Beckylane. She was a finalist for the Edna Staebler award for creative non-fiction, and the serial poem, *what the auntys say* (2002), was a finalist for the League of Canadian Poets' Gerald Lampert Prize for best first book of poetry. She has a recent collection of poetry, *she is reading her blanket with her hands* (2008) and an epic historical fiction poem that was years in the making, *she walks for days / inside a thousand eyes / a two-spirit story* (2008). Sharron's work appears in several anthologies and journals.

Martin Quigley is a lecturer at undergrad and postgrad levels in Art at Waterford Institute of Technology. As regional arts officer for the South-East of Ireland in the nineteen eighties, he was instrumental in setting up an arts infrastructure for the region and the establishment of art centres. On the international front, he re-established links between Waterford, the South-East Region and Newfoundland, which had all but died. He is both artist and writer. His works are in numerous collections nationally and internationally, including Canada. His recent exhibitions include *Plus 4*, Kenny's Art Gallery in Galway, *Darkness and Light*, Waterford Healing Arts Trust and the Patrick Kavanagh Centenary Show, where he collaborated with poet Michael Coady. Recently Collins Press published his novel, *Drifting with the River Gods*.

Matt Rader is the author of two books of poems: *Miraculous Hours* (2005) and *Living Things* (2008). His poems, stories, and non-fiction have appeared in journals and anthologies across North America, Australia, and Europe and have been nominated for numerous awards including the Gerald Lampert Award, the Journey Prize, and two Pushcart Prizes.

Monty Reid's *The Luskville Reductions* is his fourteenth book. His previous books include *Crawlspace, Flat Side*, and *Disappointment Island* which was shortlisted for the Ottawa Book Award and won the 2007 Lampman-Scott Award. Born in Saskatchewan, and a long-time resident of Alberta, Reid now lives in Ottawa and works at the Canadian Museum of Nature.

Harold Rhenisch has published poetry, creative nonfiction, memoir, essays and translation since 1978. He is the winner of the ARC Magazine Poem of the Year Prize, the CBC Literary Prize, and two *Malahat Review* Long Poem Prizes, the *George Ryga* Prize for Social Responsibility in Literature for his prose memoir, *The Wolves at Evelyn*, and, most recently, the Canadian National Playwrighting Award. After fifty years in the mountains and grasslands, he now lives in Campbell River on Vancouver Island.

Shane Rhodes's first book, *The Wireless Room* (2000, NeWest Press), won the Alberta Book Award for poetry. His second and third books, *Holding Pattern* (2002, NeWest Press) and *The*

Bindery (2006, NeWest Press), both won the Lampman-Scott Award for poetry. Shane's work has been widely published in Canada and is also featured in the anthologies *New Canadian Poetry, Breathing Fire II, Seminal: Canada's Gay Male Poets, Best Gay Poetry 2008*, and *Best Canadian Poetry in English 2008*.

Mansel Robinson is primarily a playwright based in Saskatoon. His work includes *Colonial Tongues, Collateral Damage, The Heart As It Lived, Downsizing Democracy, Spitting Slag, Ghost Trains, Street Wheat, Scorched Ice* and *Picking Up Chekov*. He has been writer-in-residence at the Pierre Berton House in Dawson City, Yukon, Northern Light Theatre, Edmonton, The University of Windsor and Regina Public Library. His play, *Bite the Hand*, was presented as a staged reading at the Saskatchewan Playwrights Centre's 2005 Spring Festival of New Plays.

Janet Marie Rogers is a Mohawk/Tuscarora poet and spoken-word performer. She lives on Canada's west coast in traditional Coast Salish territory in Victoria British Columbia on Vancouver Island. Janet draws from the richness of her own Indigenous heritage as well as the cultural life around her as inspiration for her poetry. She records her poems with music and has one published collection to date titled *Splitting the Heart* (Ekstasis Editions, 2007). Janet's website includes mp3 samples and video samples of her spoken word poems.

Peter Sanger has published seven collections of poetry including *Earth Moth* (1991) and *Arborealis* (2005). This latter was a collaborative project with photographer Thaddeus Holownia. His most recent book of prose is *White Salt Mountain* (2005). He has been the poetry editor of *The Antigonish Review* since 1985. He lives on a farm in South Maitland, Nova Scotia.

Crystal Sikma is a writer based in Regina. She has an honours degree in English from the University of Regina, with a Women's Studies minor and a specialization in Creative Writing. She has twice attended the Sage Hill Writing Experience and she also attended the 2006 Saskatchewan Writers' Guild mentorship programme with Judith Krause. Her poems have been published in *In Medias Res*.

Sue Sinclair's latest book of poetry, *Breaker*, was published by Brick Books in 2008. Her work has been nominated for various national awards including the Gerald Lampert and Pat Lowther awards. Sue is currently working on a PhD in philosophy, studying theories of beauty. Previous collections by the author include *The Secrets of Weather and Hope* (Brick, 2001), *Mortal Arguments* (Brick, 2003) and *The Drunken, Lovely Bird* (Goose Lane Editions, 2004).

Carolyn Smart is the author of five volumes of poetry, including *The Way to Come Home* and *Hooked*. An excerpt from her memoir, *At the End of the Day*, won first prize in the Canadian Broadcasting Corporation Literary Contest in 1993. She is the founder of the Bronwen Wallace Award for Emerging Writers, and since 1989 has been the Director of Creative Writing at Queen's University in Ontario. She lives in the rocky woodlands of the Canadian Shield country with her husband and their three sons.

Gerald Squires was born in Newfoundland. Artist, art activist and teacher. Much of Squires' large body of work finds its inspiration in the landscape and culture of Newfoundland. In 1984, Squires earned the Newfoundland and Labrador Arts Council's Ted Drover Award for Achievement in the Visual Arts; in 1992, an Honorary Doctorate from Memorial University; in 1999, election to the Royal Canadian Academy of Art; in September 1999, appointment as a Member of the Order of Canada; and in 2003, the Golden Jubilee Award from Her Majesty Queen Elizabeth. He has acted as a juror for Canada Council Arts Grants "B" and was appointed as a juror for two years on the Newfoundland & Labrador Arts Council. He is an Honorary Member of The Drawing Society of Canada. Some of his major exhibitions have traveled across Canada and his works have been included in over 300 group exhibitions in Newfoundland, Canada, U.S.A., Great Britain, France and India, including: "Political Landscapes #1" at the Royal Canadian Academy Gallery, Toronto, and the Tom Thomson Memorial Art Gallery, Owen Sound, ON, 1989; "9 Peintres Terre Neuviens" at the Salle de la Renaissance, Bordeaux, France, 1992; "Hidden Values: Atlantic Corporations Collect", Art Gallery of Nova Scotia, 1997. He exhibited in Waterford in 2008 in a one-man show and met students of Art in masterclass.

Andrew Suknaski is a poet and visual artist from Saskatchewan. He has published six collections of poetry and his work has appeared widely in anthologies. He has worked as a researcher for the National Film Board, contributing to such films as *Grain Elevator* (1981) by Charles Konowal and *The Disinherited* (1985) by Harvey Spak. Suknaski's Polish and Ukrainian heritage, his concern for First Nations, as well as the people and place of Wood Mountain feature strongly in his poetry. His *Wood Mountain Poems* originally published in 1976, edited by Al Purdy, was re-issued by Hagios Press, with a new introduction by Tim Lilburn, in a thirtieth anniversary edition in 2006.

Anne Szumigalski was born in London in 1922 and grew up in a Hampshire village. Having worked as a Red Cross nurse and interpreter during the Second World War, she moved to North Wales in 1947 with her husband, a Polish refugee. In 1951 they emigrated to Saskatchewan, living in the remote badlands of the Big Muddy before settling permanently in Saskatoon in 1956. Her first book of poems, *Woman Reading in Bath*, was published by Doubleday in New York in 1974. Thereafter she chose to publish only with western Canadian firms. Among her 18 books are *Voice* (winner of the Governor-General's Award in 1995), *On Glassy Wings: Poems New and Selected* (1997) and the posthumous *When Earth Leaps Up* (2006). Anne Szumigalski died in 1999.

John Terpstra lives in Hamilton, Ontario, where he works as a writer and cabinetmaker. He has published seven books of poetry, including the GG-nominated *Disarmament* (2003) and the Bressani Award-winning *Forty Days & Forty Nights* (1987). He is also a distinguished prose author. *Falling Into Place* (2002) is his creative investigation of the Iroquois Bar, the geologic formation that supports one of Canada's busiest transportation corridors. In 2005, he published *The Boys, Or, Waiting For the Electrician's Daughter*, honouring the lives of his wife's three brothers, each of whom lived with muscular dystrophy until their early twenties. This book was shortlisted for the Charles Taylor prize and the BC Award for Canadian Non-Fiction.

Mildred Tremblay was born in Kenora, Ontario. She has won many awards for her writing including the League of Canadian Poets Award, The Arc National Poetry Award and the Orillia Award for humour as well as the Vancouver International Writers' Festival Award for poetry. Her collection of short fiction, *Dark Forms Gliding*, was published by Oolichan Books, as were her two collections of poetry: *Old Woman Comes out of Her Cave* and *The Thing About Dying*. She lives in Nanaimo, BC.

Yvonne América Truque née à Bogota, en Colombie, elle est arrivée à Montréal en 1984 et y a vécu jusqu'en 2001, année de son décès. Elle est aussi l'auteure de livres de poésie publiés de 1982 à 1991dans son pays d'origine et au Québec. Elle a reçu en 1987 le prix de prose et de poésie Humanitas. A paru à Montréal, en 2008, *Hojas de sol y Recorriendo la distancia/Feuilles de soleil suivi de Franchir la distance* (Adage/Enana Blanca), dont sont extraits les poèmes figurant dans cette anthologie. De plus, elle a été, dans les années 1990, représentante au Canada de la revue internationale *Vericuetos*. Deux autres livres inédits verront le jour, dont *Los olvidados en la tierra/Les oubliés de la terre*, prévu pour 2010, est en voie de traduction.

Michael Trussler received a PhD from the University of Toronto, completing his doctoral thesis on the contemporary American short story. He has published literary criticism, poetry, and fiction. His short story collection, *Encounters*, won the City of Regina and Book of the Year Awards from the Saskatchewan Book Awards in 2006. His collection of poetry, *Accidental Animals*, was short-listed for the same awards in 2007. He teaches English at the University of Regina in Saskatchewan and was the Editor of *Wascana Review* from 2002 to 2008.

Diane Tucker was born and raised in Vancouver, British Columbia, where she earned a Bachelor of Fine Arts in Creative Writing from the University of B.C. in 1987. Her first book, *God on His Haunches* (Nightwood Editions, 1996), was shortlisted for the 1997 Gerald Lampert Memorial Award, an annual award given to the best first book of poems published in Canada. Her second poetry book, *Bright Scarves of Hours*, was published by Palimpsest Press in 2007. More than fifty journals in Canada and abroad have published her poems and Thistledown Press will release her first novel in September 2009. Diane lives in Burnaby, BC, with her husband, their two teenagers and Doxa the spotty dog. You can find more information about her at www.dianetucker.info.

Jacqueline Turner is the author of *Into the Fold, Careful*, and *Seven Into Even*. She lives in Vancouver, B.C. Her work has appeared in *absinthe, West Coast Line, Rampike, qwerty, Tessera*, and *Fireweed*. She was a founding editor of *Filling Station* magazine. In 2005, Turner was Queensland's inaugural poet-in-residence at the Judith Wright Centre of Contemporary Arts in Brisbane, Australia. She teaches at Emily Carr University of Art and Design.

Alan R. Wilson was born in New Brunswick and now works at the University of Victoria in British Columbia, Canada. His writings have appeared widely in North American periodicals and anthologies. He has degrees in Physics and Creative Writing and often incorporates modern science into his work. His first book, *Animate Objects*, is a poetry collection that probes the covert nature of things. For reasons never fully explained, the second book he decided to write, *Counting to 100*, is a bestiary of 100 poems about the numbers from 1 to 100. His third book, *Before the Flood*, is set in Woodstock, New Brunswick, and won the Chapters / Books in Canada First Novel Award. It is the first of what will be a quartet of novels, all set in Woodstock at different times in the town's tumultuous history. The second in the series, *Lucifer's Hair*, is almost complete. His most recent volume, *Sky Atlas*, is a sequence of 88 sonnets, some more traditional than others, based on the 88 constellations. He still looks through the astronomical telescope he bought in high school, and is currently teaching his four-year-old daughter the names of the constellations.

David Zieroth's most recent book of poetry is *The Village of Sliding Time* (Harbour, 2006). He has also published *Crows Do Not Have Retirement* (Harbour, 2001), poems, and a memoir, *The Education of Mr. Whippoorwill: A Country Boyhood* (MacFarlane Walter & Ross, 2002). He won the Dorothy Livesay Poetry Prize for *How I Joined Humanity at Last* (Harbour, 1998). In 2009, *The Fly in Autumn* will appear from Harbour Publishing and *Berlin Album*, a chapbook, from Rubicon Press. His poetry has appeared in dozens of anthologies, and he taught at Douglas College in New Westminster, BC, for many years before retiring and founding The Alfred Gustav Press, a micro press for publishing poetry. Born in Neepawa, MB, he lives in North Vancouver, BC. More information can be read at www.davidzieroth.com.

Notes from Contributors (Student Artists)

Mark Adams - Sir Wilfred Grenfell College
Joe Batt's Arm, Newfoundland and Labrador
Come-by-Chance by Carl Leggo
"Carl Leggo's *Come-by-Chance* struck me with the first stanza that mentions coming across a gas station. Gas stations are peculiar, aren't they? These little stops we make from going at break-neck speeds to refill, to rest for a bit. Their usual stature and design has always fascinated me. I used to work at a gas station and much like my service work in a gallery, you see a lot of people whiz by you in the run of a day, with yourself remaining as stationary as the station itself [p.251]." http://www.markadamsart.com

Gwen Aker - Sir Wilfred Grenfell College
Sydney Mines, Nova Scotia
Aubade for St. Brigid's Day by Alice Major
"I want to learn to work with every medium. Every day I want to learn something new. Keep learning. I was interested in the way the poem read: it created a flow of images. The poem almost drew itself for me [p.302]."

Rachel Anstey - Sir Wilfred Grenfell College
Torbay, Newfoundland
Strawsmoke by George Johnston
Rachel received the Canadian Coast Guard Newfoundland Region Alumni Association Bursary in 2006. "I am primarily interested in printmaking and drawing. I hope to continue printmaking as well as my education aiming for a Masters in Fine Art. I was drawn to the poem by the strong imagery of smoke turning to curtains [p.231]."

Lindsay Brennan - Sir Wilfred Grenfell College
Torbay, Newfoundland
The Maiden by Alice Major
"I am mainly interested in drawing but since I have been introduced to print for the first time I think I've been more inclined to print right now in my life. I am also interested in sculpture and I would like to broaden my knowledge in that area. In the future, I hope to be happy and enjoy my job whether it be as a practicing artist or helping people in communities find creative solutions to their problems. I chose this poem in particular because it is a topic that will always be modern, it also deals with the choices and struggles a young woman has to deal with [p.306]."

Jonathan Cohlmeyer - Sir Wilfred Grenfell College
Corner Brook Newfoundland
www.jrc9.ca<http://www.jrc9.ca/>
Avoiding Airports by Mildred Tremblay
Chief Scout Award / Bronze, Silver and Gold Duke of Edinburgh Award / Aaron Bradbury Memorial Scholarship Sculpture, Installation, Performance, Photo, Digital Media (Photo, Video, Web & Interactive Programming), "I hope to attend grad school at Emily Carr University of Art + Design (Master of Applied Arts in Media Arts), and become a product / web designer and / or university professor. I was attracted to this poem at first by the title. I am myself apprehensive about flying, so could relate to why someone would want to avoid an airport. This after a

particularly stressful trip in / back from Europe and the United Kingdom. After reading the poem, I began to relate with the figurative meanings in the poem, relating to letting go of our strict society. I wanted the image I created to become free of these bonds, represented in a physical way. I wanted a free and open image-making technique, becoming free from strict representationalism. The result is an abstract representation of someone breaking free from literal bonds, that represent the bonds and restrictions of society [p.543]."

Jessi Dearborn - Rhode Island School of Design
Bristol, VT
Charcoal Pencil)
forbidden to go barefoot blues by Rosanna Deerchild.
"I have always loved drawing, the tight control that one has using a pen or a pencil. I chose this poem because I loved the sense of humor. I can relate to the feeling of constraint with uncomfortable shoes and I love how the narrator attempts to make a break for it [p.120]."

James Doran - Waterford Institute of Technology
From Enniscorthy, Co. Wexford. "Waterford is my home working as a graphic designer. I love incorporating illustration into my designs whenever I can. I normally specialise in concept-driven illustration using inks or on scraperboard."

Dinner at the Priest-House: "The story of Terry Sawchuk is one that inspired me instantly. Having read the work of Randall Maggs, I got a real feel for the character of Sawchuk. He was always at war with himself. I could picture Sawchuk in the church trying to make peace with himself when the priest spots him and dwells on whether to disturb him [p.289]."

New York Hospital I.C.U. "For this illustration I chose to focus on Emile Francis, the man in waiting by Sawchuk's bed. His coach, a former goaltender, someone who understood the mindset of Sawchuk. Waiting alone [p.281]."

Molting Time, Van Gogh after Rembrandt, Stephanie McKenzie: "For this illustration I focused on simplifying Van Gogh's painting of the Raising of Lazarus, which in itself had simplified Rembrandt's version [p.327]."

Lenore Gale - Sir Wilfred Grenfell College
Stephenville, Newfoundland
Along a Snake Fence Riding by W. H. New
"My main interests are painting and printmaking. When I finish my degree, I hope to do the Masters in Philosophy of Humanities program at MUN and then be a working artist incorporating my philosophical ideas into my artwork. The poem I chose attracted me because it discusses youth and the fleeting of time, which is something I become more aware of constantly. I created the image to express fleeting time in the background with the moment of the couple in the foreground silhouetted, for soon it will be but a memory they are holding on to [p.375]."

Martha C. George - Sir Wilfred Grenfell College
Brookfield, Nova Scotia
Sous la pluie by Yvonne-América Truque, translated by Jean-Pierre Pelletier
Martha is studying sculpture and printmaking.
"I chose this poem because my parents are French Canadian and therefore French has been a big part of my upbringing. Also the poem is about love, and all the feelings and emotions that go along with that wonderful rollercoaster experience. I chose my image because I wanted to have a silhouette of someone waiting by the door as the rain pours down outside. Waiting for that

special someone to come and bring the sun in with all of those warm feelings [p.545]."

Erin Gerrity - Rhode Island School of Design
Williamstown, Massachusetts
Graphite on paper
Tower Song (A Poem in Celebration of Darwin's Birthday) by Jan Conn
"My artwork reflects a longstanding interest in animals. I use watercolor and graphite to create small intricate illustrations. I chose *Tower Song (A Poem in Celebration of Darwin's Birthday)* by Jan Conn. I enjoy the rhythm of her writing, and connected to the subject matter of this poem. *Note: The images can be strewn or split among the lines of poetry or overlapped into a layered single piece as shown here* [p.75]."

Amanda Goodyear - Sir Wilfred Grenfell College
Mount Pearl, Newfoundland
Bones in the Wings by Sheri Benning
Amanda is a recipient of the Millennium Excellence Awards Scholarship. She hopes to become a graphic novelist. "I felt the poem, *Bones in the Wings,* by Sheri Benning was both concise and fully illustrative in its curious mix of tender moments and temporal vulnerability. As a depiction, it is far less a literal rendering as it is an image inspired by the poem's text. I chose this method of depiction because I felt the idea of an X-ray alludes to the fragility of health and reminds us of our limited time on earth. It is about how these limitations, our very lack of immortality, makes a moment in time very precious [p.46]."

Ida Floreak - Rhode Island School of Design
Providence RI
Ink on Paper
Poems by Rosanna Deerchild
"I chose Deerchild's poems for their simple language and imagery, and the feeling of displacement conveyed therein. Growing up in a sometimes ugly world, it is easy to feel that there is a part of the big picture that I am missing. Deerchild illustrates meaningful life experiences with a little flourish from the naive eyes of a small girl. Symbols crop up repeatedly throughout the pieces that, seemingly mundane, carry weight for the poet and for her small northern town. Uncomplicated illustrations of selected symbols will carry their own weight for me, for the poem, and for the reader [pp.115, 122]."

Chamisa Kellogg - Rhode Island School of Design
Sebastopol, California
Poems by Barry Dempster
"I find poetry fascinating in its rigid fluidity. I think this aspect is more the experience of the writer than the experience of the reader, however. I enjoyed Dempster's poems because they attracted me with their subject matter, but also I found myself trying to imagine the process of writing them. It was this curiosity that inspired my illustrations. They are an effort to portray this particular creative process through a different medium [p.140]."

Inna Komarovsky - Rhode Island School of Design
Providence, Rhode Island
Ink pen
Ardent by Carolyn Smart
"I hope to continue to study illustration and learn about the ways that mental imagery and visual images can interact. Smart incorporates memories in her poems in a way that interests me because the past and present seem intertwined as certain images from the past live on in our experience. She uses vivid imagery to make her memories come to life and communicate her own involvement with them [p.489]."

Michelle Lee - Rhode Island School of Design
Vancouver, Canada
The Clipped Language of Mathematics by Jan Conn
Between You and the Weather by Mary Dalton
"I work in most mediums, but I enjoy oil painting the most. I am interested in both environmental science and illustration. As I develop as an artist, I would like to integrate my environmental science background into my work. I also hope to be able to do some jewelry design. Jan Con's poem *The Clipped Language of Mathematics* inspired me the most because of the way she linked mathematics and astrology with love [p.68]. Furthermore, I was drawn by Mary Dalton's clever use of metaphors in *Between You and the Weather* [p.94]. I used pen and pencil to illustrate for both poets."

Brian Macbeth - Waterford Institute of Technology
Pensacola, Florida
Brian Macbeth was born in Pensacola, Florida, where early on he developed a fascination with the brilliant turquoise and ultramarine colours of the Gulf of Mexico. This attraction is present in his work which involves building layers of depth and color volume in mixed media. He studied art at the University of Georgia, Athens. As an international artist, Brian has exhibited his work in the United States and Ireland. Currently he is pursuing a Research M.A. in Painting in Waterford, Ireland.

"Themes in my art involve compositions on urban culture blending figurative, abstract and architectural forms in subjective landscapes of measured closeness. I am interested in describing islands of nature surrounded by concrete man-made objects. The paintings can be seen as self-portraits emerging from the interior landscapes of my imagination."

Mary Hill by Elizabeth Bachinsky
"For me this poem conjures early memories of driving, the responsibility, recklessness, freedom, speed and danger teenagers experience in their first car. I use an antique car floating in a barren landscape with the girl's face and eyes superimposed beneath a black sun [p.25]."

Of a Time by Elizabeth Bachinsky
"The scene of a horse swimming was so vivid in my mind's eye I chose to illustrate it exactly as I imagined it; in collage from dream imagery his expectant ears pricked forward / forward, as he glides through the murk. Behind the horse lies a representational image of the mind's eye imbedded in the bark of a tree [p.17]."

Letter to Grandma by Brenda Leifso
"This poem struck me as a sincere, honest confession. An example of insecurity and the desire for reassurance we all hunger for in moments of self doubt. I offer the image of the child and grandmother fused into one by the lightning in the tree behind her chair. Her arms are crossed reassuredly and her face is meditative and calm [p.259]."

Blackness by Keita Demming
"For me it is a poem about separation and defining of self from the isolation of racism. In my image, I have a beautiful woman of color, an immigrant, separated from home looking out from a foreign shore [p.132]."

Cametá by Jan Conn
"The native girl is surrounded by the river of mist with the eye above representing the dreamer of the unconscious mind [p.80]."

Spanish Insane Asylum by Jan Conn
"My painting depicts the manic mind of the artist's asylum. One of my favorites, I see a claustrophobic psyche trapped in a surreal nightmare. 'my mind is alive with ghosts... [p.71]'"

Eros by Jan Conn
"On the lip of a volcano, exploring the ruins of Cuicuilco in the searing Mexican sun."
I offer here the Aztec jaguar god, in contrast to Eros, as an icon of pre-Columbian Mexico. Appearing as a feminine force, a woman is staring down Eros, a tip of the hat to the Virgin of Guadalupe, if you will [p.78]."

Rumour of Silk by Jan Conn
"For *Rumour of Silk,* I have depicted the "green-eyed beauty" as a rainforest goddess. She is accompanied by a dog skeleton stalking a Day of the Dead sugar skull [p.82]."

Heather McCarthy - Sir Wilfred Grenfell College
Corner Brook, Newfoundland and Bridgetown, Nova Scotia
Reincarnate by Alice Major
"I'm into everything, but my main interest is Sculpture, followed by Painting. I hope to become a teacher and eventually further my education to become a Professor of Visual Arts. Since I was a child, I've been interested in Egypt, especially Egyptian art. I found the poem very evocative. Powerful imagery came into my mind when I read it [p.310]."

Sofia Omelkovica - Waterford Institute of Technology, Ireland
I think the soul is really... by Monty Reid
Pencil, collage, ink pen, watercolor and digital.
"Isn't it exciting to be able to make invisible thoughts visible? The strive for love makes us suffer, reality kicks in, yet we keep looking and searching for something true. I hope that my illustration captures the essence of this beautiful piece by Monty Reid [p.427]."

Maria Penny - Sir Wilfred Grenfell College
St. John's, Newfoundland
Untitled (It's Morning) by Anne Szumigalski
"My main study interests are in visuals arts, sculpture and photography. I felt a strong relation with this poem, it has a dark and eerie feeling to it. The sixth line of the poem 'to build myself a lover' — I imagined a mechanical but evil woman that someone has created. I have always been infatuated with Medusa the ultimate chthonic female monster. I felt that the image of Medusa is a modern depiction of the unspecified someone that has designed and created his own lover [p.519]."

Marken Shed - Rhode Island School of Design
Wellesley College, Wellesley MA
Etching and Aquatint
Poems by Alan R. Wilson
"I wasn't tied to any one particular poem in making these images. Rather, I was thinking of interconnectedness and nebula in the first print; self+memories in the second [pp.573, 583]."

Katherine Slauenwhite - Sir Wilfred Grenfell College
Truro, Nova Scotia
The Small Lion by Alan Wilson
Katherine works with photography, sculpture and digital print. "I hope to have at least some success as an artist, but I can see myself involved in a museum or gallery as well. I have a long-standing fascination with mythological, astrological and varying erotic subjects. This poem interested me for both its erotic and astrological references and I could easily see possibilities for the other poems by this author. I used a series of photographs I had previously made as the basis for this image and went from there [p.575]."

Catherine Yuan Chi - Rhode Island School of Design
Hong Kong, China and Providence, Rhode Island
Ink, color pencil, marker and digital
Rumble by Barry Dempster
Hymn for Small Engine Repair by Harold Rhenisch
Ukrainian Bones by Randall Maggs
"As a child I was hopelessly bewitched by the idea of living the life of a destitute painter in a musty garret. My fascination with all things dusty and antiquated, I think, stems from this childhood fantasy. Older now, I would love to be able to make a living off painting and illustration. The deeply personal nostalgia of *Rumble* [p.137], the unexpected but very effective combination of the religious and mechanical in *Hymn for Small Engine Repair* [p.430] and the familiarity of the self-consciousness in *Ukrainian Bones* [p.283] drew me to these poems."

Permissions / Acknowledgements

Complementing the titles of poems included from each particular publication, the publishing house and year of publication noted in the Contents for each author, as appropriate, a summary record of acknowledgement is here provided for the various permissions granted:

Abley, Mark for permission to reprint two poems as listed from the estate of Anne Szumigalski and published by Coteau Books in 1997;

Breakwater Books for permission to reprint poems by Tom Dawe and Carl Leggo as listed; for permission to quote from "St. Leonard's Revisited" by Al Pittman from *An Island in the Sky*, Selected Poetry by Al Pittman edited by Martin Ware and Stephanie McKenzie (2003), by permission of Breakwater Books and the estate of Al Pittman;

Brett, Heather for permission to reprint her poems listed;

Brick Books for permission to reprint poems listed from Sheri Benning, Jan Conn, Barry Dempster, Don Domanski, John Donlan, Barbara Klar, Brenda Leifso, Randall Maggs, Elizabeth Philips, Monty Reid, Sue Sinclair, Carolyn Smart and Anne Szumigalski;

Catalano, Francis for permission to reprint his listed poems;

Coach House Books for permission to reprint the listed poems of Jeramy Dodds;

Demming, Keita for permission to reprint his poem "Blackness";

Desbarats, Michelle for permission to reprint her listed poems;

Écrits Des Forges for permission to reprint the listed poems of Dominique Gaucher;

ECW Press for permission to reprint the listed poems of Jacqueline Turner;

Éditions Adage Inc. for permission to reprint the listed poems in French Translation by Jean-Pierre Pelletier from the original Spanish of Yvonne América Truque;

Ekstasis Editions to reprint the listed poems by Mike Doyle;

Fitzhenry & Whiteside to reprint the listed poems of Eric Miller and Alan R. Wilson;

Fronterac House to reprint the listed poems by Sharron Proulx-Turner;

Gaspereau Press to reprint the poems as listed by John Terpstra and Peter Sanger;

Hagios Press to reprint the poems as listed by Beverley Brenna, Neal McLeod, Jeff Park, Mansel Robinson, Crystal Sikma, Andrew Suknaski and Michael Trussler;

Harbour Publishing to reprint extracts from *The Village of Sliding Time* by David Zieroth;

Hollett, Matthew for permission to reprint his listed poems;

House of Anansi Press for permission to reprint the listed poems of Kevin Connolly;

Kerr, Don for permission to re-print his poem "Editing the Prairie" from *A Sudden Radiance*: *Saskatchewan Poetry*, edited by Lorna Crozier and Gary Hyland (Regina; Coteau Books ,1987);

McClelland & Stewart for permission to reprint from the listed poems of Tim Lilburn;

NeWest Books for permission to reprint from the listed poems of Shane Rhodes;

Nightwood Editions for permission to reprint from the listed poems of Elizabeth Bachinsky, Jay MillAr and Matt Rader;

Oolichan Books for permission to reprint the listed poems of David Manicom, George McWhirter, W. H. New and Mildred Tremblay;

Palimpsest Press for permission to reprint the listed poems of Diane Tucker;

Porcupine's Quill for permission to reprint the listed poems of George Johnston;

Ronsdale Press for permission to reprint the listed poems of Joanne Arnott, Graham Good, Garry Gottfriedson and Harold Rhenisch;

Running the Goat Press for permission to reprint the listed poems of Mary Dalton;

Salmon Press for permission to reprint the listed poems of Stephanie McKenzie;

Signature Editions for permission to reprint the listed poems of Andrea MacPherson;

The Muses Company for permission to reprint the listed poems of Rosanna Deerchild;

Turnstone Press for permission to reprint the listed poems of Carla Funk and extract from *she walks for days inside a thousand eyes: a two-spirit story* by Sharron Proulx-Turner;

University of Alberta Press for permission to reprint the listed poems of E. D. Blodgett, Elis Juliana's haiku as listed and translated by Hélène Garrett, extracts from *Continuations* by Douglas Barbour and Sheila A. Murphy, Alice Major's poems as listed, and photographs and text by John Conway from *Saskatchewan Uncommon Views* (2005).

Index of Poets

Index of Poems

Notes on the back room team

Liam Rellis is an arts professional based in South-East Ireland. He specializes in arts event management, particularly the management and administration of festivals. He operates an arts consultancy agency, Liam Rellis Arts Consultants, to professionally advise arts organisations in production and company administration. Liam is currently taking a Masters Degree by Research in Waterford Institute of Technology. He operates as co-ordinator for the Centre for Newfoundland and Labrador Studies, Waterford Institute of Technology.

Samantha Thomas is a Caribbean-American poet and recent graduate of the Poets' House Creative Writing Program at Waterford Institute of Technology. Her MA thesis focused on the history of sugar and poems from that work were published in the *The Echoing Years* anthology. She is currently pursuing further postgraduate studies at the University of Oxford as well as teaching in the School of Humanities at Waterford. She has been living in Ireland since 2005.

Hannah Butler, "the Mysterious Hannah Butler" (Brenda Leifso), was born in Waterford, Ireland. Hannah has been working in Waterford Institute of Technology, in the School of Humanties, since 2005, having previously worked in Éircom for many years. Hannah was involved in the previous anthology *The Echoing Years* with Dr. John Ennis. Her hobbies include reading, walking, aerobics. She enjoys being a loyal supporter of the Waterford Hurling Team. She currently resides in Waterford with her husband Seamus and children Patrick and Niamh. Up The Deise!!!

Caroline Phelan was born in Waterford, Ireland. She has been working in the Waterford Institute of Technology since 2006. Having worked in the Estates Office, School of Business, she works presently in the School of Humanities. She has also worked in the Waterford City Council, working in the City Archives and Arts Office as well as in the Environment and Planning Office. She has studied Photography and is currently studying Business and was awarded a Licentiate Membership of the Royal Photographic Society in 2002. Her hobbies include Photography, Swimming and Walking. She resides in Waterford with her husband Gerard and children Sarah, Neil and Rachel.

A Note on the Collaboration of Poets and Artists

Mol an óige is tiocfaidh sí . . .   so goes the old Irish proverb / *Praise the young and they will prosper. . .* Something of that perception informed the rationale for *How the Light Gets in.* Purely as a student project, it enabled young artists in Canada, the U.S. and in Ireland to engage firsthand with the work of living Canadian poets expressing themselves in recent, even forthcoming, publications. An extra in the process was the opportunity given to young artists to get to know the respective styles of their own contemporaries. The door remains ajar to future collaborative work and exchanges.

The role of professor, or lecturer, with the student has long changed from the old authoritarian stance to one of the former facilitating the learner at every turn. Today, students are variously seen through the lens of customer, client and peer. The latter concept offers the most exciting possibilities. Using the peer approach, students work side by side with their tutors in projects of research and discovery. This approach, pioneered by MIT, is more generally espoused today at third-level. The harvest reaped can be great in terms of performance; the process instils growing confidence, energy and independence in the learner. For this anthology, young artists have worked side by side with experienced practitioners, — Susan Doyle, Kent Jones and Martin Quigley, for instance. The work achieved in corresponding to or complementing the various poems stands in its own right as independent art, in no way subservient to the literary. This is an old tradition, in Ireland stretching back to *The Book of Kells.* It sometimes works the other way as well. Auden's poem "Musée des Beaux Arts" is no less a fine poem because it was inspired by Breughel's *The Fall of Icarus.*

In pursuing this project, I was fortunate that it coincided with the exhibition *Darkness and Light* which featured artwork by staff at Waterford Institute of Technology on display along the corridors of Waterford Regional Hospital as part of a Healing Arts Initiative. I'm grateful to Sheila Naughton, organiser, for her support in making available two of the art works featured at the exhibition for this book: one by Lorenzo Tonti and the other by Tony Ryan, who imagines the face of his son lighting up on first viewing early First Nations artwork. "In 1998, my son was a student in Brigham Young University in Utah and it was a time of discovery for him. In this drawing I imagine what it would be like for my son to discover Native American cave drawings by torchlight in Dead Horse Canyon, Utah." *Discovery* (Pastels, p.395). I thought it fitting to locate this work beside the poems of Sharron Proulx-Turner, who herself celebrates her children with such vibrant imagery. An example of one art form illuminating another.

Of his own art work, *Where Water Falls* (Oil and Wax on Primed Panel, p.643), Martin Quigley adds:"Light falling on water is an ongoing theme in my work. Rivers: Suir, Nore, Barrow and midland lakes Owel, Ennel and Derravarragh are my habitat. I am spellbound by water." Martin is also a novelist, once again celebrating water, in *Drifting with the River Gods.*

"Looking at you, one would never think you have a brain tumour," Lorenzo Tonti records as something of the kind he hears many times. Duality of perception is a constant presence in his life and art as in *Self-portrait 1 & 2* (Diptych, p.261). The poem comes before Tim Lilburn's "Getting Sick".

Susan Doyle's image is a lithograph (p.643) on the subject of self-knowledge and self-deception. Courtesy of Ken'ichi Matsumura, I have added a famous haiku (by Anzai Fuyue) on the subject of transience, a butterfly out on the straits of Dattan, where the convergence of fonts attempts to explore further the ineffable in a small space. On the general subject of higher and lower case in poem headers in the anthology, we attempted to adhere to what was visible in the original text of publication, such being obviously important to the poet artist in each case.

Throughout the volume one may note that certain poets also compose as fine artists; examples include Garry Gottfriedson, Neal McLeod and Andrew Suknaski. The work of Matthew Hollett is particularly exciting. In the poet's own words:

" 'rabbit-track alphabet' and 'soliloquies' [pp.222-224] in particular most definitely occupy a grey area between visual art and poetry, and are my attempts to explore language, typography, and the intersection of language and image: 'rabbit-track alphabet' is from a series of drawings called 'alphabetica' that explore poetic typography and alphabet design. Through drawings, letraset, collage, and found lettering, I've composed a variety of visual poems based on the alphabet. These are not fonts - they are attempts to tinker with language at its most basic level, deconstructing and reconstructing each alphabet in an attempt to better understand this ubiquitous system of glyph; 'soliloquies' is another series of visual poems I assembled, this time inspired by the chance encounter of my magnetic poetry kit and my scanner. Each image is an unaltered digital scan; the distortion effects are caused by moving the objects as they are being scanned. Experimenting with different gestures and movements, I tried to find an effect that suited the meaning of each chosen word.

The three 'answers' poems [p.225] are taken from a small artist's book I made which consisted of twenty-five solutions clipped from the back of various puzzle books, snipped out of context and transferred onto tea-dyed paper. While the idea is perhaps most effective as a book, these three excerpts also work well as a group of found poems."

Kent Jones, a colleague of Matthew Hollett at SWGC, elaborates on the creative process involved for his students in producing the prints:

"These prints were produced using Intaglio printmaking processes which involved establishing images on metal plates, which were subsequently etched with acid and hand-printed on intaglio presses. The student artists used traditional hard ground, soft ground and aquatint techniques as well as more contemporary open-bite techniques. Also, drypoint, a direct drawing technique which does not require acid etching, was employed by some of the students.

Intaglio printmaking traces its roots back to the great German artist, Albrecht Dürer, and others from the early 16th century who realised that the process of etching armour might be useful for reproducing all sorts of images.

Rembrandt, whom history records as having been released from relentless painting commissions, found and developed his original style of art-making through experimentation with the Intaglio Printmaking process. The process itself is ideally suited to illustrating poems, broadsheets and books, and there is an extensive history of print artists collaborating with poets and novelists which stretches back for hundreds of years."

A range of prints and art work contained in the book will be featured in an exhibition on display during the Seán Dunne International Festival of Arts and Culture in Waterford in March 2009.

Hopefully the reader will come away with his or her own mental gallery having read the poems. Two of my favourite portraits from these "unacknowledged legislators" of the Canadian psyche are Dunc and Babe McPherson extending their garden in old age and Tom Dawe's "The Last Keeper" telling ancestors and Ottawa to "go to hell." Perspectives more out of Hesiod than out of Vergil. The Joycean epiphanic is everywhere to be found. As in a John Conway prairiescape, poets and readers are caught off-guard, stumble on the astonishing, pondering paradox and disquieting memory as in *St. Michael's Retreat House* (p. 477). I am as grateful for a John Conway to conclude the book as I am for a Gerald Squires (the Jack B.Yeats of Newfoundland) to open it.

And Wesley Bates remains open for business on the main street of Clifford, SWO.

At the heart of all this, I hope there has been a fun element for the young artists. Certainly, when the pressure was on students to integrate this work with the rest of their year's portfolio and growing lives, it was the only approach that could have worked. In working like this, the artists probably were exposed to a basic in composition whether in the fine arts, music or verse. Tchaikovsky's heart may have been breaking when he was writing the *Le Pathétique Symphony* because of the particular set of circumstances he found himself in, yet he used the waltz to propel his spirit in the growing darkness gathering round him. In the same mode in his own life, and verse, Kavanagh wrote, "All true poems laugh inwardly / out of grief-born intensity". Bachinsky's poem "Drive" is sometimes numb with pain, but with its jocular speed you'd hardly believe it.

In reading the work of certain poets on display, I could not but be struck by future possibilities as their work develops: in Elizabeth Bachinsky's "Drive", again, some characters encountered ache between the lines to tell their stories. Even as it stands, that fine poem could be illustrated in many ways, not least with an illustrative flourish of the unmentionables like pennants in the wind. On reading Matt Rader's "Trees of Canada" in *Living Things*, I wondered why he didn't place the tree sequences together: until I recalled what I saw from a high-rise window in a UBC student residence during Congress: a Vancouver cityscape dominated by trees where buildings and streets appeared to nestle in between the trees, just like the other poems in Rader's book. What a difference from a Dublin cityscape where every square inch is concrete and money, and where the greed of speculators sown in the past now reaps its own whirlwind.

Some day, somebody should publish a coffee-table size book of the Trees of Canada with Matt Rader's poems in between. That way we could all smell the resin.

Kent Jones, The Madwoman of Cork

"[Y]ears ago I illustrated Patrick Galvin's poem *"The Madwoman of Cork"* with eight original colour lithographs and eleven pages of text. Sets are in the collections of the Arts Council of Northern Ireland, The Tyrone Guthrie Centre at Annaghmakerrig, the Ulster Museum, Harvard University, Princeton University, Emory University (Atlanta, Georgia), St. Mary's University (Halifax, Nova Scotia), The National Library of Ireland, University of Lethbridge (Alberta, Canada), the Art Gallery of Nova Scotia, Boston College, The Rooms / Provincial Art Gallery of Newfoundland and Labrador, University of Delaware and others, as well as private collections in Ireland, Britain, Canada and the States."

Martin Quigley, Where Water Falls